THE MAKING OF
"JEW CLUBS"

STUDIES IN ANTISEMITISM
Alvin H. Rosenfeld, editor

THE MAKING OF "JEW CLUBS"

Performing Jewishness and Antisemitism in European Football and Fan Cultures

—ᴍ—

Pavel Brunssen

INDIANA UNIVERSITY PRESS

This book is a publication of

Indiana University Press
Office of Scholarly Publishing
Herman B Wells Library 350
1320 East 10th Street
Bloomington, Indiana 47405 USA

iupress.org

First Printing 2025

Cataloging information is available from the Library of Congress.

ISBN 978-0-253-07337-2 (hdbk.)
ISBN 978-0-253-07338-9 (pbk.)
ISBN 978-0-253-07340-2 (ebook)
ISBN 978-0-253-07339-6 (web PDF)

In loving memory of
Eberhard, Egon, Erna, and Juliane

CONTENTS

CONTENTS

PREFACE AND
ACKNOWLEDGMENTS

WHEN I WAS GROWING UP as a kid in Bremen, becoming a supporter of the local football club Werder seemed unavoidable. I remember looking at the floodlit stadium from my bedroom window and attending my first game when I was five years old. A few years later, aged twelve or thirteen, I became aware of the connection between football and politics. At the Weser stadium, I stood next to fans chanting about building a subway from Hamburg—the city of Werder's main rival, Hamburger SV—to Auschwitz. I was troubled.

I encountered a fan culture that had long been defined by neo-Nazi hooligans. But around that time, a new ultras fan culture developed. Ultras were primarily concerned with flags, banners, and singing. During a complex process of repoliticization, ultras clashed with hooligans across the country, often for political reasons, and this also happened in Bremen. This was the time when my parents took me to the stadium, even to away games, and my grandparents gave me a wonderful present: my first season ticket. Today, the fan cultures in Bremen and other German cities have changed and—while still an exception in Europe—fans participate in antidiscriminatory campaigns. In the 1990s and the first decade of the twenty-first century, I witnessed the social

potential of football firsthand—even though the political hegemony remains contested across the different fan groups.

I left Bremen to study social work and social pedagogy in Düsseldorf, where I also cofounded *Transparent Magazine*, which became a significant voice in the German discourse about football
and society and introduced me to many people and topics surrounding the politics of football cultures. I continued to work
for *Transparent* as I moved from Düsseldorf to Berlin to pursue
an MA at the Center for Research on Antisemitism, where my
particular interest in the connections between antisemitism and
football developed further. In 2015, I attended the first international conference on antisemitism in European football at Amsterdam Arena, a place to which I returned several times during
my research for this dissertation and book. At the conference,
we discussed the "Jew Clubs"—Ajax and Tottenham—and I was
immediately fascinated.

At the Center for Research on Antisemitism, the center's chair,
Professor Stefanie Schüler-Springorum, shared my interest in
the connections between antisemitism and football. I am forever
grateful to her for long and critical debates about antisemitism in
football fan culture (among many other things). What led me to
this project initially was, however, the fact that she trusted me
to organize the international conference The Beautiful Game?:
Identity, Resentment, and Discrimination in Football and Fan
Cultures in 2018, at which we continued our discussions from
Amsterdam. We invited Emma Poulton and Andrei S. Markovits
as the conference keynote speakers.

At the time the conference took place, Professor Markovits
had already become "Andy" to me, and I was accepted to pursue a
PhD at the Department of Germanic Languages and Literatures
at the University of Michigan, where I intended to work with him
and where the journey to this study really took off. This study,
while initially crafted as a dissertation, has been a ride that has
truly altered my understanding of the space that football cultures

have in contemporary European societies and of what working through the past means for the present moment and creating a potentially less antisemitic future. I am deeply indebted to all those who supported my research.

I could not have undertaken this journey without my wonderful dissertation committee, namely, Andrei S. Markovits, Julia Hell, Scott Spector, and Robert Mickey. I am extremely grateful for their continual encouragement, their wise counsel, and their unique enthusiasm concerning not only my research project but also my development as a scholar and as a person.

I would like to express my deepest gratitude to Julia Hell. Rarely have I seen someone engage with texts and images as she does. Her brilliance in theory and close reading techniques have influenced this project in many ways, and it would not be the same without her. I am extremely grateful to Scott Spector, who was supportive in many ways; our conversations on minority subjectivities and the "Jewish question," among other topics, significantly inspired my work. I am also thankful for the valuable feedback from the committee's cognate member, Robert Mickey.

And then, there is Andy. He shows a devotion to his students—and I had the privilege to be one of them—that I have never seen before. Andy's scholarly brilliance was the initial reason why I applied to the University of Michigan, and I do not regret that decision for one second. I had expected intellectual genius, but I encountered a mensch in the best sense of the word. His mentorship has been beyond words, and he has been a source of inspiration and encouragement for every page of this study. Andy not only supported me in publishing my first book, *Antisemitismus in Fussball-Fankulturen: Der Fall RB Leipzig,* and became a wonderful coauthor, but most important, he welcomed me with open arms in Ann Arbor. Together with his wonderful wife, Kiki, and their fantastic dog, Emma, they truly made me feel at home in Michigan, and I am delighted to call them close friends. I will never forget what you have done for me and continue to do!

I would like to extend my sincere thanks to the Department of Germanic Languages and Literatures and the Frankel Center for Judaic Studies. I am deeply grateful to the faculty, students, and staff of both institutions for their invaluable support, suggestions, and comments. Along with various fellowships provided by Rackham, among others, they enabled me to carry out the necessary on-site research for my dissertation. I am extremely grateful to have had the opportunity to visit various places in Germany, Austria, the Netherlands, and England, which the reader will encounter in this book. During these trips, I met many people to whom I wish to express my deepest appreciation.

The chapter on FC Bayern Munich has greatly benefited from conversations with Michael Brenner, Stephanie Dilba, Jutta Fleckenstein, Alexa Gattinger, Gregor Hofmann, Anton Löffelmeier, Simon Müller, Laura Nicolaiciuc, Fabian Raabe, Dietrich Schulze-Marmeling, and Volker Stör, I wish also to thank a number of people who introduced me to various aspects concerning the chapter on FK Austria Vienna. Many thanks go to Georg Spitaler as well as Michael Bonvalot, Bernhard Hachleitner, Matthias Marschik, Agnes Meisinger, Thomas Pöltl, Laurin Rosenberg, Nicole Selmer, and Daniel Shaked. Roman Horak, whom I had the pleasure of meeting several times in Vienna, introduced me to the city's coffee house culture and generously shared his knowledge of local football history. He sadly passed away shortly before the publication of this book. His presence and insights are deeply missed. As for the chapter on Ajax Amsterdam, thanks are due to Steven Burger, Olaf van Muijden, Ronald Pieloor, Menno Pot, Jasmin Seijbel, Jurryt van de Vooren, Joram Verhoeven, and Willem Wagenaar. Further thanks are due to those who helped me with the Tottenham Hotspur chapter: Charlie Eccleshare, Alan Fisher, Chris Gibbons, Lee Harpin, Bonnie Lunn, Rachel Martin, John Mann, David Newman, and Christine Schmidt. Special thanks go to Frank Brunssen, Danielle LaVaque-Manty, and Naomi Silver for their comments on parts of this manuscript.

I also owe thanks to Max Antpöhler, Martin Endemann, Andreas Kahrs, Daniel Lörcher, Catarina Rodrigues, Daniel Schneider, Hannah Ulmrich, and Nora Zirkelbach. Furthermore, I wish to acknowledge the contributions of scholars and writers who have explored aspects regarding the "Jew Clubs" before such as John Efron, Simon Kuper, and Emma Poulton. I want to pay special tribute to Evelien Gans, whom I had the privilege of meeting once before starting this project but who has, sadly, passed away. Finally, I wish to thank the anonymous reviewers for their thoughtful comments as well as Indiana University Press and Andrew Hodges for excellent editorial work.

To my friends and colleagues Richard Bachmann, Émilie Duranceau-Lapointe, Felix Hempe, Jonas Knatz, and Yanara Schmacks: I am deeply thankful for your encouragement and support. Special thanks are also due to Hedda B.

This endeavor would not have been possible without my parents, Christiane and Michael: I cannot express how thankful I am to them for not only tolerating my often-unreasonable devotion to football but also for even encouraging me to pursue it. None of this would be possible without you.

Above all, I wish to thank Gesa for supporting me in moments of exhaustion and for sharing moments of joy and beauty. I am looking forward to everything ahead of us.

THE MAKING OF
"JEW CLUBS"

INTRODUCTION

WHEN THE TWENTY-YEAR-OLD ISRAELI DUTCH filmmaker Nirit Peled moved from Israel to the Netherlands in the early 1990s, she soon found herself surrounded by Dutch football fans in an Amsterdam streetcar.[1] The fans were wrapped in Israeli flags and had tattoos on their arms depicting the Star of David. They chanted Jewish folk songs such as "Hava Nagila" and shouted, "Super Joden," which means "Super Jews," in a reference to the supposedly Jewish football team Ajax Amsterdam. The fans—most of them not Jewish whatsoever—confused and scared Peled, who questioned what these people were doing with the Israeli flag: "What are they doing with my flag? Is this about me?"

When Peled was in that streetcar, she was well aware of what had occurred in these Amsterdam streets fifty years earlier. In May 1940, German Nazis marched through Amsterdam, occupying the Netherlands. They forced Jews to wear a badge known as the Judenstern in public, a yellow star with the letter *J* on it. The Nazis deported around 100,000 of the 140,000 Dutch Jews to concentration camps and death camps, with about 60,000 of them ending up in Auschwitz. The majority of Dutch Jews—104,000 of 140,000—did not survive Nazism, resulting in a death rate of 75 percent, higher than in any other West European nation. The image of a streetcar full of "Jews" evokes the cattle wagon that came to symbolize the deportations. Peled may have thought about all of this while passing through the streets where most of these Jews lived, but now, she was surrounded by Dutch football fans who were bizarrely celebrating some kind of fan culture that inexplicably featured a heavy Jewish hue. Peled was dumbfounded by it all.

At the time the Nazis invaded the Netherlands, Walter Benjamin was writing his last major work, *On the Concept of History*.[2] Shortly after, he died by suicide while fleeing from Nazi persecution. Benjamin wrote that "perhaps revolutions are not the train ride, but the human race grabbing for the emergency brake."[3] At times, Benjamin suggested, it is necessary to stop moving and reflect on the human condition. This all occurred in 1940. After the Holocaust, however, most Europeans moved on with their lives, although Nazi terror and the Second World War had left Europe in ruins. Amsterdam, once a vibrant center of Jewish life, had changed completely. For millions of Jews, no one had grabbed the emergency brake. Those who returned were met with skepticism, reparations were denied, and their suffering was ignored. The strange behavior Peled encountered in that Amsterdam train was a form of engagement with the history of the Holocaust and its consequences. Despite all the memorials and the commemorations that were erected all over Europe toward the end of the twentieth century, the past remains unmastered, and the performances of European football fans are one space in which the unmastered past comes to the surface.

In 1959, Benjamin's colleague Theodor W. Adorno wrote an essay entitled "The Meaning of Working Through the Past."[4] After his return to Germany from exile, Adorno observed that Germany's collective narcissism was "severely damaged by the collapse of Hitler's regime." Yet, he argued, "the damage occurred at the level of mere factuality, without individuals making themselves conscious of it and thereby coping with it."[5] This is, Adorno continued, "the social-psychological relevance of talk about an unmastered past." Today, Germany is often seen not only as a world champion in football but also as the world champion in *Vergangenheitsbewältigung*, which literally translates as a "struggle to work through the past."[6] Yet, the problem of what Adorno called a "collective unmastered past" can still be observed in different forms—for instance, in the performances of European football fans.

On the Amsterdam streetcar, an encounter between different perspectives of history occurred—namely, between those of the filmmaker Neled and of Ajax's fans. Outside the streetcar, both may have encountered fans of Ajax's rival football clubs, such as Feyenoord Rotterdam. Feyenoord supporters may well have chanted "Jews to the gas" on their way to the stadium, a chant that is, as most Feyenoord fans argue, "not antisemitic" because it supposedly refers only to Ajax and not to Jewish people. As horrific as a chant like "Jews to the gas" sounds, those who chant it are not limited to hooligans, neo-Nazis, and convinced antisemites, and the antisemitic chants cannot be taken literally, as if those who are chanting are promoting another Holocaust. Still, many Jews are, understandably, shocked by the demand that they should be gassed. During a 2015 conference on antisemitism in football, the Dutch Holocaust survivor Joop Waterman expressed his shock when he witnessed antisemitic chants during the derby between Feyenoord Rotterdam and Ajax Amsterdam: "I was shocked when I saw the hatred in the eyes of the Rotterdam supporters."[7] Jewish football supporters like Waterman stopped attending live games because of these chants. While such open expressions of antisemitism seem to have been cut short in the public sphere, if at least to a certain degree, they persist in European football stadiums. The chants are a reminder of what occurred in the streets, in the trains, and in the camps. My study of these performances aims to uncover how the Holocaust past is still "unmastered." It offers a glimpse into current debates around memory cultures and collective identities, and it reveals the consequences of the ruptures and transformations of the twentieth century.

Ajax is a football club people often refer to as a "Jew Club." This term describes clubs that are associated with Jews and Judaism, although they are not explicitly Jewish. Throughout this book, the term "Jew Club" appears in quotation marks to emphasize its distinction from Jewish clubs, a concept I will explain in the next section of this introduction. Likewise, throughout this book, I use the term *Jew* without quotation marks to denote the group of people and "Jew" with quotation marks to denote an abstract category of representation in my analysis.

A club is a "Jew Club" not because it is Jewish but because certain images, stereotypes, and stories are linked to that club. The "Jew Club" conundrum incorporates the complex relationships that exist between past and present, between memory cultures and collective identities, and between historical and contemporary antisemitism.[8] This book uses the discourses around "Jew Clubs," such as Ajax, as case studies through which to analyze the connection between collective memories and identity formations in post-1945 Europe. Additionally, this book is about the function and space of "the Jew" (as an image for the Other), and Jews (as a minority) in contemporary European societies. In this book, I investigate how European societies engaged with Jews after World War II and how Jews navigate their identities in these societies.

In addition to Ajax, the European football clubs FC Bayern Munich, Austria Vienna, and Tottenham Hotspur (London) are known as "Jew Clubs." Yet none of these clubs was or is explicitly Jewish. The identification of these clubs with Judaism has historical roots, but it is also a misconception, an illusion that requires explanation and that has consequences not only for the football clubs but also for Jews, clubs, and local and national cultures.

My book focuses on the relationships between histories, memory cultures, and identities. It aims to answer why non-Jewish

European football clubs are known as "Jew Clubs." Furthermore, it asks how this misconception affects the clubs' memory cultures and identities today while also considering the effects these labels have on contemporary Jews. My transnational study shows how football serves as a contested space for questions of identity, subjectivity, and belonging, including localism, nationalism, cosmopolitanism, and xenophobia as well as anti-antisemitism and other forms of antidiscrimination activities. It illustrates how sports clubs and fan cultures perform memory cultures and thus function as an important societal arena for the construction of collective identities.

This book is an archaeological dig through the various layers of meaning that encompass several levels of time and space.[9] It involves (a) a dig into the local histories of Munich, Vienna, Amsterdam, and London; (b) a transnational dig into the national histories of Germany, Austria, the Netherlands, and England; (c) a dig through the various layers of German-Jewish, Austrian-Jewish, Dutch-Jewish, and English-Jewish relations; (d) a dig through the respective memorial cultures; and (e) a dig through the development of football in Europe, showing how football has been and remains a primary site for groups and individuals to navigate their identities.

This study is based on textual, visual, and audio sources. My focus is on primary sources such as fanzines, fan chants, banners, films, videos, photographs, online discussions, blog posts, podcasts, statues, memorials, street names, and newspaper articles. I visited Munich, Vienna, Amsterdam, and London, and I consulted fans, club representatives, journalists, and scholars. Working with this huge and diverse corpus requires a combination of methods from a variety of fields, such as German studies, Judaic studies, history, visual studies, sound studies, performance studies, and memory studies. I apply appropriate methods and theories for each chapter and each source. The book's unifying thread is its conceptual and qualitative interdisciplinary analysis of the

"Jew Club" conundrum. The next sections will outline the most significant terms, theories, and assumptions of this study.

WHAT IS A "JEW CLUB"?

"Jew Clubs" must not be confused with Jewish football clubs and Jewish sports organizations. In contrast to "Jew Clubs," *Jewish clubs* are explicitly Jewish. This may be because they accept only Jewish members or because their club culture is Jewish (for example, because they celebrate Jewish holidays). Many Jewish clubs are integrated sports clubs, meaning that they are open to everyone, but they still express their Jewishness publicly through Jewish names, such as Maccabi or Hakoah, and Jewish symbols, such as the Star of David, on their football uniforms. In contrast, "Jew Clubs" have never been explicitly Jewish, never wore Jewish symbols, and, as a rule of thumb, never had more Jewish officials, players, and fans than other clubs. As earlier mentioned, the term "Jew Club" appears in quotation marks to emphasize its distinction from Jewish clubs such as Hakoah and to indicate its contested nature.

This book, which is based on four case studies, examines how and why these clubs became "Jew Clubs." The four clubs presented in this book were selected because they are all known to be "Jew Clubs." One common assumption is that this is because they all have or had more Jewish players or Jewish chairs than other clubs. Empirically, however, they did not. While Jews were involved in all these clubs, the same can be said about many other clubs from each of the four countries where these clubs are located. The label "Jew Club" is therefore misleading. To understand the "Jew Club" phenomenon, it is important to recognize that this label does not result from an empirical core. Nonetheless, "Jew Clubs" are an empirical reality because people consider them as such. This study thus aims to uncover the processes and meanings underlying the making of "Jew Clubs." I assert that these clubs function as a space for post-1945 societies to engage with ideas about Judaism, antisemitism, the history of the Holocaust, memory cultures, and collective identities.

Each of the four clubs mentioned—FC Bayern Munich, Austria Vienna, Ajax Amsterdam, and Tottenham Hotspur (London)—is presented in an individual chapter. This book is thus a transnational study that strives to clarify the common features and distinctive characteristics of each of the four "Jew Clubs." The chapter on FC Bayern Munich analyzes the "Jew Club" as memory culture. It shows how the former German Jewish club president Kurt Landauer became central to the club's identity in the early twenty-first century. The chapter on FK Austria Vienna (FAK) highlights the "Jew Club" as a "cultural code."[10] It shows how the idea of the "Jew Club" is linked to antisemitic tropes about cosmopolitanism, rootlessness, and urbanism. The chapter on Ajax Amsterdam presents the "Jew Club" as fan performance. It elucidates the case of a club attacked as "Jewish" by fans of rivaling clubs and whose fans, in response, started to self-identify as "Super Jews." The chapter on Tottenham Hotspur discusses the "Jew Club" as a problem. In London, Tottenham's fans appropriated the antisemitic epithet "Yid" in the 1970s, which rival supporters shouted at them. This chapter analyzes how the public perception of the underlying problem has shifted from a focus on the rival fans' antisemitic chants, such as "Hitler's going to gas 'em again," to the Tottenham fans' self-identification as "Yids."

The selected cases are both comparable yet distinct because their histories and memory cultures are intertwined and because their development as "Jew Clubs" is somewhat parallel. Each of the four chapters discusses the "Jew Club" phenomenon in the context of national and local histories: Germany as the former Nazi empire; Austria with the "Anschluss"; the Netherlands with its myth of resistance despite its compliance with Nazi Germany; and England, which fought against and triumphed over Nazism. Each case is also a study of local histories and memory cultures, and I seek to account for and better understand both how these various national histories influence the respective "Jew Clubs" and also how the "Jew Clubs" influence the contemporary societies they operate in. It is my hope that this study will lead to further research on football clubs with the "Jew Club" label, namely, AS Roma (Italy),[11] Cracovia (Kraków, Poland),[12] RSC Anderlecht (Belgium),[13] Club Atlético Atlanta (Buenos Aires, Argentina),[14] and MTK Budapest (Hungary).[15]

THE "JEW" IMAGINARY FRAMEWORK

In the Netherlands, any spectator of a football derby between Ajax Amsterdam and the club's bitter rival Feyenoord Rotterdam will encounter both anti-Jewish and pro-Jewish songs, flags, and banners. Feyenoord's fans will likely chant "Hamas, Hamas, all Jews to the gas," whereas Ajax's fans will likely celebrate their "Jew Club" identity by chanting "Joden! Joden!" In England, a spectator of a football derby between Tottenham and the club's city rival Chelsea may encounter Chelsea fans chanting phrases such as "Spurs are on their way to Auschwitz," which Tottenham fans will respond to with "Yid Army!" These performances have sparked widespread public interest but have not been extensively studied by scholars. Commentators have labeled them as *either* antisemitic *or* anti-antisemitic. I contend that the antisemitic and philosemitic performances are intertwined: both contribute to the making and remaking of "Jew Club" identities. "Jew Clubs" are a space for negotiating ideas about real Jews, abstract "Jews," and collective identities.

This book is about Jews (as actual people) and "Jews" (as an abstract category). In this study, the word *Jew* is used in all its connotations, ranging from a term for Self to a word that connotes the Other. It can be used as an expression of pride or as a slur. Some consider it a neutral term, while others "politely" avoid it. The word *Jew* may have an antisemitic connotation related to

stereotypes about modernity, greed, or cosmopolitanism. Jewish identity may relate to a religion, a culture, a nation, or family
heritage. Jews may identify themselves as secular, religious, or
something in between. This study is an investigation of the processes of the inclusion and exclusion of Jews and Jewish perspectives associated with the term and that materialize in football
fans' performances.

The meanings and connotations of the terms "Yid," "Jew," the
German "Jude," and the Dutch "Joden" are contested. Cynthia
M. Baker's study *Jew* shows that these terms indeed have a long
history of debates surrounding them.[16] Baker's core claim is that
the term "Jew" has been used for most of its history by non-Jews
to define an Other and to shape the identity of a Self. The word
"has served as a cipher for materialism and intellectualism, socialism and capitalism, worldly cosmopolitanism and clannish
parochialism, eternal chosenness and unending curse."[17] The
word "Jew" in "Jew Club" thus represents an image of both the
Self and Other. Clubs like Ajax and Tottenham are frequently attacked antisemitically with chants like "Jews to the gas." Yet fans
of these clubs—Jews and gentiles—chose "Joden" and "Yids"
as markers for their collective identities. The "Jew Club" conundrum thus offers a promising opportunity to study not only the
complex entanglement of Self and Other in the creation of group
collectives but also the multifaceted relationship between antisemitism and philosemitism.

Philosemitism is "commonly understood as the defense, love,
or admiration of Jews and Judaism."[18] This book, as a transnational comparison of "Jew Clubs," attempts to contribute to a
newly emerging body of literature on philosemitism, a topic that
has so far received little attention.[19] I agree with Maurice Samuels
that philosemitism and antisemitism are not opposites. Rather,
Samuels argues that they are dialectically linked and "partake of
a similar process of generalization and stereotyping."[20] Inquir-
ing into the dialectics between antisemitism and philosemitism

shows that both have something in common—namely, that "Jews" are viewed as "not Self."

Scholars continue publishing numerous monographs, handbooks, and edited volumes that aim to define antisemitism. They disagree on whether to spell the term with or without a hyphen (*anti-Semitism* vs. *antisemitism*) or suggest speaking of anti-Judaism, Jew-hatred, or Judeophobia. They disagree on whether the development from religious anti-Judaism to modern antisemitism in the late nineteenth century was defined by continuities or discontinuities in religious prejudices, secular ressentiment, or both. From today's post-Holocaust perspective, scholars of antisemitism face specific challenges. For instance, whether and when statements about Israel are antisemitic is a particularly heated discussion. Furthermore, the (belated) awareness for and education about the Holocaust has, as a side effect, led to new difficulties in defining antisemitism in the present, for as the literary scholar Dara Horn notes, "anything short of the Holocaust is, well, not the Holocaust."[21] The bar for what *really* counts as antisemitism, Horn notes, is rather high. While antisemitism still exists in post-Holocaust societies, anyone made aware of an antisemitic action refuses to "be an antisemite" and claims a misunderstanding or ill-intended accusation. We are living in an age of "antisemitism without antisemites."[22] Antisemitism no longer is a legitimate cultural code, and everyone (except for a few neo-Nazis) would fervently deny having any antisemitic intentions. Yet, antisemitism still exists.

Although those who use antisemitic language or performance deny antisemitic intentions, researchers and commentators on antisemitism still focus predominantly on the motivations of those who are suspected of an antisemitic act. A common strategy used to study antisemitism is to focus on the explanations given by those who express potentially antisemitic stereotypes, such as an account by Gijs van Delft, the head of Feyenoord Rotterdam's supporters club De Feijenoorder who legitimized the

"Jews to the gas" chants against Ajax with the following statement: "It is not that everyone thinks that Jews must be gassed. We are always talking about 'football Jews.'"[23] I find it especially important to complicate interpretations of antisemitism in football as "not really intended," as "humor," "banter," or as a "natural" and thus unproblematic part of football rivalries. Studying the "Jew Club" conundrum from this perspective means that any analysis of "Jew Clubs" must consider that antisemitism is more than intentional acts of hate speech.

Recently, scholars have attempted to build bridges between competing frameworks in the field of antisemitism studies. Dov Waxman and colleagues distinguish four approaches that identify antisemitism.[24] There is (a) the focus on the perpetrator's motives, (b) the emphasis on the victim's perception, (c) the spotlight on objective effects or outcomes, and (d) the concentration on discourse and representation. Public debates—not only in the context of football—usually focus on intention and motives to determine whether something (most often: someone) is antisemitic, therefore ignoring that antisemitism today is often an "antisemitism without antisemites." Motives are hard to determine. In a societal context that perceives antisemitism as taboo, the speaker of an antisemitic idea probably finds any reason for their expressing such an idea more plausible than hatred toward Jews. This study thus focuses perceptions of Jews, the effects, and a close reading of the discourses and representations produced in chants, flags, and banners. My research thus aims to consider the meanings and consequences of fan performances beyond their supposed intentions.

In my previous publications, I have attempted to analyze antisemitism from different angles. In a recently published journal article titled "Hitler's American Countermodel: The United States and the Making of Nazi Ideology," I delve into how the Nazis viewed the United States not only as a model to emulate but also as a countermodel for dealing with the "Jewish

question."[25] While admiring America's racist laws and techno-
logical advancements, the Nazis despised Americans for what
they perceived as Americans' failure to address the so-called
Jewish threat. Through an intertextual analysis of visual and textual primary sources, I demonstrate how the Nazis claimed that
an allegedly Jewish world conspiracy was behind the replace-
ment of "Aryans" with "Black people." I argue that antisemitism
and racism are overlapping yet distinct ideologies: racism legiti-
mizes inequalities from a position of power, while antisemitism
is often perceived as a rebellious challenge to perceived injustice.
In contrast to racist ideology, where the object of hatred is seen
as inferior, antisemitism operates on the belief in a world conspiracy, with the antisemite searching for someone responsible
for all individual and societal ills.

In my previous book on antisemitism in German football fan
cultures, I argue that antisemitism includes but is not limited to
discrimination against Jewish people or institutions. I analyze
a distinct form of hatred within German football fan cultures
that emerged after the foundation of RasenBallsport Leipzig (RB
Leipzig) in 2009. This animosity is fueled by various factors, such
as the club's ties to Red Bull as its founder and sponsor (reflected
in its name and stadium) and its deviation from the 50+1 owner-
ship rule, which states that at least 51 percent of a club must be
owned by its members. Amid contempt for the club, criticism
turns into ressentiment: hatred identifies RB Leipzig as the personification of capitalism, infused with antisemitic stereotypes
rooted in a rejection of modernity and globalization. Although
not being perceived as a "Jew Club," RB Leipzig became an object
in the antisemitic imagination. The club's identity is constructed
in opposition to one's own club, supposedly rich in history and
tradition—RB Leipzig is modern, global, and unauthentic—
things imagined as Jewish in antisemitic ideology.

To understand the antisemitic communication of ressentiment
against RB Leipzig, I refer to Reinhard Rürup, who posits that

antisemitism served as an explanatory model and offered possible solutions to the economic, political, and cultural crises of late nineteenth-century Germany. He has convincingly argued that antisemitism is a distorted image of society.[26] Similarly, Moishe Postone describes how certain forms of anticapitalist thinking tend to perceive capitalism only in its abstract form, equating it with money and personifying "Jews" as representatives of capitalism. This form of anticapitalism, as Postone argues, lays the groundwork for manifest antisemitism through personalized and moralized critiques of capitalism.[27] Jean-Paul Sartre further characterizes antisemitism as a comprehensive attitude toward not only Jews but also toward people, history, and society—a passion intertwined with one's worldview.[28]

This book is different. The "Jew Clubs" are neither accused of world conspiracies like "American Jews," nor identified as the personification of capitalism like RB Leipzig. They are celebrated as "Yids" or "Super Jews," and they are targeted with blatant antisemitic chants but are not singled out for being too commercial, too global, or too inauthentic. Instead, the "Jew Clubs" are spaces in which the complex web of ideas about "Jews" and false representations of them are negotiated—a web constantly reproduced through antisemitic and philosemitic performances.

Some scholars discussing the "Jew Club" identity of Tottenham Hotspur argue that the focus should be on the *real* antisemites, that is, the fans of rival clubs who engage in chants like "Jews to the gas" against Tottenham, instead of the Tottenham fans who use "Yid" as a nickname.[29] This book complicates understandings of *real* antisemites based on supposed intentions and suggests a different approach that I call the "Jew" imaginary framework. It aims to illuminate the web underlying and connecting antisemitism and philosemitism in order to analyze the performances of both. In so doing, it considers the fans of the "Jew Clubs" and their rivals, the antisemitic and philosemitic chants, and how they are connected. Scholars such as

Zygmunt Baumann and Lisa Silverman note that the concept of antisemitism can be limited or limiting.[30] Silverman introduces the concept of "Jewish difference" to redirect attention to the "hierarchical ordering system of constructed ideals of the Jew and non-Jew" that underlie antisemitism.[31] While Baumann and Silverman understand the abstract Jew as the Other in a hierarchical binary framework of Jews and non-Jews, my proposed concept—the "Jew" imaginary framework—also highlights the role of ideology in antisemitism, such as an imaginary space of "Jews" as a third Other.[32] The sociologist Klaus Holz understands the figure of the "Jew" in modern antisemitism as symbolizing a *Figur des Dritten*, which literally translates as a figure of a third person, category of person, or concept.[33] Holz describes how the emergence of nation states arranged the world in binary frameworks of we-they oppositions between national collectives competing for resources and influence. The "Jew" thus adds a third Other to this binary framework that justifies and stabilizes the contemporary world order: the "global Jews" are perceived as a threat to collective identities and the differences between them; "they" are not "down" in a power structure, but "up" and "dangerous." Ultimately, all that remains to be done to save the world is removing this third Other. The concept of Jewish difference, understood as a "hierarchical framework that encompasses the relationship between the socially constructed categories of 'Jew' and 'non-Jew,'" can also be limiting.[34] If it is reduced to a binary framework of us versus them, the conceptual framework of Jewish difference may lead to claims like "the figure of the Jew can also be replaced with a different other—such as, in recent examples in Germany, the Muslim."[35] I maintain that ideologies such as antisemitism and anti-Muslim ressentiment are coexisting and overlapping; they do not replace one another, but rather, there is an intersectionality of ideologies present.[36] Taking power dynamics, binaries, and the potentially narrow focus of antisemitism into account, the "Jew" imaginary

framework considers the imaginary space of "Jews" in antisemitic ideology and examines the interrelatedness of antisemitism and philosemitism.

The "Jew" imaginary framework highlights the symbolic, cultural, and historical dimensions that inform the making of "Jew
Clubs" and the construction of the imagined figure of "Jews."
The "Jew" imaginary framework encompasses a complex interplay of societal perceptions and stereotypes of "Jews," which are
constructed within an imaginary realm of cultural and historical
narratives, leading to the emergence of "Jews" as symbolic and
moral constructs reflecting broader cultural and social concerns.
Let me now detail the three key elements: "Jew," imaginary, and
framework.

First, the term *"Jew"* refers to the abstract "Jew" and the cultural constructs embedded within this figure. In the "Jew" imaginary framework, the concept of "Jew" surrounds an individual
just like I have chosen to retain quotation marks surrounding the
word "Jew." Jean Améry illustrated the process of being signified
as a "Jew" in his 1966 essay "On the Impossible Obligation to Be a
Jew." Améry read the Nuremberg Laws in a Viennese coffeehouse
in 1935 and remembers: "I only needed to skim through them to
realize that they applied to me. Society . . . had just made a Jew
of me" although "I was no more Jewish now than I had been half
an hour earlier."[37] Améry contemplates his complex identity as a
Jew, which was forced on him by historical circumstances rather
than personal choice. An imagined Self (non-Jew) projects an
imagined identity onto an Other (Jew) to develop (collective)
identity, leaving a significant effect on the Other's identity. This
book, while focusing on the process of (re)creating the abstract
"Jew," does not leave Jews out of the question: I analyze the subjectivity and agency of Jew(s), albeit in the context of the quotation marks, which denote the societal situation, of the "Jew"
imaginary framework.[38] What "Jew" signifies is dependent on
social and historical context and is not stable. This framework

does not (alone) determine how Jews (people) experience their identities, and how they respond to or partake in the framework.

Second, the term *imaginary* denotes the realm in which ideas surrounding "Jews" are constructed.[39] I understand this as the constant (re)production of images about Self and Other, about Jews, "Jews," and non-Jews. These images are collective and imaginary; they link Jews (as people) to "Jews" as an abstract category; they are distorted images through which individuals and collectives perceive themselves and Others. This constant (re)creation of the imaginary occurs within the realm of a symbolic order governed by symbols, language, and performances, functioning as signifiers representing concepts such as Jew and "Jew." The making of "Jew Clubs" is a constant practice in which language, symbols, and performances (re)produce a web of meanings associated with the "Jew" imaginary framework.

Third, the term *framework* refers to the societal context in which the imaginary identification of the "Jew" occurs. It highlights local contexts, historical events, political structures, and cultural values. A framework helps interpret a cultural phenomenon such as the "Jew Clubs" in a specific context, allowing us to explore how it is shaped by and contributes to the dynamics of the societies to which the respective "Jew Clubs" belong. This approach also allows me to study how Jews and non-Jews respond to and contribute to the "Jew" imaginary framework. In sum, the "Jew" imaginary framework demonstrates the connection between antisemitism and philosemitism, and how "Jew Clubs" serve as a platform for negotiating Jewish identities, ideas about "Jews," and collective identities.

JEWS, FOOTBALL, AND CLAIMS TO MODERNITY

Football is a space through which contested concepts about belonging, origin, and worldviews are expressed. Sport was—and remains—more than just an occasional pastime for many Jews in Europe. For them, "sports served as a weapon in their various fights."[40] It may not surprise, then, that "Jewish history cannot be reduced to intellectual history."[41] Studying Jewish-gentile relationships in the context of sports in general and the "Jew Club" phenomenon in particular shows how Jews made claims of modernity far beyond avant-garde culture, as has been described in canonical works such as George L. Mosse's *German Jews beyond Judaism*.[42] In other words, researching Jewish-gentile relationships through the lens of football adds more nuance to an understanding of Jews as having been isolated from the masses and consequently "committed to the pursuit of a higher culture, making contact with the masses increasingly difficult."[43] Particularly in the early twentieth century, Jews participated in sports as officials, players, fans, doctors, and in many other roles.

My book engages with current studies such as Marline Otte's *Jewish Identities in German Popular Entertainment, 1890–1933* by discussing how Jews participated in football and how their perception in football shaped and was shaped by the "Jew" imaginary framework. Otte criticizes a scholarly overemphasis on German Jewish contributions to high culture and notes that—as a side effect—many studies of the German Jewry have echoed the anti-semitic stereotype of the "smart Jew."[44] Otte challenges the "contributionist" paradigm, which entailed a focus on elites and elite culture. Furthermore, Otte criticizes the scholarly focus on assimilation into German society although "no preexisting, homogenous German mass culture into which Jews chose to assimilate existed." On the contrary, "mass entertainment evolved in conjunction with the massive involvement of Jewish actors, artists, directors, screenwriters."[45] What Otte found about Jewish participation in the context of the circus, Jargon theater, and revue theater holds true for football, too. The sport's success story cannot be written without the contributions of Jews. Football clubs such as the "Jew Clubs" analyzed in this study offered Jews a space in which they could contribute to modernity (rather than assimilate). Indeed, sports "has occupied and continues to occupy, an important place in the modern Jewish world."[46] In and through sports, Jews navigated their identities, negotiated contemporary political questions, and responded to current debates within and beyond Judaism such as Zionism and Max Nordau's notion of muscular Judaism (*Muskeljudentum*),[47] that is, the idea of the "new Jew" who is the antithesis of the supposedly weak "old Jew," which was previously commonplace in the antisemitic imagination. Even today, the "Jew Clubs" are a central societal space for Jews to negotiate their identities in the context of post-Holocaust societies in which the "Jew" imaginary framework remains powerful. Traditionally, studies of Jews in sport concentrate on officials and players. My book—the Tottenham chapter in particular—also highlights the perspectives of Jewish fans.

The "Jew" imaginary framework is a powerful societal structure that impacts how Jews navigate popular cultural spaces and that is also impacted by their actions. The notion of the abstract "Jew" influences the experiences and identities of Jews, without dictating them to them. Klaus Hödl, an Austrian historian, critiques the reliance on binaries in German Jewish studies and suggests that the field shift away from its focus on dichotomies. Hödl argues that historical accounts of Jewish–non-Jewish binaries "do not correspond with actual historical life-worlds."[48] Hödl proposes the concept of similarity to eliminate the notion of "a deeply anchored and seemingly fixed otherness of Jews."[49] Instead, his notion of similarity maintains that Jews can be "both-and-one": their experiences are not limited to differences—they may identify simultaneously as Jews, Germans, football fans, and so on. From the perspective of binaries, the "Jew Clubs" reproduce the "Jew" imaginary framework and encompass antisemitic and philosemitic stereotyping. Yet from the perspective of subjectivity, "Jew Clubs" offer room for interaction, empowerment, and agency. Taken together, this book investigates how the "Jew" imaginary framework functions in the context of "Jew Clubs," without determining individual and collective experiences and identities.

Before Nazism, many European football clubs stood in stark contrast to, for instance, the Turner movement, a national movement in nineteenth-century Germany. "By the end of the nineteenth century many gymnastics and sports associations made it clear that they would not welcome Jewish members."[50] The Jewish body was "not considered equal with the 'Aryan body.'" In football, however, there was a sense of modernity, a sense of belonging among Jews. In contrast to the antisemitic Turner movement or the anti-Jewish German fraternities (*Burschenschaften*), sports clubs like FC Bayern Munich, Austria Vienna, Ajax Amsterdam, and Tottenham Hotspur in London offered liminal spaces in which a gentile-Jewish symbiosis seemed possible for a short period of time, at least for some European-assimilated bourgeois Jews. Michael Brenner and Gideon Reuveni argue that "Jews could show that they belonged to the surrounding society by participating in the sports associations of their neighborhood."[51] Yet, as Silverman has shown for the Austrian context, "the parameters of Jewish participation . . . were carefully circumscribed."[52] While sports offered a space for Jews to participate in society, there was no space for the Jewish. As Silverman notes, "unspoken rules of behavior . . . constantly and irrevocably shaped the experiences of Jews."[53] Sports clubs attempting to distance themselves from the "Jewish"—among them the "Jew Clubs" of this study—attracted Jews who were "seeking to distance themselves from associations with that category."[54] On the other end of the spectrum were sports clubs embracing Jewishness as a reaction to what Silverman calls the framework of Jewish difference. This book engages with the histories of those Jews who joined the "Jew Clubs" and investigates the perception of their participation from a modern-day perspective.

Whatever these Jews had found in their respective sport organizations changed drastically in 1933. Football clubs in Germany were quick to expel Jewish club members, according to the
racially antisemitic definition that the Nazis enacted.[55] Jews in
Austrian and Dutch football clubs had similar experiences after
Austria's "Anschluss" in March 1938 and the occupation of the
Netherlands in May 1940. In Germany, Jewish clubs like Maccabi
and Schild had record numbers of new members for a short time
because of the expulsions from other clubs.[56] Yet the antisemitic
policies of the German government, the rise in everyday antisemitic incidents, and soon also the deportations and the murders
of Jews made the Jewish clubs disappear. Jews were also expelled
from "Jew Clubs" like FC Bayern, and whatever one understands
as "Jewish football" in Europe fundamentally changed with the
Holocaust. Even the once world-famous Jewish sports club SK
Hakoah Vienna vanished, although it was reestablished in 1945
(when only five thousand Jews lived in Vienna); however, it discontinued its football section in 1950. In 2008, seventy years after
the "Anschluss," Hakoah finally reopened its sports complex in
Vienna, although still without a football section. The "Jew Clubs"
had also changed; for instance, FK Austria Vienna, a club that
was partly built by assimilated bourgeois Jews, was fundamentally different as only those Jews who returned to clubs like FK
Austria Vienna or FC Bayern Munich remained the exception.

There are three historical moments in which the supposed
Jewishness of the "Jew Clubs" was particularly important. First,
before Nazism, "Jew Clubs" offered a space of belonging for
Jews and non-Jews. Although the "Jew" imaginary framework
influenced their experiences, Jews did not experience their lives
in a zero-sum logic of inclusion or exclusion. They were proud
Bavarians, Amsterdammers, and so on. Second, the Nazis sys-
tematically discriminated against, expelled, and murdered Jews,
including officials, players, fans, and sponsors of the "Jew Clubs."

In contrast to Jewish sports clubs like Hakoah, however, the "Jew Clubs" were not systemically disadvantaged by the Nazis; they continued to exist, and even participated actively in the expulsion of Jews from their clubs. Fellow sports players turned into enemies. Third, the making of "Jew Clubs" is a recent phenomenon that predominantly began in post-Holocaust societies. Tottenham and Ajax, for instance, had almost no antisemitic chants directed against them before the 1970s, and the memory of Kurt Landauer did not become central to FC Bayern's club culture until the early twenty-first century.

COLLECTIVE MEMORIES AND COLLECTIVE IDENTITIES

There are two primary reasons why football offers a uniquely promising opportunity for the study of collective memories and collective identities: (1) being a fan of a football club is by definition impossible without a strong sense of collective identity, and (2) the sense of belonging to a football club collective is predominantly fueled by a shared sense of tradition. The victories and the defeats, the titles and the failures, and anecdotes from fan experiences are part and parcel of collective football identities. In many European stadiums, such as Munich, Vienna, and Amsterdam, one will encounter graffiti in and outside the stadium, displaying club heroes and the greatest successes. Many of them have been created and paid for by the fans themselves, and some even portray the fans—often referred to as "the twelfth player." Collective football memories are also expressed in the form of statues. Indeed, there are so many of them that a whole website has been created to collect, categorize, and map them: the Sporting Statues Project.[57] Graffiti, statues, and other material forms of collective sporting memories generate collective identities. They create a sense of shared history—something that becomes more important as the sport itself becomes increasingly commodified and global.

In Germany, for instance, many fans even perceive it as more significant to belong to a traditional club than to win championships. When Red Bull announced the foundation of the football club RB Leipzig in 2009, German football fans reacted with an unprecedented wave of hatred against the club. For them, the club represents everything that a traditional club is not: RB Leipzig is new, commercial, and global. In my previous book, I argued that the ressentiment communication[58] directed at RB Leipzig reveals structures of antisemitic thinking and feeling.[59] The fans project tropes onto RB Leipzig that have been—traditionally—projected onto Jews, such as rootlessness, cosmopolitanism, and modernity. They construct their self-image as traditional clubs in opposition to RB Leipzig's supposed lack of tradition. The fans understand tradition as something one is, as what one has, yet also as something that one can never acquire. Although tradition is a central value for them, they remain vague about what tradition means: fans from Cologne claim, for instance, that "every football fan recognizes a traditional club right away."[60] The traditional club is something felt and recognized, yet it requires constant enactment. I have described this process as *doing tradition*. Doing tradition is the constant performative practice of "inventing traditions," a process, as Eric Hobsbawm writes, "of formalization and ritualization, characterized by reference to the past."[61] Invented traditions are powerful specifically because they are vague and unspecific.[62] *Doing tradition* is a key practice for the construction of collective identities, and fans are doing tradition through manifold collective performances in and outside the stadiums. Studying their performances, their doing tradition, is a central approach to understanding the making of "Jew Clubs." This study ultimately shows that the making of "Jew Clubs" is an active process in the present rather than the automatic result of events in the past.

The football stadium is a key site for the (re)production of collective identities. Here, collective memories are enacted through collective representations,[63] such as the fans' graffiti, stickers, and flags, and in the club's museums or statues. Lately, a memory boom has created the interdisciplinary academic field of memory studies, with its own journals, institutes, and yearbooks. Yet the interconnection between memory and sport cultures has so far been overshadowed by the field's focus on the realms of museums, memorials, politics, and tourist sites. My work explores memory cultures in the realm of sports and thus also provides a study of *memory in action*. I understand collective memories in a similar sense to Andrei S. Markovits and Simon Reich as "bridges linking history (as fact) to ideology (as myth)."[64] Collective memories are therefore a central key to understanding the "Jew Club" phenomenon as they link the history of Jewish contributions to and participation in these clubs (fact) to today's "Jew Club" identities (myth). In Munich, the "Jew Club" identity is constructed through memory culture. Here, the former club president Kurt Landauer is remembered as one of the club's great presidents. By foregrounding Landauer's Jewish background, however, the club produces a collective identity as a "Jew Club" and links itself to the glorification of an alleged German-Jewish symbiosis. The bridges built through collective memories produce the (self-)identifications of "Jew Clubs" in European football stadiums.

FOOTBALL AND SOCIETY

Football is a contested space for belonging, participating, integrating, and excluding. Even the choice of term used to describe the sport—"football" or "soccer"—is the subject of heated debates. In most countries, "football" refers to association football, with local variants such as the German *Fußball* and the Spanish *fútbol*, imbuing the term with widespread clarity. However, in the United States and some other countries, "football" denotes a sport related to but distinct from association football, and it is the dominant variant in these regions. To distinguish these leading forms of "football" from association football, the term *soccer* is used.

The name and identity of the sport have been contested since the late nineteenth century. Until the 1980s, *soccer* was commonly used in Britain alongside *football*. For instance, Manchester United coach Matt Busby titled his 1974 autobiography *Soccer at the Top: My Life in Football*, and we also see that English newspapers still talked of "soccer" when discussing Tottenham's "Jew Club" identity in the early 1980s. However, with the modernization of the game and the rise of American soccer from a peripheral to a more prominent position, the term *soccer* has acquired a negative connotation in Europe that continues to this day. Despite its British origin, where it was used alongside *football* in reference to the same game, *soccer* is now often viewed in Europe as inauthentic and an unwelcome Americanism. In this book, although published in the United States, I use the term *football* to align with its common usage in Europe, as the book focuses on four European clubs.[65]

The football stadium embodies the connections between sport and society, between football and politics. As Norbert Elias argues, "Studies of sport which are not studies of society are studies out of context."[66] The stadiums are "spaces of political discourse."[67] I understand football as a microscope under which societal phenomena become observable in a particularly rich yet specific way. To decipher the game's language, it is important to consider "that sports are communicative forms with clearly delineated rules and regulations that have a bevy of meanings, nuances, and levels."[68] Sport today is important because it matters culturally. Richard Giulianotti writes in one of the many handbooks on the sociology of sport that, socially speaking, "sport dominates much of everyday public discourse and anchors many of our social identities."[69] This is, Markovits argues, what makes a sports culture hegemonic: such sport cultures are defined by "watching, following, worrying, debating, living, and speaking a sport rather than merely playing it. . . . The very crux of all hegemonic sport cultures occurs off the playing field or court and centers on ancillary matters between the games or matches proper."[70] In other words, football is a significant cultural space that follows a particular logic and requires understanding a certain language. Football is "a form of popular culture that reaches massive audiences and permeates the national and global imagination in many parts of the world."[71] The club Tottenham Hotspur, for instance, "gave the emerging middle class something to identify with."[72] Fans' collective identities are tied to spaces; in the case of the Spurs, the stadium White Hart Lane represents their collective identity—it "brings a sense of place, of feeling at home, of belonging."[73] Sport events are televised globally and followed by millions across the globe. Yet football, although globalized, always remains local. The sport is, as Roland Robertson puts it brilliantly, always "glocal."[74] Studying collective memories of Jews and the Holocaust in the realm of football is particularly pertinent at a time when Holocaust memory has become globalized as well.[75] Bringing together the study of a glocalized sport and the globalized collective memory of the Holocaust illustrates that Holocaust memory is just as local as it is global. The four case studies I gather show that collective memories are not just globalized but are rather best understood as glocalized.

FOOTBALL CLUB CULTURES AND FAN CULTURES

Usually, we think of the players as central to the culture of a football club and perceive the fans as those who follow them. For me, it is the other way around. I assert that the fans are not only one active part of the spectacle but also the most important one. It is because of the fans that football is hegemonic, not because of the players. While millions of fans follow stars like Lionel Messi or Cristiano Ronaldo on Instagram, I am most interested in what I call "active fandom," that is, the fans who follow the club actively, visit the stadium, and aim to participate in their club cultures, for instance in the form of club membership or participating in collective fan performances. A club's culture is, I claim, more defined by active fandom than by players (who transfer from club to club every other year anyway) or by the clubs' public relations departments.

Individual bodies become one through engaging in collective actions of jumping and singing. The atmosphere in a football stadium "is a ritual that is actively performed by the fans."[76] Active fans "are willing to embody the collective by removing traces of their individuality, as the individual and group become one organic body."[77] The football chants I analyze in this book "arise from the tradition of folk songs, popular plays, burlesque rhymes, and ballads, and they are related to local, patriotic or nationalistic songs and chants celebrating the supremacy of the singer's home town, county, or country."[78] The mass singing unifies; it creates "an atmosphere of sociability rather than communication."[79] Within these "sonic landscapes," "traces of history and identity are registered"; the songs of fandom offer a way of representing "locality and social life in the realm of metaphor and symbolism," through which a notion of "home" is produced.[80] Through the fans' performances, clubs become "small mother countries."[81] Active fandom lets groups feel as one and thus function like collective memories, which, as Maurice Halbwachs argues, offers the group a self-portrait that "allows the group to recognize itself."[82] Collective identities and collective memories intersect in the practices of fandom. The practices of fandom are so meaningful because of football's high status in society, as embodied in the architectural frame of a stadium.

All the fan groups studied in this book are not only emotionally attached to "their" clubs but are also invested in contributing to their respective club cultures. Many fans participate in membership meetings or protest against overly expensive tickets. Nearly all football fans are neither hooligans nor neo-Nazis. Indeed, as I discuss in this book, many of them—for instance the hardcore fans of FC Bayern—are praised with awards for their engagement on behalf of democracy and against neo-Nazism. Studying the (dis)continuities of National Socialism, such as antisemitism, in contemporary football fan cultures thus allows me to investigate the possible continued relevance of Adorno's claim: "I consider the survival of National Socialism *within* democracy to be potentially more menacing than the survival of fascist tendencies *against* democracy."[83] The "survival of National Socialism within democracy" can, I argue, be studied through sport cultures and by discussing how memorial activities in this context understand, reflect, and influence the present moment.

Active fandom is overwhelmingly masculine, even though women make up a sizable proportion of spectators. Football cultures operate within a masculine grammar, and this aligns with the sports' masculine ideals such as toughness, physicality, camaraderie, and heterosexuality. Football masculinity is associated with loyalty, honor, competition, and hierarchy. Camaraderie and community are predominantly seen as male domains. Sexist comments and the overstepping of physical boundaries are part of a sexualized football culture, creating a space that women often navigate cautiously, imposing certain rules on themselves.[84] Sexism shapes women's experiences of football, and so there have been continual attempts by those participating in football culture to undo genderized standards and for women to be perceived as fans rather than as female fans.[85] Scholarship on fan cultures has tended to portray sport as a male domain, thus potentially making female fans invisible.[86] Although the male football fan remains the norm, female fans are no longer unusual, and in recent years, a rapid increase in scholarly publications "discovering" female fan perspectives has emerged.[87] Despite the increased presence and visibility of female fans, the masculine grammar of football remains powerful; it depicts women as unauthentic, untraditional, and unusual, intersecting in various ways with the "Jew Club" identities.

The masculine grammar of fan cultures involves performative practices that not only construct collective club identities in opposition to or as "Jew Clubs" but that also constantly engage in practices of doing gender—more specifically, doing masculinity and undoing femininity. Football provides a unique context and a specific opportunity structure for such performances because this sport allows for collective emotional practices that are not similarly available to men in other societal spheres. Men embracing each other and crying or publicly praying together are rarely encountered outside football contexts. In the football context, however, there exists an emotionality mandate.[88] Fandom is a strategy for intensifying emotional experiences.[89] The emotionality mandate also serves as an authenticity mandate: emotional fan practices promise to be a spontaneous expression of the "authentic" (masculine) person. The terms *football*, *masculinity*, and *emotions* often overlap in football-related discourse. Almut Sülzle's ethnographic field study of German football fans argues that emotions in football primarily belong to men, while women are aware of the male prerogative to possess "true" football emotions.[90] Gender stereotypes can sometimes take on reversed meanings in football. The sociologists Nina Degele and Caroline Janz argue that while women typically defend themselves against the prejudice that they are irrational and emotion-driven compared to men who are seen as rational and objective, this is reversed in football. Here, it is women who "cannot genuinely celebrate and cheer along."[91] Football culture is only perceived as authentic when it has a masculine connotation. In this context, female fans are making constant choices to appear as "authentic" fans, for instance in relation to their clothing, which is supposed to look not too female.[92] Female fans are constantly navigating their identities in the framework of a predominantly masculine and sexist sport culture. This book touches on these gendered performances of fan cultures, expressed in banners such as "Jews and Pussies" (directed at Tottenham supporters) or the portrayal of Ajax Amsterdam supporters as "unmanly Jews."

In the vibrant world of European football fandom, a remarkable degree of coordination and self-organization among supporters defines the fervor that accompanies every game. Unlike the scenes witnessed in the US in Major League Baseball, National Football League (NFL), National Basketball Association (NBA), and National Hockey League games, where fans often congregate in smaller groups and the support has a different level of organization, European football enthusiasts take center stage in crafting the stadium atmosphere. These fans infuse every game with independently orchestrated performances, with their chants resounding throughout the stadium, their flags waving proudly, and their songs echoing in unison. In stark contrast, events in the NFL, NBA, and similar leagues are typically choreographed by dedicated event teams, disseminated through loudspeakers, and displayed on video walls, creating a manufactured ambiance that differs significantly from the atmosphere of European football fandom. In other words, the atmosphere in the "Big Four" US sport leagues is organized top-down, whereas the atmosphere of European football is created bottom-up by independent fan organizations. Despite these differences, fans of various teams such as the NFL team Kansas City Chiefs engage in a ritual called the tomahawk chop (also known as the arrowhead chop) during which thousands of fans make a chopping motion while chanting rhythmically. Here, the organization does not orchestrate the performance and even prohibited fans from wearing headdresses or face paint that mimics Native American cultures. Nevertheless, the chop endured. More often, fans of NFL teams were used to encountering Native American mascots or halftime show performers "playing Indian" at the arena, staged and hired for them by an organization that creates the atmosphere ready to be consumed by its fans.[93] Fans of "Jew Clubs" in European football, such as Ajax Amsterdam or Tottenham Hotspur, create a "Jew Club" identity through their performances even though the management boards are opposed to such performances or appropriations.

Fans who embrace Native American mascots and those af-filiated with European "Jew Clubs" share a common thread of what Renato Rosaldo terms "imperialist nostalgia." In both scenarios, societies grapple with their histories, collectively mourning "the passing of what they themselves have trans-formed."[94] By playing Indian or enacting a "Jew Club," these communities keep the abstract Other alive, albeit bound to an imaginary realm, while simultaneously seeking reconciliation with the past. "Imperialist nostalgia" evokes an "innocent yearn-ing," serving to establish one's innocence while also acknowl-edging the destruction wrought by one's predecessors. As the contentious issue of Native American mascots in the US reaches "a moment of change,"[95] European nonfootball sport teams are increasingly adopting such mascots, often divorced from these critical discussions in the US.[96] This underscores the ongoing global conversation about the appropriation of cultural symbols and the complex interplay between sports, historical memory, and collective identities.

THE "VIRTUALLY JEWISH" FOOTBALL STADIUM

Benedict Anderson famously defined the nation as an imagined political community, a community that is "imagined because the members of even the smallest nation will never know most of their fellow-members, meet them, or even hear of them."[97] Those participating in an (imagined) football community not only hear but also see each other in the stadium. The stadium is an important site for the development of collective memories and the construction of identities. The sense of a football ground as sustaining historical continuity, Les Back argues, "is underscored by the request often made by fans to have their ashes scattered on the pitch itself after their death. The playing surface provides a connection to past and future heroes who perform on it but it also serves literally and metaphorically as an altar of memory and commemoration."[98] The stadium connects the past and the present. The stadium is a *lieux de mémoire*[99] where collective memories are produced and enacted. Collective memories need a public medium.[100] As Michal Bodemann writes, commemoration "always takes place in contexts similar to the theater." It needs "a stage, spectators, actors, stage designs, the drama and the staging itself."[101] The football stadium, as I understand it, is a medium comparable to the theater: Both are public spaces where the performances take place at specific times and under specific rules. Both the theater and the stadium are architectural spaces with specific forms of "gaze guidance and eye control."[102] While the building architecture matters, it is the crowd that gives significance to an otherwise empty building. When Johann Wolfgang von Goethe reflected on the amphitheater in the Verona chapter of his Italian travels, he observed that the building's purpose is "to impress the people with itself."[103] When "crowded together" in the arena, the people find themselves "united as one noble assembly, welded into one mass, a single body animated by a single spirit." If empty, however, "there is no standard by which to judge if it [the amphitheater] is great or small."[104] Even today, the stadium is an ideal space in which to observe collective identities in action.

The collective memories of football fans in Munich, Vienna, Amsterdam, and London have a public medium—their fan performances. While all clubs have their forms of engaging with history, they share a perception of Jews as "nahe Fremde," that is, the Other among us.[105] The abstractness, anonymity, and perceived absence of Jews is crucial for these forms of the fans' performances. They developed different forms of reinventing the "Jew," which tell us more about collective memories than about objective histories—this is more about how non-Jews see "Jews" than about what Jews are like. These performances are a form of meaning making in the present that always relates to history. They lie in the middle of a tension between collective memories and the creation of (imagined) communities. Through studying the practices of fandom, we can understand how the past is made present in distorted ways.

The practices described in this book turn the football stadium into a space where collective memories, histories, and identities intersect. The stadium evolves into a non-Jewish "Jewish" space, similar to the "virtually Jewish" spaces studied by Ruth Ellen Gruber in her 2002 book *Virtually Jewish: Reinventing Jewish Culture in Europe*, in which Gruber identifies a "longing for lost Jews or for what Jews are seen to represent."[106] This longing, Gruber argues, emerged around the 1980s, roughly alongside the rise of the "Jew Club" identities by fans of Tottenham and Ajax, and parallel to the emergence of hooliganism and the related rise of antisemitism in football. The central thesis of Gruber's book is that the longing for lost "Jews" resulted in a virtual Jewish world. The concept of virtually Jewish spaces is related to the concept of cyberspace, a space into which people can enter and move around without leaving their "real-world" identities behind. Cyberspace allows them to "assume other identities, play other roles, and be, or act as if they are, whoever they want."[107] Gruber identifies the virtual Jewish world, for instance, in Jewish-style restaurants that sell a supposedly authentic Jewish atmosphere; in such restaurants, one encounters allegedly Jewish elements such as "subdued lighting, tastefully arranged antique furniture, scattered menorahs, background klezmer music, and dark oil paintings of old fashioned Jewish scenes," all of which are intended to "conjure up a vanished world." However, they only "bear scant resemblance of what most real prewar Jewish eateries looked like."[108] In the context of football, one can find virtually Jewish symbols not only inside the stadium, where fans paint the Star of David on their flags or chant "Hava Nagila," but also in de facto virtual spaces such as Tottenham Hotspur online fan forums, where fans may end their posts "with an emoticon character wearing a *shtreimel* (large black hat) with beard and sidelocks, waving an Israeli flag."[109] Whether in the stadium or online, these fan practices in and around football create a virtually Jewish space in which people develop and confirm their understanding of the "Jew" imaginary framework.

Performances of Judaism in the virtually Jewish stadium can thus be defined as enacting representations of Judaism without Jews. At the same time, however, skepticism toward any essential definition of a person or space as either Jewish or, for instance, German, is a problematic presupposition. The common models of definite identities are, as the historian Scott Spector argues, "themselves powerfully ideological instruments of segregation, rather than descriptors of a cultural condition."[110] Spector's project of "introducing subjectivity to German–Jewish history" has inspired two core assumptions for this study.[111] First, Jews, like FC Bayern's president Kurt Landauer, "did not experience their relationship to Jewishness (or to Germanness, for that matter) in the zero-sum-game terms of the politics of assimilation."[112] From a post-1945 perspective, the complexities of secular Jewish identities are too often ignored. More awareness of the historical situations of these Jews in their contexts is required. Second, to acknowledge the complex experiences of Jews, researchers must understand that the "Jew Clubs" are more than either philosemitism or antisemitism without Jews.[113] The "Jew Clubs" are "with Jews" although the club's identities do not rely on an empirical core. Many Jews are offended by antisemitic chanting, while others see "Jew Club" performances as acts of solidarity and empowerment. Jewish subjectivities are diverse and ambiguous. This understanding allows for a perspective that is more nuanced than binary frameworks of these clubs as either Jewish or not Jewish.

The memory cultures described by Gruber share with the realm of football that they are a "means of rethinking and redefining personal identity and national histories."[114] Yet they differ because the spaces analyzed by Gruber typically are commercial tourist sites where everything is already arranged when the consumer enters the space; in football, the stadium is an empty architectural space that gains its cultural relevance to a large degree through fan performances. While the clubs have a commercial interest, the "Jew Club" identities are performed by football fans rather than by the clubs. In the cases of Ajax and Tottenham, the clubs—commercial entities in and of themselves—pushed against the use of Jewish symbols by their fans because they feared they would trigger antisemitism among the club's opponents and thus blemish the club's corporate identity. This book is thus also concerned with questions of policing the virtually Jewish space and of mapping the various actors, such as clubs and fans, and their relationships not only to Judaism but also to one another.

Gruber developed her concept of virtually Jewish spaces in reference to Diana Pinto's notion of the "Jewish space," which Pinto defines as "containing a multitude of 'things Jewish,'" but as "not dependent on the size or even presence of a living Jewish community."[115] Gruber argues that "this 'universalization' of the Jewish phenomenon" and "this emergence of a 'Judaizing terrain'" is "a 'filling' of the Jewish space," "a process that in turn encompasses the creation of a 'virtual Jewishness,' a 'virtual Jewish world.'"[116] My study is concerned with how the virtually Jewish stadium is filled, and with the question of how clubs and fans are working through the past. They do so, I argue, through their different performances and policing and in ways very different yet connected to how people engage with Judaism at virtually Jewish restaurants. The hungry eater at a virtually Jewish restaurant encounters something staged for them. The purpose of the restaurant is to sell an authentically Jewish atmosphere to the customer. The opposite is the case in the stadium. The fan who arrives at the stadium on game day encounters an otherwise empty stadium that gains its significance only through the meaning that is produced through their actions. The fan in the stadium has, I argue, more agency than the customer in the restaurant.

The virtually Jewish stadium offers a promising opportunity to investigate the long-term effects of Nazism on European societies. In 1986, the historian Dan Diner argued that the idea of a German-Jewish symbiosis had finally materialized after Auschwitz, although negatively.[117] Diner asserted that Germans and Jews are finally bound together because the Holocaust has become the central focus point for both identity collectives. Auschwitz would, Diner argued, "make its most lasting impact on . . . the future."[118] The "Jew Club" phenomenon appears to be one space where the unconscious impacts of the unmastered past come to the surface. Ultimately, this study takes up Diner's concept and asks about the consequences of both the Holocaust and the subsequent memory culture on contemporary European societies.

OUTLINE OF CHAPTERS

This book is divided into four chapters, each of which presents the case of one "Jew Club." The first chapter analyzes the German football club FC Bayern Munich through the lens of the "Jew Club" as memory culture. It shows how fans and club rediscovered FC Bayern's German Jewish club president Kurt Landauer at the turn of the century. It investigates local and national memory cultures through a study of the club's belated turn to Landauer. More precisely, it studies German memory culture through what the historian Ulrike Jureit calls "victim-identified memory culture," that is, a memory culture in which identification with the victims tends to obscure the perpetrator's past.[119] Furthermore, it argues that the new club icon, Landauer, helps the fans uphold their local identity while the club becomes more and more global.

The second chapter, on the football club FK Austria Vienna (FAK), highlights the "Jew Club" as a cultural code. It shows how supposedly Jewish traits such as cosmopolitanism, modernity, and rootlessness became associated with FAK in the interwar period. This case is particularly thought-provoking because the club has a neo-Nazi fan base despite being known as a "Jew Club." After 1945, the club portrayed itself in ways congruent with the nation's myth as Hitler's first victim, thus paving the way for neo-Nazi fan culture. Today, FAK is rediscovering its Jewish heritage in order to get rid of its neo-Nazi fans.

The third chapter, on Ajax Amsterdam, analyzes the "Jew Club" as fan performance. It illuminates a club attacked as "Jewish" by rival fans and whose fans, in response, began calling themselves "Super Jews." This chapter analyzes how these fan performances flourished in the particular context of the carnivalesque culture of the football stadium and based on the unique Dutch memory culture that evolved around the founding myth of Dutch resistance.

The fourth chapter studies the "Jew Club" as a problem. Like the fans of Ajax Amsterdam, the mostly non-Jewish supporters of Tottenham Hotspur (London) began calling themselves "Yid Army" in the late 1970s. They took over the slur "Yid," which was used by rival fans to denigrate Tottenham. Jewish Tottenham fans expressed how they had never felt such solidarity and cohesiveness anywhere else in society. Yet public opinion shifted from identifying the blatant antisemitism—such as gas chamber hissing by rival fans—as the issue to classifying the fans' "Jew Club" identity as the main concern. This chapter focuses on the public arguments surrounding the "Jew Club" conundrum and how the understanding of why it is problematic has developed.

Last of all, the conclusion has three parts. First, it provides a concise summary of each chapter's contribution to solving the "Jew Club" conundrum. After this summary, the conclusion identifies the similarities and differences among the four "Jew

Clubs" studied. Finally, the conclusion points to the broader implications of this book; the final pages use the results of this study
to reconsider the concept of a (negative) German-Jewish symbiosis after Auschwitz—one of the scholarly frameworks that has
significantly influenced how we understand the consequences of
the Holocaust for the present. Ultimately, the conclusion presents
the argument that the concept of a negative symbiosis can be
advanced in two directions: the concept needs to be decentered
from its sole focus on Germany, and it does not determine the
subjective experiences of Jewish and non-Jewish football fans.

As a final point, this book—researched and written prior to
October 7, 2023—includes an afterword that examines how the
events of October 7 and their aftermath have affected the "Jew
Clubs." By connecting these recent developments to the book's
broader arguments, it invites readers to consider how the ongoing dynamics of football fandom, antisemitism, and collective
memory continue to shape identities and societal debates in the
present.

ONE

FC BAYERN MUNICH
The "Jew Club" as Memory Culture

IN MAY 2012, FC BAYERN MUNICH opened *Erlebniswelt*, one of the largest sport exhibitions in the world (see fig. 1.1). The plan to open a museum was made in haste, leaving the curators less than eleven months to fill an empty space of over three thousand square meters in the heart of the club's stadium, Allianz Arena—one of Europe's finest stadiums, built for the 2006 World Cup. In 2010, the club had first appealed to readers of its publication *Bayern Magazine* to provide objects for the evolving club archive. At this point, the club's collection consisted of only a few objects, mainly trophies, not least because its main office had been fully destroyed by an air raid in 1944, and the club had little interest in its history. About ten years later, in January 2023, I came across a professional club archive consisting of more than seven thousand objects; the *Erlebniswelt* exhibition had been renamed the FC Bayern Museum,[1] a change that also signals the club's shift toward a more serious approach to its history.

The club's collective memory developed late and unhurriedly, even reluctantly, but it is moving fast today. When I visited the FC Bayern Museum in January 2023, new revisions were planned, designed to adapt the club's historical narrative to the outcomes of historian Gregor Hofmann's 2022 book about the club's history

Figure 1.1. The FC Bayern Museum. Photo by author.

during the Nazi period.[2] The book resulted from a doctoral project that had been fully funded by the club and independently
commissioned by the renowned Institute of Contemporary History. When I walked through the exhibition space as one of its
350,000 annual visitors, I could still read that the club had supposedly been "reviled as a *Judenklub* [Jew Club]," and that "the
men in red suffered systematic discrimination and soon lost their
place at the summit of German football" during Nazism.[3] It is
uncertain whether this narrative will be part of the revised exhibition, but it will probably persist in and around the club culture;
over the last two decades, the club's collective identity has been
marked by a memory culture built on the "Jew Club" concept.

FC Bayern identified itself as a "Jew Club" at two historical
moments. First, when the Nazi regime fell. At this time, the club
was hoping to gain the mayoral office's favor, and club members
underwent a denazification process. The second period, ranging from 1997 to about 2017, but lasting into the present, was

characterized by a turn to Kurt Landauer, the long-forgotten German Jewish club president who led the club to its first national
title in 1932, survived Nazism in exile, and returned to Munich in
1947, where he served as FC Bayern's president again until 1951.[4]
For decades, FC Bayern had no clue about the important contributions Jews made to the club. In 1997, two publications mentioned Kurt Landauer.[5] It took much longer, however, for fans,
the club management, and the public to turn Landauer into a
club legend. The turn to Landauer finally occurred, as I show in
this chapter, in 2009, and it was not until 2013 that the club posthumously granted him an honorary presidency. The club's memory culture developed late, rapidly, and with enthusiasm.

The turn to Landauer led to the club's self-perception as Germany's "Jew Club," and, paradoxically, the more the club culture
remembered, the more it seemed to forget about the perpetrators
in its ranks. In 2017, the club's collective memory shifted again:
the turn to Landauer was followed by a turn to history after an
article in Germany's leading magazine *Der Spiegel* attacked the
club's historical narrative.[6] The article foregrounded how the club
had expelled its Jewish members, something that was (partly)
known before but had found little to no space in the club's historical narrative; it was buried under a fascination for Landauer and
pride over FC Bayern's "Jew Club" history. An article published
by *Die Zeit* proudly claimed, for instance, that "there is a reason
to love FC Bayern after all: The story of a club that stood by its
Jewish president."[7] *Der Spiegel*, however, stirred a public debate
about FC Bayern's role during Nazism.[8] Around eighteen months
later, the club made an unprecedented and highly unusual announcement for a football club: it provided complete funding for
a research project intended to work through the club's history
during Nazism.

This chapter is organized into two parts: the club's turn to
history (2017–2023) and the club's turn to Landauer (1997–2017).
It begins with the club's recent turn to history, which includes

a discussion of FC Bayern's self-identification as a "Jew Club" in the context of denazification. The club became aware that its members included Nazis, Jews, and many others, and it began to ask itself whether the "Jew Club" narrative was still accurate. This chapter traces these changes and also discusses the findings of Hofmann's study, namely, the club's actions (or nonactions) during Nazism. Finally, it discusses the post-1945 moment through the lens of today's memory culture. Ultimately, this chapter argues that the club's reintegration of both perpetrators and victims after 1945 made it particularly appealing for later generations to turn Landauer into a symbol of the club's collective identity.

The second section analyzes the turn to Landauer that occurred between 1997 and 2017. Before 1997, Landauer had been long forgotten; today, it has become impossible to study the topography of Munich's memorial culture without recognizing the various sites dedicated to Landauer. This part of the chapter aims to answer why the turn to Landauer happened so quickly and what the club's memory culture reveals about the memory cultures in the city (Munich), the nation (Germany), and German football more broadly. Furthermore, it discusses the different functions the turn to Landauer has had for the club's management and its fans.

FC BAYERN AND THE TURN TO HISTORY (I)

Several authors, when looking back on the 1930s from a post-Holocaust perspective, have portrayed FC Bayern's 1932 championship game against Eintracht Frankfurt as a "showdown between two 'Jew Clubs.'"[9] The 1932 trophy, won by FC Bayern under President Kurt Landauer, became a symbol of the supposedly last highlight of "liberal" German football because Jews had significant positions at both clubs.[10] In addition to its president, FC Bayern's club coach, Richard "Dombi" Kohn, was Jewish. The FC Bayern Museum has a large exhibition board about the

Figure 1.2. "Deutscher Meister 1932" exhibition board at the FC Bayern Museum. Photo by author.

1932 title, including panels on both Landauer and Kohn (see fig. 1.2).[11] Furthermore, FC Bayern's fan group Schickeria hosted an event in 2010 for which 250 fans gathered to celebrate the 1932 title.[12] The title's symbolic space in the club's collective memory invited misconceptions of continuity: The prevalent image was that FC Bayern had always been, as the club museum claims, "an open society."[13] In his preface to the 2014 Landauer biography, FC Bayern's honorary captain Philipp Lahm states that FC Bayern was always *weltoffen*, a term that translates as "cosmopolitan" but is also used to mean "tolerant" or "progressive."[14] Lahm suggests a continuity symbolized by Landauer, who led the club as its president before and after Nazism. Yet, as the recent turn to history clearly shows, FC Bayern was not weltoffen at all times.

In June 2021, the historian Gregor Hofmann completed his study, which was finally published in 2022. Its title signifies the interventions and corrections it attempts to make: *Teammate of the Volk Community: FC Bayern and National Socialism* [*Mitspieler* der *"Volksgemeinschaft"*: *Der FC Bayern und der Nationalsozialis-mus*].[15] A *Mitspieler* is both a teammate and also someone who plays along in the *Volksgemeinschaft*, which refers to the racially defined community of the "German" people. A Mitspieler does not just stand on the sideline of societal events but is also some-one who acts. A Mitspieler is influenced by a larger web of norms and rules and also shapes this framework. In sum, FC Bayern was not simply a perpetrator, bystander, or victim but a companion of Nazism.

Hofmann's study describes how Landauer resigned as the club president quickly after Germany handed over power to the Nazi Party. The book foregrounds that Landauer did so as one of over thirty Jews in the club between February and August 1933.[16] It describes in detail how FC Bayern adapted to the new system immediately: in 1933 it had already established the *Führerprinzip*, a club structure that mirrored the dictatorship, and it had signed the Stuttgart Declaration, also known as the club's first "Aryan clause," a declaration by fourteen football clubs that welcomed the new dictatorship and declared their willingness to expel Jew-ish members.[17] The study shifts the focus: FC Bayern is no longer portrayed as a club that resisted Nazism but as a club that will-fully declared its participation in the Nazi project without being forced to do so.

Although the club quickly adapted, the exclusion of Jews was initially contested within the club, and it excluded them later than others, such as the local rival 1860 Munich, a club that rushed to be "cleansed" of Jews and that the Nazis significantly shaped even before 1933.[18] FC Bayern's new club führer, Siegfried Herrmann, established a council of elders [*Ältestenrat*] in June 1934, a group consisting of old club members who were to be excluded from expulsion, with several Jews among them. At this time, Jewish members were even mentioned in the club notices, something unimaginable in other clubs at the time.[19] However, in March 1935, the club incorporated a second "Aryan clause" in its statutes without the Nazi regime insisting on it.[20] The club left no space

for Jews. In sum, FC Bayern was a club that participated will-
fully and without compulsion in the National Socialist project, although its adaption to Nazism was contested and the club aligned
itself with Nazism later than others. After Nazism was defeated,
however, FC Bayern did not portray itself as a Mitspieler but as a
"Jew Club" disadvantaged by Nazism.

The "Jew Club" as Denazification (1944–1951)

FC Bayern's turn to Landauer began in 1997 with two publications: a book by Dietrich Schulze-Marmeling and a book chapter
by the historian Anton Löffelmeier that first used the phrase "Jew
Club" in a subtitle.[21] Löffelmeier was the first to discuss a source
from Munich's city archive that seemed to justify the phrase;
when the club won the Gauliga championship in 1944, it was suggested to the mayor that the club's triumph should be celebrated
at the town hall. The mayor's office refused to invite the champions, noting that "FC Bayern was led by a Jew until the seizure of
power."[22] For at least two decades, the discourse was dominated
by Löffelmeier's notion that FC Bayern was stigmatized throughout Nazism.[23] The historian Hofmann suggests that the mayor's
office disfavored FC Bayern not because the Nazis discriminated
against FC Bayern as a "Jew Club," but because a sporting celebration was considered inappropriate, bearing Germany's difficult military position in mind, and because the major's office
(with Director Obermaier) favored FC Bayern's local rival 1860
Munich.[24] Hofmann notes that this is the only known evidence
of discrimination against the club during Nazism. It illustrates,
however, that a connection between FC Bayern and Jews was
probably common knowledge for contemporary Bavarians, at
least for those who loved football.

The phrase "Jew Club" first appears in connection to FC Bayern
in the mid-1940s during the denazification process.[25] Hofmann
quotes numerous FC Bayern officials who, after 1945, said that
they were loathed as a "Jew Club" at various Bavarian football

grounds. The youth manager, Heinrich Lämmle, claimed during denazification that FC Bayern's youth teams had been deni-
grated everywhere as a "Jew Club" (*Judenverein* or *Judenclub*).[26]
The Spruchkammer categorized Lämmle as a "fellow traveler"
[*Mitläufer*],[27] and it noted in its reasoning that FC Bayern "was
called a 'Jew Club' during the Nazi era because its former president, Landauer, was a Jew."[28] As early as in May 1945, about two
weeks after the US Army occupied Munich, the club wrote to the
mayor's office: "We are ready to follow you unconditionally and
loyally because, with your assumption of office, a time of new
construction has also begun for us 'Bayern.' So far, we, as a 'Jew
Club' that rejected having a National Socialist club leadership
enforced on it, have been run down with all means."[29] The club
president, Siegfried Herrmann, addressed a letter to a former club
member in August 1946, persuading him to renew his membership. In this letter, Hermann complained that the club had to dis-
card all its activists, and that FC Bayern had, like all other clubs,
some restrictions: "In any case, the much decried 'Jew Club' in
Munich has to fight for its existence in the new democracy."[30] The
club's portrayal of having been discriminated against as a "Jew
Club" is questionable because the claims, written amid ruins and
turmoil, were aimed at gaining the support of the authorities
or the goodwill of former members. At the same time, however,
the claims do show that various individuals considered the "Jew
Club" image to be a credible argument to bring out in front of
their target audience. The "Jew Club" association was more than
a defense strategy during denazification.

Later testimonies suggest that FC Bayern members themselves
felt proud to be part of a "Jew Club." Flori Schuster, grandchild
of the former FC Bayern member Josef Mauder, stated, "Even in
my younger years, it was never a secret to me that my grandfather
was always proud to have found admission to no other but the
'Jew Club.' And to belong to it. The reason for this was the liberal,
intellectual, and artistic (in addition to the sporting) aspirations

and the environment of the members there."[31] Kurt Landauer's
nephew Uri Siegel reported that he had never heard anything
antisemitic in the context of FC Bayern, although the club was
called a "Jew Club." "But," he continued, "this was meant both
more mockingly and lovingly. Nobody thought anything of it."[32]
Both Mauder and Siegel were probably referring to the pre-1933
period, for which no source proves that FC Bayern was called a
"Jew Club." During this period, contemporaries, however, most
likely shared a latent common understanding of FC Bayern as a
"Jew Club." As early as 1935, FC Bayern's *Dietwart* (a term used
to denote a regime-imposed ideological indoctrinator and guardian),[33] Theodor Slipek, remarked in the club notices that the club
was, "from earlier times, not exactly considered to be built on
a purely *völkisch* basis."[34] While not naming Landauer or Jews
explicitly, his remark suggests that FC Bayern was somehow considered the opposite of völkisch before 1933.[35]

The "Jew Club" as Cultural Code (1900–1932)

From today's perspective, it strikes me that FC Bayern was not
only associated with its Jewish president Landauer but also with
values and spaces that contemporaries associated with Judaism.[36]
The term "Jew Club" is, in this sense, a cultural code,[37] which is a
core concept examined in chapter 2. Through identifying a club
as a cultural code for "Jews" or "Jewish" things, the terms "Jew
Club" and "FC Bayern" become associated with particular values
and a certain space. FC Bayern has been associated with professionalism, a technical style of football, an international orientation, the bourgeoisie, an openness toward Jews, and the area of
Schwabing. I contend that even before 1933, an antisemitic mind-
set connected the club with "Jews," an idea to which people would
later allude. First, FC Bayern was connected to Schwabing, a section of Munich that was and still is associated with the Bohème
and the avant-garde, "a quarter that was nothing but 'Jewish' for
völkisch contemporaries."[38] Second, the club was associated with

a significant share of Jewish club members and key figures like its Jewish president. Third, the club was modern and cosmopolitan. It was at the forefront of attempts to internationalize German football at a time when sports were supposed to be national and adhere to conservative amateurism.

FC Bayern was closely linked with Schwabing: "Bayern and 1860 were attuned with their quarters: Bayern was Schwabing," as the former player Herbert Moll remembers.[39] Meanwhile, 1860 was and still is linked to the former working-class district of Giesing. FC Bayern was, as the FC Bayern Museum informs, "originally based in the Bohemian quarter of Schwabing and its players and officials were mostly members of the educated middle class or academics."[40] The author Dietrich Schulze-Marmeling vividly describes how the club's modern orientation is also a product of Schwabing, "a center for artists and intellectuals."[41] It is here, Schulze-Marmeling argues, that the club's cosmopolitanism developed, where artists, literary authors, and other intellectuals flooded the coffeehouses that characterized the club's neighborhood.[42] Club members wore straw hats as an outward symbol of extravagance. As a result, Bayern was known as "the gentlemen's club" [Der Kavaliersklub].[43] The club's entertainment committee organized large societal events, for instance at the German theater,[44] and the family of President Kurt Landauer maintained relationships with artists and writers.[45] The club was known as a coffeehouse club, and coffeehouses were advertised frequently in FC Bayern's magazine Clubnachrichten.[46] The coffeehouse club image was also linked to the "Jew Club" image.[47] Yet Schwabing leaned increasingly toward Nazism and its coffeehouses were soon abandoned by the cultural scene that used to frequent them in the 1920s.[48] Hofmann argues that FC Bayern was a football club from Munich before anything else, and, in its entirety, "barely an artists' club."[49] In its early years, however, the club was connected to the area, and it remained attached to the idea that Schwabing represents.

Looking back on the club's foundations, the FC Bayern Museum created a special exhibition entitled Between Atelier and

Football Field: The Founders of FC Bayern Munich. Even today, fans place stickers in the streets of the town, which exemplify how important the cultural concept of Schwabing remains for the club's collective identity. Schwabing thus occupies a considerable space in the club's collective memory, a notion that significantly contributes to its "Jew Club" identity.

Today, FC Bayern proudly looks back on those who founded the club in 1900. They were all *Zuagroaste*, a Bavarian term for foreigners, and they included two Jews—Edward Pollack and the club's first president, Franz John.[50] At the time, football was perceived as a modern game that stood in stark contrast to the nationalist and conservative gymnastics.[51] Football was perceived as English and often despised as anti-German. For secular Jews like Landauer, football clubs were alternatives to, for instance, nationalistic fraternities in which antisemitism was rampant. Schulze-Marmeling characterizes FC Bayern before 1933 as a "cosmopolitan and liberal club, at which Jews could find a home."[52] Arguably, few social spaces came as close to the ideal of a German-Jewish symbiosis as some football clubs did. About 130 of FC Bayern's members were Jews, approximately 10 percent—a notable share, compared with Munich's population, of which approximately 1.2 percent were Jews.[53] FC Bayern members had diverse political orientations ranging from favoring the Social Democrats (SPD) to favoring the Nazi Party (NSDAP).[54]

Jews have been integral to the development of football, and the sport's journey toward modernization cannot be understood without their contributions. For football, Jews played an important role as pioneers of modernity, shaping the sport's evolution.[55] For Jews, football provided a platform to actively engage with and contribute to the broader cultural and societal advancements of the time. Figures like Landauer, with their international outlook, were instrumental in developing a more technical and modern style of play.[56] The club FC Bayern in general and Landauer in particular were directly related to attempts to professionalize and internationalize football in the early twentieth century. Landauer is known today as one of football's great visionaries.[57] He had a modern, professional, and cosmopolitan approach to the sport and was influenced by Walther Bensemann—the German Jewish founder of *Der Kicker*, which continues to be Germany's most important football magazine.[58] Landauer organized international friendly games against some of the world's best football teams such as the "Jew Clubs" MTK Budapest, Tottenham Hotspur, and Ajax Amsterdam. Many of these clubs came from a similar bourgeois milieu and were also influenced by Jews.[59]

Landauer continually pushed for the professionalization of football.[60] His modern idea of football, however, stood in direct opposition to the nationalist amateurism of the German Football Association, and resulted in vicious conflicts with the Deutscher Fußball-Bund (DFB) and the Westdeutscher Fußball Verband (WSV). The club's strivings for more professionalization, commodification, and the internationalization of sports have probably been associated with Judaism; materialism, greed, and cosmopolitanism were not only accusations made against Landauer but also attributes that became projected onto "Jews" as antisemitism developed into a cultural code.[61] In sum, FC Bayern was bound up with Schwabing, associated with its Jewish members, and tightly linked to attempts at professionalization and internationalization. Taken together, these factors resulted in FC Bayern being linked with Landauer and Jews, connections that gained importance during Nazism, in the immediate post–World War II context, and during the turn to Landauer.

From Ruins to Glory and the Promise of Reconciliation

The 2014 feature film *Landauer—Celebrated, Banned, Forgotten* [*Landauer—Gefeiert, Verbannt, Vergessen*] contributed significantly to the turn to Landauer.[62] The film begins with FC Bayern's 1932 championship, where Landauer was celebrated, but turns to the post-1945 moment after only three minutes.[63] The

Figure 1.3. Kurt Landauer's ruin walk. Screenshot; ARD, 2014.

film suggests a continuity between the pre- and the post-Nazi period, which is introduced by displaying Landauer sitting in a train on his way back to Germany after a period of Swiss exile. His gaze is directed outside the train window; he seems to be lost in thought. At passport control, the letter *J* is clearly visible in his passport, marking him not only as Jewish but also as banned. Back in Munich, Landauer walks through the ruins (see fig. 1.3).

This scene, of Landauer walking through and viewing the ruins, invites audiences to reflect on the history of this place, including "the nature of the event" and "the meaning of the past for the present."[64] Landauer has the ticket for his intended, but never completed, onward journey to the United States in the pocket of his suit. He walks through the ruins of Munich with a suitcase in hand, this action potentially symbolizing his exile, his return, or his possible onward journey. Landauer looks at the ruins, and, it seems, the ruins stare back at him. The film's audience experiences the sense that cinema and ruins share the common function of "visualiz[ing] time and history in modernity."[65] Ruins "move us" because they "evoke imaginations about a moment in which the ruin as the material face of human destruction will be replaced by a new human creation."[66] Ruins invite us to "project onto them our wishes, desires, and hopes for the future," and they ask us "to see them as a space that is still in becoming rather than a site that merely marks what was."[67] They are the remnants of the past, but they also provoke imagination about the future. As Landauer walks through the city's ruins, the film suggests various possibilities: Will Landauer unpack his belongings in Munich or elsewhere? Has his connection to Munich been destroyed much like these buildings? Should he move on? Is there hope for him and the city somewhere in this rubble?

The film's central theme is the resurrection of football in Munich, and Landauer is depicted as the central hero of FC Bayern's revival. He even manages to unite the club with its local rival 1860 Munich; they collaborate to rebuild the football stadium from the rubble (see fig. 1.4), even though FC Bayern represents the "Jew Club" and 1860, the Nazis. "We can only do it together," Landauer claims. The president is turned into a symbol of continuity, reconciliation, and progress. The short ruin scene at the film's beginning is followed by Landauer's encounter with children playing football: a sign of continuity and optimism for the future amid the heavily bombed city. There are few who can connect the past with the present like Landauer, who, these images imply, symbolizes tradition and continuity but also reconciliation and an orientation toward the future.

At the time of Landauer's return to Munich in August 1947, "Germany lay in ruins," as the club museum states.[68] There was not much left of FC Bayern either: "There was a team, but no club."[69] In this context, Landauer "was of invaluable importance to Bayern—as a victim of the Nazi regime, the Allied authorities regarded him as a strong advocate for democracy. His reputation and standing facilitated a swift transition back to normality."[70] The US occupying forces suspected club organizations of Nazi affiliation, and so football clubs needed to research how to receive the licenses they required. Landauer, who could help the

Figure 1.4. Stadium reconstruction. Screenshot; ARD, 2014.

club's case with the Allies, was long thought to have returned to Munich because of FC Bayern, until a biography that includes letters exchanged between Landauer and a woman, Maria Baumann, was published in 2021, revealing another reason for his return: "But I am not returning for the club, there is a wholly different attraction there."[71] Baumann eventually became his wife. Nonetheless, Landauer's picture fits the club, city, and national self-perception of resurrection.[72]

Immediately after his reelection as the club president in 1947, at the club's fiftieth anniversary celebration, Landauer promised he would draw a line under the difficult past: "We want to forget the recent years, and we want to show mercy."[73] FC Bayern not only reintegrated expelled club members—Landauer was one of thirteen Jews who renewed their membership—but also re-admitted (former) Nazis, even against the protests of other club members. FC Bayern's archive includes a letter exchange between the club and its former president, Hans Bermühler, concerning Bermühler's refusal to accept the club's invitation to its fiftieth anniversary celebration. In 1950, Bermühler hesitated to accept the club's suggestion of drawing a line under the Nazi past and wrote this message to Landauer: "I gladly forgo the honor of sharing a table with such politically blind people from back then, of whom there are yet again enough fanatics in Germany."[74] The club responded regretfully that the fiftieth anniversary was the perfect opportunity to shake hands and reconcile with some FC Bayern members who had been "misguided."[75] Three years later, Bermühler received another letter from the club, which sought to recruit him as a member (it succeeded). The letter explained "that the club cannot forever maintain the ban against all former Nazis in the club."[76] Bermühler "should know that many old and really impeccable Bayern were National Socialists," and one could easily give him "many dozens of names." The club "has accepted many, although not all [of them] back into its ranks as members and drawn a thick line under everything that happened." FC Bayern's attempt to draw such a line was contested yet successful.

FC Bayern practiced amnesia by reinstalling a sense of the "old Bavarians" (*alte Bayern*). The club's core should consist of long-standing club members who had made up the club before and for whom the club has supposedly always had priority. At the time, FC Bayern officials used to sign their letters with "old, loyal Bayern greetings."[77] After 1945, the club even functioned as an exoneration network for those who went through the denazification process.[78] Community spirit offered them the opportunity to gain a denazification certificate known as a *Persilschein*—club members helped each other.[79] Nazism and perpetrators were externalized: FC Bayern officials like Landauer portrayed Nazism as something that had destroyed the club's community spirit from outside. The club's fifty-year anniversary publication features seventeen pages on the "Third Reich," stating that "Hitler's seizure of power meant a very enormous intervention in the club's innermost structure," although "the club had always held the view that any decent person, regardless of race or religion, could find a place in sports."[80] This sporting community spirit foregrounded the club, which was supposed to always come first:

"Despite many difficulties, the club management tried, above all, to maintain the club's inner unity."[81] And as the anniversary publication's author, the former president Siegfried Herrmann, argues, "Whoever did not live through these times has no right to judgment ... the life and existence of FC Bayern were at stake."[82]

Collective memories are always selective and thus always constitute forms of forgetting. Collectives remember to become groups, nations, football clubs, or other forms of (imagined) communities. To imagine one's group as homogeneous, forgetting is just as essential as remembering. "Working through the past," Theodor W. Adorno claims, "does not mean seriously working upon the past, that is, through a lucid consciousness breaking its power to fascinate. On the contrary, its intention is to close the books on the past and, if possible, even remove it from memory."[83] Memories are not only coupled with forgetting, but they are also always selective: As Andrei S. Markovits and Simon Reich argue, "Collective memory is the selective use of the past to legitimate present conditions."[84] In football, where invented traditions are crucial for collective identities, "certain aspects of the group past will be prioritized over others."[85] Some scholars of collective memories go so far as to claim that "forgetting is the rule and remembering the exception" when working through their reality, and that "memories are small Islands in a sea of forgetting."[86] In the context of Holocaust memory, "the initial impulse to memorialize events like the Holocaust may actually spring from an opposite and equal desire to forget them."[87] Forms of collective memories are also forms of forgetting.

For FC Bayern, the impulse to forget stems from the post-1945 moment and is directly linked to Landauer himself. Remembering the sense of alte Bayern helped the club members forget that the club had excluded its Jewish members. Although the process was contested, both victims and perpetrators longed for continuity and reintegration into a football club that had been liberal

Figure 1.5. The *Kurt Landauer* statue (1). Photo by author.

and open to Jews before 1933. However, the reintegration resulted in decades of forgetting, in which the club only wanted to look forward. After the club was reestablished and denazification was over, the "Jew Club" identity and Landauer were soon forgotten.

Kurt Landauer was already established in Munich's memorial landscape when his statue was unveiled in March 2019. The bronze statue, funded by the Kurt Landauer Foundation and created by the local artist Karel Fron,[88] is located at the club's practice facilities at Säbener Straße (see figs. 1.5 and 1.6). The statue sits on a concrete bank designed to invite visitors to sit down and take pictures with it. Just in front of the statue is the team's primary practice field; another practice field is right behind the memorial. There is an advertisement board to the right and a small beer garden to the left, although the practice facilities are usually not open to the public and the statue is thus inaccessible.[89]

Figure 1.6. The *Kurt Landauer* statue (2). Photo by author.

The Kurt Landauer Foundation's website provides a guide to the statue's intended meaning: the statue's left hand, referencing the pose of Michelangelo's famous *David*, is supposed to symbolize the victory of the underdog over Goliath and to signify Landauer's Jewish background.[90] The "David versus Goliath" metaphor is today often used to describe the task of playing against FC Bayern because the club has dominated the league for many years and won back-to-back championships between 2013 and 2023. In this case, the sculptor, Fron, referenced *David* to portray Landauer's bravery in returning to Munich and

becoming FC Bayern's president even after Nazism.[91] The concrete bank below him is shaped like a home stand, or *Fankurve*,
with Landauer sitting among the fans.[92] The curved shape of the
bank and the half circles in front symbolize FC Bayern's memory
culture. They stand "for the fact that history has returned to him,
for his rediscovery." The bank furthermore consists of a crevice,
representing a break with civilization, the Holocaust.[93] The right
hand stretches across the gap and calmly reaches over to the
other side, thereby reconciling the past with the present, and
the statue's pose is calm. With his jacket over his left shoulder,
Landauer seems to have sat down to rest. His work is done, FC
Bayern is playing again—and it is highly successful. The statue
is, however, only one part of FC Bayern's turn to Landauer, a turn
that is widely praised today and that occurred late but quickly
and with enthusiasm.

THE "JEW CLUB" AS MEMORY CULTURE:
THE TURN TO LANDAUER

Munich, March 2001. The atmosphere at FC Bayern's main office
is awful. The team has just lost 0–3, and the club president Franz
Beckenbauer has just called the players a shit team; right now,
the club has no interest in Landauer. A journalist's call from the
London magazine *Totally Jewish* was answered with the remark
that the club is "not interested in this old shit," and manager Ulrich Hoeneß stated his disinterest by saying he was not alive at
that time.[94]

Munich, September 2009. The South Stand, or Südkurve,
home to FC Bayern Munich's most passionate fans, is covered in
red and white. A large portrait is at the center of the image, displaying the face of Kurt Landauer, visible to tens of thousands in
the stadium and millions at home who are following the game's
live television broadcast. The football fans' performance is about
to place Landauer at the center of debates around fans' collective

identity, FC Bayern's club culture, and Munich's memory culture. The display is an impressive commemoration ceremony for Landauer, funded and created solely by the fans. The huge visual image is framed by two banners that read, "FC Bayern was his life—nothing and no one could change that."[95]

Munich, May 2019. The mood is ceremonial at FC Bayern's Säbener Straße practice facilities. Supporters, club officials, and Kurt Landauer's nephew Uri Siegel have gathered to unveil a statue of Kurt Landauer.[96] While Ulrich Hoeneß claims to be very proud and happy, the Kurt Landauer Foundation is now rather informal when it speaks about its former president: "Today Kurt is sitting here once more, full-size, looking at his FC Bayern. Welcome back, Kurt," a representative of the foundation says.[97] For almost fifty years, Landauer and the "Jew Club" identity had been forgotten. Today, however, Landauer is a central part of the club's collective identity and is inextricably linked with its "Jew Club" image.

FC Bayern Munich's Memorial Landscape

The club's stadium, the Allianz Arena in Ottmaning, is a good thirty-minute train ride away from Marienplatz, Munich's famous central square. Those willing to travel the twelve kilometers or so north will not only arrive at a hypermodern arena but may also notice Kurt-Landauer-Platz, the square in front of the stadium named after the former president. Twelve years earlier, the club and the city were still reluctant to remember Landauer. A motion by Bündnis 90/Die Grünen—the German Green Party—in 2003 to rename the street by the arena after Kurt Landauer resulted in a short, small, and almost-hidden escape path named Kurt-Landauer-Weg in 2005. Located on the city outskirts beside a highway and a sewage plant, the path was criticized for not memorializing Landauer appropriately.[98] Yet, it was the Kurt-Landauer-Weg that put Landauer on the map of Munich's memorial landscape (see fig. 1.7).

Figure 1.7. Kurt-Landauer-Weg and the sewage plant. Photo by author.

Just as the Kurt-Landauer-Weg may be easily overlooked, Kurt Landauer's legacy was left unrecognized for many years. After Landauer died in 1961, the club still laid down wreaths at his grave for a couple of years, but Landauer was soon forgotten. In 1975, the club's seventy-fifth anniversary book devoted one single sentence to Nazism and did not mention Jews at all.[99] In 1990, the club chronicles written for the ninetieth anniversary used just ten additional characters to describe the club's history during Nazism.[100] In 2000, the club's hundredth anniversary publication provided five sentences and mentioned "Jewish members" directly.[101] In 2002, the Institute for Judaic History and Culture at Ludwig-Maximilian University, Munich, hosted a conference called Jews and Sport: Between Integration and Exclusion (*Juden und Sport: Zwischen Integration und Exklusion*). The conference organizer, Michael Brenner, attempted to cooperate with FC Bayern—unsuccessfully.[102] The local film project *Kick It like*

Figure 1.8. The Kurt Landauer plaque at Allianz Arena. Photo by author.

Kurt had a similar experience: two letters to the club remained unanswered. It appeared the club was still uninterested in its history, or at the very least, its leadership was hesitant to confront that history.

The club's view on memory culture finally changed on July 28, 2009, at an event organized by the Dachau Lutheran Church of Reconciliation and the Jewish sports club TSV Maccabi, which commemorated Landauer's 125th birthday at the Dachau Concentration Camp memorial site. The event triggered a veritable wave of memory.[103] Today, Landauer is one of the most commemorated individuals in Munich's memorial landscape. In addition to the statue (2019), the Kurt-Landauer-Weg (2005), and the Kurt-Landauer-Platz at Allianz Arena (2015), the sports grounds of TSV Maccabi Munich are named Kurt-Landauer-Platz (2010).[104]

The club's museum has thematized Landauer since its opening in 2012, a plaque has been placed near the Kurt-Landauer-Weg (2012; see fig. 1.8), and a rooftop football field was named Kurt-Landauer-Platz in 2020.[105]

In 2009, the club's ignorance and reluctance had finally transformed into proud identification. Two years later, the club's chairman Karl-Heinz Rummenigge said, "FC Bayern has a Jewish past, a very rich and successful one. We are proud of this Jewish past, and together with our Jewish friends we will also have a proud future."[106] Since then, several books on Landauer and the club's (Jewish) history have been published.[107] The local film project *Kick It like Kurt* aired in 2010,[108] and the ARD broadcasted *Landauer—Der Präsident* in 2014. The film was accompanied by a documentary and a roundtable discussion, both of which aired on Bayerischer Rundfunk, as well as the LandauerWalk—an augmented reality app.[109] During my research in Munich, I went on a walking tour narrated by a fictional Kurt Landauer who guided me through Schwabing and the nearby areas while informing me about FC Bayern's foundation in 1900.[110] To understand why and how the club's memory culture emerged so strongly and quickly, it is important to consider the club's collective memory within a broader context.

All memories are cultural and are thus shaped by social contexts. Collective memories need a public medium, one that allows different individuals to come together to create, share, and negotiate public memories.[111] I assert that football offers one such space: it is highly public and consists of diverse forms of expression staged in and beyond the stadium. As earlier mentioned, commemoration is a creative and dramatic act comparable to a theater play, unfolding in contexts similar to the theater, "with a stage, spectators, actors, stage designs, the drama, and the staging itself."[112] Specific to the theater (and the stadium) is the fact that it "is not part of everyday practices, it seems to be located outside the 'stream of history.'" Public memory, Michal Bodemann reminds us, is a creative process in which remembrance and imagination are one and the same.[113] Memory cultures are malleable like a wax tablet, as a metaphor used in Plato's *Theaetetus* exemplifies.[114] The late but rapid construction of Landauer as central to FC Bayern's memorial landscape was shaped in context. Memory occurs in a variety of dialogical and dialectical relationships. Before discussing the role of the club, its fans, and the 2009 event in more detail, I review the context in which the turn to Landauer occurred—namely, the memorial landscapes of German football, the city of Munich, and the overall German republic.

Football's Memorial Landscape: From Ignorance to "Die Welt zu Gast bei Freunden"

While it was a long journey from ignorance to identification with Landauer for FC Bayern in particular, the path that German football more generally has taken to acknowledging its own history was in no way shorter.[115] For decades, football's relationship to the Nazi past was represented through Carl Koppehel's 1954 book, *Geschichte des deutschen Fußballsports*.[116] It neither acknowledged the expulsion of Jews from German football nor mentioned the leading role that Germany's football governing body—the DFB—and its clubs played in this process.[117] From the 1960s, early studies—for instance, by the historian Hajo Bernett—challenged the narrative that sport had functioned as an apolitical island, but these remained ignored.[118] The perception of sports as apolitical changed only in the late 1990s. Despite researchers having been denied access to the DFB archives, two books were published that began to put pressure on the DFB.[119] When it became clear that Germany would host the 2006 World Cup, the DFB assigned the task of working through its archives to the historian Nils Havemann in 2001. The outcome was a study published four years later that was widely contested because Havemann made the bold and surprising claim that the stakeholders of German football aimed to remain on the sidelines of Nazism.[120] Detlev

Claussen criticized Havemann's study as a "final stroke that was 473 pages bold."[121] It perpetuated the alleged binary between sports and politics. On the contrary, the publishing house Die Werkstatt, which has published numerous books on football and Nazism since the turn of the century, has played a leading role in connecting the study of Nazi history with football.[122]

In 2004, the Christian Democrat Theo Zwanziger became the DFB's president, and during his leadership, which lasted until 2012, the DFB saw progress. He established the Julius Hirsch Preis, an award named after a German Jewish player who was murdered in Auschwitz.[123] The annual award has honored initiatives, campaigns, and projects against discrimination in German football since 2005. Furthermore, the foundation of the DFB Kulturstiftung, established in 2007, documents a shift of focus in German football from denial to action.

In 2005, the !Nie wieder or !Never Again campaign was initiated by the Dachau Lutheran Church of Reconciliation. Since then, it has become an annual ritual for football clubs to participate in Holocaust Remembrance Day, on January 27, by reading statements or displaying videos in their stadiums, such as in Munich's Allianz Arena. The commemoration of Jewish club members has become common in not only Munich but also many stadiums across Germany. Most often, individual historians or fan groups have initiated the memory work, sometimes against the wishes of their clubs. In Bremen, the Werderaner remember the Jewish club president Alfred Ries; in Mainz, club and fans commemorate Mainz 05's first president, Eugen Salomon, and the Clubberer in Nuremberg honor the Hungarian Jewish coach Jenő Konrád.[124] These activities created a memory boom in German football, and fan groups across the country began to celebrate former Jewish club members. The German football magazine 11 Freunde published the brochure "Verlorene Helden" (Lost heroes) as a supplement to their magazine, consisting of short biographies of German Jewish "football heroes."[125] Today, there are more than thirty memory initiatives in German football.[126] FC Bayern's turn to Landauer is part of this memory boom in German football.

Munich's Memorial Landscape: Tradition and Continuity

FC Bayern's memorial landscape is part of Munich's memorial landscape. Both take a conservative approach to memory, emphasizing local tradition and continuity. The club and the city both emphasize their strong ties to tradition. In the city, very few examples of extravagant modern architecture disrupt the city's historical exterior. Almost no World War II ruins are to be found, nor are there noticeable Nazi buildings.[127] Munich's historical appearance mirrors the city's way of dealing with the Nazi past. Munich's memorial discourse, as the historian Gavriel D. Rosenfeld argues in his book *Munich and Memory: Architecture, Monuments, and the Legacy of the Third Reich*, did not identify the cause of Nazism as rooted in local history but instead foregrounded abstract, modern, and supposedly non-German causes. Rosenfeld's work shows how Munich's architecture and the city's memorial landscape are shaped by a traditionalist perspective that legitimized reconstructing the prewar architectural conservatism after the city's destruction: Munich's post–World War II society was, Rosenfeld argues, characterized by a longing for continuity. This longing not only led to a rapid reconstruction of the city but also came with the consequence that Munich remembered and remembers selectively. In other words, a longing for tradition and continuity led to the avoidance of remembering the city's history as *Hauptstadt der Bewegung* (the movement's capital). Cities are not only "built memory" but also "sites of forgetting."[128]

The immediate post-1945 years in Munich took a conservative and restorationist approach marked by the repression of guilt.[129] Munich "acquired the image of a city without perpetrators, a city only of victims, bearing no responsibility for the events of the recent past."[130] As I previously stated, FC Bayern's club culture in the post-1945 era involved the readmission of alte Bayern and the drawing of a line under the Nazi era by emphasizing tradition and continuity between the pre- and post-Nazi eras. During the Wirtschaftswunder period (1958–75), when Germany enjoyed strong economic growth, Munich saw a traditionalist countermovement, a monument preservation movement that aimed to avoid Munich's "second destruction"[131] and resulted in the 1973 Bavarian Denkmalschutzgesetz: a law on preserving monuments that emphasized the city's reawakened traditionalism.[132] During this period, the club had little to no interest in working through or even remembering its relationship to Nazism. The contemporary postmodern era began in 1975 and is marked by a direct continuation of the city's love of tradition.[133] Munich's city development has emphasized local space, history, and identity. Meanwhile, history has been reembraced nostalgically.[134] In the postmodern era the number of new memorials almost doubled.[135] This started to change Munich's image as a city of repression and forgetting. Still, when something is remembered, something else is forgotten. The acknowledgment of perpetrators was still excluded from Munich's memory culture, which centered on the German resistance and victims of Nazism were finally recognized.[136] It took much longer for football clubs in general and FC Bayern in particular to begin to commemorate Kurt Landauer and other Jewish figures.

FC Bayern's memorial landscape of today is part of Munich's memorial landscape. Both focus on local tradition and continuity. The club's return to tradition and the rediscovery of Landauer mirrors the city's return to tradition in the postmodern era. The boom in memorials and the shift from commemorating non-Jewish Germans to commemorating Jewish victims are typical features in both the city's macrolevel and the club's microlevel discourses.

Germany's Memorial Landscape: A Victim-Identified Memory Culture

All these memorial landscapes—the club, the sport, the city—increasingly, albeit slowly and reluctantly, shifted their focus to Jewish victims. The turn to Landauer is thus part of a belated turn to the victims at the national level, a process that took shape in the 1960s and that was critically described by Ulrike Jureit and

Christian Schneider as "identifying with the victim." Jureit and Schneider argue that this memory culture has two main characteristics. First, a wish to identify oneself with the victims. Second, a promise that if a person only commemorates genuinely, they can hope for redemption and reconciliation.[137]

Jureit argues that this victim-identified memory culture results in an objectifying memory culture: "Six million Jews are not remembered as victims of the genocide committed by Germans, but are ritually co-opted as their own dead."[138] This identification with the victims is simultaneously fueled, Jureit claims, by making the perpetrators publicly invisible. The tendency of identifying with the victims instead of with the perpetrators has important implications: whoever identifies with the victims also begins to view the perpetrators from this standpoint.[139] Consequently, the perpetrators are removed from the memory collective, and the individual who identifies with the victim is now on the "right" side of history.[140] On the one hand, the victim-identified memory culture embraces the victims. On the other hand, the perpetrators are anonymized, deindividualized, and condemned. It follows, Jureit argues, that German memory culture not only loses its subversive potential but also risks being turned into a culture of forgetting with compulsive remembering paradoxically its main characteristic.[141] Remembering as such, Jureit continues, is thus neither valuable in or of itself, nor is it the opposite of forgetting.[142] In summary, turning to the victims was a necessary step in working through the past, but it has also resulted in selective memorialization. A memorialization that also used the victims for a memory culture that risks forgetting the perpetrators. The slogan "Remembering to Never Forget" may become "Remembering to Forget."[143]

FC BAYERN MUNICH'S MEMORY CULTURES

Contemporary tourists interested in Hitler and the NSDAP in Munich may have read the 2018 book *111 Orte in München auf den Spuren der Nazi-Zeit*. In the book, each of the 111 places is briefly described. One of them is titled "The 'Jew Club': The Nazis' Hatred of FC Bayern," and it guides the book's readers to the club's former headquarters.[144] Readers, however, do not have to travel to Munich to learn that FC Bayern is a "Jew Club." The club holds an office in New York City, and it has a US-wide touring exhibition with the "Jew Club" notion included. The exhibition is called *Venerated—Persecuted—Forgotten: Victims of National Socialism at FC Bayern Munich*.[145] During the club's US tour in 2019, the exhibition was presented at the Los Angeles Holocaust Museum. It was well received by local media who transmitted the "Jew Club" concept to the American audience.[146] During its 2022 Audi Summer Tour to the US, the exhibition was presented at the Capitol in Washington, DC. The FC Bayern president at the time, Herbert Hainer, referred to Kurt Landauer in his opening address to highlight the club's supposed continuity as both "familial and cosmopolitan."[147] The exhibition even toured several high-quality US academic institutions, such as Columbia University and Penn State, where the exhibition was on display in January 2023.[148] The "Jew Club" identity became known globally not least through the exhibition's international touring (although the club did not show the exhibition in Qatar, despite its close relationship to the country).

FC Bayern's memory culture emerged in the context of connected memorial landscapes, but, as the historian Peter Burke notes, societies consist of different "memory communities."[149] For FC Bayern and its fans, two distinct yet entangled regimes of memory emerged. While both the club and its active fans have participated in the project of identifying with Landauer and rewriting its Jewish members into the club history, different factors have motivated them.

Ultras and the "Rediscovery" of Kurt Landauer

As the closing scene in the 2014 film *Landauer—Der Präsident* claims, it was the fan group Schickeria that reminded the world of Kurt Landauer, by displaying images of a (second) large fan choreography (a coordinated display by supporters, often involving flags, banners, and other visual elements, typically during prematch or halftime) devoted to Landauer.[150] Quoting Landauer, it reads, "FC Bayern and I simply belong together and are inseparable from each other."[151] The large flag shows images of Landauer, the dates of his birth and death, the symbol of the club, the city, and the 1932 championship trophy. The 2014 choreography demonstrates the place Landauer came to occupy in the club's collective identity.[152]

Schickeria stands out in its engagement with the club's memory culture. This group was founded in 2002, has well over one hundred members, and is part of the ultras movement, the most vocal and most visible fan culture in German football stadiums since its appearance in the 1990s.[153] Ultras can be understood as "extreme fans" who travel to every away game of their respective clubs to show support with chants, banners, flags, and choreographies. In the first few years of the new millennium, the young ultras movement developed a political consciousness, for instance, by supporting local charity organizations or by opposing neo-Nazi fans in their home stand.[154]

Schickeria articulated most clearly in a 2005–6 fanzine how the club's collective memory informs its collective identity in the present, stating that "as a group, we stand by and behind the history of the 'Jew Club' FC Bayern Munich."[155] The fanzine's cover presented a picture of Landauer, the club's former symbol, and the Star of David.[156] The title read, "Star of David and Red Shorts ... Kurt Landauer and the Success Story of the 'Jew Club' Bayern Munich."[157] The feature article was titled "The (Forgotten) History of the 'Jew Club' Bayern Munich."[158] The ultras produced a graphic in which the Star of David and FC Bayern's symbol merged. FC Bayern became the "Jew Club," and Landauer became its key figure.

When the ultras were writing about this topic, the club was not commemorating Landauer. About four years later, in July 2009, Schickeria celebrated Landauer's 125th birthday. They visited his grave, organized a large choreography in the stadium, got together for a celebratory dinner at a Bavarian beer hall in his honor, and even released a press statement.[159] Furthermore, they attended an event at the Dachau Concentration Camp Memorial Center, which, from today's perspective, appears as the precise moment in which the club turned to Landauer. The event was organized by the Dachau Lutheran Church of Reconciliation and Maccabi Munich. After a commemoration at Baracke 8 in Dachau, where Landauer was imprisoned in 1938, the event continued at the reconciliation church, where there was a discussion between Landauer's nephew Uri Siegel and FC Bayern's former president Willi O. Hofmann.[160]

The 2009 event is remarkable for two reasons. First, FC Bayern board members turned to Jews as an important part of the club's history. Witnesses described to me how uncertain the club management was at the event. The chairman, Karl-Heinz Rummenigge, and the vice-chairman, Karl Hopfner, seemed out of their comfort zone and, according to those accounts, were quite uncertain about how to represent the club in this context. Yet they realized that Landauer mattered to the club's fans and other local organizations. Second, reports from immediately after the event offer a glimpse of the encounter between the fans and the club representatives. Walking from the commemoration at Baracke 8 to the church, members of Schickeria addressed Rummenigge and Hopfner, suggesting that the club's management should engage publicly with its history, saying, "This [event] can only be the beginning!"[161] According to Schickeria, event participants criticized "how FC Bayern is coming to terms with its history far too late and still far too little, although the club can be particularly proud of its history."[162] Positive feedback for its participation in the event most likely inspired the club's decision to turn to Landauer at a time when the club was already considering constructing a museum and an archive to tell its history.

Progressive Traditionalism: Kurt Landauer as a "Vehicle"

Like almost all German ultras groups, Schickeria consists mainly of young men. FC Bayern's ultras mostly belong to the middle class, and many of them are students.[163] Membership is by invitation only, after a person has proven themself through continual and frequent attendance at games and in-group activities, such as creating choreographies or helping organize the Kurt Landauer tournament, which the group hosts every year. Since the approximately 250 group members are expected to attend almost every game—home and away, national and international—class is a factor for potential members. Ultras groups, even more progressive ones like Schickeria, tend to be homogeneous in terms of class, gender, and nationality, yet heterogeneous in terms of political orientation and group roles: while some group members prepare choreographies, others focus more on acoustic support or write texts for fanzines, organize events, or participate in fights with fans of rival clubs.

Because of the diverse interests and political orientations of their members, ultras groups face the challenge of whether to be political at all, and if so, to what extent they want to and can be. The spectrum ranges from far right through "apolitical" to far left, with most groups, broadly defined, somewhere between apolitical and left. If they are political, they must contend with fellow fan groups with a different political stance. In the home stands of Borussia Dortmund, Werder Bremen, and several other clubs, progressive ultras and reactionary fan groups clashed in the early years of the twenty-first century.[164] At this time, Schickeria in Munich brought antiracist banners to FC Bayern's home stand for the first time. Several group members had been socialized in a fan scene replete with racism, sexism, and antisemitism. The fanzines of FC Bayern's fan clubs from the 1980s and 1990s frequently displayed the swastika and other far right symbols, a fact that provides a fresh perspective on the cultural shift in the fan culture that Schickeria brought about.[165] At this point, the club and its fans did not have a "Jew Club" identity at all.[166]

On average, seventy-five thousand fans attend a regular Bundesliga game at Allianz Arena, including approximately four or five hundred ultras. Although just a minority, they are core fans. Ultras almost always stand behind one of the two goals, and the group positioned right behind the goal in the center of the home stand usually leads the internal fan hierarchy. In Munich, this is Schickeria, which has two or three groups standing nearby. The main group leads the chants with one or more group members. They face the fans, not the field, organizing the fans' chants and choreographies throughout the game. Fan scenes and ultras groups are complex social organizations, and an in-depth study would be far beyond the scope of this book.[167] What is crucial to understand is this: Schickeria's turn to Landauer happened at a time of political tension in German fan stands, and Schickeria needed to find a way to justify its leading status in the still traditional FC Bayern fan scene, while retaining its general political orientation. In this context, Schickeria not only turned to Landauer because they considered it important to remember him as the club's former German Jewish president but also because, for them, Landauer had become a symbol of the club's open-minded, antiracist orientation. Landauer was a "vehicle" used to transmit the values Schickeria had in mind for the club and its fan base to a larger audience. All German clubs and their fans understand their club cultures as rooted in the city and marked by tradition. Landauer was both: a local and a central figure in the club's history. No fan disagrees that Landauer is a central part of the club's legacy. Because Landauer was also excluded from society as a "Jew," commemorating him furthermore promoted the club's identity as progressive. Schickeria writes: "Due to this open-minded, cosmopolitan, and tolerant tradition of our club, we as Bayern fans feel obliged to speak out against racism and discrimination in the stadiums and in society and to get involved."[168]

For ultras, local rootedness is a central value. They express their localism through flags displaying the city's colors in the stadium. Schickeria also gave itself a name that aims to express

Figure 1.9. A Kurt Landauer sticker. Photo by author.

their rootedness in Munich.[169] Outside the stadium, ultras mark their territory through graffiti and stickers. Throughout Munich, stickers by FC Bayern's ultras offer a glimpse into their priorities and values. Stickers expressing their memorial regime display for Kurt Landauer (see fig. 1.9) or for Sophie Scholl and the symbol of Scholl's resistance group the White Rose movement (see fig. 1.10). Both stickers express a sense of local and anti-Nazi traditionalism. Other stickers display the number 72, sometimes together with the word *Südkurve*, which means South Stand. This symbol refers to the home stand in the club's former stadium, which was built for the 1972 Olympic Games. Schickeria members perceive the old home stand as a symbol of the roots of their group and a symbol of the unity of all fans standing in the South Stand today: "Südkurve München 72—origin and future."[170] Additional stickers display the group name and their love for the city, for instance: "Schickeria—Wir lieben München" [We love Munich]. More stickers display the group's political orientation; they read, "Ultras against Nazism" or "Love Bayern—Hate Racism." In sum, Landauer is embedded in a web of symbols expressing the group's love for the club, its localism, and its progressive traditionalism.

Figure 1.10. A Sophie Scholl sticker. Photo by author.

Memory Culture as Rehabilitation

Ultras, like many youth cultures, have a complicated relationship with authorities and so-called deviant conduct, such as violence, drugs, and the use of pyrotechnics at stadiums. Ultras are the most visible fan culture. They stand as a collective in the home stand or away sector, and they travel and walk collectively to and from the stadiums, which may seem intimidating to others. They demand the gaze of fans, players, and the public, while authorities and journalists react with fascination but also with disdain and repression. The spectrum in the complicated police–fan relationship ranges from reactions to crimes to unprovoked police violence.[171] Bavaria is known as a state that enforces its laws firmly, and Schickeria has struggled from its foundation in 2002 with police repression and conflicts with the club management.[172] Just one year after its foundation, the club attempted to ban Schickeria and two other groups from the stadium entirely and for good.[173] In 2006, fifty-nine FC Bayern fans received stadium bans after clashes broke out during FC Bayern's away game in Duisburg.[174]

One year later, FC Bayern's club management issued seventy-three stadium bans after riots occurred between fans of FC Bayern and their rivals 1. FC Nuremberg at motorway services near Würzburg. During this incident, a flying bottle injured the bus driver's wife, who lost one eye. After Würzburg, the club took away the season tickets of 530 FC Bayern fans who had filed their tickets via a Schickeria-compiled list for the South Stand, and the club also requested them to separate themselves from the group. Several FC Bayern fans were sentenced and barred from even contacting the group. A judge compared the ultras to an assault troop.[175] "This will probably mean the end for the group," Germany's leading magazine for football culture wrote at the time.[176]

Schickeria struggled to survive. For its members, Würzburg was "just another welcome reason to attack the active fan scene in Munich once more, hoping to deal them the death blow."[177] While the details regarding ultras and violence go beyond the scope of this chapter, it is crucial to emphasize that ultras have a complicated relationship with violence that separates them from the violent and often far right hooligans that frequented stadiums in the 1980s.[178] There are ultras who refuse to take part in violent actions, while being a hooligan without fighting is impossible. What is significant for the turn to Landauer is that Schickeria faced a vital decision on how to proceed.

About six months after Würzburg, the group published an essay in the German fanzine *Blickfang Ultra* entitled *Quo vadis Ultras? On the Future of the German Ultras Groups*. They asked, "Is it possible to create acceptance for our Ultrà subculture among the general public through skillfully presenting our topics and through our own media and press?"[179] This question "became an existential one for the group's immediate survival after the incident at the Würzburg motorway services."[180] The group's public perception as a security concern made it tough for them to continue with their game day routine: "An organized collective that travels by bus and a cohesive group appearance have always played a central role in our understanding of an ultras group. . . . But a large police force welcomes our group at almost every away game and checks over all travelers, although nothing happened before. Because of this massive change for the worse, we can no longer organize buses to away games."[181] Even more significantly, the group did not display its main banner between 2006 and 2022 because of all the stadium bans against its members. To an ultras group, no object is more "sacred" than its main flag, which is always placed in front of them in the stadiums. It displays their presence, and if this banner gets lost, an ultras group usually ceases to exist. Instead of its main flag that read "Schickeria München," the group displayed banners such as "The banned are always with us" or "Bayern München" at Allianz Arena.[182] Schickeria concluded the 2007 *Blickfang Ultra* article by asking how ultras could continue to exist while "staying real," with the demand that ultras should "think about it and find their own way."[183] Shortly after, it was the turn to Landauer that, for the first time, led to a more complex, even celebratory, perception of the group. Today, the Schickeria is an important part of the club culture that is particularly praised for its visual and acoustic support of the club but, most importantly, for bringing Landauer to the public's attention.[184]

WORKING THROUGH THE PRESENT: MEMORY IN ACTION

Arguably, people have worked off the past in Munich. At least, this is the conclusion of Gavriel D. Rosenfeld's book *Munich and Memory*. Although many historians argue that coming to terms with the past is a never-ending process,[185] according to Rosenfeld, this has been disproven by the reality of Munich's postwar urban development because, "in certain areas of the city, the past has been fully mastered in the sense of the so-called *Schlußstrich* [drawing a line under it]—that is, mastered in the sense of being finished, or left aside as a matter over and done with."[186] The reconstruction process has come to an end; no further controversies are to be expected; traditional architectural styles have finally been rehabilitated. This process, Rosenfeld suggests, may, in fact, mean the end of working off the past (Vergangenheitsbewältigung). Rosenfeld's observation is supported by the fact that "the only open question" remaining at the time of his writing—the Munich Documentation Center for the History of National Socialism—has finally been established.[187] The Munich of today, including the documentation center, also remembers the perpetrators.

But did working through the past (Aufarbeitung der Vergangenheit) really come to an end in Munich? Through the memorialization process, the past that is supposed to be remembered may, in fact, be obscured by this memory work taking the form of memorials.[188] In architecture, the past may be worked off. In the case of FC Bayern, however, a surprising actor has appeared on the memorial landscape, aiming to prevent memory culture from freezing. Sport fans are often associated with rude behavior. To FC Bayern's most passionate fans, the ultras, however, there is more than meets the eye. While the FC Bayern memorial landscape, with its paths, football fields, signs, and statue, may be the materialized end product of a long process, this working through the past remains an active process first and foremost because of the club's fans who use Landauer's legacy as an inspiration to work through the present (Gegenwartsbewältigung).[189]

As earlier mentioned, Schickeria, founded in 2002, developed a political position against Nazism and discrimination. During the 2008–9 season, for example, Schickeria initiated a Refugees Welcome action day, for which they invited refugees to the stadium, distributed flyers, and collectively displayed the slogan "Refugees welcome" at the stadium.[190]

Schickeria has hosted an annual football tournament named after Kurt Landauer since 2006, and thus three years before the turn to Landauer, which came to a peak at the Dachau Lutheran

Church of Reconciliation. The ultras invite fan groups from Munich's Südkurve as well as fan groups from FC St. Pauli, VfL Bochum, Italy, and other places where Schickeria have friendships. The Kurt Landauer tournament is more than a football tournament. In fact, these gatherings have become the most active space for doing memory in the club's culture. In 2006, the ultras organized showings of the films *KZ Dachau, Nacht und Nebel*, and *Schindler's List*, and they hosted workshops about repression against football fans and racism in football. Furthermore, the fans went to visit the Dachau Concentration Camp memorial site.[191] In 2009, they organized a workshop on homophobia in football and went on a guided city tour about Jewish life in Munich. Three years later, Charlotte Knobloch, president of the Israelitische Kultusgemeinde München und Oberbayern since 1985, was among the tournament's guests. The ultras also invited Schulze-Marmeling, author of many books on FC Bayern and Kurt Landauer, to give a lecture during the tournament. Schulze-Marmeling had expected drunken and rude football fans, but as he remembers, "I was sitting in a beer tent in front of three hundred people. There was complete silence. I have not felt such an interest in my reading anywhere else."[192] Repeatedly, the ultras have invited refugee teams to the Kurt Landauer tournament, which serves as a space of enacted memory through the ultras' various activities. The memorialization of Landauer becomes an active engagement with the past that functions as a statement about the present and a vision for the future.

When the DFB handed the Julius Hirsch Preis to FC Bayern ultra Simon Müller in 2014,[193] he attended the ceremony wearing a T-shirt that displayed the slogan "No One Is Illegal" ["Kein Mensch ist Illegal"], and thus used the spotlight to make a statement about contemporary racism and about refugees—a statement about the present based on the memory of the past.[194] The prize fund they received was used by Schickeria to found the Kurt Landauer Foundation. The message that "Landauer is a vehicle to convey messages," as stated by Michael Linninger, a representative of the Kurt Landauer Foundation,[195] was transmitted across the German media through the "Kein Mensch ist Illegal" T-shirt at the DFB ceremony. In fact, the fans' working through the present may serve as an example of how multidirectional memory is put into praxis.[196] The foundation is explicit about using the memory of a Bavarian Jewish club president as a method of multidirectional engagement for equality in the present. Its aim is, as the foundation's statutes, say, "to fund projects promoting a cosmopolitan, progressive, liberal, and antiracist society and the peaceful and equal coexistence of all people regardless of their nationality, citizenship, ethnic, and cultural origin."[197]

The statutes explicitly state the support of intercultural football teams as one of the foundation's goals, alongside the integration of refugees, for instance, through stadium visits or historical city tours completed by fans and refugees together. The tournament and the Kurt Landauer Foundation are ways of doing memory that connect the commemoration of Landauer with political engagement in the present. Instead of coming to an impasse, FC Bayern's ultras put memory culture into practice. Through their various forms of doing memory, the impasse has been turned into various multidirectional opportunities. Yet, the fans' working through the present neither counters an identification with victims nor challenges the obscuring of Munich's tradition as "the Nazi Movement's capital city." Although memory is turned into action, it simultaneously remains selective and includes a form of forgetting.

Mia san Mia: Mia san Landauer

Football clubs perceive and portray themselves as locally rooted, often conveyed through the German word Heimat, which roughly translates as "home" or "homeland."[198] In Munich, the club FC Bayern advertises its localism with the slogan "Mia san Mia," which translates as "We are who we are."[199] Today, the slogan is imprinted in large letters on the West Stand of the Allianz Arena, and it also features prominently in Dirk Kämper's 2014 book on Kurt Landauer. The second paragraph of the book's preface—written by FC Bayern's honorary captain, Philipp Lahm—deals solely with this maxim and thereby places Landauer's legacy within the realm of tradition, of *Heimat*, and thus also at the center of the club's collective identity in the present: "FC Bayern's identity can be summed up by the maxim 'Mia san mia.' These three words express one's connection to one's Heimat, and a sense of tradition. These nine letters stand for identification, they express cohesiveness, and a certain pride. A pride in the club's Bavarian character, in preserving one's roots, and, finally, of course, in the successes and trophies won. A pride that is often interpreted as arrogance, which polarizes and thus creates a community."[200] The prominent positioning of "Mia san Mia," the initial words any reader interested in Landauer's biography will encounter, frames Landauer's past as an integral part of the club's identity in the present. Landauer becomes the personified idol of this maxim: "Mia san Landauer." He is turned into a figure that embodies localism, traditionalism, identification, preservation, continuity, and gemeinschaft. The image built of Landauer has become a symbol for the club's collective identity in the present. *Mia san Mia* becomes *Mia san Landauer*.

The club's collective identity is about tradition and presenting Bavarian culture. Each year, the players, dressed in lederhosen, visit the local Oktoberfest. Furthermore, a member of Schickeria offers bicycle tours for the players of FC Bayern's youth teams about the history and the values of the club. During these tours, Landauer is also discussed.[201] While being oriented toward tradition and the local, the club has also become "the fastest growing football brand in the world."[202] Its website has been translated into Chinese, English, and Spanish. The club holds an office in New York Manhattan where its US subsidiary resides, FC Bayern Munich LLC.

In 2011, two years after the event at the KZ Dachau memorial site and a year before the FC Bayern Museum opening, FC Bayern and Qatar's relationship took off, starting with the relocation of the club's training camps to Doha, which led to an official partnership that lasted from 2018 until 2023. During that period, FC Bayern's annual revenue more than doubled.[203] Fan groups like Schickeria strongly criticized the club management for its connections to Qatar, a country known to violate human rights, and this also led to global calls for boycotting the Qatar World Cup in 2022. The club's ties to Qatar were highly contested publicly, and they caused conflict between the club and its fans. In 2020, fans of the club organized a roundtable discussion at EineWeltHaus Munich titled "Qatar, Human Rights and FC Bayern—Hands Open, Mouth Shut?" At this discussion, two migrant workers from Nepal, one former activist from Human Rights Watch, and a fan representative discussed the catastrophic violations of human rights in Qatar.[204] The fans had reserved a seat at the roundtable for a club representative, but the invitation remained unanswered, the seat empty.[205] One year later, fans filed a petition at the annual club members meeting, demanding an end to the club's ties to Qatar because they stood in stark contrast to the club's values. The club's board rejected the petition and refused to discuss the issue, leading to vocal protests at the membership meeting.[206] The conflict between fans and the club over Qatar also signifies different approaches to memory culture. For the fans, criticizing Qatar's human rights violations and demanding the discontinuation of the club's business relationship is part of commemorating Landauer. The petition claimed: "Kurt Landauer would turn in his grave."[207] For the club, which faced a "legitimacy gap,"[208] between its social values associated with its "Jew Club" identity and its sponsorship deal with Qatar, Landauer fulfills a different function.

Football cultures are always glocal.[209] While the game is understood universally and those who play it professionally have become global entities, the game's authenticity is always defined through its local embeddedness. While football clubs have become immense global businesses, they still rely on local marketing strategies to keep their local fans attached to the club. Local fans perceive the clubs as representatives of their city or region on football's global stage. In this context, the club's turn to Landauer becomes relevant for two reasons. First, FC Bayern's identification with Landauer provides the club with a sense of rootedness in local tradition. Second, the club's recognition of its former German Jewish club president—and with it the sense of having been disadvantaged by the Nazis as a "Jew Club"—frames the club as anti-Nazi. To a certain degree, Landauer compensates for the club's global aspirations and criticism of its ethical standards.

In light of the increasing globalization of football, the great challenge of the time is to be a business organization while maintaining a football club, the club's chairman Oliver Kahn says in the 2021 Amazon series *FC Bayern—Behind the Legend*.[210] Chairman Karl-Heinz Rummenigge similarly claims that connecting the past with the future is "a balancing act";[211] a point that also applies to the tension between the values of FC Bayern as a "Jew Club" and its association with Qatar. Schulze-Marmeling asked whether the club's memory culture will conflict with the Qatar sponsorship.[212] In contrast to Schulze-Marmeling, I believe that FC Bayern's relationship to Qatar actually strengthened the club's memory culture. I argue that the turn to Landauer happened not despite but, to some degree, because of Qatar. Turning a Jew into the club's symbolic figure allows it to remain morally intact while moving close to a state strongly criticized for antisemitism, human rights violations, and homophobia.

The deal between FC Bayern and Qatar benefited both sides but was discontinued after Qatar refused to renew the contract after it ended in 2023.[213] FC Bayern has doubled its annual revenue since Qatar started to invest in the club. Qatar, a country that also invests in other clubs such as Paris St. Germain and FC Barcelona, made positive headlines through football. Qatar profits because the club provides global recognition. The state of Qatar—located in one of the most conflict-ridden areas globally with an army of only twelve thousand soldiers—has developed one of the costliest soft power strategies the world has ever seen. Qatar invested billions in culture, science, and sports. Football is a kind of diplomacy for Qatar, putting the small but wealthy country on the map of global affairs.[214]

The memorialization of Kurt Landauer thus has multiple meanings and functions: For the club, the turn to Landauer grounded FC Bayern within local tradition and continuity at the very moment when the club was going more and more global. For the fans, Kurt Landauer allows an identification with the club's tradition and localism and thus provides an opportunity to focus more on the local than on the global side of the club. The tension between the global and the local, between clubs and fans, has found common ground in "Mia san Landauer," the identification with the former president. Landauer is the link between the club management and the active fan groups, which are increasingly divided on how they perceive the continued development of football as a global commodity.

FC BAYERN AND THE TURN TO HISTORY (II)

FC Bayern is still coming to terms with its past. In January 2023, the club jointly organized an event with the Israelitische Kultusgemeinde München und Oberbayern (IKG) at the Jewish Community Center in the heart of Munich on Holocaust Memorial Day. The event featured high-ranking speakers from both organizations and presented the revised special exhibition *Venerated—Prosecuted—Forgotten: Victims of National Socialism at FC Bayern Munich* to the two hundred guests. The event made it clear that both history (as fact) and collective memory (as myth) can potentially coexist in the future.

The first speaker, Charlotte Knobloch, president of the IKG since 1985, opened the event by praising FC Bayern's memory work, and asked the audience to applaud the club several times. Besides

Knobloch, the moderator, Guy Fränkel, declared how significant the club's embrace of Landauer is for local Jews: "I am so happy! My community and my club together!"[215] Knobloch, who also made no secret of her love for FC Bayern, declared: "The great Kurt Landauer would have been proud that his FC Bayern is so engaged."[216]

The second speaker, FC Bayern's president Herbert Hainer, opened his address by thanking Knobloch for her praise.[217] He then found remarkable words about Hofmann's study on FC Bayern during Nazism that demonstrated his commitment to the club's turn to history: "The study has clearly shown that there were also perpetrators at FC Bayern."[218] Hainer highlighted the importance of external and independent studies, saying that this is the only way to draw conclusions, and he declared the club's aim as being to "work through the past instead of working *off* the past."[219] He said that the club is also future-directed. Hainer concluded by saying that commemoration is not enough.[220] Above his head were the symbols of FC Bayern and the IKG and the event's theme "Remember Together, Shape the Future Together!" as stated in German in figure 1.11. The phrase's design emphasizes the future and stresses that, after the study, the next task is to draw conclusions from it.

It is too early to tell how the study will shape the club's collective identity in the future, and in how much detail the club wants to talk about the inglorious aspects of its history. Even though Gregor Hofmann, author of the study, was present at the event, he was missing among the speakers. The club, however, used the opportunity to present the book and to hand out free copies to guests at the event. The touring exhibition was updated and now includes exhibition boards on exclusion, radicalization, and the Holocaust. In addition, the club published an interview with Hofmann in its own museum catalog, which suggests that the club's turn to history will also inform its memory culture in the future. The club critically asked the historian: Was the club influenced by Jews? To what extent does he [Kurt Landauer] represent the

Figure 1.11. "Remember Together, Shape the Future Together!" Photo by author.

club? To what extent was FC Bayern generally considered a "Jew Club"?[221]

CONCLUSION

This chapter has addressed how FC Bayern Munich became known as a "Jew Club" through memory culture. The turn to the club's German Jewish former president Kurt Landauer was a substantial turnaround for the club, as, after 1945, it drew a firm line under the Nazi period and offered reintegration to both Jews and Nazis. The club management was reluctant at first, but it finally joined the turn to Landauer in 2009. Since then, the club, its fans, and the general public have told themselves the story of a "Jew Club" resistant to and therefore discriminated against by the Nazi regime.

Two memory regimes developed in FC Bayern's memory culture: The ultras fan culture and the club both contributed in different ways and for different reasons to the turn to Landauer. The memory work of the ultras was influenced by two aspects, which primary sources like fanzines revealed. First, they developed a strategy that I call "progressive traditionalism"—because the ultras' progressive politics contrasted with the historically reactionary fan culture in Germany, they needed to appeal to a shared identity. They turned Landauer into a symbol for their politics to highlight antidiscrimination activities as part of the club's heritage. Second, their successful memory work involved public rehabilitation at a time when the ultras considered whether they could even survive. For the club, the turn to Landauer offered them the chance to become locally rooted while creating a global marketing strategy, including the contested relationship with Qatar. The turn to Landauer allowed the club to globalize its identity, balancing its global ambitions with local rootedness. Fans and club unite in memory culture: "Mia san Landauer."

FC Bayern's memorial landscape evolved in a dialectical way with other memorial landscapes. First, it shared its traditionalist approach with Munich. The city's memorial landscape emphasizes continuity. Ruins were built over, and the remnants of the past have been replaced with new buildings that have old-fashioned appearances. Second, the club's memory culture also developed in relation to German football's memorial scene. The club's and the sport's memorial landscapes both emerged belatedly after the 2006 World Cup. Finally, a desire to identify with the victims had come to define the nation's memorial landscape when FC Bayern's memory culture began to take shape. These memorial landscapes succeeded in writing the victims into their histories, even if this was long overdue. Yet as a byproduct, they identified with the victims and obscured the history of the perpetrators. In summary, collective memories are selective and always also constitute forms of forgetting.

The "Jew Club" narrative was significant in two historical moments. Initially, during denazification, the club sought to portray itself in a favorable light to the new authorities. After the post-1945 moment, the club never looked back. In the context of the turn to Landauer, the club rediscovered its "Jew Club" identity and contrasted Nazism with its own past. It highlighted Landauer as a symbol of reconciliation and continuity and promoted itself as Germany's former "Jew Club," which had supposedly always been liberal-minded and cosmopolitan.

The club FC Bayern, the city of Munich, the nation of Germany, and the sport of football all established institutionalized and ritualized ways of commemorating Jews. After two decades of "Mia san Landauer," the club's memory culture shifted again; the turn to Landauer was followed by a turn to history, initiated by a public debate in 2016 that led FC Bayern to fund an independent investigation into its NS history. The club began updating its historical narrative once the book was published in 2022. Yet it remains unclear how the club and its supporters will change their version of history.

TWO

FK AUSTRIA VIENNA

The "Jew Club" as Cultural Code

WHEN THE AUSTRIAN NATIONAL FOOTBALL team played against Israel on November 12, 2021, it was not Austria's 4–2 win that made global headlines.[1] The day before, representatives of both states, their football federations, and the football club FK Austria Vienna (FAK) had gathered at Judenplatz in central Vienna to celebrate the club's and the national football federation's adoption of the International Holocaust Remembrance Alliance's (IHRA) definition of antisemitism, which VIPs and news agencies hailed as a huge step forward in the fight against antisemitism.[2] Journalists gathered around the small group. Pictures were taken, interviews given. The crowd assembled in front of Austria's central Holocaust Memorial, the "Nameless Library." Less than a century ago, Austrians had cheerfully celebrated Hitler when he announced Austria's "annexation" in 1938 from a balcony at Vienna's Heldenplatz—just half a mile away from Judenplatz. Two days before, on November 9, FAK's football team had already gathered at Judenplatz to commemorate the Jewish victims of Nazism, and—notably—also to self-assert the club's Jewish history. Despite its "Jew Club" image and antisemitic attacks from rival fans, FAK has a far right presence among its own fans. The club had long ignored all of this. Now, the club increased its memorialization of its historical association with Vienna's bourgeois Judaism to counter antisemitism in the present. The events highlighted the importance of football in Austria, the ongoing process of overcoming the nation's long-held myth of being Hitler's "first victim," and the issue of antisemitism and neo-Nazis in contemporary Austrian fan cultures.

In what follows, I first discuss how people in the interwar period associated FAK with a particular cultural code.[3] This code covered things supposedly Jewish, namely, modernism, cosmopolitanism, coffeehouses, urbanism, and rootlessness. In the second part of the chapter, I examine how FAK and its fans construct their collective identity in the present in a way that is grounded in the club's collective memory. I argue that both FAK's fans and the supporters of rival clubs are reinventing the "Jew Club" in distinct ways: FAK supporters, on the one hand, reverse the club's former allegedly Jewish features by reinventing FAK as a rooted, traditional club. Rival supporters, on the other hand, have rediscovered FAK's "Jew Club" reputation and engage in antisemitic fan performances. The final section of this chapter focuses on the clubs' memory cultures as manifest in museums and publications. I address how FAK portrays itself in a manner congruent with the nation's victim myth, and I discuss how FAK commemorates its previous Jewish managing director Norbert Lopper; president Emanuel Schwarz; and player Matthias Sindelar. The latter has long been lauded as a resistance hero despite having profited from the "Aryanization" of a coffeehouse. Finally, this chapter demonstrates how FAK transforms the "Jew Club" notion into a new cultural code to combat its neo-Nazi supporters.

THE "JEW CLUB" AS A CULTURAL CODE IN
EARLY TWENTIETH-CENTURY VIENNA

A statue stands in front of the football stadium of FAK's local rival, Rapid Vienna (see fig. 2.1). Dionys "Mister Rapid" Schönecker,

Figure 2.1. A statue of Dionys Schönecker. Photo by author.

Rapid Vienna's club manager from 1910 until his death in 1938, is fundamental to Rapid's collective identity. The statue presents him as the "father of the Rapid spirit" and is accompanied by a plaque that reads, quoting Schönecker, "Who sticks together, wins!"[4] The wall behind the statue also displays the club's corporate identity: "Together. Fighting. Winning." This is derived from Schönecker's quote and provides the core concept for the club museum.[5] Schönecker is known for developing Rapid's "working-class club" ethos and reputedly instructing his players before every Derby versus FAK: "Guys, listen, we are playing against the Jews today. You know, beat them, then they are where they belong."[6]

How can we understand Schönecker's—at the time unquestioned—association of FAK with Jews? Was Schönecker a hateful antisemite? Given his antisemitic criticism of the Austrian football federation's (ÖFB) Jewish general secretary, Hugo Meisl, this posthumous interpretation is intriguing.[7] Yet, antisemitism was anything but institutionalized in Rapid's club culture before 1938.[8] Schönecker supported the admission of the actually Jewish club Hakoah Vienna to the Austrian football federation, and Rapid had Jewish players, officials, and sponsors during and before Schönecker's reign.[9] The words "Jew Club" contain much more than vicious antisemitism. Rather than understanding "Jew Club" in terms of either antisemitic hatred or an anti-antisemitic identity, I understand this Othering as part of the "Jew" imaginary framework, in which the "Jew Club" stands for the modernism, cosmopolitanism, and intellectualism of the early 1920s metropolis—all things associated with "Jews" and despised by antisemites. The making of the "Jew Club" FAK has four main components: the Jews in the club, FAK's modern style of football in the early twentieth century, the concept of the coffeehouse club, and FAK's image as a city club.

What Is Jewish about the "Jew Club?"

"If you grew up in Vienna's Jewish community, you'll know there is only one club people talk about: FAK," the photographer and freelancer Daniel Shaked told me.[10] Shaked, a lifelong supporter of the "Jew Club" FAK, was among the first football players for the Jewish lower-league team Maccabi Vienna. Although the foundation of SC Maccabi Vienna in 1996 expressed "a renewed [Jewish] self-confidence in the Austrian public sphere," as Adam Sutcliffe notes, FAK has remained by far the most important sports club for Vienna's Jews.[11] As Daniel Shaked says: "At Maccabi, we used to play at ten or eleven in the morning so we could make it to FAK's stadium after our games. Between half and three-quarters of our team went to see FAK. You cannot compare the significance of Maccabi to the importance of FAK. Maccabi is the club where you do sports, but the topic of conversation in the community is FAK."[12] Shaked, the son of an Israeli mother and an Austrian father, grew up in 1990s Vienna, where friends took him to the stadium. His memories of FAK are linked to Jewish spaces such as the synagogue or the coffeehouse: Shaked remembers the Café de l'Europe, for example. Scenes of older men from the Jewish community who frequented the coffeehouse left an imprint on Shaked: "This was the first time I saw concentration camp numbers on forearms, but what they spoke about was FAK." At the synagogue one day, Shaked recalled sitting close to an older man who always used to discuss FAK. Shaked said, "He did not pay attention to the prayers. One would meet there and simply talk about FAK." Every Saturday or Sunday, the old man walked the long distance from the synagogue to the stadium. Shaked added, "You grew up there, and everyone around you talks about the club." Jews have always been important to FAK and the club was always important to Jews, while, at the same time, others used FAK as a projection screen to construct their own collective identity along the notions of supposed "Jewish difference" and by contrasting their imagined community with the "Jew Club."[13]

In 1911, when FAK—then known as Wiener Amateur Sportverein or simply as Amateure—was established, it held significance for the Jews in Vienna, albeit not as an explicitly Jewish club. Jews held key positions in the club: FAK's inaugural president, Erwin Müller, was an "assimilated" Jew, and the famous Hugo Meisl, the coach of Austria's revered Wunderteam, served on the club's management board and as its sporting director.[14] From its inception, FAK embraced its identity as a bourgeois football club, providing a space for Jews and non-Jews alike.[15] Karl Geyer, a former player and coach, fondly recalled the early days: "When I joined FAK, half of the team was Jewish, and the other half were 'Aryans.' But it did not matter. You knew it, but nobody talked about it, it was uninteresting! . . . There was no fuss. They didn't say, 'You Saujud [pig Jew], you.'"[16] Primarily, the club prioritized its football pursuits, with identity distinctions revolving more around class and gender than around Jewish and non-Jewish backgrounds or political leanings.

Jewish participation, as in Germany, was a core aspect of sports in Vienna. Jews played important roles in Vienna's football federation and in all the city's major football clubs—except for the Wiener-Sport club.[17] More than one-third of all sport officials in Vienna were Jews, exceeding the proportion of Jews in Vienna's population.[18] FAK had more Jewish officials than other integrated Austrian clubs between 1926 and 1938, yet FAK was never explicitly Jewish.[19] FAK was a *Gesellschaftsverein*, a cultural organization based in Vienna's Bohemia, the city's vibrant coffeehouse culture, and linked with theaters and writers.[20] While Jews could do sports in various clubs, it was FAK in particular that became important among assimilated bourgeois Jews.

Football became Austria's leading sport in the early twentieth century. It had more spectators and more media attention during Vienna's interwar years—a period of rapid transformation that offered workers more leisure time and new mobility within a rapidly changing city expanding quickly in terms of size and population. Earlier, at the turn of the century, Vienna had also witnessed the development of a genuinely Jewish sports movement—a reaction to the increasing exclusion of Jews from sports clubs.[21] The Sports club Hakoah, founded in 1909, not only offered a variety of sports for its Jewish members but also organized events to foster Jewish self-confidence. Non-Jews were only permitted as coaches; members had to be Jewish.[22] This period saw the rapid growth of new Jewish sports clubs such as Kadimah, Hachawer, and Hasmonea, all of which had a Zionist orientation and thus proximity to Hakoah.[23] Jewish clubs, however, existed far beyond the Zionist ideal of muscular Judaism propagated by Max Nordau at the Second Zionist Congress in 1898, at which Nordau discussed the necessity of creating a "new Jew" with the mental and physical fortitude to attain Zionism's aims.[24] Hanizachon was, while short-lived, an Orthodox Jewish sports club. The Jewish

Athletic Club and the Young Jewish Sporting Club were linked to the Viennese Social Democrats.[25] While all these sports clubs offered Jews a space to do sports, two were most significant for Jews in Vienna: the clubs people discussed, debated, and spoke about were Hakoah and, of course, FK Austria Vienna.

Nowadays, all of Austria recognizes Rapid vs. FAK as the most important football game in Vienna. It was not always like this. In the early twentieth century, Rapid's uttermost rivals were Wiener-Sport Club, Floridsdorfer Athletiksport Club, and the Wiener Association Footballclub. One of the city's most important rivalries was FAK vs. Hakoah, or, put differently, a game played between Austria's "Jew Club" and Austria's Jewish club. The former FAK coach Karl Geyer said the following: "The spectators shouted, 'You, *Saujud*, you,' one Jew to another Jew; they were all Jews. They are not brawlers; they just scolded each other. It's different when people start to brawl and hit one another with all sorts of stuff until blood flows. But they just scolded: 'You, *Saujud*, you're filthy!' or 'Isidor, horrible, ugh!' And so, it was occasionally funny in the stands, when it was too loud, or when the ball was outside the pitch, and we looked up."[26] Although exaggerated, Geyer depicts how two concepts of Judaism clashed when Hakoah and FAK entered the pitch: Here, the Jewish sports club of the Zionist Jews; there, the integrated "Jew Club" representing the "assimilated" bourgeois Viennese Jews. One key difference between the two clubs was class, as the former FAK player Geyer noted: "We only had the righteous ones as we had our office at the Ring—or Domcafe, and the poor, small Jews did not go there."[27] Like Hakoah, FAK was called a *Juden-klub*. Geyer said the following: "I played for the 'Jew Club,' so to speak, we were also called the 'Jew Club,' although I was Aryan. We were the Jews, just like Hakoah. . . . And when Hakoah played against FAK, there was always a rivalry."[28]

The rivalry between Hakoah and FAK vanished with the "Anschluss." Almost immediately, the Nazis shut down the sports club that had so proudly advocated Zionism during its world tours and that had produced world-class athletes who used to compete at the Olympics. A real sensation, Hakoah became the first continental European club to defeat an English team on its home ground.[29] Only two years later, Hakoah clinched the 1924–25 national title and thus moved to the rank of a national elite competitor such as FAK, which had won the title the year before and the year after Hakoah. All of this came to an immediate end with the annexation. While the Nazis prohibited Hakoah, FAK continued playing, although with an entirely different managing board. The Nazis, in short, drew a clear distinction between the Jewish club Hakoah, and FAK, a club with Jews in leading positions.

Playing Smart, Playing Modern: FAK and Donau Football

The "Jew Club" concept as a cultural code includes this particular club being associated with Jews and Judaism. Similarly crucial is the association with modernity, often expressed through the link with an innovative style of playing football. FAK stood for such a particular modern style of the game: Donaufußball, that is, Donau football, which was associated with bourgeois culture and stood in direct opposition to Hakoah's or Rapid's supposedly proletarian working-class style. The centers of Donau football were Hungary (with the "Jew Club" MTK Budapest), Czechoslovakia, and Austria.[30] In these countries, football was more advanced than, for instance, in Germany. Donau football was known for professionalism, a cosmopolitan orientation, and a quick-passing game.

Vienna was "the metropolis among the metropolises of Donau football."[31] No other city had as many excellent football teams as Vienna, a football culture that also profited from Jewish Hungarian migrants who had escaped the antisemitic Horthy regime.[32] At least since then, FAK has been known for technically oriented football. This style is known as *Scheiberln* in the Viennese dialect,

Figure 2.2. Sticker "Scheiberlspiel." Photo by author.

which means "playing smart." Instead of chasing the ball, players used fast passes to shift it around the pitch, thus moving it quickly to open spaces on the field. FAK was proud of Scheiberln, for as Karl Geyer noted: "We were an intelligent team."[33] FAK was known as the "intellectuals" or as the "intellectuals' club."[34] During one of the club's many tours through Europe, FAK promoted itself in a brochure, published in the summer of 1919, as "its own brand in Austrian football." The club "was never what one would call a 'hard team,' perhaps because the club was just as eager to be a social club as a football club. . . . The club was almost always led by a doctor or a professor," the brochure proudly claims.[35] And this image lasted. Throughout the 1930s and 1940s, newspapers elaborated on FAK's "skillful and tricky style of football" and admired "the most intellectual way of playing football."[36] It was alleged that FAK never scored goals by force.[37] Even today, fans place self-designed stickers around the stadium to display their collective identification with the Scheiberlspiel, the club legend Matthias Sindelar, and a club that supposedly "always plays and never fights" (see fig. 2.2).[38] The president of the Austrian football association said: "FAK is not the history of a team consisting of diligent football workers, but of creative football artists."[39] Although many of its players were proletarians, the image of the artists' team is still prevalent today, as Daniel Shaked told me: "If you were to ask a FAK fan: 'What style of football do you wish to see?' they would answer: 'We want to keep the ball on the ground. We want passes, we want to dribble. And if we lose, we lose.' If you asked a Rapid supporter, they would say: 'We want a dirty win. We want our team to fight!'"[40]

Many spectators appreciated FAK's Donau football, while others despised the club's professionalism and association with commerce, which they called *Gagenfußball*.[41] Referencing Hugo Meisl, FAK, and Hakoah, the *Salzburger Volksblatt* wrote in 1938 that much of the German spirit had been destroyed by foreign professionalism.[42] Connecting FAK with money, rootlessness, and intelligence was a crucial component in the making of the "Jew Club" FAK. The "Jew" imaginary framework connected "Jews" with capitalism, cosmopolitanism, and intellectualism— all of which were embodied by FAK's "Jew Club" identity.

FAK itself was and still is proud of its intellectual style, a style that used to reflect FAK's aspiration to represent Viennese football and Austrian football, since the league consisted only of Viennese clubs. It also reflected the club's professionalism, modernism, and cosmopolitanism, which stood in stark contrast to the ideal of German amateurism. FAK's image as a smart and modern club lasts to the present—and the club is proud of it. The Hugo Meisl memory room at the FAK Museum honors the famous coach and former player in the most untypical way one expects from a football museum: it displays Meisl's piano and bookshelf, which

Figure 2.3. The Hugo Meisl memory room. Photo by author.

includes works by authors like Goethe and Schiller (see fig. 2.3). The museum does not mention that Meisl was a Jew, but it proudly states that "Meisl was not a power athlete." Instead, his weapons were skillfulness and mind; people called him the *Hirnfußballer*, which roughly translates as a brainy football player.[43] FAK is a "Jew Club" because FAK is coupled with professionalism, not having a place to call home, and being smart—things that the Austrian imaginary associates with "Jews."

A Hot Cup of "Jewishness": The "Jew Club" and the Coffeehouse

Most authors describe FAK in one way or another as the prototypical Viennese city and coffeehouse club.[44] Even today, fans place stickers around the stadium celebrating the "Kaffeehausklub Austria Wien" (see fig. 2.4). In fact, the club's management operated from the Dom Café, where the Amateure were founded in 1911, and the club was later renamed Austria. During

Figure 2.4. Sticker "Kaffeehausklub." Photo by Daniel Shaked.

the 1920s, fans bought tickets for FAK's football games at coffeehouses. In-town coffee shops were frequently used for discussions with supporters and meetings with sponsors.[45] Emanuel
Schwarz, FAK's former Jewish president, lived only a few minutes
away from the Dom Café.[46] Football historians have described
him as the incarnation of the Gesellschaftsverein, because he
came from the Viennese coffeehouse's social and cultural environment.[47] Vienna residents in the early twentieth century had a
choice of over six hundred coffee shops: young authors and young
social democrats went to Café Griensteidl (until 1896), and Café
Central welcomed a mélange of poets, writers, actors, and doctors

(such as Sigmund Freud) and Austro-Marxist politicians (such as Otto Bauer and Max Adler).[48]

The coffeehouse was not only "intimately associated with the development of modern urban culture" but was also crucial for the city's Jewish communities and individuals.[49] As a pivotal site for the dismantling of social hierarchies,[50] the coffeehouse proved vital for the emergence of Viennese Donau football, a football style deeply associated with modernism, cosmopolitanism, and its Jewish protagonists. Football became Vienna's leading sport in the 1920s: more spectators, a growing media presence, and international successes quickly transformed the stadium into an arena of mass spectacle. Football in Vienna, however, gained its relevance not so much in the stadium but in the coffeehouse, in the *Fußballklub-Cafés*.[51] Dozens of these coffee shops existed, and each club's fan knew which one to visit in order to meet a favorite player. Almost every sports club had its favored coffeehouse or tavern, often located close to its respective sports ground.[52] As is the case with all hegemonic sports codes, the clubs and their Fußballklub-Cafés were masculine spaces, even though women had finally been allowed entrance to coffeehouses in 1918.[53] The public imaginary associated the coffeehouses with Judaism.[54] The "Jew" imaginary framework became attached to the supposedly Jewish space of the coffeehouse. While other clubs frequented coffeehouses too, FAK in particular was associated with the coffeehouses and thus became known as a "Jew Club."[55] Of equal importance as the coffeehouse was FAK's designation as a city club.

The City Club: Rootless in the City

A central antagonism of Austrian football was the binary opposition between the city and the *Vorstadt* (an industrial, proletarian, and rural space).[56] Both concepts were linked to certain football clubs: FAK represented the city, while Rapid embodied the Vorstadt. FAK stood for rootlessness, while Rapid represented localism and nature. The headline of the sports weekly *Illustriertes Sportblatt* in 1927 read "Die Vorstadt führt," which means "The Vorstadt is leading."[57] The subheading reads: "Why the city clubs are falling behind." The article describes Rapid as the prototypical *Vorstadtklub*, or "suburb" club. It is rooted, close to the people, and dedicated to its home ground. "Rapid is rooted in the people and never neglects the domestic soil. The green-and-whites are a Vorstadtklub in the best sense of the word."[58] Rapid represents the domestic soil—an idea that imagines Rapid as the embodiment of nature, Heimat, and *Bodenständigkeit*. Other Vorstadtklubs included football clubs like Admira, whom the article celebrated after Admira's 6–0 win over FAK: "On Sunday, the goals of the Admira roared like bat strokes in FAK's goal. The aspiring, healthy youth bombed the defensive position of a rotten formation. Sport triumphed over business. The fresh Jedlesee meadow air has blown away the stuffy haze of the coffeehouse. The team has ironed down the sell-out team [*Gagenfußball Mannschaft*]."[59] The author links FAK to the business world and the coffeehouse. Admira, in contrast, is portrayed as young, lively, on the offensive, and related to nature. In short, this is the coffeehouse versus nature, sport versus business.

Until 1949, there was no national football league, so local identities were magnified between Viennese teams.[60] Globally, all Viennese teams represented the city. Locally, people emphasized the differences between them. This city-suburb binary was part of a larger Austrian city-province binary, in which the concept of Jewish difference was essential.[61] While the city-province discourse did not always reference Jews explicitly, it nonetheless "often relied upon references to Jewish difference."[62] The article "Die Vorstadt führt" exemplifies the opposition between city and suburb: "The healthy, unconsumed suburb leads physically, morally, and materially."[63] The article praises Rapid, "the representatives of local football,"[64] for its strong players [*Spielermaterial*] who are "almost exclusively homegrown." For Rapid, any "adventurous business policies" are "foreign." The locally based football club also stands in contrast to commercialization.

Notably, the author speaks of city clubs in the plural and provides a second example for this category: Hakoah. We thus find the Jewish club presented next to the "Jew Club": "Vienna's Jews were to Vienna as Vienna was to Austria: a critical symbol as 'Other' necessary for self-definition."[65] To the provinces, Vienna seemed to be a "dangerous 'Jewish' metropolis," perceived as "superficial, ugly, crass, corrupt, depraved, socialist, capitalist, materialist, decadent, modern, and immoral" in contrast to the provinces, which "functioned as the site of all that was pure, good, beautiful, respectable, and moral."[66] The connection between antisemitism and city hatred is well studied.[67] In 1948, the sociologist Arnold M. Rose considered it "worth noting how the popular image of the Jew is related to the city in many ways."[68] Rose states that in much of America, "'New York' and 'Jew' are almost interchangeable epithets." Rose suggests that Jews are hated primarily "because they serve as a symbol of city life" and he observes that "the city man's picture of country life excludes the Jew." For the city man, "the symbolic projection of hatred of the city onto the Jews allows ... [one] to destroy the city and to escape the city, and at the same time to keep it and live in it."[69] The 1927 *Illustrierte Sportzeitung* article must be understood in this context. That clubs like Admira and Rapid represent the Vorstadt and, in absolute contrast, FAK represents the city is part of a city-suburb divide with antisemitic undertones that presents itself in the contemporary language of "Jewish difference." Vorstadtklubs perceived themselves as authentic because they constructed their identities in opposition to the "Jew Club."

Antisemitism is contradictory and ambivalent. Antisemites have accused Jews of capitalism and communism, of urbanism and globalism. FAK is imagined as representing both rootlessness and the city. In the "Jew" imaginary framework, the club is a root-less city club: FAK is a city club because its only stable location was its main office at the coffeehouse. FAK is imagined as rootless because the club did not own a sports ground between the 1920s and the 1970s and played, unlike Vienna's other teams, at various sports grounds. All other clubs were associated with a particular area of Vienna; FAK, however, seemed to be rootless in the city.[70] When FAK objected to the city handing over the Weststadion to Rapid, representatives of Rapid responded with an old antise-mitic stereotype: They said that FAK had a pathological drive to migrate. Even though FAK is now based in Favoriten, Rapid fans still refer to FAK as the "eternal guest" in the city.[71]

Clubs like Rapid and SC Admira from Floridsdorf created their collective identities in opposition to FAK, placing an "authentic" and locally rooted aura around their clubs. Most importantly, these clubs counted as "native" and "down to earth" (*bodenstän-dig*) because they compared themselves to FAK. Bodenständig-keit is a value, or concept, associated with someone or something deeply rooted in one's Heimat. The German term Heimat em-bodies a profound sense of belonging, identity, and cultural heri-tage tied to a specific place. The term is linked to nationalism, na-ture, and the concept of the *Volk* (people). It emphasizes regional pride and cultural unity. Its emotional and cultural ties make it difficult to translate into English, as "home" or "homeland" fail to capture its full meaning. Heimat and Bodenständigkeit stand in stark contrast to cosmopolitanism. The bodenständig-cosmopolitan binary draws a distinction between the Vorstadt and the city, between the local and the cosmopolitan or global. In the antisemitic imaginary, the "always wandering Jew" serves as Bodenständigkeit's counterimage. In Austria, Bodenständigkeit became a key political, societal, and cultural concept in debates around inclusion and exclusion during the interwar period.[72] In 1933, Austrian citizens increasingly used the term to imagine a national community,[73] and the Zionist newspaper *Die Neue Welt* noted only four years later that the term bodenständig had become a substitute for antisemitic: "If one wishes to avoid saying frankly that one is against the Jews, one states that one favors the Bodenständigen."[74] The concept, however, already had antisemitic undertones in the early 1920s, when, for instance, the *Sport-Tagblatt* claimed that "nothing is bodenständig" about FAK.[75] The connotation that FAK is a "Jew Club" is thus loaded with antisemitic images and cannot be explained by FAK's rootedness in Vienna's bourgeois (Jewish) culture. Floridsdorfer AC, for instance, had consecutive Jewish presidents, but no one called it a "Jew Club." Why? Simply because Floridsdorfer AC presented itself as a Vorstadt club and was therefore perceived as totally bodenständig. The "Jew Club" identity does not rely on an empirical core, but it is a reality because of the identities ascribed to certain clubs.

The "Jew Club" connotation was—and still is—a distorted image created by FAK's self-understanding as an urban club, a Gesellschaftsverein; by antisemites; and by the club's rivals Hakoah and Rapid. Even Rapid's Jews thus participated in the discourse of Jewish difference that portrayed FAK as a rootless and greedy city club. Rapid's former president Hans Fischer claimed in 1929 that "nothing is more important than the fact that Rapid has always built its teams out of bodenständig player material."[76] Fischer constructed Rapid's Bodenständigkeit in contrast to FAK: "There have been clubs in Vienna who, although they have won championships because of their top-class style of play, sent almost no players to the national team because they mainly consisted of foreigners."[77] Similarly, Rapid's Jewish board member Leo Schidrowitz claimed that FAK's social image "has brought a certain following that still characterizes the club: The disappearing in number but financially quite powerful society from the Kai district, rich Jewish merchants, who can twist everything more easily than be lumped together with the Jews of Hakoah."[78] Schidrowitz accuses the club of "adjusting its entire sport business only to the abundance of its wallet."[79] While Jews in Austria had, the historian Lisa Silverman argues, "a platform . . . to shape mainstream culture," Austria "had little room for the 'Jewish' when it came to forming new conceptions of the 'Austrian.'"[80] Interestingly, many of those who consciously avoided overt displays of Jewish identity often inadvertently highlighted Jewish difference, by avoiding or rejecting overt Jewish markers.[81]

FAK's "Jew Club" identity was formed during the interwar period when it became associated with the antisemitic cultural code of the time, namely, money, capital, coffeehouses, modernity, intelligence, rootlessness, and the city. Even though the "Jew Club" image became irrelevant during the Nazi era and only subtly persisted after 1945, it never went away and is yet again part of the club's identity.

REINVENTING TRADITIONS: HOW TO (UN-)JEW THE "JEW CLUB"

The making of the "Jew Club" FAK occurred in stark contrast to the "workers' club" Rapid, epitomizing a rivalry steeped in symbolism and embodied by key players such as Rapid's Josef Uridil and FAK's Alfréd Schaffer and Matthias Sindelar. These players personify the distinct identities of their respective clubs. Uridil supposedly embodied Rapid's famous "fighting spirit" and earned the moniker "the tank."[82] He was revered by Rapid supporters as the quintessential working-class hero, and he symbolized their ethos. In contrast, FAK's Sindelar, dubbed "the Paper Man [*Der Papierene*]," was celebrated for his finesse, creativity, and nimble footwork, earning comparisons with the genius of Mozart. In addition, fans compared the "rooted" Uridil with the "rootless" FAK player, Schaffer. In contrast to Uridil, who was born in the Viennese suburb of Ottakring, and who was known as "a loyal Rapid man," the Hungarian FAK forward Schaffer played for twenty-one clubs during his successful career. Even today, Austrian football historians describe Schaffer as a Wandervogel—a migratory bird—who celebrated an elegant style of football (in contrast to other players such as Uridil).[83]

In the realm of club identity, mythology often eclipses reality. Although the legendary players of both clubs participated in the professionalization of football, FAK alone has come to represent commerce. For example, Uridil was just as crucial as Sindelar in turning football into a hegemonic sport in the 1920s. Uridil participated in advertising campaigns, starred in films such as *Duty and Honor* (*Pflicht und Ehre*) (1924), and the famous Viennese composer Hermann Leopoldi dedicated the song "Today, Uridil Is Playing" ("Heute spielt der Uridil") to him in 1922. Uridil even established his own brand of beer (Uridil) and a sugar brand (Kracheln). Despite his popularity, little is known about Uridil's political position except that he joined the Nazi Party in 1938.[84]

Uridil and Sindelar serve as living embodiments of their respective football clubs' identities, a fact vividly illustrated in the exhibitions of the club museums (see figs. 2.5 and 2.6). At the Rapid museum (*Rapideum*), visitors are greeted by a bold image of Josef "the tank" Uridil captured in pursuit of a ball. Meanwhile, FAK's museum proudly showcases a life-sized figure of Sindelar at the heart of its display. At first glance, the images may appear similar, depicting the players engaged in action on the field. However, closer inspection reveals profound distinctions between them. Uridil's portrayal captures the essence of raw power and determination, as he strains to reach a ball suspended in the air—an arduous feat that suggests a struggle for control. His body contorts with effort, his left hand outstretched in unbridled exertion. The absence of his right foot from view hints at the challenge of maintaining precision in his movement, while his closed eyes imply a reliance on instinct rather than on calculation. In such a scenario, a forceful kick seems inevitable.

In contrast, Sindelar exudes an air of graceful finesse and calculated precision. With the ball under his command, poised to

Servus im Rap

Herzlich willkommen im Museur
Wandle das grün und weiße Banc
heute vereint. Entdecke die spanr
österreichischen Rekordmeisters u
haben, von den Anfängen im Jal
den ewigen Rapidgeist, der hier i
»Gemeinsam«, »Kämpfen« und »Si
sonst nur im Stadion, wenn die Rapic
Das alles ist Rapid, das alles sind wir,

Servus!

Welcome to the Museum of SK Rapid Vienna –
Stroll along the green and white band which unite
present. Discover the exciting and glorious history of th
people who have influenced them from the beginning, in
Experience the "Rapidgeist", the eternal spirit of Rapid, with
"Fighting" and "Winning". This spirit is as palpable here in the Rapideu
"Rapidviertelstunde", the last fifteen minutes of a game, is applauded in
This is all Rapid, this is all us, you too can be all this!

Josef »Pepi« Uridil, 1920

Figure 2.5. Josef "the Tank" Uridil. Photo by author.

receive a gentle touch from his right foot, he exudes tranquility and composure. His relaxed facial expression belies the intensity of the moment, suggesting serene mastery of his craft. Every aspect of Sindelar's form is in harmony, each movement flowing seamlessly as if choreographed. Witnesses to his play were often reminded of the elegance and sophistication of Mozart's compositions. In essence, both museums expertly capture the essence of their club icons in alignment with their respective identities: Uridil, the embodiment of blue-collar grit and relentless pursuit, contrasted with Sindelar, the epitome of technical brilliance and artistic flair.

The images of these two players serve as potent symbols of their respective club identities. Here, we see the embodiment

Figure 2.6. Matthias "the Paper Man" Sindelar. Photo by author.

of the Vorstadtklub: a club deeply entrenched in its local roots, embodying the authentic spirit of the working class. In stark contrast stands a representation of the cosmopolitan, intellectual city club—rootless, yet imbued with a sense of sophistication and worldly allure. Football clubs, in their essence, are what Benedict Anderson termed "imagined communities," forged through a shared sense of camaraderie and belonging.[85] A club culture's sense of community relies on shared traditions that must be comparable to those of other club collectives yet have to be specific enough to belong to one club only. Such traditions are tied to spaces like the stadium or the coffeehouse. Similarly, a club's colors or its insignia serve as rallying points, evoking a sense of pride and belonging among supporters. Yet these identities are invented and selective.[86]

Any visitor to Rapid's museum will hear all the details of the famous Rapid-Viertelstunde, which literally translates as the Rapid quarter hour. As the clock ticks down to the final fifteen minutes of every game, thousands of individual fans unite to clap in synchrony, transforming into a singular, thunderous mass. This ritual, known as the Rapid quarter hour, serves a dual purpose: to rally the home team with an infusion of energy and to unsettle the opponents with a display of unwavering support—a tactic aimed at securing a crucial advantage when playing at home.

A football game lasts ninety minutes, and as football is a low-scoring sport, a game is often decided long before it is over. Not so for the fans of Rapid. Here, the fans put all their faith in the last fifteen minutes of a game because they expect their players to have a unique fighting spirit and to gain momentum at the end of a game when the other squad is thought to be exhausted. The origins of this tradition are shrouded in folklore, with tales tracing its inception to the club's former home ground at Rudolfsheimer Platz, nestled beside the imposing Rudolfsheimer church. The resonant tolls of the church's tower clock are said to have provided the rhythmic backdrop to the ritual, a tradition that persisted when the club relocated to a new stadium in 1912.

Indeed, Rapid was frequently able to turn games around in the last quarter hour, but almost as frequently, they failed to do so. As with other rites, the Rapid quarter hour is a myth that becomes powerful through its ritual character, the collective fan experience, and the surrounding stories. The cult goes so far that fans filed a motion in 2011 to list the Rapid quarter hour as a UNESCO World Heritage Site (the motion almost succeeded).[87] Other legends claim that Rapid's functionaries were the only club representatives avoiding the Ringcafé, where the national team's Jewish club manager Hugo Meisl used to hold office.[88] Today, stories are told about Rapid fans who would rather walk many miles than take the U2 subway line, which is painted with FAK's club color, violet.

The first official championship game between the two clubs took place in 1911, when the games between FAK and Hakoah were more relevant. In the 1930s, the most important Viennese derby was arguably played between Rapid and Admira. During Nazism, Rapid took on the successful "Vienna," while it was not until the 1950s that Austrian newspapers officially christened the encounters between Rapid and FAK as a derby.[89] However, in the realm of myth, the derby portrayed a timeless narrative of the grounded working-class club from Hütteldorf pitted against the cosmopolitan "Jew Club"—a clash of fighting spirit against finesse. In fact, this myth does find its roots in reality: Rapid's origins as the 1. Wiener Arbeiter Fussball-Club starkly contrasted with FAK's bourgeois beginnings. But exceptions to these distinctions have always existed. While Rapid's leadership boasted bourgeois credentials, many FAK supporters hailed from the city's working-class neighborhoods. The cultural scholar Matthias Marschik astutely reminds us that while myths often harbor kernels of truth, they always construct history themselves.[90]

By the 1950s, as the rivalry crystallized into the derby, the two clubs found themselves more aligned than ever before. Football had undergone commodification, and the once-local Viennese league had evolved into a national organization. Paradoxically, as football's commodification blurred actual differences between the clubs, the distinctions between FAK and Rapid grew more pronounced—a testament to the enduring power of rivalry and myth in the ever-evolving landscape of football.

Austrian football has undergone several transformations throughout its history. In the 1920s, the sport ascended to a position of dominance, becoming the undisputed favorite pastime of the nation. However, the Nazi regime followed this era, and it saw the expulsion of Jews from the sport and a radical transformation of the game's landscape. By the 1950s, Austrian football had undergone yet another evolution, transitioning from a local to a national league.

Austrian football fans experienced another transformation when Red Bull took over SV Austria Salzburg (founded in 1933) in 2005. The new owners wasted no time in rebranding the club, altering its name and colors, and stripping away the very symbols that had long served as touchstones of identity for its fanbase. In response, many supporters felt a profound sense of betrayal and loss. This prompted them to abandon the newly christened Red Bull Salzburg and instead rally around a newly formed, fan-operated club in a lower league, proudly preserving the old name and colors.

The takeover by Red Bull sent shockwaves through the Austrian football community, igniting fears that other clubs could suffer a similar fate, losing their cherished identities in the pursuit of commercial success. Red Bull Salzburg has won the title in almost every season since the club took over SV Austria Salzburg in 2005. Before Red Bull Salzburg was established, Rapid and FAK dominated the league. Since 2005, all experts have predicted that Red Bull will win the championship, with Rapid and FAK vying for second place. National titles are no longer a central component of Rapid's and FAK's identities. Consequently, both clubs and their fan collectives have begun to look for identities elsewhere. Rapid amplified its identity as a local and traditional club, whereas FAK slowly began to rediscover its "Jew Club" identity. FAK's fans, however, reinvented the club's tradition in a different way.

Traditionsklub: Performing the Non-Jewish "Jew Club"

A piece of graffiti shines in the heart of the FAK's fan section at Generali Arena (see fig. 2.7). The word Traditionsklub— traditional club—written in capital letters, indicates that the club, once perceived as modern, has now been reinvented as traditional by its fans. What was formerly associated with a "Jewish" identity has been woven into the fabric of tradition. While the club cautiously embraces its partly Jewish history, the fans appear to

Figure 2.7. The "Traditionsklub" graffiti. Photo by author.

adopt a "Jew Club" identity without Jews: they consider what was once new, modern, and "Jewish" as traditional and local, yet they barely, if at all, mention that its key protagonists were Jews. They embrace, for instance, the skillful and intellectual playing style, as expressed in stickers or the graffiti they wrote at FAK's practice field: "Austria Vienna stands for commitment, playfulness, and magic."[91] Once perceived as a bastion of modernity, FAK has now been reimagined as a beacon of tradition, all meticulously crafted by its loyal fanbase.

Within FAK's fan scene, distinct groups emerge, each wielding its own influence and shaping the club's identity in unique ways. The hooligan group Unsterblich has a formidable presence within FAK's fan scene, notorious for its hooliganism and repeated neo-Nazi expressions. This group, known for its violent tendencies and staunch adherence to the principle of the law of the strongest—that is, the idea that stronger people should

impose their will over the less powerful—commands a significant space in the hierarchy among fan groups. However, its influence is not without controversy, as its members actions have
sparked both concern and condemnation. They have mobilized
against refugees and drawn the ire of both supporters and observers alike. Despite the notoriety, the club has enacted recent
measures that seek to curb the neo-Nazi presence and eliminate
right-wing symbols and ideologies from the stadium environment. While the fans are not embracing a "Jew Club" identity, the
club's cautious rediscovery of its "Jew Club" identity is an explicit
reaction to Unsterblich and the associated headlines.

Headlines such as "A 'Jew Club' and Its Neo-Nazis" may sound
catchy, but they do not do justice to the diversity of the club's
fanbase.[92] While the club's far right hooligans are still powerful, other supporters, albeit less organized and weaker, oppose
their ideology. Walking around the club's stadium, I encountered more antifascist messages than signs of far right groups or
far right content.[93] The fan scene's political hegemony is—and
remains—contested.

Founded in 2001, the Fanatics once reigned as the leading ultra
group within FAK's fan culture. Officially apolitical but open
to the far right, they have played a leading role in orchestrating
fan chants and fostering a sense of camaraderie among supporters. Despite attempts to appear apolitical, their ties to far right
groups like Unsterblich helped create a space in which neo-Nazis
could express themselves. The dissolution of the Fanatics in 2023
marked a pivotal moment in FAK's fan culture and left a void that
the KAI2000 group swiftly filled.

Emerging as a new force within FAK's fan scene, Kampfastllln
Inzersdorf (KAI2000)[94] ascended to prominence after the dissolution of the Fanatics. KAI2000, positioned as a politically more
neutral alternative to the far right ideologies of Unsterblich,
aims to distance themselves from the divisive politics that have
plagued previous groups. Their style is less aggressive, and they

engage in broader subcultural activities such as the painting of graffiti in and around the stadium. This has included portraits of the former Jewish club icons Norbert Lopper and Emanuel Schwarz and the legendary player Matthias Sindelar. Yet they seem to still believe that a fan group can be apolitical and adhere to such an ideal, although this stance often prevents any attempts to critically address discrimination and masculinity.

Finally, nestled in the periphery of the fan section, the *Pickerlecke* (sticker corner) serves as a refuge for those seeking to avoid the fervor of Unsterblich and related groups. Here, a loosely organized group of supporters, including several Jewish fans, express their fandom through antifascist stickers and symbols of local pride.[95] While they may stand on the outskirts of the fan scene, their presence serves as a reminder of the diverse tapestry of political orientations and identities within FAK's supporter base. Stickers referring to the club's history, such as the playing style called Scheiberlspiel or FAK's supposed Bodenständigkeit (see fig. 2.8), were produced by these supporters. They engage with the club's collective identity and even produce stickers targeting Unsterblich directly: "A real Viennese is not a Nazi—Rather dead than Unsterblich [immortal]" (see fig. 2.9). When I returned to the stadium in late 2023, I even encountered newly produced stickers depicting a Star of David with the inscription "Austria [FAK] Oida" (see fig. 2.10). *Oida* is an Austrian slang term that can mean various things depending on the context, similar to "dude" or "mate" in English. It is a versatile term and can express excitement or emphasis, too. Yet this open expression of Jewish symbols remains an exception that proves the rule: when it comes to FAK supporters, they are reinventing the club's tradition as non-Jewish while referring to the cultural code of the "Jew Club" of the interwar period.

The graffiti of Norbert Lopper and Emanuel Schwarz, two Jews of significance in the club's history, signify their important space in the memory culture and collective identity of the fans, but they

Figure 2.8. Sticker "Bodenständig." Photo by author.

are not remembered or celebrated as Jews like Kurt Landauer is in Bavaria. The (officially) apolitical stance of groups like Fanatics and KAI2000 have prevented the fans as a collective group from revering the club's partly Jewish heritage. Instead, the fans have rebranded what was once considered new, modern, and "Jewish" as traditional and local, largely devoid of explicit Jewish connotations. Jewish connotations have now been relegated to the annals of history for most FAK supporters.

FAK's collective identity in the present is fueled by the memory of legends and the club's alleged playing style. The club and fans navigate an identity between tradition and modernity. This is also noticeable at the entrance to the stadium's away stand,

Figure 2.9. An anti-Nazi sticker. Photo by author.

where automatic ticket-scanning machines are located next to a
mural that reads "Chess Club—Hooligans Austria Wien." This is
a playful twist on the assumption that Rapid used to have a fighting sport section, while FAK had a chess section (see fig. 2.11).[96]
Now, the hooligans who are proud to "fight for FAK" also gather
under the name "chess club," while they are, of course, doing "the
opposite," that is, fighting with rival hooligan groups. Principles
that were originally seen as the antithesis of Bodenständigkeit
were transformed by FAK supporters into proof of this very idea,
as stated plainly on stickers placed around the stadium: as local,
traditional, and rooted. They reinvented the club's "Jew Club"
tradition as bodenständig, rooted in tradition.

Figure 2.10. Sticker "Austria Oida." Photo by author.

Iron Vienna and Antisemitism as Rivalry

As FAK's fans strive to redefine the club's traditions as bodenstän-dig, usually devoid of any overt references to Jewish heritage and sometimes co-opted by far right sentiments, their counterparts among Rapid supporters have revived FAK's "Jew Club" identity. This resurgence dates back to the early 1980s when Rapid fans boldly inscribed "Don't buy from FAK Jews!" ("Kauft nicht bei Austria Juden!") in prominent letters at FAK's home stadium. This provocative act harked back to the antisemitic boycott campaigns orchestrated by the Nazis, who once defaced Jewish-owned busi-nesses with the slogan "Don't buy from Jews!" ("Kauft nicht bei Juden!").[97] In the stadium, Rapid's fans shouted, "One, two, three, four—FAK to the gas!" ("Eins, zwei, drei, vier—Austria ins Gas mit Dir"),[98] or "Zyklon B for FAK people" ("Zyklon B für Austri-aner"),[99] invoking the gas used by the Nazis during the Holocaust. These antisemitic expressions emerged within the developing

Figure 2.11. Chess Club graffiti. Photo by author.

hooligans' fan culture.[100] Hooligan groups, adopting names like Terrorszene ("terror scene"), Streetfighters, or Hooligans, drew inspiration from British hooliganism. However, hooliganism was not the sole fan culture in Austria. In the 1970s, earlier fans had established the first regular fan clubs, primarily gathering to enjoy the games and support their teams.[101] Nonetheless, the rise of hooliganism ushered in a wave of antisemitism directed at FAK, and other fans also joined in the chorus.

In the 1980s, neo-Nazis aimed to infiltrate Rapid's fan culture, and antisemitic fan performances became ritualized. Even young fans of Rapid considered it appropriate to participate in antisemitic chanting against the club's local rival, as the author Domenico Jacono remembers from experience: "I know what I'm talking about because I, too, shouted, 'Jewish pigs!' with a boyish falsetto voice and a clenched fist as a thirteen-year-old, back in the fall of 1980, at the first derby I was allowed to attend without adult guards. It may have been a statement that was, in the words of the British behavioral scientist Desmond Morris, 'not so much antiracial as antirival,' but it says a lot about the political and historical consciousness of a quite average Viennese teenager from the lower middle class during these years."[102] Although antisemitism today is less frequent than it was during the 1980s, fans continue to label FAK as the "Jew Club." Graffiti by FAK fans has repeatedly been covered by Rapid supporters with a Star of David.[103] Antisemitism toward "Jew Clubs" is not limited to the stadium; it expands from the football arena to other public places such as streetcars and pubs, and it is written onto the walls of the cities (see figs. 2.12 and 2.13).

Football hooligans differed from the football-oriented fan clubs because they came to the stadium for violent clashes with other hooligan groups or the police, sometimes attacking "foreigners" whom they also sought to encounter outside the stadium. The new fan culture, manifested in Austria almost only on the Rapid and FAK terraces, arose in the context of changing social conditions such as urban development concepts and the rupture of traditional social environments.[104] Even though most hooligans preferred to keep a certain distance from neo-Nazis, it was "no coincidence" that far right groups such as the Aktion Neue Rechte attempted to recruit members among football hooligans.[105] Neo-Nazis from the Volkstreue Außerparlamentarische Opposition (VAPO) used to invite Rapid fans to neo-Nazi gatherings.[106] Although the hooligan fan culture has waned since then, its influence remains potent; hooligans are still respected by younger fan generations, and they can still gather up to one hundred men for particular games, such as the rivalry game between FAK and Rapid.

During the 1990s, the prevalent antisemitic atmosphere coincided with a notable rise in the presence of neo-Nazis. Far right activists extended their influence beyond the confines of football rivalry, unifying hooligan factions from both FAK and Rapid.

Figure 2.12. Antisemitic graffiti (1). Photo by Matthias Marschik.

Figure 2.13. Antisemitic graffiti (2). Photo by Matthias Marschik.

After a game between the two teams in the early 1990s, hooligans from both clubs marched together to attack immigrants.[107] They chanted "Germany for the Germans! Foreigners out!" ("Deutschland den Deutschen! Ausländer raus!")[108]—a reference to Nazism and to racist attacks against refugees in Germany. Hooligans from Rapid and FAK fought with the slogan "Iron

Vienna," with the German word for iron—*Eisern*—also meaning steadfast, stout, and impenetrable. This is a slogan that can still be heard today at far right demonstrations and rallies organized by Austria's right-wing populist party, the Freiheitliche Partei Österreichs (FPÖ).[109] When football hooligans participated in far right antirefugee demonstrations during the humanitarian crisis in 2015 all over Europe, some hooligans from both clubs marched side by side.[110] While Rapid's hooligans attacked their local rival in an antisemitic manner, they became allied with far right FAK supporters. Although countermovements exist in both fan scenes, neo-Nazi supporters remain a component of both fan scenes today.

The atmosphere around the stadiums altered in the 1990s as a result of greater police activity and the aging of many hooligans. European football underwent a process of gentrification, including the founding of the Champions League, police repression against hooligans, and increased marketing and media coverage. A gap emerged in the fan areas and ultras fan culture entered the scene. New fan groups were less concerned with violence and focused on organizing the acoustic and visual support in the stadiums. Hooligans are characterized by violence; ultras are defined by their passionate support in the stadium. The ultras groups claim to represent the fans of the respective clubs, and indeed, they decide which songs are performed in the stadiums and which banners are presented. In contrast with Munich, FAK's ultras—the Fanatics and KAI2000—did not develop a "progressive traditionalism" (see chapt. 1), but a supposedly apolitical orientation, which is also a strategy used to prevent completing any antidiscrimination activities, leaving the space open for discriminatory fan performances and the presence of neo-Nazis.[111]

The group Ultras Rapid declared in the late 1980s that all politics should be kept out of the stadium.[112] While this declaration has created a climate in which neo-Nazis no longer openly show their politics or recruit fans, this apolitical position also evades critical engagement with their less visual presence and influence. The purportedly apolitical stance serves to minimize instances of discrimination as mere football banter. Even in the face of homophobic or sexist banners, which Ultras Rapid and other fan factions still display, these actions are often dismissed as harmless banter and therefore deemed nonpolitical. Those who dare criticize such discriminatory displays are frequently accused of "introducing politics into the stadium" and of jeopardizing the unity of fans. However, while neo-Nazis may refrain from openly expressing their ideology, their presence and influence linger beneath the surface, restrained but ever present. Open performances of antisemitism have decreased in a societal climate that associates antisemitism mostly with neo-Nazis. Allegedly, Ultras Rapid even removed an antisemitic banner displayed by other Rapid fans during a game against the Israeli team Hapoel Petah Tiqwa in the 1990s.[113] But the group's stance toward antisemitism in the context of the rivalry against FAK remains an issue. In the late 1990s, a founding member of Ultras Rapid proudly revealed in a television interview how Rapid fans yell "Jewish pigs!" ("Judenschweine!") at FAK fans and players.[114] Even though the fan organization has distanced itself from far right activists and neo-Nazi ideas, the term "Jew pigs" appears on occasion, as in 2017 during a football game between the FAK and Rapid youth teams.[115] In essence, Ultras Rapid's allegedly apolitical position defines what can be said in the club's stadium; while it limits public expressions of neo-Nazism, it also creates room for discriminatory performances by framing them as apolitical football banter. Occasionally, this includes antisemitism if directed against the "Jew Club" FAK.

"NOT HISTORY PROFESSORS": FAK AND THE TURN TO MEMORY

Sports clubs are big business. They are concerned about their corporate identities, their market value; a club either needs to be successful or it needs a unique identity, something that stands out. For FK Austria Vienna, whose last national title was clinched in 2013, the dominance of Red Bull Salzburg looms large. With the new sports authority, Red Bull Salzburg, dominating the league, and headlines linking neo-Nazi hooligans to FAK, the club's management has sought new avenues through which to carve out a distinct identity. In this quest for uniqueness, FAK embarked on a process of reinvention, gradually claiming its "Jew Club" identity, not least to counter the club's neo-Nazi fan groups.

As part of the club's turn to memory, FAK's players and board members have gathered more or less every year since 2018 at Judenplatz to commemorate those Jews who fell victim to the antisemitic pogroms of November 1938. Likewise, the club agreed to sign the IHRA definition of antisemitism, a step that is supposed to help organizations first define and then tackle antisemitism. The participants in the symbolic IHRA definition adoption ceremony at Vienna's Judenplatz in November 2021 were transferred by bus from the city center to FAK's stadium, Generali Arena, in Favoriten where they attended a Global Conference on Football's Role in Combatting Antisemitism, which was jointly organized by the Israelitische Kultusgemeinde Wien and Chelsea Football Club (from London). Curiously, FAK was neither the host of the event, nor did any representative of the club participate in the event for more than the few minutes required to publicly sign the IHRA definition. Only the club's symbol and its corporate slogan, "Aspiration and Style," remained. Despite FAK not hosting the event and the club's limited participation, the symbolic gestures underscored the club's changing perception of its "Jew Club" image and its evolving stance on confronting antisemitism, albeit with a lingering reluctance.

Those who took the twenty-minute bus ride from Judenplatz to Generali Arena met a club still uncomfortable with but grudgingly ready to highlight its Jewish members. This club was starting to build a memory culture like that of FC Bayern Munich's Mia San Landauer and was also starting to embrace the "Jew Club" concept. FAK is a club about whose history many myths are recounted, whose history under Nazism has only just been examined, but whose self-image as a victim of Nazism continues to be a part of its memory culture. It is anticipated that embracing the club's past Jewish members and their destiny during Nazism, alongside emphasizing their vital contributions to the club's accomplishments, will further disassociate the club from far right fan organizations.

The inherent tensions between the "Jew Club's" memory culture and its present issue with neo-Nazis became visible to participants in Chelsea's event at FAK's stadium. Coming from the Judenplatz to the Generali Arena, the group passed a thirty-meter-long piece of graffiti presenting the name of FAK's fan area, Ostblock, and got off the bus between other pieces of graffiti: with portraits of the former Jewish managing directors Norbert Lopper and Emanuel Schwarz on one side and a Celtic cross—a symbol used by fascists in Europe and white supremacists in the United States—on the other side (see fig. 2.14).[116]

Despite its efforts, FAK is caught between its desire to combat neo-Nazism and its conception of football as a nonpolitical arena. The club has also struggled financially for years, and its board of directors has changed multiple times. Furthermore, embracing the "Jew Club" image openly may cause rival supporters to engage in antisemitic behavior. Perhaps, FAK's managing directors also fear stirring conflict with the club's fan groups, such as Unsterblich. In 2009, Unsterblich presented a banner at the stadium, blatantly reminiscent of the neo-Nazi network Blood and Honour. FAK's head of security told the Austrian newspaper *Der Standard* in an interview that the club's board members are "not history professors."[117] He maintained that this is why he had personally permitted them to display the far right banner. For years, FAK alternated between speaking with Unsterblich and

Figure 2.14. Graffiti at Generali Arena. Photo by author.

banning the group from the stadium. It seems the club is still not quite sure how to deal with its neo-Nazi fans as it battles to reconcile its own past.

Between Myth and Reality: FAK's Contested Memory Landscape

During the first commemoration ceremony at Judenplatz in 2018, the club declared that it is "strongly against any form of racism, discrimination, or homophobia." Although FAK did not mention antisemitism specifically, the statement continued: "The Jewish history is an important part of FAK. It is therefore of particular importance to us as a club that our players know and understand what this history means to us, and that they also take a couple of minutes to commemorate it."[118] The players had gathered at the

Holocaust memorial, designed by Rachel Whiteread, a massive concrete cube resembling a library, with its books turned inside out. The hundreds of books in the Nameless Library evoke images of a rich cultural archive and of many individual stories, too. The books' spines face the inaccessible center of the cube and thus remain distant, although they are physically close to those visiting the Judenplatz. "In this library," Simon Wiesenthal observes, "the books remain closed, and the onlooker is forced to find his or her own words."[119] The monument reminds us that even though history appears right in front of us, it is our responsibility to interpret it.

Until recently, FAK had interpreted its history in a manner consistent with the nation's "victim thesis." Austria gained questionable fame for its victim thesis, which stated that the nation was Hitler's first victim. This "master-narrative of the Second Republic"[120] originated in the 1943 Moscow Declaration, which branded Austria as "the first free country to fall a victim to Hitlerite aggression."[121] The victim thesis became Austria's "guilt-free founding myth," leading to "a climate of selective and deleterious amnesia," in which Jewish victims were marginalized.[122] Jews were "discriminated against in the name of equality," creating an environment in which Jews avoided expressing themselves as victims because they feared antisemitism.[123] The few FAK Jews who returned to Vienna after World War II were celebrated for "not making a fuss" about their suffering.

In 1938, immediately after the "Anschluss," a swastika flew over every sports ground in Vienna, and players had to give a Hitler salute before every game.[124] All of FAK's board members were Jews according to the Nuremberg Laws and were immediately forced out of office, as were Jews from other clubs.[125] FAK lost its management and many supporters. In turn, these people also lost their club, which had adapted to the new regime. While the lives of these individuals changed dramatically, their clubs and teammates continued with their lives. During Nazism, FAK was not treated differently from other integrated clubs, except for being renamed SC Ostmark for a brief period of time.[126] After 1938, FAK's club culture was fundamentally different, and the transformation was spurred not only from external sources but also from within. At least, many club members adapted quickly and participated in the new system. Many of the new board members were connected to the club before the "Anschluss."[127] After the expulsion of Jews from the club, FAK remained a "strong brand" during National Socialism,[128] and the Vienna edition of the *Völkischer Beobachter* mentioned FAK in the same breath as the Nazi flagship club FC Schalke 04, when the two clubs faced each other in the summer of 1938: "The two teams are often seen as the best playing teams of German football."[129] The Nazis understood football as a propaganda tool used to keep Vienna's population happy, but football was also a tricky terrain, as it was one of the few societal spheres in which the city felt superior to the Germans.[130] As a result, the Nazis carefully supervised football and sought to capitalize on FAK's popularity. For the most part, the Nazis simply ignored the FAK's "Jew Club" image.

In the 1980s, the nation finally debated its Nazi past. In what became known as the Waldheim affair, the Austrian public debated revelations that Kurt Waldheim, who was running for president in the 1986 elections, served in the German Wehrmacht. The late 1980s saw the emergence of Jewish studies as a scholarly field, the restoration of synagogues, and the opening of the Jewish Museum.[131] In the 1990s, memory culture became institutionalized and Austrian Jews developed a new self-confidence. Former chancellor Franz Vranitzky finally rejected the victim thesis publicly in 1993. A new generation of Jews demanded participation. This included the establishment of the Jewish culture festival (1992), the inception of regular Jewish street fairs, and the founding of the Jewish Maccabi sports club in 1996.[132] In 2000, the memorial to Austrian Holocaust victims was unveiled at Judenplatz (see fig. 2.15).

Figure 2.15. The Nameless Library. Photo by author.

Austria's reconciliation with its past occurred gradually, with football culture lagging behind. It was not until the release of the 2019 book *Ein Fußballverein aus Wien* that numerous myths surrounding FAK as a detached victim of Nazism were thoroughly addressed. These misconceptions, previously criticized by author David Forster in his insightful 2014 book chapter titled "Opfer Österreich, Opfer Austria?" were finally challenged, although not corrected.[133] The Nameless Library at Judenplatz encourages people to interpret history. Another arena where history is interpreted is in the forewords of history books—a potent space for knowledge production. Forewords hold authority, as they are typically written by respected figures or experts in the field. Their words lend weight and credibility to the content that follows, guiding readers and shaping their understanding of the book's subject matter. The book *Ein Fußballverein aus Wien* (2019), which finally addressed FAK's history during Nazism in detail, had no less than seven forewords.

The first of the seven prefaces was written by FAK's president in 2018, Wolfgang Katzian, who was also the president of the Austrian Trade Union Federation.[134] Katzian describes the book as part of Austria's official memory year 2018, which commemorated the "Anschluss" as one of many historical events in years ending with an "8": 1848, 1918, 1938, 1948, 1968.[135] FAK has, Katzian writes, never supported the Nazis: "Like all football- and sports clubs, FAK was forced under Nazism's administrative authority, and for a few months it was called SC Ostmark. But it kept its distance from the authorities, so it could not be co-opted. Some players succumbed to opportunistic temptations, others adapted, the FAK center-half and *Wunderteam* player Hans Mock was celebrated as a member of the SA by the newspapers."[136] Katzian, very much in the spirit of the post-Waldheim Austrian Republic, acknowledges that some players adapted to the new system, yet remnants of the victim thesis persist. Katzian holds on to the myth of apolitical sport even though the distinction he draws between the sports club and the regime is disproven by the very book his preface introduces. Notably, his exclusive mention of Mock serves to separate the individual (SA Nazi Mock) from the club's structure, preserving FAK's supposedly untarnished image.

Katzian refrains from explicitly identifying those who "succumbed to opportunistic temptations," but his wording strongly implies star player Matthias Sindelar, who was bestowed an "Aryanized" coffeehouse. Notably, discussions surrounding Sindelar often eschew terms like *perpetrator, Nazi,* or *collaborator,* instead portraying him as a passive victim who yielded to Nazi pressures. Absent from Katzian's narrative is any mention of the previous owner, Leopold Drill, who perished in a concentration camp. In his preface, former player and club legend Herbert Prohaska directly addresses Sindelar's legacy, questioning, "What did he really do back then? Like many people at the time, he may have looked after his own interests, and who are we to judge him eighty years later?" Although the victim thesis remains in these lines, Katzian formulates the club's ongoing (and reluctant) turn to memory: "We have a duty to face our responsibility for our contribution to this checkered history."[137]

Much like forewords, museums serve as pivotal arenas for knowledge production, playing a crucial role in shaping memory politics through the collection, presentation, and interpretation of selected artifacts. The FK Austria Vienna Museum lies behind the club's fan shop at Generali Arena in Favoriten (see fig. 2.16), and it stands as a testament to this concept. The museum perpetuates the prevailing myth of Austria as Hitler's first victim.

The museum meticulously showcases certain players, coaches, and pivotal events in the club's history, although some display boards have fallen and remain unrepaired, indicating financial struggles within the club. Notably, the museum offers a sobering portrayal of the "Anschluss" that refrains from critically mentioning the event was celebrated by many Austrians and instead describes it as a moment orchestrated by the Nazis that plunged "Austrians and their culture to the edge of the abyss."[138] This particularly striking exhibition board aligns the club's history with that of the nation within the framework of the victim thesis, thus portraying FAK as a long-standing bastion of Vienna's liberal-bourgeois football tradition. Notably, the board states that FAK, with its diverse supporter base, including Jewish and antifascist individuals loyal to Austria, immediately posed a challenge to the new rulers.[139] This reinterpretation of history, setting FAK and Nazism in fundamental opposition to one another, becomes even more apparent on another exhibition board that boldly declares

Figure 2.16. The FAK Museum. Photo by author.

the period from 1938 to 1945 as "the years of darkness," stating that
Austria and FAK suffered from forced "Aryanization" and the renaming of FAK to SC Ostmark. However, this portrayal certainly
overemphasizes Austria and FAK as victims; FAK did not suffer
more than other football clubs, although its Jewish members and
fans sufferend significantly during this time.[140]

The museum's perpetuation of the prevailing myth of Austria
and FAK as Hitler's first victims can be attributed, at least in part,
to its opening in 2009, which occurred before comprehensive
research projects on the role of clubs like Rapid and FAK during
Nazism. Furthermore, as of December 2023, the museum has
not been updated, thus perpetuating this outdated narrative de-
nying any complicity and overstating the club's role as opposed
to Nazism. The museum narrative becomes even more apparent when compared with Rapid's Rapideum. The "modern" club
FAK presents an old-fashioned museum, while the "traditional"

club Rapid offers a novel Rapideum.[141] FAK's museum opened in 2009, and its simplicity and bad condition reflect the club's financial struggles in recent years. Rapid's museum opened in 2016 and reflects everything that happened between 2009 and 2016, most notably the 2011 release of a detailed study of Rapid during Nazism (eight years earlier than the study of FAK).[142] Rapid has long commemorated its German championship, which it won over the Gelsenkirchen-based team FC Schalke 04 in 1941. When the club announced it would celebrate its centennial with a game against Schalke, criticism arose about the club's deafening silence over the context of its 1941 championship. This resulted in research being completed on the club during Nazism and a well-designed exhibition at the museum, where the drawer on Nazism is the only one that does not completely close, symbolically presenting the message of never forgetting to the museum's visitors.

Just as museums shape memory politics through artifacts and exhibitions, books on the football clubs' histories construct the meaning of the past in the present. In various publications linked to the club, FAK promotes a self-image as Hitler's first victim, without embracing its "Jew Club" identity. FAK's journey to understand itself has been marked by numerous myths and periods of silence. Notably, earlier publications, such as the club's fifty-year Festschrift in 1962, do not even mention the "Anschluss" as an important event.[143] Later works, such as the sixty-year Festschrift or Jo Huber's 1975 publication *Das große Austria Buch*, portray Matthias Sindelar, who profited from taking over an "Aryanized" coffeehouse, as both a resister to Nazism and a victim of circumstance.[144] These publications also underscore a long-standing reluctance within the club to address its "Jew Club" tradition. This trend extends beyond FAK, as evidenced by the Austrian football federation ÖFB and local rival Rapid's similar omissions of Jewish victims and Nazi perpetrators in most of their publications.[145] ÖFB's first canonical work, published by Leo Schidrowitz in 1951, portrayed football as a "victim of its circumstances."[146]

The second canonical book, published in 1972 by Karl Kastler, understood National Socialism as a "fateful intermezzo" and the year 1945 as football's zero hour.[147] Finally, the centennial ÖFB book, published in 2004, places a greater focus on Nazism—the chapter on Nazism has a black background, making it stand out from the rest of the book.[148] Yet, it still claims that football players tried to "stay out," and it continues to portray Sindelar as a victim of his circumstances: the "Aryanization" was, the authors claim, a result of an attempt to woo him.[149] In the aftermath of 1945, FAK remained largely silent on the connections between football and Nazism and on its previous association as a "Jew Club."

Matthias Marschik's *Wiener Austria: Die ersten 90 Jahre*, published in 2001 to commemorate the club's ninetieth anniversary, marked a shift toward a more nuanced examination of FAK's history during Nazism.[150] However, the book's preface by Austria's Chancellor from 2000 to 2007, Wolfgang Schüssel, perpetuated an idealized image of the club as open-minded and cosmopolitan since its inception in 1911, even amid the "difficult times" of the 1930s and 1940s.[151] Marschik even claims that the Nazis despised FAK because of its Jewish officials and players, although FAK in fact had no Jewish players in 1938.[152] Despite the fact that Marschik was among the first to write that the coffeehouse had been "Aryanized," the book maintains the victim thesis by portraying Sindelar as a resister. Sindelar, Marschik claims, did "not use 'Aryanization' to his profit, but paid the former owners a decent price."[153] The myth of the "fair price" persists despite having been ultimately debunked in 2019. In 2008, the journalist and historian Peter Pelinka, who served as FAK's vice president from 1998 to 2006, wrote, "The incorporation of Austria into National Socialist Germany hit FAK the hardest of all Austrian football clubs: Among the players and officials were many Jews, not only the legendary President 'Michl' Schwarz, who had to emigrate immediately after the invasion. The image of the 'Jew Club' still stems from this time, and it was 'cultivated' in antisemitic chants by opposing fans until recently."[154] Pelinka's statement perpetuated several myths as the "Jew Club" image predates Nazism and no players in 1938 were Jewish.[155] Additionally, his assertion that Nazism "hit FAK the hardest of all Austrian football clubs" ignores the fact that the Nazis immediately shut down Jewish clubs like Hakoah or marked Jewish sports clubs as "not-Austrian."

Publications and the club's museum have collectively painted a portrait of FAK as a bastion of resistance populated by Jewish Austrian anti-Nazis. Despite corrections made by a book-length study, these myths persist and perpetuate the notion that the Nazis held a particular animosity toward FAK.[156] This narrative echoes the memory culture in Munich, which often centers on identification with victimhood, risking the portrayal of FAK's former Jewish members solely through this lens. After the commemoration event in 2021, the club published a report on its website stating, "The year 1938 almost vanquished FAK, whose eight-person management board consisted completely of people of Jewish faith until the Anschluss."[157] The use of the term "people of Jewish faith" ("Menschen jüdischen Glaubens") suggests a reluctance to use the term *Jude*, which aligns with a broader trend among German speakers. While this declaration signals the club's commitment to combating discrimination and acknowledging Jewish history, its avoidance of the term *Jew* in present contexts reflects a lingering uncertainty over how to navigate its "Jew Club" identity and the continuing power of the "Jew" imaginary framework in which "Jews" are perceived as different.

On its website, the club makes a bold claim, asserting that during Nazism, it never appointed a new president after Emanuel Schwarz's escape into exile.[158] "The stadium had visible war injuries, and jerseys and shorts were missing in the locker room," the website states, as "it was the zero hour."[159] This narrative, however, diverges from historical reality, as the Nazis treated FAK no differently than other Austrian clubs, besides briefly renaming it SC Ostmark.[160] Moreover, the notion of reserving the presidency for Emanuel Schwarz was debunked, as the position itself was not provided for in the new Nazi club regulations, which mandated that football clubs be led by a Vereinsführer—a football club leader during Nazism, voted in by members but ultimately approved by the Nazi party. Emanuel Schwarz remains a prominent figure in the club's collective memory, alongside Norbert Lopper, a former Hakoah player who assumed the role of FAK's club secretary in 1956. Together with the legendary player Matthias Sindelar, who is often hailed as a resistance hero despite benefiting from the "Aryanization" of a coffeehouse, these three figures represent the complex ambiguities that distinguish FAK's engagement with its own history.

Norbert Lopper: From the Anschluss to Better Times

Norbert Lopper's legacy looms large over FK Austria Vienna. He has been immortalized in graffiti that adorns a wall adjacent to the club's stadium (see fig. 2.17). His remarkable life story received public attention thanks to Johann Skocek's 2014 book, whose title translates as *Mister Austria: The Life of the Manager Norbert Lopper; Player, Concentration Camp Prisoner, Cosmopolite*. Born in Vienna as the second of five children to Leo and Regine Lopper, Norbert honed his skills as part of the Hakoah youth teams. After the annexation of Austria, he fled to Brussels, where he continued his football career with Étoile and Maccabi. In August 1942, the Nazis deported Lopper to Auschwitz, and he was finally liberated by US forces at Mauthausen concentration camp. After going through the horrors of the camps, his physical abilities were never the same, and he never played football again. Lopper's wife, Rebecca Cige, his sister Klara and his father, Leo, were all murdered by the Nazis. He lived in Belgium after the liberation and then returned to Vienna in 1953. In 1954, he founded the FAK supporters' club and assumed the role of secretary in 1956, a position akin to today's manager or sports director, a post he held until 1983. Lopper, who also gave testimony in the process against SS officer Gottfried Wiese in 1984, remained in Vienna until his death in 2015.

Figure 2.17. Graffiti "Norbert Lopper." Photo by author.

Norbert Lopper's contribution to FAK cannot be overstated. He is credited with discovering the talent of Herbert Prohaska, who stands as one of Austria's greatest footballers. With Lopper and Prohaska, FAK achieved remarkable success, clinching four national titles and securing three cup victories. Despite these monumental achievements, Lopper's role in shaping the club's memory culture remained largely overlooked until the publication of Skocek's book in 2014, which finally accorded him recognition. However, even as Lopper's story gained prominence, the book inadvertently perpetuated enduring myths.

The book's preface by the ÖFB's president from 1984 to 2002, Beppo Mauhart, portrays the post-1945 Austria to which Lopper returns as a nation of "rebirth (or reincarnation) and new birth."[161] The experience of dictatorship, war, and prison, Mauhart claims, has been turned into a "hard school of reason."[162] In other words, a new and better Austria has emerged because of the nation's suffering. Nazism becomes an "experience" and antisemitic suffering a "school." Football, according to Mauhart, occupies a distinctive and significant position at this critical national moment. "Football creates," he argues, "a symbolic *Anschluss* to 'better times' amid the efforts of *working through the past*."[163] Curiously, Mauhart manages to mention the word *annexation* alongside the idea of working through the past. The recontextualization of these concepts stresses continuity rather than a break and rupture. Likewise, in the preface by former FAK president Wolfgang Katzian to the same book, he states, "Norbert Lopper . . . decisively and self-sacrificingly shaped the history of Vienna's FAK. Football has determined his life and vice versa— he has determined the football of FAK for more than three decades. Although the Nazi regime landed in his life like a meteor striking . . . he played a crucial role in the success of 'his' FAK, whose impeccable reputation has always been his goal, principle, and drive."[164] Each of Katzian's sentences is significant for understanding FAK's memory culture. The first sentence acknowledges Lopper's close ties with FAK and his achievements for the team. The second sentence is about his exile, his experience in the concentration camp, and the loss of his family members. The undertone is critical: a meteor is a falling star, creating heat and light while burning out in the Earth's atmosphere. A meteor, unlike a meteorite, has no influence on Earth since it does not "survive" its fast journey through the atmosphere. Despite being an inaccurate comparison between Nazism (which certainly affected Earth) and meteor (which does not impact Earth), the metaphor evokes the image of something that comes from far away and whose origin is unknown. In this metaphor, the Nazis appear like aliens who came out of nowhere and left as quickly as they came. By portraying the Nazis as ephemeral invaders, the metaphor obscures personal continuities, such as that of Mr. Eckerl, the club president during and after Nazism. Finally, the assertion that Lopper's pursuit of FAK's "impeccable reputation" encapsulates his essence insinuates a moral high ground for the club, positioning it as a victim rather than a collaborator in the annals of history. Thus, the narrative about Lopper exemplifies FAK's enduring quest for continuity, its portrayal as "Hitler's first victim," and the deliberate separation of the club's legacy from the taint of Nazism.

The book's foremost achievement lies in its elevation of Norbert Lopper to a central figure within the club's collective memory. Through the inclusion of numerous direct quotes, it grants Lopper a voice, allowing readers to glimpse his experiences. A noticeable dissonance, however, emerges between Lopper's firsthand testimony and Skocek's interpretative lens. Those who focus solely on Lopper's words may discern a narrative of enduring physical and psychological struggle, extending far beyond his liberation. Conversely, readers attuned to Skocek's narrative thread may perceive the book as a tale of reconciliation, perhaps even redemption: "Lopper's testimony is the story of a happy life enriched with many anecdotes and encounters, which only experienced a turning point with the forced stay in Auschwitz. If he was following someone with resentment, I asked him. It was one of our last conversations for this book. 'Thank God I didn't find anyone in Vienna who did me evil, I couldn't be angry at anyone,' Lopper stated. 'I was not present during "Kristallnacht." I could have directed my anger at the regime, but at the people? Should I shoot myself and not return? I owe FAK so much.'"[165] Lopper never "made a fuss of his pain," Skocek claims.[166] If we listen to Lopper's voice, however, the impeccable optimism of a man who had "not even lost his confidence in the future when in the concentration camp"[167] turns into resignation and frustration here and there, even suicidal tendencies: "I had such terrible pain in 1973 that I would have killed myself, if I had had a gun."[168] For Skocek, however, Lopper lived a life in which no wishes or desires remained unfulfilled, all because of his reconciliation with FAK: "He gave his heart to this club and received a successful life in return, filled with external successes and inner satisfaction, which left no wishes unfulfilled."[169] At various junctures,

Lopper's story is reframed within the broader context of Austria's collective narrative, as symbolizing the nation's "Wiedergeburt und Neugeburt," that is, Austria's "rebirth (or reincarnation) and new birth." When it was published in 2014, the book was nothing but a milestone for FAK's memory culture. It is, in many ways, a respectful and honoring portrait of "Mister Austria" Norbert Lopper, but the book also illustrates that memory is always also selective, involving a form of forgetting, too.

Emanuel Schwarz: Selective Memory

At Generali Arena, alongside Norbert Lopper, various other club legends are celebrated through graffiti. The fan group KAI2000, responsible for the artwork, also pays tribute to the former FAK presidents Joschi Walter and Emanuel Schwarz and the player Ernst Ocwirk (see fig. 2.18). Interestingly, Lopper and Schwarz are not explicitly acknowledged as Jewish in this tribute, although many in Vienna believe that linking their Jewish heritage to their significant contributions to the club could serve as a powerful counter to the presence of neo-Nazis in the stadium. While FAK's museum briefly mentions Lopper as the founder of the supporters club, Schwarz features more prominently for his role in renaming the club from Amateure to Fußball Klub Austria in 1926. Born in Vienna in 1878, Schwarz embodied the club's identity as a societal institution, and he lived in proximity to the club's headquarters at the Dom Café. He became the club's vice president in 1931 and finally its president in April 1932. As a student, the merchant's son had learned from the city's most distinguished doctors. As a doctor, he was frequented by the city's upper middle class.[170] Schwarz, who was married to a Catholic woman, trusted his local network and perhaps his "mixed marriage" status when the Nazis took over Austria in March 1938. Despite facing discrimination under Nazi rule, he continued to work as a doctor, although the Nazis permitted him to treat only Jewish patients and forced him to work under the derogatory label of *Krankenbehandler*, which

Figure 2.18. Graffiti "Emanuel Schwarz." Photo by author.

translates as treater of the ill.[171] Schwarz, who had volunteered as a military doctor in World War I, stayed even after the November pogroms but finally escaped in May 1939 to Bologna, with the assistance of Giovanni Mauro, whom Schwarz knew thanks ot Mauro's role as president of Italy's football federation. Schwarz was arrested in France in 1944, escaped again, and survived in hiding in Paris. Schwarz is said to have been able to escape from internment only because a camp commander who knew Schwarz as a significant Viennese football figure gave him a chance.[172]

Almost immediately after the liberation, a newspaper reported that Schwarz had survived the Nazispuk—that is, the Nazi haunting—in Paris, and he was hoping to return to his hometown, his *Vaterstadt*.[173] Josef Gerö, president of the Austrian football federation (1927–41 and 1945–54) and justice minister (1945–49 and 1952–54), soon wrote to the French authorities, who assured him that Schwarz would be one of the first to return to Austria.[174] FAK's management board wrote to Schwarz personally, expressing its hope that he would return soon. Football had provided him with the opportunity to escape the Reich, and it was football, too, that brought him back to Vienna: When France's national team embarked on an airplane in December 1945 to play against the Austrian national team in December 1945, Schwarz got on the same flight to Vienna, where he would take over FAK's presidency again. Schwarz, who led FAK to three national and three cup titles, remained FAK's president until 1955. Schwarz's and Lopper's life stories, intertwined with their involvement in football, are undeniably captivating. Myths have been woven into them, often portraying them as figures of resilience and reconciliation. The historian Wolfgang Maderthaner writes that Schwarz seamlessly assumed the presidency of FAK, seemingly destined for the role, despite the challenges he faced. Yet as previously discussed, this myth warrants deconstruction, as a more nuanced reality lies beneath the surface.

The 2019 book *Ein Fußballverein aus Wien* argues that the common story of Schwarz's return portrays the years 1938–45 simply as a disruption and not as the final break with the pre-1938 FAK that Nazism caused.[175] This narrative, the authors argue, mirrors the Austrian post–World War II storyline: "The [implicitly also German] Nazis have gone, and everything continues like before. It has been forgotten, however, that the Jews—except for very few exceptions like Schwarz—were still missing because they had been murdered or expelled."[176] Manager Robert Lang and Secretary Heinrich Bauer were among the victims of the Holocaust. At the same time, myths about the persecuted club and its resistance are told: the club's centennial book, published by FK Austria Wien Merchandising GmbH, concocts the idea that the club was despised by the Nazis, that the remaining club members were always resilient, and that the "Aryan" players and officials quickly organized a refuge for the Jewish club members.[177] The club's memory was—and remains—selective. Any overlaps between FAK members and Nazism are ignored, among them the honorary president Ernst Kaltenbrunner as well as the associate director and Dietwart (a term used to denote a regime-imposed

FK AUSTRIA VIENNA 141

ideological indoctrinator and guardian), Walter Münch.[178] When Bruno Eckerl, after Nazism, became the club's president for a second time, the club did not even discuss his presidency during Nazism. Similarly, the players Karl Sesta and Matthias Sindelar both took part in the "Aryanization" of Jewish property but were honored for being resistant and for being advocates of the Austrian nation. The gaps in the club's working through the past are, the authors of the 2019 study conclude, closely linked to the comfortable victim thesis.[179] Notably, Matthias Sindelar emerges as a central figure in perpetuating this narrative, symbolizing the complexities of FAK's collective memory and identity.

Matthias Sindelar: Contested Memory

Matthias Sindelar, the forward who played for FAK from 1926 until his unexpected death in 1939, is also honored with graffiti near the stadium (see fig. 2.19). Sindelar was voted best Austrian player of the twentieth century.[180] The club has not only devoted a large exhibition board at its museum to Sindelar, where FAK also displays a large Sindelar figure, but also named the stadium's south stand after him in 1999. Since his curious death, Sindelar has been the figure of many myths. On January 23, 1939, Matthias Sindelar and his girlfriend Camilla Castagnola were found dead at their apartment after—according to the official verdict—carbon monoxide poisoning. Speculations arose over whether their death had been an accident, suicide, or murder. His death immediately turned Sindelar from a legend into a myth, and he was buried in an honorary grave. The Nazis celebrated him as an idol, and his funeral was politicized by the Nazis and attended by more than ten thousand people despite the rainy and cold weather.[181]

After World War II, Sindelar remained important. As early as in 1946, the author Franz Blaha published a biography that idealized the player.[182] Two years later, the cultural councilor Viktor Matejka from the Vienna branch of the Communist Party of Austria suggested a Sindelar statue.[183] In a shifting post–World War II society and a club culture that experienced ups and downs,

Figure 2.19. Graffiti "Matthias Sindelar." Photo by author.

Sindelar remained a stable symbol of identification, and when the millennium approached, people posthumously honored him with more awards and additional honors: the club hosted Sindelar events at the fan shop, where you could also buy a coffee pot with the player's portrait. In 2004, the club organized a bus nostalgia tour in honor of Sindelar, which stopped at his former home and his coffeehouse.[184] However, amid the Sindelar millennium celebrations, a public debate erupted in 2003 over how to deal with the fact that Sindelar's coffeehouse had been "Aryanized."[185]

What had happened? The journalist Peter Menasse publicly accused Sindelar of stealing the coffeehouse from its Jewish owner, Leopold Drill, by putting pressure on him while collaborating with the Nazi authorities.[186] Not many details about this "Aryanization" are known, and the public debate arose quickly and became heated. In newspapers, online comments, and roundtable discussions, people debated one of the "real fathers of the nation," as the journalists Skocek and Weisgram had crowned Sindelar in 1996.[187] The Nazis allocated "Aryanized" businesses like coffeehouses to respected party members and to renowned football players who had lost their income after the Nazis abandoned football's professionalism. But in April 1938, the Sturmabteilung (the "Storm Division," that is, the Nazi Party's original paramilitary wing) member Franz Reithner forced the Jewish owner Leopold Simon Drill and his son, Robert, to "sell" the coffeehouse.[188] At first, Drill resisted. In May, however, when the Nazis sent half of the coffeehouse's Jewish guests to the Dachau concentration camp, with the owner's son—who had been running the business for the last few years—among them, Leopold Drill finally "accepted" and set the price at around 54,000 Reichsmarks. Two weeks later, Sindelar offered less than half of the shop's market value and shortly after moved into the apartment above the coffeehouse, which he soon reopened.[189] The whole house had belonged to Drill, who was deported to Theresienstadt on July 22, 1942, where he died a year later, on March 26, 1943.[190] Whether Sindelar had struggled morally or whether he shared the Nazis' ideology is unknown and remains contested. What is known, however, is that Sindelar became a part of the Nazi system when he had the chance to take over the coffeehouse. Sindelar profited. Drill died. Although it is unlikely that Sindelar was a member of the NSDAP, and the Wiener Gauleitung—the regional Nazi Party leadership—described him as "Jew friendly" after his death, he became part of the antisemitic regime: a *Mittäter*, a coperpetrator.[191]

Portraying the club and the nation as Hitler's first victims allowed a specific breeding ground to emerge on which myths about Sindelar could flourish. The idea of the appropriate purchase price is widespread.[192] For instance, Norbert Lopper, who had heard many stories from Sindelar's mother Marie, reported, "Sindelar knew the former owner, Leopold Simon Drill, very well. . . . He wanted to limit the damage for Drill."[193] FAK's former vice president Peter Pelinka writes that Sindelar bought the "Aryanized" coffeehouse "for a decent price."[194] The club's museum distinguishes between the Nazis and Sindelar and remains silent about Drill: "The purchase of a coffeehouse, 'Aryanized' by the Nazis, provided Sindelar with a second career."[195] Various cultural products went even further: Wolfgang Weisgram's biographical novel portrayed the "Aryanization" (and thereby implicitly also Drill's death) as a "blöde G'schicht," an "unfortunate event."[196] Willem Pellert's 2006 theater play *Sindelar* tells the story of a football player who buys the coffeehouse as a favor to a friend (Drill) and then portrays Sindelar's suicide as an act completed together with his "Jewish girlfriend." Finally, he has the coffee owner, Mr. Goldberger, return to Vienna from the camp.[197] Nello Governato crowns Sindelar in his biographic novel *La partita dell'addio: Matthias Sindelar, il campione che non si piegò ad Hitler* as the "champion, who did not bow to Hitler."[198] The "resistant hero" myth became a global phenomenon, as the political scientist David Forster shows in his article *Café Sindelar Revisited: Verlauf und Folgen der Sindelaar-Debatte*.[199] The unproven story about his friendship with Drill, and the "friendly buying price" story, were two of the many claims made in Sindelar's defense during the 2003–4 debate.

Sindelar's absolution is often linked to Emanuel Schwarz. The FAK Museum states, "When FAK president Michl Schwarz was removed from office and it was forbidden to even greet him, Sindelar told him: 'I, Mr. Doktor, will always greet you.'"[200] This story has been repeated many times.[201] And although it originates from Schwarz's eyewitness account in June 1946, it has fueled the myth that Sindelar was a popular antifascist.[202] Consequently, Norbert Lopper would not accept Sindelar being portrayed as right wing.[203] In addition to Lopper, other Jews participated in the mythmaking: the author Alfred Polgar wrote that the "good Sindelar" had died by suicide in the "squelched, broken, and tormented city" out of "loyalty to his home country."[204] Friedrich Torberg wrote a famous poem "On the Death of a Football Player" that portrays Sindelar as a naive football player.[205] Jews and gentiles both looked to Sindelar as a national hero who was supposed to bring normality, stability, and reconciliation to post–World War II Austria, a nation that otherwise did almost nothing to make amends to Jewish victims.

Another important myth centers on the so-called reconciliation game played between the Ostmark and the Altreich on April 3, 1938, at Prater stadium, which the Ostmark won 2–0, allegedly "celebrating" its win "demonstratively" and "enthusiastically."[206] The myth suggests the two teams had agreed to a draw but that both Sindelar and Karl Sesta (who was also involved in the "Aryanization" of Jewish property) broke the promise by scoring one goal each.[207] Furthermore, Sindelar allegedly insisted on wearing jerseys in the Austrian national colors and refused to play for Nazi Germany's national team.[208] There is no evidence for any of this, yet the ideas of Sindelar are more significant than facts. After his death, Sindelar as an icon served a unifying function for Austrians. According to the myths, he fit perfectly into the cozy "victim thesis."

The graffiti at the stadium celebrates Sindelar as one of the greatest FAK players of all time, and the exhibition board at the museum proudly claims: "He was FAK!" Indeed, Sindelar represented the club FAK, called "Austria," and thus also represented the Austrian nation. And the club was a "good" one: somewhat resistant, somewhat Jewish. As the FAK Museum claims, "Austrian football was practically at its end when the German troops invaded and annexed Austria in 1938. 'Jewish clubs' such as FAK were banned, and many of the officials and players fled immediately after the Anschluss."[209] Sindelar remained good, and therefore, so did the club. He, the exhibition board reminds us, still greeted Emanuel "Michl" Schwarz.

The club's memory culture remains contested, and the "eternal journey to itself" is anything but over.[210] The sports historian Matthias Marschik concludes that the Sindelar debate of 2003–4 was a "missed opportunity." "What remains" in Austrian society, he argues, is "discontent because one of the rare opportunities to publicly discuss 'Aryanization' and everyday Nazism . . . remained stuck between repression and bloodless guilt confessions."[211] David Forster summarizes the outcome of the debate by quoting the Austrian saying, "Guat is gegangen, nix is gschehn" ("It went well, nothing happened").[212] The myths will prevail, and FAK is—and will remain—a contested space for collective memories and collective identities.

In conclusion, the narratives crafted by publications and museum exhibitions allocate specific roles to figures like Lopper, Schwarz, and Sindelar within FAK's collective memory, often framed within the context of the "Jew" imaginary framework. While these individuals hold significant positions in FAK's history, their portrayal in the club's collective memory tends to emphasize themes of continuity and reconciliation, obscuring the profound impact of Nazism. Antisemitism is often externalized, relegated to the past, and attributed to entities outside the club's culture.

CONCLUSION

Graffiti depicting the club's legendary player Matthias Sindelar, and its Jewish executives Norbert Lopper and Emanuel Schwarz are all located by the stadium.[213] Norbert Lopper and Emanuel Schwarz are on metal containers (the kind used for shipping, here used as storage) on the stadium square, and Sindelar's portrait beckons from a wall just a few meters away at the small stadium used as a practice facility. The Sindelar graffiti is on one side of the square (the left or right, depending on where you enter from), and the Lopper and Schwarz graffiti are on the opposite side. The perception of the club's icons remains a matter of perspective. Football cultures long for club legends and symbols with which to identify. After FAK lost its position as one of the main contenders for the national championship in 2005, it slowly rediscovered its "Jew Club" image from the pre–World War II era.

In the 1920s, FAK offered a space for Jews who wanted to participate in an integrated Gesellschaftsverein with a cosmopolitan orientation. The club thus cultivated its rivalry with Hakoah—in the 1920s, the Vienna derby was not yet played between FAK and Rapid but between FAK and Hakoah. The "Jew Club" against the Jewish club, or, put differently, the modern bourgeois Jews against the Zionist Jews. FAK was famous for playing smart and modern football—the club's style was called Scheiberln, or Donau football. Furthermore, the club was known likewise as a coffeehouse club and a city club. For those associating themselves with FAK, their club stood for modernity. For antisemites, the "Jew Club" FAK had become an antisemitic code, associated with everything they despised about "Jews" and offering a means to define their sports clubs as bodenständig in opposition to FAK's alleged rootlessness.

In the 1970s and 1980s, newly emerging fan cultures brought antisemitism against the "Jew Club" back to the stadiums. FAK, too, has struggled since then with some of the club's own fans, who display antisemitic and racist behavior. In a slowly shifting nation, which gradually began to value Jewish life and commemorate Jewish victims, FAK begins to embrace its "Jew Club" image. The club's turn to memory, however, is in part a continuation of the victim thesis through different means. While the Jews are hailed as part of the club's tradition, its Nazis and collaborators are either ignored or idealized. Consequently, Sindelar's status as a club icon remains untouched, although his role in the

"Aryanization" of Leopold Drill's coffeehouse has been public knowledge at least since the early years of the twenty-first century. Sindelar's graffiti, as well as those of Lopper and Schwarz, are not mutually opposed but rather complementary. Celebrating Sindelar despite the "Aryanization" and the act of commemorating Jews like Lopper and Schwarz is not a contradiction. Sindelar had supposedly been tempted. Lopper and Schwarz returned. All three are appropriate club icons beyond their legendary contributions to the club's successes. They all fit into FAK's emerging memory culture. The new cultural code of the "Jew Club" is anti-Nazi. Something that adheres to the images built of Sindelar, Lopper, and Schwarz as individuals and to the image of the club FAK.

The Jewish photographer and freelancer Daniel Shaked, who spoke to the club at the Judenplatz event, sees the increasing memory culture as part of the club's new orientation toward tolerance and against neo-Nazi fans. "To communicate the club's to some extent Jewish history conveys the message that FAK stands for something other than neo-Nazism."[214] The club's collective memory is thus part of its contested collective identity in the present and is tied to hopes about the future. The club's collective identity is shifting and the "Jew Club" image is at the center of attempts to disassociate FAK from the club's far right groups, which continue to make headlines.

In the next chapter on the Dutch football club Ajax Amsterdam, I take up the analysis of collective identities by focusing on the fans' performances as "Super Jews." In Amsterdam, fans began to embrace the Ajax's "Jew Club" image by bringing Israeli flags, Star of David symbols, and Jewish chants such as "Hava Nagila" to the stadium. Such performances have not been seen in Vienna, although they are not unheard of. Indeed, as Daniel Shaked told me, "We have always dreamed of bringing a Star of David, painted in FAK's club color, purple, to the stadium, as they do at Ajax or Tottenham. As teenagers, we discussed the idea of a fan club. We drafted banners and scarfs, but we always dismissed the idea. We did not dare do it. I do not know whether it would work today, but I believe that such performances would be more accepted than twenty years ago."[215] In recent decades, Jewish fans of FAK have feared displaying Jewish symbols or have relocated to the fringes of the fan section to avoid confrontations with far right fan groups. These groups have sought to redefine FAK's identity under the banner of a Traditionsverein, a traditional club, thus reinterpreting the "Jew Club's" cultural code as non-Jewish. During my last visit to the club's stadium in December 2023, I observed several stickers featuring the Star of David intertwined with the club's name and colors, suggesting a potential evolution in fans' collective identity. This development coincided with the disbandment of the Fanatics fan group and the club's tentative embrace of its "Jew Club" identity. FAK's "eternal journey to itself" continues.

THREE

AJAX AMSTERDAM

The "Jew Club" as Fan Performance

WHEN TWO RISING STARS OF Detroit techno's second wave, Richie Hawtin and John Acquaviva, traveled to the Netherlands in 1992 to perform at Rotterdam's club Parkzicht, the Rotterdam audience yelled something strange. The DJs realized, "with slowly dawning horror," that they were chanting "Joden," the Dutch word for "Jew," a chant that was then used by fans of Feyenoord Rotterdam and directed at their rivals, Ajax Amsterdam.[1] The two DJs had arrived at the epicenter of the emerging gabber scene, a form of hardcore techno that developed in 1992 Rotterdam in and around the Parkzicht club. The same year saw the founding of the label Rotterdam Records, which released the Euromasters album *Amsterdam Waar Lech Dat Dan*, famous as one of the first gabber releases ever. The titular song asks, "Amsterdam, where's that then?" This phrase highlights the rivalry between Amsterdam and Rotterdam that is part of both music and football. And the evolving gabber scene was tied to Feyenoord's fan culture, which strove to reinforce Ajax's "Jew Club" image.[2]

According to Acquaviva, their Dutch friends assured them on that day in Rotterdam that they would not have to worry because the chant about "Jews" would be nothing more than an innocent "football chant." Acquaviva, however, recalls being concerned about the interaction: "But I'm like, 'Fuck that, that's not who I am. I'm not a Nazi, I can make people rock without making them hostile.'"[3] Indeed, Hawtin and Acquaviva's label, Plus 8, completely changed tack after this experience, with their trajectory changing from "faster and harder" to "bringing back the funk and the soul of electronic music."[4] Feyenoord's fans, meanwhile, continued to shout "Joden" at their rivals from Amsterdam, and they still celebrate gabber, with gigantic raves taking place outside the De Kuip stadium in Rotterdam before some Feyenoord games and at Legioenzaal, a small club located inside the stadium just beneath the main fan stand run by Feyenoord fan groups (see fig. 3.1).[5]

One year after the Detroit techno DJs had visited Rotterdam, the Amsterdam-based label Mokum was founded. Like Rotterdam Records, Mokum chose a local term for its name: the word comes from Yiddish and means "place." Although Amsterdam's Jews introduced the term, all Amsterdammers use it today. The label was among the first to introduce the slogan "Hardcore united against fascism and racism." Mokum was known to be more intellectual than competing labels.[6] Like the two football clubs Feyenoord and Ajax, the local gabber scenes tended to represent the respective cities, with Rotterdam usually presented as a working-class city with a port, and Amsterdam as cosmopolitan and modern; an antagonism significant for the performances of Jewishness and antisemitism.

Amsterdam is famous for tolerance, bikes, art museums, Anne Frank, and the local football club Ajax. Ajax, the city's biggest football club, is renowned for its fantastic era of *total foetbal*, an intense, offensive style that has helped Ajax win many European titles. Ajax is also legendary for its youth academy, producing dozens of world-class talented young players. The club, too, is known as one of Europe's "Jew Clubs." All over the world, people wondered, as in a *New York Times* article, why Ajax "became known as a Jewish club" since there seems to be "no clear reason why."[7]

Figure 3.1. The Legioenzaal. Photo by author.

Any visitor to Ajax's stadium, specifically those who made a trip
to Amsterdam in the 1990s, must have thought they were attending some kind of Jewish pride festival. "Welcome to the weirdest,
least kosher Hebrew tribe in the world," the author David Winner
writes.[8] At times, it seems as if even Ajax's fans are confused. In
a famous chant that the whole stadium joins in at every game,
thousands of fans ask:

Waar komen Joden toch vandaan?	Where do the Jews come from?
Israel hier ver vandaan	Israel far away
Wonen daar ook Super Joden?	Do Super Jews live there too?
Ja daar wonen Super Joden	Yes, Super Jews live there too
Vinden Joden voetbal fijn?	Do Super Jews like football?
Als ze maar voor Ajax zijn	Yes, but only if they are for Ajax

The ritualistic ending to the chant consists of the entire stadium singing "Amsterdam, Amsterdam, Amsterdam" together. Ajax Amsterdam is the Netherlands' most famous and most successful football club; it has won more than thirty-five national and several international titles. The Ajacieden (supporters or players; sing., Ajacied), as they like to call themselves, are most proud of having achieved the "impossible" task of winning three consecutive European Cups, which grants Ajax the honor of keeping the trophy in Amsterdam (it is usually handed over to the new winner after each season). Today, the trophy is showcased at Ajax's club museum.

The Ajax Museum is immensely popular, although it can only be visited as part of a stadium tour. Just before the COVID-19 pandemic began, in 2019, the Johan Cruijff ArenA Tour had an estimated 2.3 million visitors, making it the second-most-visited attraction in Amsterdam after the famous Rijksmuseum, which 2.67 million people visited that year.[9] For the sixteen euros the club charges for the arena tour, visitors get to see the stadium, the locker room, and the media area. The museum—basically a trophy room—is also included. Only a single paragraph informs visitors of the German occupation; the respective text covers the years from 1940 to 1965 and is titled "Hard times," referring to the club's meager successes while remaining silent on World War II and the Holocaust.[10] Nowhere does the museum inform visitors about something many of them probably wonder about: Ajax's "Jew Club" identity. At the club's former museum, the Ajax Experience, this was not the case. The overambitious Ajax Experience opened in 2011 at Rembrandtplein but closed just two years later after a reported loss of 9 million euros. There, the club discussed yet denied its "Jew Club" identity. Perhaps referring to the fans' question about where the Jews are coming from, the club asked, "Wie Zijin We? Ajax, Jodenclub?" which translates as "Who are we? Ajax, a Jew Club?" and denied any such association because, the museum explained, Ajax never had more Jewish players than other football clubs.[11]

Indeed, the "Jew Club" Ajax was never an explicitly or predominantly Jewish club like the Amsterdam clubs Blauw Wit '34, Allen Eén Doel (AED), Hortus Eendracht Doet Winnen (HEDW), and Wilhemina Vooruit (WV).[12] Although a "Jew Club" identity is predominantly based on myths, the making of "Jew Clubs" relies on collective memories shaped by events in the past. In the case of Ajax, the "Jew Club" image refers to the predominantly Jewish area around the club's stadium.[13] Until 1941, Ajax was, as many commentators note, "more Jewish" than most other sports clubs.[14] Yet being Jewish was not the point, at least not before the Germans invaded the Netherlands in May 1940, as pre–World War II Ajax fan Abraham Roet explains.[15] Judaism, Roet says, "was never a problem in the Netherlands. You never felt different." At least to him, Ajax was more a "melting pot" than a Jewish club. Many academics believe that Jews in Amsterdam were more integrated and welcomed than in other European towns. It was in the Netherlands, however, that the Nazis murdered a higher percentage of Jews than anywhere else in Western Europe: 3 out of every 4 Dutch Jews—104,000 of 140,000—did not survive Nazism. Before the Germans invaded the Netherlands, more than half of them had lived in Amsterdam. In total, 75 percent of Dutch Jews were killed in the supposedly least antisemitic city— a contradiction that historians have named the Dutch paradox.[16] Amsterdam's Jewish history, the Holocaust, and the consequent Jewish absence have had a lasting impact on Dutch society. An analysis of the "Jew Club" Ajax demonstrates the conscious and unconscious ways in which the effects of the Holocaust still resonate today.

In Amsterdam, Nazism and the Holocaust changed everything, including Ajax. In 1996, the club's ninety-fifth anniversary book claimed that, nevertheless, for Ajax, "the misery of war remained relatively limited," because "there were no deaths to mourn among Ajax members."[17] But this is a truism, as Ajax had already expelled its Jewish members in the fall of 1941.[18]

Furthermore, most Jews associated with Ajax were fans and neither players nor members because most could not afford a club
membership (the club's neighborhood, East Amsterdam, was
a largely proletarian neighborhood).[19] After the war, very few
Jews, such as the goalkeeper Jopie de Haan and Jaap van Praag,
who later became Ajax's chair, returned to the club. Others, like
the New York–born player Edward Hamel, were murdered in
Auschwitz. It was mainly the fans who did not return, more so
at Ajax than at any other of Amsterdam's football clubs.[20] Yet
Ajax also had a (partly) Jewish club culture, particularly between
the 1950s and 1970s, that remained hidden to the public because
of fear of antisemitism. Ajax had back-to-back Jewish chairmen
between 1964 and 2011. Although Jews had important roles in
and around Ajax, the "Jew Club" was never predominantly or
explicitly Jewish.

The question of where the Jews come from had been asked in
many ways long before the establishment of academic fields like
Judaic studies and long before Amsterdam's football fans began
to call themselves "Super Jews." In this case the question is particularly tricky: Why is it that the Johan Cruijff ArenA became a
"virtually Jewish" space—a place where Jewishness is performed
almost always without Jews?[21] Where does their "Jew Club" identity come from? The fans' performances are often portrayed as
"strange" and tend to be observed with a voyeuristic gaze. This
has led to some misconceptions, such as that Ajax's fans would
potentially prefer to root for teams from Israel over Ajax. This
chapter's task is thus to understand the fans' performances in
their particular context, namely, the specifics of Dutch fan culture, Dutch memory culture, and Dutch antisemitism. This discussion is grounded in the analysis of primary sources such as
fanzines and chants. It begins with an analysis of the fans' performances, followed by a discussion of the reasons for the club's "Jew
Club" identity in the 1970s—of which there are many. The first
reason was the emergence of the *zijdes*, a form of fan culture that

involve introducing frequent chants and banners to the stadiums with a carnivalesque quality. This fan culture resulted in new nicknames for clubs and their followers, including that of "Jews" for Ajax. Second, the club's location in East Amsterdam resulted in a significant number of Jewish fans and with Ajax being understood as a "Jew Club" by away fans. Third, the "Jew Club" identity must also be explained in the context of Dutch memory culture and post-1945 antisemitism. Fourth, the rivalry between Ajax and Feyenoord Rotterdam is crucial and is, in many ways, like the cultural code that FK Austria Vienna assumed in opposition to Rapid Vienna (see chapt. 2): Ajax came to be seen as a "Jew Club" from a cosmopolitan and modern city while Feyenoord came to represent a *volksclub*, a term that means "people's club," not unlike the Traditionsklub, with a working-class mentality. This chapter discusses the "Jew Club" as an opportunity for anti-antisemitism and as a space of belonging for Jewish Ajax supporters. Finally, I examine how common theories of linguistic reclamation fail to grasp the case at hand, and I introduce a new model of linguistic appropriation. The chapter concludes with a discussion of the emergence of a less carnivalesque fan culture that recently led to a decline in "Jew Club" performances, although the fans' philosemitism lives on in their friendships with supporters of other clubs, namely Cracovia (Kraków, Poland), Maccabi Tel Aviv (Israel), RSC Anderlecht (Belgium), and Tottenham Hotspur (England). All four clubs are similarly known as "Jew Clubs."

PERFORMING JEWISHNESS: HOW THE STAR OF DAVID BECAME THE STAR OF AJAX

The museums of Amsterdam deal with the fans' "Jew Club" performances in different ways. While the club's museum (or, rather, trophy room) at the Johan Cruijff ArenA totally ignores the fans' "Jew Club" identity, the Jewish Museum exhibits a hat with the Star of David that references the F-Side, Ajax's supporters. In contrast to the official club museum, the online Ajax museum displays a private collection of jerseys and other Ajax-related items.²² It also offers a glimpse into the various "Jew Club" performances, such as the fans' tattoos, many of which feature the Star of David.²³ Even today, fans sometimes use the Star of David when leaving the initials AFC (Ajax Football Club) on walls across the country (see fig. 3.2).

Ajax's "Jew Club" identity is first and foremost constructed through the fans' performances. They frequently display the Star of David, which is recognized globally as the most important symbol of both Jewish identity and Judaism. The link between Ajax and the Star of David has become so common, an anecdote goes, that customers have even asked a jeweler from Amsterdam whether he sells Ajax stars.²⁴ Ajax's fans named one of their fanzines *De Ajax Ster* (*The Ajax Star*), displaying both the Ajax logo and the Star of David on each of the thirty-nine issues the fans produced between 1996 and 2001 (so did the fanzine *Dapp're Strijders* [*Brave Warriors*], which ran from 2003 to 2005) (see fig. 3.3). In 1999, *De Ajax Ster* produced a two-page article on the history of the Star of David.²⁵ It was meant to provide information about the symbol because "probably 99% of the Ajax fans wearing a Star of David do not know its origin or history." The text distinguishes between the antisemitic connotations of the *Jodenster* and the proud *Davidster*. The fans thereby raise awareness of the symbol's antisemitic connotations but also open up space for positive references, connecting one proud identity collective (Ajax fans) to another (Zionists): "The Star of David has become the symbol of a proud nation and a sign of hope for every Jew who seeks protection in his land."²⁶ Performing Jewishness is aimed at constructing a cohesive and proud identity collective and the appropriation of the Star of David is a welcome sign of belonging and unity to the Ajax collective.²⁷

Ajax's fans introduced the Star of David in the late 1970s or early 1980s. The exact date remains unknown; what is clear is

Figure 3.2. AFC graffiti in Utrecht, the Netherlands. Photo by author.

that they appropriated the "Jew Club" identity in response to antisemitic insults by rival supporters, which they refer to by their
differentiating the positive *Davidster* from the negative *Jodenster*.
The Ajax fan Peter, interviewed by van Bemmel, explains this as
follows: "Since increasing amounts of people started to 'insult'
us as Jews, we started to call ourselves Jews. In the 1970s we were
more and more 'the Noses' or simply 'the Jews' of Ajax. . . . we
just adopted that name and presented ourselves as 'those Jews'
of Ajax, to be able to silence the opposing fans and to take away

Figure 3.3. *De Ajax Ster.* Courtesy Jewish Museum Vienna (Photo: Tobias de St. Julien).

their ammunition."[28] During an away game in Utrecht in April 1983, Ajax supporters displayed a banner with the words "Joden worden kampionen" ("Jews will be champions") and an Israeli flag stating, "Jews is no longer a slur, it is a nickname."[29] Similar banners were displayed multiple times, for instance during a game against Feyenoord in 1985 (see fig. 3.4). Menno Pot, the author of several important books on the history of Ajax, told me that "when the antisemitic chanting started, the supporters adopted that as a name of pride. And it never disappeared."[30] The antisemitism came first and Ajax's "Jew Club" identity followed. Dutch football fans often claim that because Ajax's fans call themselves Jews, chants like "Jews to the gas" would simply refer to "football Jews" in response to Ajax's "Jew Club" identity and thus could not be antisemitic. The rhetorical strategy behind this is to base the determination of whether an expression is antisemitic to a question of intention, and intentions are easily deniable. It becomes a matter of perspective whereby every

Figure 3.4. The "Jews will be champions" banner. Courtesy Rob Bogaerts / Anefo.

statement about the expression's potential antisemitic quality is supposedly equally valuable. A focus on intentions obscures the antisemitic effects or content of an expression. Furthermore, the order of events—antisemitic performances first, use by Ajax's fans second—disproves the assertion that targeting Ajax as "Jews" is a response to Ajax fans' identification as a "Jew Club." However, the notion that Ajax's fans adopted the label to "silence the opposing fans and to take away their ammunition," as suggested by Peter, seems unlikely. The fans appropriated the "Jew Club" identity in a moment of intense rivalries and fighting between different supporters' groups—not least as a means of provocation and to intensify the opposition.

On the surface level, fans altered the meaning of the word "Jew" in the specific context of football identities: fans from both sides—Ajax and their rivals—claim they had or have little to no knowledge of Jews. The Ajax fan Tom, who describes himself as the first to bring an Israeli flag to the stadium, says: "It was just a flag . . . the symbolism eluded me."[31] Through their performances, however, the fans brought philosemitic and antisemitic notions that had survived in the "Jew" imaginary framework to the surface. Both sides contributed to the reemergence of the abstract "Jew" in the public sphere. In 1979, Feyenoord supporters chanted that Jews should be gassed. Months later, they attacked a television bus because it was allegedly affiliated with the "Jew Club." They sang blatantly antisemitic chants and displayed anti-Jewish banners.[32] Other fan collectives, such as those in Utrecht, joined them.[33]

Ajax's fans appropriated the Star of David on flags (see figs. 3.5 and 3.6) and the word "Jew" in chants, which soon spread out from the fan section to the whole stadium.[34] Fans even began to send letters to the fanzines, complaining that there were more chants about "Jews" than about Ajax at the stadium: "I am a little bothered that almost all chants today are about 'Jews.' I hardly hear AJAX anymore," as one fan put it.[35] Another fan argued that the Jew chants are meant to be playful and therefore should only be performed on special occasions, for instance when the opponents chant anti-Jewish songs, to celebrate a special goal, or to create a unique atmosphere during a special game such as a cup final.[36] Another fan complained that the proud club colors, red and white, have been replaced by blue and white, the colors of Israel. He wrote "IK SCHAAM ME DOOD!" ("I am ashamed to death!") in capital letters and wondered whether Ajax's fans are still being taken seriously.[37] Individuals experience shame as an emotion in relation to how others perceive them. Football fandom often seeks to be loyal toward one's club, its name, and its colors—something that the "Jew Club" performances seem to negate. If fans want to be respected by other fan groups, they can accomplish this through uniqueness, such as a "Jew Club" identity, or through "realness," for instance by "remaining true" to one's colors, one's club, and one's city. The issue of "Jew Club" performances was, still is, and will remain contested, although

Figure 3.5. Flag of Ajax supporters. Courtesy Jewish Museum Vienna (Photo: Tobias de St. Julien).

Figure 3.6. Ajax supporters displaying the Israeli flag (1987). Courtesy Bart Molendijk / Anefo.

the phenomenon today appears on a much smaller scale than in the 1990s or early years of the twenty-first century.

Fan Competition: Chanting "Super Joden" during the Second Game

One key practice for the construction of the fans' "Jew Club" identity is their chants. "Where do Jews come from?" is one example, while the chanting of the Jewish folk song "Hava Nagila" is another. Fans chant in the stadium to support their team, display their pride of a home team or hometown, and impede the opponent or the referee. Chanting also appears outside the stadium when fans travel to an away game, or on their walk to the stadium. The virtually Jewish space thus extends from the stadiums to any place occupied by supporters, such as restaurants, pubs, and train stations.

Fan chants are central for creating collective identities and fans are aware of their importance.[38] I suggest that there even exists a "second game" that takes place not on but beside the field, between supporters who compete to create louder, better, and more creative chants. If one's team loses, a supporter can still walk home proudly if their fan section has been "better" than their opponents. In 1997, De Ajax Ster produced a sixteen-page special issue entitled "Songteksten" ("Lyrics"), which provided information about a variety of Ajax's fan chants. The editorial board's introduction connects the chants to the "second game," or the competition between opposing fans: "The F-Side must become the most original in terms of songs, and the loudest and the clearest to sing; in short, they must become the most atmospheric side of the Netherlands."[39] Opponents are supposed to enter the field with "trembling knees" amid the "hurricane of noise" that Ajax's fans are supposed to produce.[40] To achieve this, the editorial board not only urges the fans to sing louder but also to slow their tempo and articulate words more clearly. Fans take their chanting seriously. The "Jew Club" identity emerges in the context of the "second game": the competition between fan collectives.

The fans' chants fall into different categories, ranging from support and celebration to insulting opponents. In a series of articles, published over three consecutive issues of *De Ajax Ster*, the fans themselves suggest dividing their chants into battle songs like "We're going to win the cup," songs about an underlying struggle like "We are the champions," and songs expressing admiration or loyalty such as "Che sera."[41] Several of the chants claim a collective identity as "Super Jews":

Langs de lijn, zingt heel het koor	Along the line, the whole choir sings
niemand kan ze stoppen en ze gaan maar door	No one can stop them, and they keep going
dan volgt het stadion	Then, the whole stadium follows
we zijn super joden	We are the Super Jews
Ajax is de naam	Ajax is the name
in heel Europa	All over Europe
met een grote faam	With a large family
zo winnen wij elk jaar een cup	So, we win a cup each year
want Ajax, Ajax is dè club[42]	Because Ajax, Ajax is the club

The chant manufactures unity by mentioning "the whole choir" and "the whole stadium" and using phrases such as *we are the Super Jews* and we are *a large family*. The union makes the club's successes possible: "So, we win a cup each year." What makes the "Jews" "super" is their union and their triumphs. Some songs refer to the entire team or the club as such; others are directed at individual players. The following chant, sung to the tune of the Irish folk song "The Wild Rover," references the British influence on fan chants all over Europe, which sometimes combines the national and the English language, as in this case:

Het is Patrick Kluivert	He is Patrick Kluivert
Patrick Kluivert is graat	Patrick Kluivert is great
He's the pride of Mokum	He's the pride of Mokum
He's scoring every game[43]	He's scoring every game

The song celebrates Patrick Kluivert, one of Ajax's great players who rose through the ranks of the club's outstanding youth academy.[44] Kluivert is, the fans claim, "the pride of Mokum." As earlier mentioned, the Yiddish word *mokum*, a nickname for Amsterdam, means "place" or "haven," and the fans make ample use of it. In the third text of the series on fan songs, the fanzine's editorial board felt the need to include warnings, printed in bold letters, before listing the songs directed at their bitter rival Feyenoord Rotterdam and before the "Jew Club" songs. In the context of their anti-Feyenoord chants, the fans "note in advance that some texts are a bit harsh" and ask readers to keep in mind that they are not meant literally but are intended to tease their rivals. The authors even omitted the hardest songs ("which most of you will know anyway") and emphasized "that we do not want to hurt anyone!"[45] One chant, sung to the melody of Herman Emmink's "Tulips from Amsterdam," claims that Ajax's fans will "throw bombs on Rotterdam" and that the F-Side is going to do to Rotterdam what the Luftwaffe did not—a reference to the German bombing of Rotterdam in May 1940, which led to the massive destruction of the city and resulted in the country's surrender to Germany.[46] When it comes to "pro-Jewish songs," the fans emphasize that they "do not intend to hurt anyone and only provide existing and sung lyrics."[47] The lyrics are "Jews will be champions"[48] and "Jews, Jews, Jews, Jews, Jews, Jews, we will be champions."[49] Another chant is "What rustles through the thickets . . . Jews, Jews, Jews."[50] This was first sung after the police aimed to hold Ajax's fans at the stadium for thirty minutes after the club's away game against FC Den Bosch, but the fans escaped "through the thickets." All three songs have various and ambiguous meanings. The first two praise Jews as superior and powerful, thereby celebrating Ajax's sporting successes and, at the same time, evoking the antisemitic stereotype of "the all-powerful Jew." The third song answers the question "What rustles through the thickets?" with "Jews," thus playing with the fans' identity but also evoking the antisemitic stereotype of the trickster Jew. Together, these philosemitic chants reinforce the "Jew" imaginary framework, the complex web underlying and connecting antisemitism and philosemitism: they celebrate "Jews," but they also reinforce the image of "Jews" as Other.

The "Jew Club" performances occur in contrast to far right and blatantly antisemitic fan performances by rival supporters. This does not mean, however, that Ajax's fan culture is free from far right or antisemitic tendencies. Around 1983, pamphlets by far right groups circulated among Ajax's fans, and a group of about twenty-five fans became far right activists. Racist jokes were considered appropriate, but some supporters considered serious statements and insults against, for instance, the few Surinamese or Jewish Ajax fans a sensitive issue. The far right group was even attacked by Ajax fans until they disappeared from the stadium.[51] Even without open neo-Nazi groups, racist fan performances persisted: when Ajax played against the Turkish club Bursaspor in 1986, Ajax fans threw garbage bags on the field, and they chanted "sweep, sweep, sweep" whenever they associated a rival club with "guest workers," that is, workers from other states employed for a fixed time in the Netherlands.[52] Even fights occurred between F-Side and "a group of Turks" in the streets of Amsterdam in the 1980s. Meanwhile, antisemitic jokes against, for instance, the Jewish Ajax player Jesaia Swart, known as Sjaak Swart, were heard.[53] Ajax's "Jew Club" identity leaves space for xenophobia and for the rivals' blatantly antisemitic chants in the performative realm of the "second game." The chants of both fan collectives foster collective identities, intensify the rivalry, and are offensive toward people perceived as Other.

Carnivalesque Fan Cultures, New Nicknames, and the Appearance of the Zijden

The stadium is not the only virtually Jewish space. Comparable phenomena exist in Jewish-style restaurants or at klezmer concerts.[54] The crucial difference between these spaces is, however, that the actors in the restaurants and at the concerts are hired performers: they serve "Jewish" food and play "Jewish" music to consumers to make a living; those who eat or listen at these virtually Jewish spaces do not bring Jewishness to the space and do nothing for it besides paying for the experience. In the stadium, it is not the club or its employees but the fans who turn a non-Jewish space into a virtually Jewish one—even against the wishes of the club. What is it about fan culture and the stadium that permits individuals who are mostly not Jewish to form an imagined-Jewish collective?

Fan cultures have a carnivalesque quality—both fan culture and carnival create a particular space, a "special, sacred time" (not work time), and a "regulated festivity."[55] Both carnival and football are to a certain degree "contained and officially sanctioned rebellion."[56] In both contexts, people may dress differently than they normally would, and individuals merge into one large group. This group shares a collective identity and a collective moment; it participates in an event that has a clearly marked beginning and end. In the case of Ajax, it is this particular situation that allows for an engagement with the "Jew" imaginary framework that would be unthinkable in one's everyday life. Words can become playful elements, "regarded as performances" detached from serious consequences such as injury or death proclaimed (for example, "bombs on Rotterdam" or "Jews to the gas").[57] The stadium differs, however, in many ways from carnival. Here, two fan groups are collectively dressed in the colors of their clubs to become two large bodies supporting their players, who are competing for the pride of their hometowns. At the carnival, countless individuals dress in countless different ways, but they become one large party—there is no competition.

Despite all the differences between carnival and football, football fandom's carnivalesque element, as suggested by Mikita Hoy, highlights fandom's playfulness and therefore also the supposed naivety of those participating in the "Jew Club" performances. Here are two examples: First, the fans have adapted the word

Joodenstreek, and it has taken on a partly new meaning. The literal meaning is "Jew trick" or "Jew prank," and it is commonly understood as deceptive trickery, most frequently used in commerce. Indeed, the combination of bribes and Jews is one of the oldest antisemitic stereotypes. Ajax's supporters started to use the term whenever someone was pranked by an Ajacied without really getting scammed. Words such as *mokum* and antisemitic words such as *Jodenstreek* have both become part of their collective identity, with Joodenstreek having lost its connection to money yet having kept its antisemitic connotation by associating "Jews" with trickery.[58] Second, when Ajax's fans cheered for their beloved goalkeeper Stanley Menzo during his last game before his retirement, they chanted, "Stanley is a Jew," therein "adopting" him as an Ajacied—as part of their fan collective.[59] Given that Menzo is Surinamese, the chant also engages with the Netherlands' colonial history and invites the once-racialized Other into the fans' "we" collective.[60] Other clubs' fan groups display similar ways of adopting players into the fan collective; for example, at FC Liverpool the Egyptian Muslim Mohamed Salah became the subject of his own song by Liverpool's fans ("If he scores another few, then I'll be Muslim, too").[61] Performing integration, however, can quickly turn into racist hate speech if the fans are disappointed with a player's performance or when a player transfers to a different (rival) club.[62] The fans' playfulness provides an opportunity to negotiate identities in the public sphere, including identity crossing and racism; fan cultures contain the potential for both inclusion and exclusion.

Nicknames in sports are neither unusual nor new. FC Bayern is also called the Rothosen (the red trousers), and FAK was known as the Kaffeehausklub (the coffeehouse club). In the early twentieth century, Dutch newspapers referred to Ajax as "the red-white team." They called the Dutch national team *oranje*, and Blauw Wit '34, one of Amsterdam's actually Jewish clubs, was called "the Zebras" because of the vertical stripes on the club's jerseys.[63]

Nicknames traditionally refer to a club's (perceived) identity. In the 1970s, European fan cultures changed, and with them, the nicknames of many clubs. A carnivalesque fan culture emerged that was playful and spontaneous, and it adopted pop music. For Ajax's fans, teams from the south were given the nickname "farmers."[64] Meanwhile, Ajax supporters called the clubs located by the German border the "krauts" [moffen], and Feyenoord supporters were called the "cockroaches" [kakkerlakken].[65] The new nicknames emerged out of the new phenomenon of the zijden, which literally translates as "sides." This included Ajax's F-Side, which appeared in the Dutch stadiums in the 1970s.[66] Most people conflate the zijden with hooliganism, but although they overlapped, they are distinct fan cultures. While hooliganism means violence, only a few affiliated with the zijden were involved in fights, and as Ramón Spaaij notes, "many young fans joined the sides merely to 'have a good time' among peers and to experience pleasurable excitement."[67] The connection between the zijden and hooliganism is, however, not entirely wrong. Before the zijden, there was little violence in Dutch football, but with the appearance of this style of fandom, the violence quickly became more planned and detached from the game itself.[68] Fan cultures became more organized and hooliganism quickly built a new juvenile subcultural identity.[69] Spaaij sees hooliganism's key characteristics as being emotions, masculinity, localism, the management of reputation, in-group solidarity, belonging, and sovereignty and autonomy.[70] Together, these features make fan cultures significantly distinct from phenomena like carnivals (not to speak of going to a restaurant or a concert). Fan cultures can be carnivalesque and playful, but they can also be serious when it comes to their collective identities—and localism is perhaps one of their most important features.

Ajax before the Invasion: Jewish Fans and De Neuzenclub

The club's association with Jews goes back to the pre–World War II period. Ajax did not have many Jewish executives or players, but

the club did have a strong Jewish support because of its location in East Amsterdam, where the majority of Amsterdam Jews
lived. The club played its home games at the "wooden stadium"
from 1907 until 1934, and then Ajax moved to a stadium called
de Meer, which was also located in East Amsterdam. Only the
wealthier Jews could afford to go to Ajax, many of them from
Amsterdam South, but Jews from the neighborhood also supported the club, whether they could afford the stadium tickets or
not.[71] Consequently, many Jewish Ajax fans traveled to the stadium by streetcar. Hans Reiss, for instance, started going to Ajax
games in 1921, when he was nine years old.[72] On game days, Reiss
told Kuper he would go with his father in a little steam streetcar
known as "the Murderer from 't Gooi," which departed every
thirty minutes from the Weesperplein metro station. "So at the
Weesperplein people would always storm it. They would be stick-
ing out on all sides. Extremely dangerous. Almost all those people
were Jews."[73] The association of Ajax with Jews has its roots in the
club's history—namely, in its neighborhood and from the Jewish
fans who came from other parts of Amsterdam.

The away fans also traveled to Ajax by streetcar.[74] Because the
streetcar passed through Amsterdam's areas, which appeared
Jewish to them, the fans started to say that they were visiting
"the Jews."[75] Ajax had a Jewish image before World War II and
was, the club historian Evert Vermeer claims, called "the club of
noses" [de neuzenclub] by supporters of other Amsterdam football
teams.[76] This label functions here as a synonym for "Jew Club,"
referencing the antisemitic stereotypes about the alleged "Jewish
hooked nose." The making of the "Jew Club" Ajax thus links to
the club's Jewish fans, antisemitic stereotypes, and East Amsterdam as a supposedly Jewish space.

When Germany invaded the Netherlands in 1940, about 10 percent of Amsterdam's inhabitants were Jews; 80,000 of the 140,000
Dutch Jews lived in Amsterdam.[77] Most of them were proletarian
laborers and street vendors. As early as in the seventeenth century,

many Jews lived in Amsterdam. The city's relative tolerance and its freedom of trade, religion, and thought attracted them—although Jews were still excluded from existing trade and professional guilds. The National Assembly emancipated Jews in 1796, granting them citizenship and thus equal civil and political rights. Jewish integration into overall Dutch society proceeded in the nineteenth century when Dutch became "the official spoken language of Amsterdam Jews," although Yiddish had sometimes influenced their Dutch to a degree that "a non-Jew or an assimilated Jew would find it hard to understand."[78] This mutual influence and partial integration characterized the Dutch-Jewish relationship, and between 1870 and 1940, Amsterdam Jews became fully integrated into Dutch society, yet they maintained their Jewish identity.[79] Until the German invasion on May 10, 1940, Amsterdam's Jews "felt they were Amsterdammers, Jews, and Dutch—in that order," and they felt "safe and secure."[80] In this situation, Ajax was an important space for the partial integration of Jewish Dutch people as Amsterdammers or, as in the words of the Ajax fan Roet (previously mentioned), into Amsterdam's melting pot, where one "never felt different."[81]

After the Holocaust, most of Amsterdam's Jews were deported, murdered, or had left, but the city's association with the "Jew" imaginary framework remained. It is no coincidence that Amsterdam's and not Rotterdam's football club is known as a "Jew Club": the city is traditionally known as the Jerusalem of the West. The equating of Amsterdam with "Jews" goes beyond the realm of football: Amsterdam youths, whose "disturbing group behaviour" has been studied by the Dutch anthropologist Jan Dirk de Jong and described by Remco Ensel, have been known to shout "We are the Jews from Amsterdam" when making trouble at a fair.[82] Jews have become a reference point for Amsterdammers; not least because the word has an outsider connotation, and it distinguishes between an in-group and out-group, between local and foreign. "Jew Clubs" have created a strong sense of belonging. The fans reproduce their collective identity through chanting, the use of Jewish symbols, and everyday interactions, for instance, when they address each other as "Dear fellow Jews" ["Geachte mede-Joden"], or when they refer to one another as a *Jodeman*, which means "Jewish man."[83] Ajax's "Jew Club" identity goes back to its historical local embeddedness in the more Jewish parts of Amsterdam and its many Jewish supporters of the past, and it relates to an awareness of Amsterdam being the Netherlands' "most Jewish town," a designation that has lasted until the present.

AJAX AFTER 1945

In 1950, Ajax Amsterdam published a poem to celebrate its fiftieth anniversary in which the club commemorated the inhabitants of the Jewish Quarter and its Jewish fans.

Menig oud historisch plekje	Many old historic places
waar men vroeger gaarne kwam	where people in the old days liked to go
is verdwenen, vormt een leegte	are missing, form a void
—letterlijk!—in Amsterdam.	—literally!—in Amsterdam.
Dit geldt wel het allermeeste	This is most true
voor de oude Jodenhoek.	for the old Jewish Quarter.
. . .	. . .
Ajax heeft—hoe kan het anders—	Ajax has always had—how else could it be—
uit het Oosten van de stad,	from the East of the city,
in de Meer steeds veel supporters	in de Meer many supporters
uit het Joodse milieu gehad.	from the Jewish milieu.
. . .	. . .
Dit was een Memento (mori)	This was a memento (mori)
van wat eenmaal heeft geleefd,	of what once lived,
bruisend leefde!—De Historie	vibrant life!—The History
kwam en heeft het weggeveegd . . .	came and wiped it away . . .
Maar wie of hen nog mocht krenken,	But who could still offend them,

| nu nóg, nu ze er niet meer zijn, | even now, now that they are no more, |
| Ajax zal hen steeds gedenken[84] | Ajax shall always remember them |

The poem commemorates the club's Jewish fans and concludes with the demand that Ajax should think of them forever. Since then, however, no vivid memory culture has evolved around the club, although the club culture was somewhat Jewish in the 1950s and up to the 1970s. Several of the club's key figures were Jews, had Jewish family members, or had Jewish friends when Ajax became a world-class team in the 1960s.[85] The Jewish club culture of the time was expressed through food, jokes, and language. Before every European Cup game, a Jewish butcher would give Salo Muller a salami, and as Muller recalls, the players said, "Oh, it's Jewish—we like it!" Whenever there was a different salami, the player Dick van Dijk would joke, "Hey, come on, throw it away—it's a Catholic salami. We only like the kosher one."[86] Before the games, Muller reports, the chair Jaap van Praag "would come and tell a Jewish joke."[87] At the time, Jewish culture influenced the club culture. The Jewish fans, however, had disappeared.

Ajax's club culture was, the historian Stefanie Schüler-Springorum writes, perhaps not so much "Jewish" as shaped by the Holocaust and occupation.[88] The players Sjaak Swart and Bennie Muller had survived as children of "mixed marriages," and the club's culture was shaped by former resistance fighters like Kuki Kral (father of the later Ajax defender Ruud Kral) and Leo Horn, one of the Netherlands' most famous referees. In short, "You knew each other, the families married among themselves and the young Ajax players worked at the factories and stores of their Jewish sponsors."[89] For the former Ajax player Barry Hulshoff, Ajax's team of the 1960s and 1970s "never felt Jewish, but it was there nevertheless."[90] It is, Hulshoff goes on, "an Amsterdam thing" as "many Jews always had a feeling for us [Ajax]."[91] For Hulshoff, Ajax was in the center of the Jewish community and "quite a few of the players were Jewish in the youth teams." He stated that this was "not an issue people thought about consciously, but things always went in this direction."[92] The club's culture after World War II was somewhat Jewish, and shaped by the Holocaust, occupation, and World War II.

It strikes me that the experience of the Holocaust and of post–World War II antisemitism formed a club culture that largely denied any Jewishness in public. The author and Ajax supporter Menno Pot explained it to me by paraphrasing what Ajax's former Jewish chair Uri Coronel had told him: "Of course we were a Jewish club. After the war, it was all Yids. We were having Jewish parties and there was a Jewish flavor to the whole club culture. It was just that we did not want to share that with people because they are turning it into something ugly."[93] Coronel may have been referring to the antisemitic cries of rival supporters that began in the 1970s, although it is possible that Ajax did disguise its Jewishness at the time because of the overall social climate after 1945. Jews in the Netherlands experienced an upsurge in antisemitism right after World War II,[94] which also influenced their experiences in football.[95] Those Jews who returned faced a bitter homecoming, as they were suspected of having betrayed those who helped them, and any Jews who wanted their property or business back were met with suspicion.[96] In the decades after World War II, Ajax denied its Jewishness because of antisemitism. About two decades later, Ajax's fans developed a "Jew Club" identity because of antisemitism. Both responses—the denial of any Jewishness and the appropriation of a "Jew Club" identity—occurred in response to antisemitism, and they both demonstrate the interrelatedness of philosemitism and antisemitism in the "Jew" imaginary framework.

Already before the emergence of the zijden, Ajax's players experienced antisemitism on the field. The "Jew Club" identity, Simon Kuper suggests, took off in the 1960s, during the period of the club's (partly) Jewish club culture.[97] In 1965, Jan Jongbloed, then goalkeeper of the Amsterdam football club DWS, called

Bennie Muller a "pleurisy Jew"—part of a tradition wherein Dutch swearing usually revolves around diseases.[98] Ajax experienced antisemitism, but the club also offered a space of belonging in a society that was often malicious toward those Jews who had survived or returned.

In his detailed analysis *Ajax, the Dutch, the War*, Simon Kuper concludes that "in a city that lost about 80 percent of its Jews, those at Ajax seem to have fared unusually well."[99] Ajax, in the sense of an informal network rather than the club, had indeed saved people.[100] According to Kuper, Jaap van Praag, who became the club's chair in 1964, hid in the apartment of Ajax player Wim Schoevaart's uncle, Jan.[101] Nonetheless, Ajax's Jews suffered like other Dutch Jews. Their club had expelled them in 1941—Jopie de Haan and Edward Hamel, who both played for Ajax, did not return after the liberation. Hamel, who is today remembered by a Stolperstein, was murdered in the Holocaust; many of the club's fans did not survive, either. The German occupation changed the whole country, and this was also the case for East Amsterdam and its local football club Ajax.

Ajax publicly rejected any ties to Jewishness because it feared antisemitism. And Ajax never kept its promise from the 1950 poem: it did not develop a vivid memory culture.[102] "Silence," Simon Kuper argues, "was best for Ajax."[103] In 1945, Ajax created a "purge committee" that expelled seventeen members and donors and suspended one for their role in World War II.[104] After the liberation, Ajax remained, above all, a football club and thus treated former collaborators primarily as Ajacieden. The club integrated both Jews and collaborators. Seventeen is a relatively large number of members to expel, yet post-1945 Ajax "was stuffed with erstwhile collaborators."[105] The club culture tied them all together. As Kuper suggests, "Belonging to Ajax was probably a clearer identity, a more tangible tie, than being Dutch."[106] Ajax's growing successes in the 1960s perhaps helped the club stick together. The club's successes are, from today's perspective, often associated with its Jews, but there were also people like the brothers Freek and Wim van der Meijden who contributed massively. The van der Meijdens were called the "bunker builders" because Freek had transformed the family business into a giant company, building bunkers and barracks for the Nazis.[107] Freek faced three years in prison but nonetheless became part of the Ajax family once more. The brothers "threw parties and bought drinks in the directors' room after matches, and soon began to strengthen the team," although the club denied them membership until the 1960s.[108] The brothers were friends of the club's Jewish chair Jaap van Praag (to the anger of the club's Jewish physiotherapist, Salo Muller).[109] Together with the Jewish sponsor, the real estate developer Maurits "Maup" Caransa, the "bunker builders" established the financial basis for the club's great triumphs. Caransa said he had "thrown himself into work"—just like a whole generation of Jews did in post–World War II Europe, looking to the future instead of the past.[110] The Holocaust was unbearable, and the presence of post-1945 antisemitism only contributed to the absence of a vivid memory culture. While Ajax contributed to the overall silence, Jews like Caransa had other reasons to remain silent; Jewish suffering reminded Dutch society of its failings and Jewish testimonies contradicted the nation's narrative of heroic resistance, which became known as the Dutch "founding myth."[111]

Dutch Memorial Landscapes: Between Namenmonument and De Dokwerker

One of the most famous museums in the Netherlands is the Anne Frank House, located at Prinsengracht in central Amsterdam, just meters away from the city's tulip and cheese museums. Anne Frank is now commemorated globally in books, films, statues, and wall paintings (see fig. 3.7). Frank is remembered as a girl who successfully went into hiding thanks to her Dutch helpers. That she was also betrayed, deported, and died is less known in the public memory.[112] The selective collective memory shaped

Figure 3.7. A wall painting of Anne Frank in Amsterdam. Photo by author.

this Dutch founding myth, a perspective in which Dutch society perceived itself as more heroic than it actually was.[113] Whereas the Austrians, as discussed in the previous chapter, portrayed themselves comfortably as Nazism's first victims, the stories of heroic resistance circulating in the Netherlands shaped "the resistance norm."[114]

As in Germany and Austria, it took time before Dutch society began to work through the nation's past. After 1945, a lack of understanding and knowledge characterized Dutch society, which treated Dutch Jewish survivors foremost as Dutch nationals and stateless Jews as German collaborators, even arresting some.[115] An existing vague sense of guilt was repressed. Immediately after the liberation, various authors emphasized how shame and repression obscured the reckoning with the past and the acknowledgment of Jewish suffering.[116] The denial of Jewish suffering after 1945 even gave rise to post–World War II Dutch antisemitism.[117] As early as 1945, the sociologist and social democrat Hilda Verwey-Jonker argued that "the majority of the Dutch people were well aware that they had behaved 'utterly miserably' towards their Jewish fellow-countrymen" and that they now "sought to justify themselves by criticising the Jews."[118] In combination with the founding myth, antisemitism was "a compensation for a lack of national pride."[119] A more nuanced reckoning with the past was still obscured by the founding myth, but this was soon followed by the notion that Dutch people had either behaved impeccably well or utterly badly.

In 1983, Hans Blom suggested, in his inaugural lecture as director of the Netherlands Institute for War Documentation (NIOD), the abandoning of the then dominant framework of either heroic resistance or collaboration,[120] thus challenging the now prevalent binary framework of *goet* versus *fout* (good versus bad). In 2022, Menno Pot said, "We are totally cured now from the idea that we were just victims and that everybody was a resistance man. Nobody believes this anymore."[121] The Dutch Resistance Museum deals so frankly with the issue of collaboration, Kuper writes, "that it might just as well be renamed the Dutch Collaboration Museum."[122] This is certainly an exaggeration, but the museum is more nuanced than its name suggests. When I visited the museum in 2022, visitors were greeted with an introductory video that emphasized the choices available to Dutch people when the Germans invaded the Netherlands, namely, to adapt, to collaborate, or to resist.[123]

Perhaps nowhere in the Netherlands is the nation's reckoning with the history of Nazism and the Holocaust so condensed as

Figure 3.8. *De Dokwerker* in front of the Portuguese synagogue. Photo by author.

in the city's Jewish Quarter around Jonas Daniël Meijerplein next to the old Portuguese synagogue and across the street from Amsterdam's Jewish Museum. At the center of the J. D. Meijerplein Square, a monument called *De Dokwerker* (*The Docker*; see fig. 3.8) proudly stands; the statue commemorates the February Strike of 1941 during which approximately three hundred thousand people joined the general strike, which lasted two days before the Germans shut it down with brutal force. The strike, initiated by the Communist Party of the Netherlands, is considered to be the largest public action against Nazism. Even today, many antiracist demonstrations start or end at the statue, where the first antisemitic raid took place, against which the strike was directed. *De Dokwerker* symbolizes Dutch resistance but also the founding myth: the statue, unveiled in 1952, was commissioned by the Amsterdam city council, which had refused permission to erect a Jewish monument in the square. Remco Ensel writes that instead, "it became mandatory that the Jewish monument should propagate 'Jewish gratitude.'"[124] Today, the area around *De Dokwerker* reveals a shift toward acknowledging Jewish suffering. The area now includes the Holocaust Memorial (unveiled in 1962; located at the memorial site for the former deportation center Hollandsche Schouwburg), the Memorial to the Victims of Auschwitz (1977), the monument to Jewish resistance (1988), the Deaf Memorial (2010), and the National Holocaust Museum (2024).

In September 2021, the king unveiled the Dutch Holocaust Memorial of Names (see fig. 3.9), one of the latest major additions to Amsterdam's memorial landscape. The memorial was contested, mostly by residents, less because of its purpose than because of its size, or so the residents argued. The memorial, designed by Daniel Libeskind, lists more than 102,000 names, each written on one brick together with the person's date of birth and age at death. The bricks together form the phrase *In memory of* in Hebrew, thus combining the general memory of the Holocaust with the commemoration of individual victims. The memorial may thus also function as a counterweight against the revictimization and deindividualization of Jewish victims. Whoever enters the memorial finds themself in a labyrinth flanked by two-meter-tall brick walls. The Namenmonument is only a two-minute walk away from *De Dokwerker*, but few of today's visitors to the Jewish Quarter would be able to guess how long a process it was for Dutch society to come from one monument to the other. Somewhere along the way, Ajax's fans started their "Jew Club" performances.

Antisemitism's New Focus Points: The Holocaust and Israel

"Hamas! Hamas! Jews to the gas!"[125] This chant, directed at Ajax's supporters since the 1970s, references two major shifts in Dutch

Figure 3.9. The Namenmonument. Photo by author.

antisemitism, over the Holocaust and Israel.[126] "Jews to the gas" calls for the killing of Jews by gassing them. Indeed, people in the Netherlands knew this was how the Nazis murdered Jews and other people during the Holocaust. Hamas is a reference to the openly antisemitic Palestinian organization that has regularly attacked Israeli soldiers and civilians for decades and is responsible for the attacks of October 7, 2023—the largest antisemitic attack since the Holocaust.

Antisemitism and memory culture reached a turning point when the fans started "Jew Club" performances in the 1970s. Antisemitism, anti-Zionism, and criticism of Israeli politics became a "fateful triangle."[127] It gradually became "standard practice to invoke Israel to support the argument that it is time to stop putting all the emphasis on 'Jewish suffering,'" as Evelien Gans and Remco Ensel wrote in their introductory essay to *The Holocaust, Israel and 'the Jew': Histories of Antisemitism in Postwar Dutch Society*.[128] "The circle is then complete," they observe, because "Jews are not just there to be gassed, they are the Nazis of today, with the Palestinians as the new Jews."[129] Dutch memory culture denied Jews a distinct place in Dutch memory culture through *nivellering*, a term that translates as "leveling,"[130] which is "the idea that Dutch society as a whole—and not Dutch Jews alone—was victimized by the Nazi regime."[131] The societal shifts have consequences for the "Jew Club" Ajax: Dutch memory culture is the breeding ground for these fan performances. Today, the Holocaust has a central space in the nation's collective memory. Yet this recognition has the side effect, Kronemeijer and Teshima argue, of potentially revictimizing Jews.[132] Jews risk becoming subsumed under an abstract concept of victimhood. The rather vague association of Jews as the "ultimate victim" and nivellering also plays out in the context of Ajax's fan culture: when Ajax's fans traveled by train to Rotterdam and were searched by hundreds of riot police officers at the Amsterdam train station, an Ajax fan shouted that it was "rather typical" that all "Ajax Jews" were forced to travel by train.[133] The fan connected his "suffering" with the images of the "train" and the "Jews," thus comparing the "Ajax Jews" to those Jews deported by the Nazis. The understanding of Jewish suffering is linked to the image of the train that has become an icon for deportation and the Holocaust. The fans' "Jew Club" identity is, although often less explicit than in this case, a way of engaging with the past and with collective memories. The "Jew Club" as fan culture is a result of the Netherlands' particular situation in the 1970s, marked by leveling, a new Holocaust awareness, transformations in Dutch antisemitism, and emerging fan cultures.

Dutch-Israeli Relationships: From Solidarity to Antipathy

Ajax's supporters began to call themselves "Super Joden" as the Dutch view on Israel shifted. Dutch society had long viewed Israelis and Jews as "weak victims," but now they became "threatening perpetrators." While the Netherlands initially denied Jews recognition at home, they showed massive support for the Israeli state. In post–World War II Dutch society, sympathy with Israel dominated, with only very few countervoices being raised "although ambivalent feelings were always lurking around the corner."[134] During the Six-Day War in 1967, the Dutch collected millions of guilders, donated blood, and sent voluntary medical and military personnel in solidarity with Israel.[135] Dutch newspapers printed full-page advertisements declaring that "Israel needs two things: money and blood," while people placed bumper stickers on their cars stating "We stand behind Israel."[136] There was enormous sympathy for Israel, but the widely held belief that the Netherlands stood shoulder to shoulder with Israel is exaggerated.[137] After the 1967 Six-Day War, sympathy began to shift from Israel to the Palestinians. This shift took place "more slowly in the Netherlands," where it occurred primarily in the 1970s—and thus alongside the emergence of Ajax's "Jew Club" identity.[138]

After 1967, anti-Israelism came to have an anticolonial touch, and it increasingly became the focus of Dutch protest movements.[139] The turning point, however, happened around the time of another war in the Middle East—the 1973 Yom Kippur War (also known as the October War or the Ramadan War)[140]—after which Jewish groups in the Netherlands highlighted an increase in antisemitism.[141] Dutch Jews were somehow held responsible for whatever the people accused Israel of.[142] The rise in antisemitism also led to a rise in Jewish activism. Protesting against antisemitism was no longer unthinkable, and Jewish agency could now be expressed "in a state of permanent alertness and militancy" and "in judicial and other kinds of protests."[143] The rise in antisemitism directed at Israel was accompanied by a new Jewish agency and visibility, which was probably also noticed by Ajax's fans and their rivals.

Even before the Yom Kippur War, antisemitism directed against Israel linked to antisemitism against Ajax. In 1970, the club was the first institution of many to receive one of approximately seven hundred antisemitic letters.[144] The letter threatened to detonate a bomb at the club's stadium de Meer: "We will destroy this imperialist Jewish sports complex," the letter read.[145] Several players, including Johan Cruijff and the Jew Sjaak Swart, received death threats. A letter to Sjaak Swart read: "They forgot to gas you and your parents. The El Fatah will put your family away. What the Germans have forgotten, we will not forget."[146] A letter asked the non-Jewish player Nico Rijnders why he played for the "Jew Club" and stated that "this cannot go unpunished."[147] The club even received phone calls about bombs being placed in the stadium. In 1972, two years after Ajax had received the first letter, the sender, Dirk K., was sentenced to six months in prison. At the trial, he reiterated his association of Ajax with Israel.[148]

The 1970s were a turbulent decade. All of this was accompanied by the emergence of new right-wing movements in the early 1970s and a new awareness of the Holocaust: The Auschwitz Memorial in Amsterdam was unveiled in 1977 and the television series Holocaust was broadcast into Dutch living rooms in 1979. These developments perpetuated the Dutch awareness of Jewish suffering that had started in the 1960s, when the National Holocaust memorial was unveiled (1962) and when the historian and Holocaust survivor Jacques Presser had published Ondergang, which had a considerable impact on Dutch memory culture.[149] In 1980, just as this turbulent decade came to an end, a local branch of the Palestine Committee distributed postcards displaying images on which they compared Israel with Nazi Germany—thus perpetuating the combination of the new focus points of antisemitism, the Holocaust and Israel, a combination also expressed in the stadium.[150]

LOCALLY ROOTED "JEWS" AND
ANTIHEGEMONIC HOOLIGANS

The figure of the "Jew" as a passive victim was no suitable icon for Ajax's emerging hooligan culture. Only its transformation "from cowardly to courageous to cruel" turned the "Jew" into an attractive symbol, as it now related to both fandom's localism and hooliganism's antihegemonic, antiestablishment attitude.[151] All collective identities of European football fan culture center around localism. A club can even become like a mini-homeland, a home. The stadium may be called a living room; the club collective, a family. Some fans even request that their ashes be scattered in the stadium after their death. The "Jew Club" identity demonstrates Ajax's local identity as a club representing Amsterdam, a city that has a long history of being associated with Jews. As football became more commodified, clubs became increasingly alike, yet they looked for things that distinguished their club collective from others. In Amsterdam, the fans referred to their city as Mokum and—since the late 1970s—to Ajax as "Super Jews." Local rootedness and Bodenständigkeit make a club "authentic."[152] One Ajax chant shows how the fans' local identity relies on the city's Jewish history:

Aan de rand van Mokum,	On the edge of Mokum,
aan de Middenweg,	at the Middenweg
stond een stadion zo sfeervol,	Stood a stadium so full of atmosphere,
het is gesloopt en dat is pech.	it is gone and that is unfortunate.
Nu in de Arena veel bobo's	Now in the Arena, many big shots,
weinig sfeer,	little atmosphere,
het vuurwerk is verdwenen,	the fireworks are gone,
ik heb heimwee naar de Meer.	I'm longing for de Meer.
Maar de echte fans die blijven,	But the real fans stay,

die houden zich niet tam.	they are not tame.
Het zijn de Ajax diehards,	They are the Ajax diehards,
het zijn de bhoys uit Amsterdam,	they are the boys from Amsterdam,
de Joden uit Amsterdam![153]	the Jews from Amsterdam!

The chant connects Ajax's localism and its history to its present. Those embodying the club's "real" tradition—linked to spaces such as Mokum, de Meer, Middenweg, and East Amsterdam—are the "Jews from Amsterdam!" The "Jew Club" identity is connected to the fans' local "rootedness." In an interesting and playful twist, the "always wandering," and "rootless Jew" is transformed into an icon that forms its opposite: local pride and rootedness.

The "Jew" would, however, not be a sufficient icon for the fans' localism if still perceived as a "cowardly" and "passive victim." To be a fan of a football team means to be part of a proud and strong identity collective. When the Dutch public identified itself increasingly with Palestinians and turned against Israel, Ajax's rival groups began to turn against Ajax as a "Jew Club." Identifying Ajax as the "Jew Club" became attractive for both sides—Ajax and its rivals—particularly because it was antihegemonic. Feyenoord's fans provoked the new state of Holocaust memory with their antisemitic chanting, such as their hissing to invoke images of the gas chambers. The fans of Ajax incited the new, negative image of Israel by waving Israeli flags and thus associating themselves with the "new devil."

Ajax and Israel: "Home Field Advantage"

Collective identities need strong images. Ajax's fans found them in Israel and Germany. According to Simon Kuper, fans of Ajax would even hand over their "home field advantage" to Israeli teams coming to play in Amsterdam.[154] Kuper describes a scene from Ajax's home game against the Israeli club Hapoel Haifa in 1999, during which he witnessed something he could not "remember ever having seen in a football ground before": the home fans, he claims, "began supporting the other team."[155] Kuper's interpretation relates to two of this study's main subjects: football fans and antisemitism. For football fans, it is completely unthinkable to root for their team's opponent. They want their team to win. Always.[156] The notion that Jewish-identifying fans root more for Israeli teams than for their local ones evokes the antisemitic stereotype of Jewish dual loyalty, which accuses Jews of being disloyal toward their nations in favor of Israel.

Kuper suggests that the fans' "Jew Club" identity led them to support an Israeli team more than Ajax. But is this really the case? Kuper leaves out that the competition between Ajax and Hapoel was played in two rounds, of which Ajax had won (3–0) the first in Haifa. Given the away goals rule (an away goal counted as double if the score is a draw after two games), Ajax was almost certain to advance to the next round. The one goal Haifa scored in Amsterdam in the second half did not risk Ajax's success. A loss of 0–1 (the result of the game), or even 0–2 or 1–4, would still take Ajax to the next round of the cup. Thus, a loss could still be considered a win. It was in this context that Ajax's fans started chanting "Olé," whenever a Hapoel player passed the ball to a teammate.

Although their advance to the next round of the cup was not in danger, Ajax's fans took their team's performance very seriously. They did not appreciate losing no matter the opponent, as the fans' written report about that game in the fanzine De Ajax Ster reveals: "Ajax does not play at all. It's only bumping along. No less than 38,000 spectators feel like they are being cheated," the fans remarked furiously.[157] "The public is ashamed of this Ajax," the fans also commented.[158] In football fan cultures, supporting may switch to mocking if the fans feel humiliated by their team's performance. The chant "Olé" has been used on various occasions to express embarrassment about a team's performance, although it is usually a form of celebration. On that day in Amsterdam, "Olé" was by far more mockery than it was friendship or an expression of a "Jew Club" identity. The fans expressed their anger in other chants: "We want to see football," "Play for your money," and "Wouters out," the latter chant being directed at the club's coach Jan Wouters. All these chants, the fans explain, were "sung out of frustration" over the players' performance.[159] Fortunately, the fans were content because Ajax had won 0–3 and Hapoel knew they could not level the score, even if they did win in Amsterdam.[160] Ajax lost 0–1 but still advanced to the next round. Even so, Ajax's fans celebrated Hapoel Haifa primarily to mock their team rather than to celebrate Ajax's opponent, their "Jew Club" identity, or Israel.

Although there was little support for Hapoel Haifa at the 1999 game in Amsterdam, the Ajacieden do indeed have some affection for Hapoel Haifa because it is an Israeli team. The fanzine's report of the first game in Haifa, which Ajax won 3–0, celebrates the game as a long-awaited "match for the Jewish championship."[161] The issue even contains a six-page account of the fans' journey to Israel, in which they lamented the "endless discussions" of their "Jew Club" performances in the Dutch media, while on the other hand, "the mood was euphoric" on the Israeli side, where the game was even called a "Jewish derby"—very much to the pleasure of the Ajacieden ("It appealed more to us than the whimpering of the Dutch scribes").[162] In the game report, published in the same issue of *De Ajax Ster*, the fans deviated from their practice to report only the number of Ajacieden and not the total number of spectators. Here, they subsumed all spectators under the term "Jews." As they themselves reported, "Aantal Joden: 15,000."[163] They enjoyed the "warm" atmosphere at Haifa: "complete strangers wanted to shake hands, and they wished us good luck," the travelogue reads.[164] The Ajacieden also made their way to Jerusalem, where they found the Western Wall to be "less imposing" than expected.[165] For them, the "great question" was whether they could approach the holy place as "non-Jewish non-Jews." They could, and they "prayed" side by side with real Jews at the

Western Wall. The travelogue concludes with the Hebrew phrase *shalom*, which means "hello" or "goodbye" and "hope to come back one day," and a full-page photograph of a Jewish man posing with a copy of *De Ajax Ster* in front of the Western Wall.[166]

When the fans traveled to Israel from Amsterdam, they transported the "virtual Jewish space" they created in the stadium on game days to actual Jewish spaces in Israel. The "non-Jewish non-Jews" encountered actual Jewish Jews and behaved as if they had just arrived in a kind of Jewish Disneyland. They experienced and comprehended their encounters within the "Jew" imaginary framework: they were looking for the abstract "Jew" among real people who were Jewish—and they found their stereotypes, for instance in the appearance of Orthodox Jews at the Western Wall, whom they photographed and messaged to their fellow Ajax supporters, for whom they also wrote the travelogue. In 2004, again, the Ajacieden became "very excited" when Ajax played Maccabi Tel Aviv in the Champions League.[167] They found this "fantastic" and announced that "we are going home to Israel," where the fans walked through the streets of Tel Aviv, proudly displaying their Ajax jerseys, waving Israeli flags, and shouting "Joooooooden! Joooooooden!"[168] In their imaginary, "Israel" becomes a space representing the "Jew" imaginary framework. Their performances reinforce philosemitic and antisemitic stereotypes but also testify to a certain ambiguity in their encounters: while they relied on and reproduced stereotypes about the "Jew" as Other, they also initiated interactions with the Jews they encountered on their journey.

Israeli perceptions of the Ajax fans' affection for Israel and their "Jew Club" performances differ. In 1999, Israeli journalist Eli Shvidler called Ajax "probably the most Jewish club in the world and certainly the most popular team in Israel."[169] On the contrary, the final scene of Israeli filmmaker Nirit Peled's film *Superjews* displays the chant "If you don't jump, you're not a Jew," to which an entire terrace of Ajax fans jumps except for Peled, who feels uncomfortable about the "Jew Club" identity. The film also portrays Israelis living in Amsterdam and liking it. Similarly, Ajax's former Jewish player Bennie Muller reports, "I talk a lot with Israelis here. They all seem to like it. They laugh about it. But for the Jewish people in Amsterdam here, it's so disgusting, it's unbelievable. Younger Jews tend to take a more relaxed view."[170] Israelis respond with mixed feelings to the fan performances, perhaps because they sense their ambiguous meanings. While the fans celebrate Super Joden and Israel, they are also reconstructing the abstract "Jew." To a certain degree, the "Jew Club" performances exclude Amsterdam's Jews from the "Jew Club" by externalizing the place where Jews belong as Israel—the land that, in the fans imaginary, is not only faraway but is also where "Jews [really] come from." The performances exoticize "Jews" as a faraway people and perhaps imagine them as a thing of the Dutch past, thus leaving little space for Jewish people in their "Jew Club" identity. To create group coherence, they tend to ignore the diverse Jewish and Israeli views on the "Jew Club" identity. Any identity group needs strong images of friends and enemies. While many of Ajax's fans view Israel positively, Germany disgusts them.

Ajax and Germany: Football as Revenge

Fans' philosemitism toward Israel is complemented by their hatred for Germany. For instance, Ajax's fans displayed the banner "Jews take revenge for '40–'45" when they played against a team from Germany in 2004.[171] A win for the "Jew Club" Ajax was regarded as revenge for the German occupation of the Netherlands and the Holocaust. The "Jews" who "took revenge" were, however, not real Jews but Ajax's "non-Jewish non-Jews." One of them, perhaps, was a fan named Arjan, whom van Bemmel interviewed and described as a "lifelong hardcore Ajax fan," a "former F-Side member" who is "talkative" and "well-informed."[172] Arjan recalls that when Ajax drew the German club Hamburger SV in the 2008–9 Europe League, many thought it was "time to get my Israeli flag out of the closet."[173] There is, Arjan says, a "link between the Jewish Ajax identity and Germany," a link with the past that also plays out when the Dutch national team plays against Germany. It is "just fun to point out the history to those Germans," Arjan declares. There is "a little bit of rivalry" between the Netherlands and Germany, intensified by imagining it within the framework of "Jews versus Nazis."

Anti-German sentiments have been commonplace in post–World War II Dutch society, and not only in football. The former Dutch football player and Ajax coach Jan Wouters, for instance, recalled in a 2005 interview that anti-German sentiment was normal for anyone growing up in the Netherlands: "In school, one learns many things about the war, and then there was 1974."[174] In 1974, the Dutch national team lost the World Cup final against Germany, in Germany. This loss became known as the "mother of all losses," and many described it as a traumatic event.[175] It took fourteen long years until they finally got their rematch. The Netherlands faced Germany for the semifinal at the UEFA Euro 1988, which again took place in Germany.[176] This time, the Netherlands were victorious. About nine million people celebrated the win on the Dutch streets. Thousands of them had traveled to Hamburg chanting, "They came in 1940, we came in 1988, Holadieh, Holadioh," and they even spoke of a counterinvasion.[177] Dutch newspapers ran with the headline "Revenge!" Some claimed a second liberation, and a former resistance fighter expressed publicly that he felt as if the Dutch "had ultimately won the war."[178] For the Germans, in contrast, the rivalry grew when Germany played the Netherlands during the quarterfinal at the 1990 World Cup, during which the player Frank Rijkaard spat on Rudi Völler's hair. In 2002, many Germans sang along to the Schlager music hit "Ohne Holland fahren wir zur WM" ("We are traveling to the World Cup without the Dutch"), when the Netherlands failed to qualify for the World Cup. Soon after, the rivalry between Germany and the Netherlands faded. About ten years later, the Ajax supporter

Arjan said that "for most people the problems with Germany are gone, maybe it is different for older people."[179] To him, the link between Ajax and World War II seems less present than it was in the last decades of the twentieth century, but the day when Ajax's fans brought their Israeli flags to Hamburg was not so long ago (November 27, 2008; Ajax won 0–1). Both the fans' affection for Israel and their contempt for Germany have been shaped by the repercussions of the unmastered past.

Ajax versus Feyenoord: De Klassieker

In the late 1970s, the Holocaust and Israel had become the leading focus points of antisemitism. Increasingly, "Jews" were linked to the gas chambers in antisemitic expressions—a link introduced when Ajax supporters "were greeted with massive hissing and 'Jews to the gas chamber'" chants by rival supporters.[180] Anti-Israel sentiments were bolstered in 1982, when the massacres in Palestinian refugee camps in Sabra and Shatila in southern Lebanon made global headlines. The Dutch streets were "filled with protest," and "Israel, Zionism and state violence became synonymous" in public discourse.[181] Amid this political climate, supporters of Feyenoord Rotterdam waved the Palestinian flag when they played against Ajax, and they also adopted slogans from anti-Israel demonstrations.[182] That Feyenoord's fans chose the "Jew" as an icon for their rivals relates to the transformation of "the Jew" figure from victim to victimizer and an awareness of the Holocaust. This complex moment assigned a paradoxical role to the "Jew," who was now imagined "not only as Janus-faced victim and perpetrator, but also as a Third [Other]" who "falls outside the apparent dichotomy of victim and perpetrator,"[183] as Evelien Gans notes (in reference to Klaus Holz).[184] The figure of the "Jew" "arouses all the more animosity and hatred because he is felt to pose as a victim while actually being a victimiser."[185] The Feyenoord fans could thus refer to Ajax as the "evil" Other (the victimizer) while also humiliating Ajax as the weak victim.

Feyenoord fans displayed Palestinian flags at the stadium when the societal solidarity shifted from Israel to the Palestinians; the intention was, however, not to show solidarity with Palestinians. "Everybody knows how Rotterdam is," one Feyenoord fan said. "We all hate those Muslims," and the flags are "really just to annoy those people from 020 [020 is the area code for Amsterdam]."[186] Feyenoord's supporters would never shout "we are the Palestinians," the fan continues, because they "do not identify . . . with the Palestinians." Palestinian flags remained rare among Feyenoord's fans, while Israeli flags became common among Ajax's fans, because "Jews" related to the localism of Ajax supporters, while Palestine or Muslims did not correspond similarly to Rotterdam's local identity. One reason why the fans of Feyenoord abstained from using the Palestinian flag as a symbol may be that racism has been a constant problem among them, although, of course, not all of Feyenoord's supporters are racists. The fans' antisemitism and racism become visible in the stadium area. When I visited Rotterdam in December 2022, I encountered several far right stickers outside the stadium (see fig. 3.10).[187] Displaying the symbols of Israel and Palestine is also a means to express rivalry for the two fan collectives. To a certain degree, the rivalry between Ajax and Feyenoord is about the opposition of two cultural codes comparable to the rivalry between FAK and Rapid Vienna.[188]

The rivalry between Ajax Amsterdam and Feyenoord Rotterdam is often described as a "clash of cultures," with Amsterdam representing the "cosmopolitan and haughty nature of the capital" and Rotterdam symbolizing "the worker spirit of the port."[189] The stereotypes associated with the cities extend to the football field: supposedly, Ajax embodies a top-notch technical game, virtuosity, and metropolitan elegance, in contrast to Feyenoord's working-class style marked by a no-nonsense attitude, diligence, and strong-mindedness. The clubs' playing styles are mirrored in their respective stadiums. Amsterdam's Johan Cruijff ArenA, which opened in 1996 and was renovated

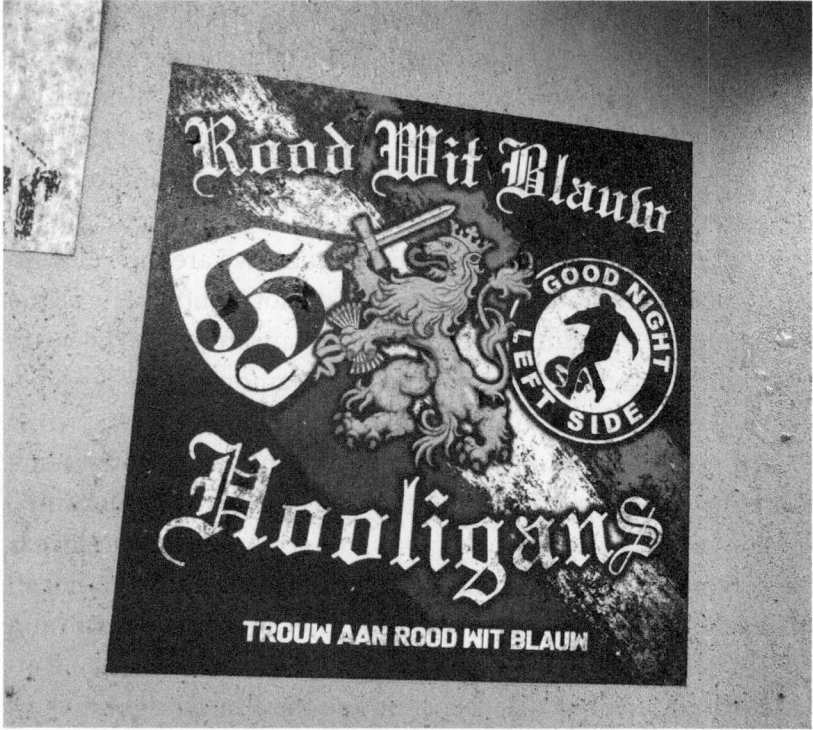

Figure 3.10. A sticker by the Hooligans. Photo by author.

in 2020, appears modern, smooth, and elegant (see fig. 3.11). Rotterdam's Stadion Feijenoord (nicknamed "De Kuip" or "the Tub") was built in 1937 and was last renovated in 1999 (see fig. 3.12). Feyenoord has made several attempts to build a new stadium since 2006 (all have failed), and it instead renovates "De Kuip" now and then. In a city largely destroyed by German bombings, the stadium has a particular traditional vibe and is built largely out of brick and steel—an architectural style that resembles the club's "hardworking" mentality—with *geen woorden maar daden* ("actions rather than words") being one of the club's slogans. Like in Vienna, the two ascribed club identities and the respective styles of play are predominantly invented traditions.[190]

Figure 3.11. The Johan Cruijff ArenA. Photo by author.

Figure 3.12. Stadion Feijenoord. Photo by author.

Both clubs are among the most successful and oldest clubs in the Netherlands. In the early twentieth century, the two cities rapidly became centers of sport.[191] Today, Amsterdam is the nation's biggest city (ca. 900,000 inhabitants), followed by Rotterdam (ca. 650,000) and The Hague (ca. 550,000).[192] Rotterdam is considered the industrial center and Amsterdam the city of artisans, commerce, and free living.[193] The rivalry between the two clubs is thus also a rivalry between two cities: the industrial center versus the cultural center.

The "Jew Club" Ajax was the perfect counterimage to the volksclub: an arrogant, elite high culture and big city club that was not only a rival competitor for championships but that also had a rival hooligan culture. Feyenoord is known as a volksclub, a concept similar to the idea of a *Vorstadtklub* in Austria or a *Traditionsverein* in Germany. A volksclub used to be known as a working-class club and stands for "the opposite of the official cosmopolitan bullshit that for many Feyenoord fans is summed up by the word 'Jews,'" Kuper writes.[194] Uri Coronel, Ajax's (Jewish) chair between 2008 and 2011, remembers how this antisemitic dualism materialized when Ajax faced Feyenoord in Rotterdam: "Before the game we [the board of Ajax] were escorted by the police to the stadium of Feyenoord. We had to walk past the Feyenoord supporters who were all standing around us and making the Nazi salute. We literally had to walk through a row of Hitler-saluting Feyenoord supporters."[195] At that time, antisemitism at Feyenoord was so common and accepted that even the player Ulrich van Gobbel initiated the chant "Who does not jump is a Jew" while standing in the center circle of the stadium.[196]

Although the club Feyenoord Rotterdam now challenges antisemitic expressions, antisemitism persists.[197] When Feyenoord player Steven Berghuis transferred to Ajax in 2021, a piece of graffiti appeared in Rotterdam depicting Berghuis with a large nose (a common antisemitic stereotype linked to Feyenoord's de neuzen nickname for Ajax), a red kippah (the color red symbolizes Ajax;

the kippah marks him as "Jewish"), and a striped shirt resembling the cloth of concentration camp inmates.[198] Furthermore, the shirt also displayed a yellow star with the letter J written on it, reminiscent of the star the Nazis forced Jews to wear in public.[199] The graffiti was accompanied by the text "Joden lopen altijd weg" ("Jews always run away"), thus blending the antisemitic stereotype of the cowardly and defenseless "Jew" with the "dishonorable" act of running away from a fight between football hooligans. The slogan recalls the infamous so-called Battle of Beverwijk between the two hooligan sides in 1997, during which one Ajax hooligan died while others allegedly ran away. The slogan is frequently used by Feyenoord fans as a chant or in banners, and is visualized in stickers (see fig. 3.13), on T-shirts, or other merchandise products.[200] Often, perhaps to avoid being "openly" antisemitic, the term *Joden* is left out or is replaced by a logo that shows an Ajax player with a long nose.[201] On social media, Feyenoord supporters commonly allude to Ajax using synonyms and codes as emoji pictures of noses that represent the stereotype of the "Jewish nose."[202]

The antisemitic visual language denigrates "Jews" as physically weak and not masculine. In the context of football cultures, honor, strength, and loyalty are associated with masculinity. Fan cultures rely on chivalrous ideals of fighting, commitment, and loyalty. Football rivalries have a reciprocal structure of competition between fans: without one's rivals, the excitement of competition would not exist. Rivalries are based on mutual recognition. Ajax supporters appropriated the "Jew Club" identity not least because it was a way to recognize Feyenoord's supporters and other fan collectives as rivals—and to be recognized. They responded to feminizing insults by reframing the "Jew Club" identity as a label of strength and local pride, thereby entering the logic of rivalries. The construction of masculinity and the collective local identities of both fan collectives—the "Jewish" Amsterdam and the "non-Jewish" Rotterdam—constantly

Figure 3.13. The "Joden lopen altijd weg" sticker. Photo by author.

intensify each other. They are connected through the "Jew" imaginary framework; they engage, perform, and negotiate ideas about "Jews" to reinforce their club identities and partake in the excitement of rivalry.

After the graffiti depicting Berghuis had appeared in 2021, a board member of Rotterdam's supporters' organization De Fei-jenoorder declared that "it is not that everyone thinks that Jews should be gassed. We are always talking about 'football Jews.'"[203] At times, though, antisemitism targets real Jews—not "just" Ajax leaders like Uri Coronel, but also random Jews on the streets of Rotterdam. As one Feyenoord fan recalls, "a while ago a Jew was walking on the street in Rotterdam and was wearing a kippah. He walked past some fans of Feyenoord and they started to insult the Jewish guy: 'Hey, fucking Ajax fan' ['Hey, kanker Ajacied']. The guy had nothing to do with Ajax, he was not wearing their jersey or anything. They just saw a Jew and immediately associated that with Ajax."[204] Antisemitism in football appears most often in the context of rivalries.[205] Fans experience games against rival teams as highly emotional. They provide the grounds for forms of hate speech to occur, which most fans do not engage in outside the stadium or at (most) other games. Sporting rivalries have recurring elements, including the frequency of competition, a defining moment, recent or historical parity, star actors, geography, relative dominance, competition over players, cultural similarity or difference, and unfairness.[206] The rivalry between Ajax and Feyenoord is so intense because the two clubs play regularly, they are close by, they represent cultural differences, and they compete over players such as Berghuis. Indeed, when he transferred from Feyenoord to Ajax, this triggered the fans' creation of antisemitic graffiti. Rivalries are also emboldened by the relative dominance of one team, in this case Ajax, which created a strong and cohesive underdog mentality among Feyenoord's supporters.[207] The underdog mentality easily merges with the volksclub and workers' club spirit, which combine to fuel the antisemitic dualism between "us down here" and "them up there," between "productive capital" and "money-grabbing capital," in which the workers' club is associated with "productive capital," that is, honest, real, material work, while the other is linked with bribery, trickery, and abstract antiwork.[208]

THE "JEW CLUB" AS LINGUISTIC APPROPRIATION

The "Jew Club" concept has become crucial for both sides of the rivalry: Feyenoord's fans use it to express their disgust for Ajax and Amsterdam, whereas Ajax's supporters use it to evoke a sense of localism and to provoke their rivals. Both sides continue and the "Jew Club" is thus a constantly reproduced praxis, although the authorities have excluded both fan collectives from visiting the away games of their clubs at the rival's stadium. The "Jew Club" identity therefore becomes "entrenched in . . . a vicious circle," as Joram Verhoeven and Willem Wagenaar argue.[209] They both work at the Anne Frank House and have developed an educational strategy together with Feyenoord that aims to break the vicious circle by appealing to the fans' collective identities.[210] The supporters engage in educational tours about local Jewish history and the Holocaust, in which cases of individual players or fans of "their" club are foregrounded, and the fans get to meet fellow Jewish supporters. Comparable approaches have been developed with other clubs, like FC Utrecht, and in other countries, for instance in Germany, where supporters and fan workers participate in educational tours to memorial sites. The approaches differ in time (several days or a few hours) and approach: while most projects in Germany address all fans, the Dutch projects target mostly those who have participated in antisemitic behavior. The tours in Germany are always voluntary, while those in the Netherlands are often offered to fans with a stadium ban.

In the Netherlands, clubs promise to decrease the time of a fans' stadium ban if they participate in the workshop. Every so often, visits to memorial sites are even mandatory and issued as punishment. The Feyenoord supporters responsible for the graffiti depicting the player Steven Berghuis were, for instance, sentenced to a mandatory visit to the Namenmonument in Amsterdam.[211] The judge did not consult the club, who would probably have explained that sending Feyenoord supporters to Amsterdam—a city they despise like no other—is most likely a counterproductive idea. Whether such a punishment is helpful remains a contested issue. Critics argue that visits to memorial sites should always be voluntary, not least because these are also sites of commemoration, and that learning about the Holocaust does not equal learning about contemporary antisemitism.[212]

The educational strategy in the Netherlands appeals to a common identity between Jewish and non-Jewish supporters. It is hoped that the encounter with Jewish fans of the same club makes the fans who participated in antisemitic chanting change their behavior. This pedagogical strategy is based on "the educational power of the encounter, of the act of meeting a person."[213]

The attendees meet with Jewish supporters of "their" club and listen to how their fellow fans have stopped going to the stadium because of the hurtful antisemitic chants. The fan performances of antisemitism are experienced as hurtful by Jewish supporters, many of whom feel excluded from the stadium experience.

While Jewish members of the fanbase at clubs where fans partake in antisemitic behavior feel excluded, the opposite is the case for several Ajax supporters. For some of them, Ajax's stadium is the only public space in which they feel comfortable displaying Jewish symbols in public, as the Jewish supporter Diana Knots explains in Nirit Peled's film *Superjews*:

> When I was a child, we had a Star of David on the wall. It scared me somehow, being a Jew. I'd rather not be one. At school we discussed the Second World War, but they were all horror stories about people going to the gas chamber or the roundups of people in hiding. Then the schoolteacher told me: "If you don't feel Jewish, you're not Jewish." Which made me heave a sigh of relief: I'm not Jewish. I'm not. Then you go to Ajax matches, where you feel the connection with the club being Jewish and me being Jewish too. . . . It's still a bit scary confessing to people that you're Jewish. I'll wear this star at home or when I go to the game but at work I won't wear it for fear of offending people. And in certain parts of Amsterdam, it's not advisable to wear it either.[214]

Knots, who has always felt uncomfortable being Jewish, has been empowered by Ajax's fan performances. At the stadium, her identity as a Jew and her identity as an Ajax supporter become one. Others have had similar experiences. The former Jewish team doctor Salo Muller states, for instance, that the fans' "Jew Club" performances make him happy: "It makes me feel warm inside."[215] Similarly, Bram, the fourteen-year-old protagonist of the 2012 short film *Cap of Keppel* (cap or kippah),[216] is both troubled and proud to be Jewish. Bram prefers to wear a cap rather than a kippah at school to conceal his Jewish identity because he wants to avoid being bullied. In contrast, Bram enjoys the stadium: "I can just walk there as a real Jew."[217] At Ajax, Bram proudly wears a kippah that displays both Ajax's club symbol and the Star of David. The film portrays Bram as excluded at school and as included at Ajax. The football stadium is a place where he does not have to balance between his identities. The vicious circle is thus a circle with two sides: it offers participation to Jewish Ajax supporters while it excludes Jewish fans of rival clubs.

In the case of the London-based "Jew Club" Tottenham Hotspur, the fans' appropriation of the term "Yid" is, according to Emma Poulton and Oliver Durell, a form of "linguistic reclamation."[218] The historian John Efron understands it as a form of value switching, during which "not merely the word, but . . . meaning and cognition evoked by the word are also turned upside down."[219] Reclamation or reappropriation of slur words, such as the N-word, are usually enacted by people of the targeted group. Reclamation is usually understood as a process of amelioration and meaning change, during which a word becomes more acceptable and less offensive, as has occurred with the words *gay* and *queer*. None of these things happened in the case of Spurs fans appropriating "Yid." They shouted it back in response to rival fans who had come to understand Spurs as a "Jew Club"—similar to the vicious circle between Ajax and its rivals. Instead of *reclaiming* the word—Tottenham had never called itself "Yids" and Ajax never called itself a Jewish or a "Jew Club"—the fans put it into a new and different context. I therefore suggest calling this process "appropriation" rather than "reappropriation" or "reclamation."

These two cases of appropriation differ from cases of linguistic reclamation. This is mainly for two reasons. First, three rather than two groups are involved. Usually, "the appropriation of an epithet" is defined as "a phenomenon whereby the targeted group takes control of the epithet, and alters its meaning for use within the group."[220] In the case of Ajax and Spurs, however, most fans belonging to the groups of attack and defense, namely, those who direct antisemitism at "Jew Clubs" and those who respond by appropriating a "Jew Club" identity, are not part of the targeted group—Jews. The process of appropriation includes the directing group (rival fans), the receiving group (Ajax or Spurs fans), and the targeted group (Jews), who may belong to both the directing and the responding group or to neither of the two. Instead of distinguishing between the rival fans as "real perpetrators" and Spurs fans as "the victims,"[221] I propose including Jews as important actors and therefore recommend understanding the "Jew Club" identities in a triangular relationship, whereby Jews are affected in different ways than (other) Ajax or Spurs fans (see fig. 3.14).[222] These interactions between rival fans and Ajax or Spurs supporters subject Jews to a third position that is paradoxically one in which they are not only victimized but also forced to be a bystander.

The second reason that makes this case distinct is its nonlinear process of appropriation. Usually, linguistic reclamation evolves more or less linearly, whereby a word is at first a slur, then becomes appropriated or reclaimed, and finally changes its meaning (see fig. 3.15). In the cases of "gay" and "queer," for instance, the appropriation process is already over in most Western countries, and the words are now open to out-groups as well.[223] These words, which have even come to signify academic fields, such as Queer studies, were at first appropriated by the targeted group and then also became, after the word's meaning changed, open to others. The word is taken from the out-group, appropriated by the in-group, and then used in society at large (the last part is different with the N-word). Generally, linguistic reclamation is "available only to in-groups, but when it is sufficiently widespread it may extend also to selected out-groups."[224] In the case of Ajax and Spurs, however, the words "Joden" and "Yid" never belonged to the in-groups as such—not when rival supporters directed it at Ajax or Spurs supporters and not when those supporters appropriated the terms. In

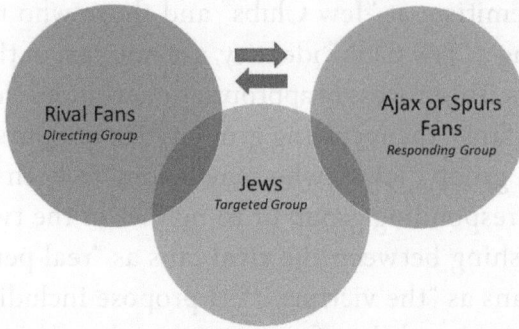

Figure 3.14. Triangular appropriation. Image by author.

Figure 3.15. Linear reappropriation. Image by author.

cases of reappropriation, the targeted group takes back an epithet to neutralize its effect and to "demarcate the group."[225] The triangular case of rival fans, "Jew Club" fans, and Jews, however, includes more than just in-group and out-group considerations. The appropriation is nonlinear: The words *Joden* and *Yid* were appropriated by a large group of fans, for whom the meaning changed. *Joden* and *Yid* became proud terms for their in-groups, consisting of both Jews and non-Jews. The meaning changed, however, and became contested again as criticism arose from (parts of) the targeted group, such as Jewish board members of the respective clubs and from Jewish supporters. The appropriation is nonlinear.

This nonlinear appropriation differs from the common understanding of linguistic reclamation. Usually, the targeted in-group dissociates from a slur's offensiveness, and the appropriation of a term and the dissociation from its offensive meaning occur in the same process. In the case of "Jew Clubs," the dissociation from the term's offensiveness is double: the fans of "Jew

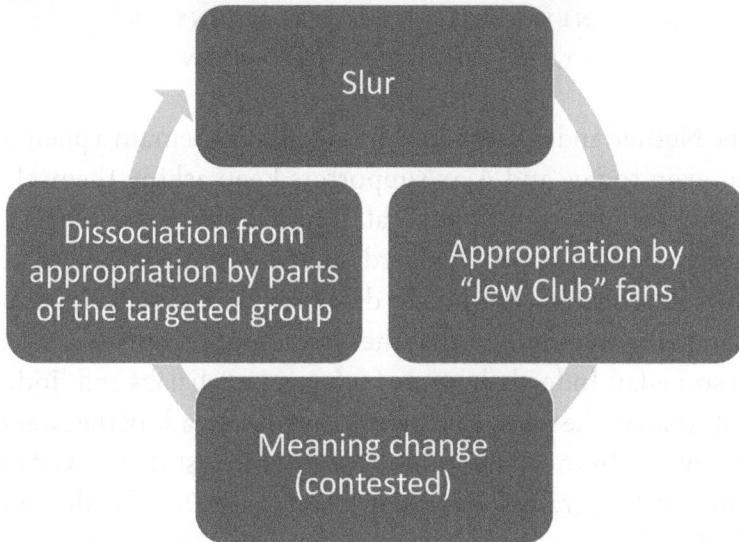

Figure 3.16. Nonlinear appropriation. Image by author.

Clubs" dissociate from the term's antisemitic use by rival fans, and in response, fellow fans, the club or the public dissociate from their use of the term, which they consider to be offensive (see fig. 3.16). The second dissociation from the "Jew Club" fans' appropriation reemphasizes that the terms themselves are understood as slurs, which makes the appropriation nonlinear. In the end, the meaning of the words has shifted for some, while remaining a slur for others. As a result, the appropriation process is stalled, and the term may be perceived as even more insulting than previously.

The value switching thus not only remains partial but is also accompanied by value reinforcement. We see in the next chapter that if Tottenham fans attempted to make the term "Yid" more acceptable, as some claim, it seems that they have failed miserably, given that various organizations and individuals consider it offensive and inappropriate. Indeed, the Y-word is arguably more stigmatized and controversial than ever before.

NEW TAKES, OLD TRADITIONS:
THE "JEW CLUB" TOMORROW

In the Netherlands, "Jew Club" performances remain a phenomenon even today, and Ajax supporters keep asking themselves
"Where do Jews come from?" at almost every game. Their answer remains the same: "Amsterdam, Amsterdam, Amsterdam."
They will probably continue to do so for the foreseeable future,
although it is not unlikely that the "Jew Club" identity will disappear someday. Indeed, there are far fewer Israeli flags and "Joden"
chants than in the 1980s, 1990s, or in the first decade of the twenty-
first century. In 2002, the author David Winner still observed that
"weird football graffiti" depicting the "Star of David with a letter
F [for F-Side]" was "scrawled everywhere."[226] This was no longer
the case when I visited the city twenty years later. Even in 2012,
the Ajax supporter Arjan told van Bemmel that a "few years ago
you could sometimes see a huge flag of Israel in the ArenA. It
covered half of the stand and it was an impressive sight. At that
time there were more songs like 'Jews, Jews,' . . . than now. It is
much less now, but hey, it remains the nickname of Ajax."[227] Ten
years later, Menno Pot told me in an Amsterdam café how, in the
1980s, the "Jew Club" identity was "in every song" and how you
could see "Israeli flags all over the stadium," but this has changed
now: "It is slowly disappearing. All I have to say to the people in
the club who want it to go is 'just be patient.' It will disappear. It
is not important to the new generation anymore."[228]

Ajax fans are less engaged in "Jew Club" performances because
the new generations of supporters are, simply put, serious in another way about their club culture, and less carnivalesque. Since
2001, Ajax Amsterdam has a new ultra-style fan group that is
about absolute support for the club and the city. This group at-
tends every game, no matter whether Ajax plays at home or away,
and no matter whether Ajax loses or wins. The ultras engage in
a "second game" that takes place in the stands, in which they

compete for the better songs, the louder chants, and the more col-
orful flags. Furthermore, ultras groups are often vocal critics of
the commodification of football, police repression, and the deci-
sions of the club's management. In short, the fan culture for ultras
is more serious than for the older, more carnivalesque generations
of fans. Ultras even have designated group members who turn
their back to the field to face the other fans and coordinate their
chants. The earnestness of this fan culture has consequences for
the "Jew Club" performances. The club magazine *Ajax Life* published a portrait of the ultras group VAK 410 to celebrate the
groups' fifteen-year anniversary.[229] This article also clarified the
decline of the "Jew Club" performances: the nickname "Jew" is
still used "here and there," the article states, but the group claims
to have "nothing to do with religion or politics" and "actually, not
much anymore with the nickname that so often causes discussions."[230] Performing the "Jew Club" identity is perhaps too playful for them, perhaps a thing of older generations. What counts
to them is only Ajax and Amsterdam.

The performances have decreased, but the fans' "Jew Club"
identity remains. The author and Ajax fan Menno Pot still has
his Ajax tattoo, which depicts a Star of David together with Ajax's
club symbol.[231] The symbol is a relic from the 1990s, and he had it
tattooed in 1994 to celebrate the club's national title. He still wears
it proudly, although he would not get the same tattoo today. The
tattoos and the chants "here and there" are not the only remnants
of Ajax's "Jew Club" identity. It also continues to live on in the
fans' friendships with supporters of Cracovia (Kraków, Poland),
Maccabi Tel Aviv (Israel), and RSC Anderlecht (Belgium) and
their sympathy for Tottenham Hotspur (England). Interestingly,
all four of these clubs are also known as "Jew Clubs," at least to a
certain degree. Cracovia has a hooligan group called Jude Gang,
and the fans of Cracovia's city rival Wisła paint antisemitic graffiti, which can be seen in many parts of the city.[232] Cracovia's fans
use stylized Stars of David as a symbol of their collective identity,

although they are neither Jewish nor anti-antisemitic or antira-cist.[233] In Belgium, fans of FC Bruges repeatedly show Nazi salutes and engage in antisemitic chants when they refer to their rival RSC Anderlecht. Although the fans of this "Jew Club" do not identify as "Jews" themselves, they are friends with Ajax supporters, per-haps because of regional proximity and because Belgium is known for a small but strong hooligan fan culture, and perhaps also be-cause both clubs are identified as "Jew Clubs" by rival support-ers. When Ajax played against Bruges in the 2003–4 Champions League season, Ajax supporters discussed their friendship with Anderlecht in the fanzine *Dapp're Strijders*.[234] Together with their friends from Anderlecht they would "defend Mokum" against the hooligans from Bruges, whom Ajax fans expected to be joined by their friends from ADO Den Haag, one of Ajax's main rivals next to Feyenoord Rotterdam and FC Utrecht. Supporters of Bruges and ADO both engage in antisemitic chants against their rivals.[235]

Only a few football friendships are shared among all the sup-porters of the clubs involved. The friendships with Cracovia and Anderlecht are, probably, mostly shared among those leaning to-ward hooliganism. The ultras of VAK 410 initiated a friendship with the ultras groups from Maccabi Tel Aviv, thus continuing the Ajax supporters' affection for Israel. The Maccabi ultra-style group the Twelfth Player talks in detail about the group's "brotherhood" with Ajax fans on its website. This "brotherhood," they write, dates back to the summer of 2002 and exists between those who are "sharing the love for Maccabi, Ajax, and of course Israel."[236] Members of both groups have visited each other regularly since then and supported the respective clubs of their friends. Symbols of Maccabi are present in the public spaces around Ajax's sta-dium, thus proudly displaying the friendship between the clubs.

In addition to their affection for Cracovia, Anderlecht, and Tel Aviv, Ajax supporters also developed a sympathy for the London-based Tottenham Hotspur, a club that has, the fans of Ajax are sure, "a lot in common with Ajax."[237] Like Ajax, the fans write, Tottenham has a large following, has won plenty of trophies, plays attractive football, and is known as a "Jew club." Spurs also comes from an area where many Jews used to live, and the team is therefore confronted with antisemitic chants from rival supporters. In London, too, the fans have taken on the name as a kind of nickname.[238] The supporters of the two clubs are, the fans write, also bound by their aversion to Feyenoord, which goes back to the UEFA Cup final in 1974, when Tottenham was defeated 2–0, and the game was accompanied by an outbreak of violence from Tottenham supporters that was unseen and unheard of in the Netherlands and in most parts of Europe.[239] More than two hundred people were injured on May 29, 1974. This caused great admiration for English hooliganism among young Dutch football fans and also "marked the beginning of a hooligan subculture at Feyenoord."[240] The admiration of English hooliganism is also evident whenever England is mentioned in the Ajax fanzines. Occasionally, Ajax's fans have traveled to London to support Tottenham. For instance, seventy Ajax fans supported Tottenham in London against Nottingham Forest in 1998.[241] Their presence at Tottenham's stadium, White Hart Lane, was announced by the stadium speaker and on the scoreboard. One year later, De Ajax Ster published a series of articles entitled "London is the place for me," announcing that there "will probably be more visits to Tottenham."[242] The texts gave advice on modes of travel, accommodation, shopping, and London's different football clubs. Various flags were painted to celebrate the friendship between Ajax and Tottenham, some of them depicting a Star of David, which became known as the Star of Ajax in Amsterdam, and which, in the context of Tottenham, has its own puzzling story that is revealed in the next chapter.

CONCLUSION

Ajax is a "Jew Club" because fans perform this identity in and through chants, banners, tattoos, fanzines, and graffiti. Although the "Jew Club" identity is often displayed with a smile, the fans can be serious about it, and they have written long texts about kosher food or the history of the Star of David in their fanzines, one of which they named after the Star of David: *De Ajax Ster.* The fans have a large repertoire of "Jew Club" performances. Since the 1970s, they have engaged in a variety of chants about "Joden," displayed Israeli flags, or described fellow supporters as "Joden" in everyday interactions. This chapter has examined the reasons for this display, of which there are five.

First, football culture provides a unique opportunity for such displays. The fan culture that emerged in the 1970s has a carnivalesque characteristic. The nicknames supporters give to themselves or to others, such as "krauts" or "Jews," exemplify the playful and spontaneous nature of fan cultures. The performances of Jewishness and antisemitism transform the stadium into a key site for negotiating memory cultures and collective identities.

Second, geographical reasons played a major role in associating the nickname "Joden" with Ajax. Amsterdam has a large Jewish history. There were more Jews in Amsterdam than in other parts of the Netherlands, many of whom lived around Ajax's stadium. Ajax therefore had a large Jewish fan base before the Holocaust and was a "melting pot" where Amsterdam's Jews mingled with non-Jews. Even away fans, who traveled to Ajax's stadium, started to associate Ajax with Jews. Today, the fans celebrate their local rootedness by performing a "Jew Club" identity—an interesting twist given that "Jews" are often imagined to be rootless cosmopolitans. Indeed, this twist also shows that antisemitic stereotypes are malleable.

Third, between the 1950s and early 1970s Ajax Amsterdam had a partly Jewish identity, albeit hidden. From the club's chairmen to the youth teams, key figures were Jews while others embraced Jewish jokes or items like kosher salami. The club's little Jewish enclave in post–World War II Dutch society remained, however, largely hidden from the public—not least out of fear of antisemitism. Furthermore, Ajax did not develop a memory culture, perhaps because the club feared antisemitism or because Ajax reintegrated both Jewish survivors and collaborators.

Fourth, the making of the "Jew Club" Ajax as it is known today appeared in a specific situation. Ajax has been targeted with anti-semitic fan performances since the 1970s. During this time, Ajax had its greatest successes and still had a somewhat hidden Jewish club culture. At this time, Dutch society became increasingly aware of the Holocaust but also flipped its perception of Israel upside down, now viewing it as a strong perpetrator instead of a passive victim. Antisemitism was on the rise and had two new focus points, namely the Holocaust and Israel, as expressed in the chant "Hamas! Hamas! Jews to the gas!" The newly emerging fan cultures—the carnivalesque *zijden* and the violent hooligans—engaged with the changing perception of "Jews." Ajax's support-ers used "Jew" as a strong and local symbol. For Feyenoord sup-porters, "Jew" had a double meaning: it evoked the stereotype of the "weak Jew" and related it to something evil, something to be against. For both sides, the new image of "Jews" appealed to the fan culture's antihegemonic attitude. Ajax's fans provoked this by associating themselves with Israel; meanwhile, Feyenoord's supporters broke the taboo of blatant antisemitism and thus pro-voked the public. Both the rejection of Jewish associations after World War II and the adoption of a "Jew Club" identity—were driven by antisemitism, highlighting the complex relationship between philosemitism and antisemitism within the "Jew" imagi-nary framework.

Fifth, the rivalry between Feyenoord and Ajax is based on what the two clubs stand for. The "Jew Club" Ajax represents cosmopolitanism, high culture, elegance, and antiwork, whereas the volksclub Feyenoord stands for hard work and rootedness. Perhaps because the concept of the "Jew Club" is the central di-vider between the two clubs, the "Jew Club" performances have become what Wagenaar and Verhoeven call a vicious circle, in which the Jewish / non-Jewish binary intensifies the rivalry for both sides and one side accuses the other of being responsible for the continued antisemitism in Dutch football.

I argue that the linguistic appropriation by Ajax's fans differs significantly from existing theories of linguistic reclamation, which typically entail two groups (the directing and the responding group, for example: racists and Blacks) and a linear evolution of a term's meaning, according to which a term is (1) a slur and then (2) reclaimed by the targeted group, which leads to (3) changes to the word's meaning. Potentially, the term (4) may be appropriated again to be used by out-groups after the meaning has changed (for instance, for "gay" or "queer") or not (for instance, for the N-word). This case involves three groups: the directing group (antisemitic fans), the responding group (Ajax or Spurs fans), and the targeted group (Jews). In this scenario, Jews find themselves in the paradoxical situation of being both victim and bystander to their own discrimination. Furthermore, the process of linguistic appropriation is nonlinear because, ultimately, the meaning change is double: "Joden" or "Yid" (in the case of Tottenham) underwent both value switching (from the perspective of "Jew Club" fans) and value reinforcement (from the perspective of Jewish fans of other clubs).

Today, performances of Jewishness are decreasing because the new ultras fan culture plays an increasingly important role among the fans of Ajax. Ultras are less carnivalesque and less playful than former fan generations, and they aim to represent the club (Ajax), its colors (red and white), and the city (Amsterdam) more seriously. Yet performing a "Jew Club" identity remains a crucial aspect of the fans' collective identity, although on a smaller scale than in previous years.

The performances have been contested many times in the club's publications and in newspapers. At the club's general assembly in 2004, the "Jew Club" identity was discussed as a trigger for antisemitic chants that should therefore be discontinued—the idea was even floated that the team should stop playing every time

"Jew Club" performances occur.[243] Michael van Praag, Ajax's Jewish chair from 1989 to 2003, has publicly criticized Ajax's fans, and the club's magazine *Ajax Life* has repeatedly reported on the issue with headlines like "Ajax Is Not a Jewish Club at All."[244] While Ajax has since ignored the fans' performances, rival fans continue to use them as excuses for their antisemitic chanting. As the "Jew Club" performances decreased, politicians publicly demanded an end to them. A VVD politician made, for instance, headlines in December 2022, by claiming that "if we cannot put an end to this, we are not going to win the fight against antisemitism."[245] The discussion of the "Jew Club" as "problem" continues in the next chapter, in which I discuss the case of Tottenham Hotspur, the club whose fans, who call themselves "Yid Army," introduced hooliganism to the Netherlands in 1974 when Feyenoord fans were beaten up by Tottenham supporters and whose club launched a campaign in 2022 to disassociate itself from its "Jew Club" identity.

FOUR

TOTTENHAM HOTSPUR

Problematizing the "Jew Club"

TRAVELING TO AN AWAY GAME by train in late 1970s England was dangerous, as rival fans often lingered at train stations, looking for a fight. It was the era of the hooligans, and the neo-Nazi organization the National Front influenced the growing fan culture. The radical security measures that followed the 1985 Heysel Stadium disaster, during which hundreds of people died, were still in the distant future. During this time, supporters of Tottenham Hotspur found themselves on a train with no windows on one side after Leeds fans had attacked them. Such attacks were not uncommon, nor were the rumors that spread from one cabin to the other before the train's arrival in London. The fans' conversation that day, published as a blog post entitled "Yid. The Man Who Gave Us the Name," was about the "usual subject of who was likely to make up any welcoming committee."[1] Such "welcoming committees" usually consisted of hooligans from any of Spurs' London rivals, West Ham, Arsenal, or Chelsea, who attacked Spurs fans on their arrival in London after away games.

Being a football fan in 1970s England meant being used to fights at train stations. And being used to the monkey chants in stadiums, which were directed at Black players.[2] Spurs, however, stood out as insults against them included the often antisemitic term "Yid." Hitler should, many rival supporters proclaimed, "gas them again," whereby "them" in this case meant the Tottenham supporters, who, according to their rivals, were England's "Jew Club." Spurs fans remember this as tiresome: "While we could defend ourselves in most ways, there wasn't much we could do about the verbal abuse and anti Semitism [sic]. We had no comeback." On the Spurs fans' journey from Leeds to London in 1978, something remarkable happened. A conversation occurred between five friends on the partly windowless train as they were preparing for the physical fights and the verbal abuse they expected upon their arrival in London:

> "Why don't we take their fire from them?"
> "What do you mean?"
> "If we embraced the word 'Yid' then we'd remove their firepower and leave them with nothing."
> "Yeah, OK, but how do we do that?"
> "We become 'the Yids.'"[3]

In a dark backstreet near the central London station King's Cross, they initiated the well-known chorus for the first time: "We are the Yids, we are the Yids, we are, we are, we are the Yids," they chanted, adapting the famous chant "We are the mods," from the contemporary mods subculture.[4] Soon, "the fire had started to spread," and during one of their next away games, "chants of 'Yiddos' rang out from the whole train as it departed the station."[5] The blog post concludes with the author questioning whether one should "apologise for possibly being instrumental in creating the monster that is the Tottenham Yids?" The author's answer is "simply no. I'm proud to be a Yid. I always will be."[6]

By the time the text went online in October 2013, English football had been transformed completely. The English Premier League, founded in 1992, has become the world's most famous football league, attracting billions of viewers worldwide tuning in to watch the best players competing in safe and modern arenas.[7]

The perception of the term *Yid* had also shifted during this time. In 1978, neo-Nazi hooligans and others chanted antisemitic and racist slurs. Today, as the sport has become a gentrified global commodity and hooliganism has faded into obscurity, the term "Yid" has become "the Y-word." As fewer antisemitic incidents against Spurs fans occur, their use of "Yid" has become the focus of antidiscrimination campaigns, comparing it to the N-word or other terms considered to be hate speech. As identity politics, awareness of cultural sensibilities, and fear of rising antisemitism are growing, so is the perception that Spurs' collective identity is anachronistic, offensive, and inappropriate. When the blog explained in 2013 how the term had been appropriated thirty-five years earlier, the author felt the need to address whether Spurs fans should apologize for capturing the term "Yid" from rival fans. Earlier that year, three Tottenham fans had been arrested, indicted, and later released for using the word during a game against West Ham while rival fans reportedly chanted about gas chambers and performed the Hitler salute. The understanding of what is problematic about the Tottenham case has moved on and now also includes the appropriation of the term by Spurs' fans.

Before Spurs' fans developed what I call a Y-identity, they had been targeted with antisemitic slurs by rival supporters wherever they went. This chapter commences with a discussion of the various forms of antisemitism they had—and occasionally still have—to endure. What follows is a brief discussion of the most recent debates and campaigns targeting their Y-identity, such as the club's The WhY Word campaign in 2022. Various stories exist about how and when people began to see Tottenham as a "Jew Club." Based on a thorough investigation of the London-based weekly the *Jewish Chronicle* (*JC*) and other primary sources such as the fascist newspapers *Action* and *Blackshirt*, as well as fanzines, blog posts, and other publications, this chapter continues with a discussion of the five most prevalent origin stories of the club's Y-identity. After a discussion of the term "Yid" in the context of debates around English dictionaries, I then analyze the various meanings of and perspectives on the Y-word, ranging from solidarity and empowerment to hate speech and antisemitism. The chapter concludes with a discussion of the different strategies used by Jewish football fans to gain agency in the debate.

ANTISEMITISM AGAINST TOTTENHAM HOTSPUR

Tottenham's fans have been concerned with antisemitism since the early twentieth century. The club, which has resided in the Tottenham area since its foundation in 1882, was attacked by the British Union of Fascists in the 1930s for having many Jewish fans. Since the 1960s, rival supporters have attacked Tottenham using the term "Yid." Fans of many clubs partake in these insults, but most often they stem from the club's local rivals Chelsea, West Ham, and Arsenal. Despite being a Yiddish term for fellow Jews, the term's antisemitic application in football was so popular that several Jewish Spurs fans were first exposed to the word in the stadium.[8] A common assumption is that this antisemitism comes from hooligans and neo-Nazis, but those who participate in it are much more diverse. By the 1990s, scholars of British football were arguing that the "racist/hooligan couplet" is misleading.[9] They criticized the idea that racism only "counts" when the perpetrators have been identified as "racist hooligans" and claimed that racism is often more subtle than the racism/hooligan couplet leads us to believe.[10] Neither are all fans hooligans nor are all those who participate in such behavior convinced racists. Like racism, antisemitism directed at Tottenham takes on various forms, such as chants, gestures, banners, flags, physical attacks, and online comments.

One form of phonetic antisemitism is hissing noises, during which parts of a stadium crowd collectively create a soundscape that imitates the sound of escaping gas.[11] The chants "Spurs are on their way to Auschwitz / Hitler's going to gas 'em again"[12] and "Never felt more like gassing the Jews / When Arsenal win and Tottenham lose" convey a similar message: Tottenham Hotspur is the "Jew Club" that should be "gassed."[13] As we will see throughout this chapter, many fans claim to distinguish between "Yids" and "Jews," as if the former would, if uttered in the context of football, refer to Spurs fans only and not to Jews. They externalize any antisemitism to "real antisemites" and legitimize their antisemitic performances as "banter" that forms, in their view, a natural part of football rivalries. The word "Jew," however, is used in chants as well:

> Good old Adolf Hitler
> He was a Chelsea fan
> One day he went to White Hart Lane
> And all the Jew Boys ran
> At last he got a few of them
> Up against a wall
> At first he laughed a little bit
> And then he gassed them all
> hahhahahahhaahhhhh, hohhohohohhoohoho, hahhahahh-
>   hahha, etc.[14]

This song expresses an awareness of the Holocaust and the identification of Jews with its victims. It exemplifies how the shift in antisemitism linked to the Holocaust occurred not only in 1970s Netherlands but also in Britain and elsewhere. The line "all the Jew Boys ran" also evokes an antisemitic stereotype of Jewish cowardice—a stereotype particularly attractive to masculine football fan cultures, comparable with the "Joden always ran away" slogan that Feyenoord fans directed at Ajax.[15] Other chants do not refer to Nazism and the Holocaust but may transmit the antisemitic stereotype of Jewish greed, as the Jewish Chelsea fan Daniel Finkelstein recalls: "'He's only a poor little yiddo, He stands at the back of the shelf, He goes to the bar, to get a lager, And only buys one for himself.' In the second verse, there was a line about hitting the yiddo with a brick, too, but I've forgotten how it goes, unfortunately."[16]

At times, fans use visual forms such as T-shirts or badges to express antisemitism. In 2012, unofficial retailers offered badges near Arsenal's stadium with the words "Fuck off yids."[17] In 2016, unofficial retailers sold T-shirts outside of Chelsea's stadium, depicting Tottenham's non-Jewish star striker and England national Harry Kane as a Hasidic Jew with the alleged respective dress and *peyot* and the slogan "He's one of your own," thus marking all Spurs as "Jewish."[18] This antisemitism is often an antisemitism without Jews—and sometimes even without the presence of Tottenham: Chelsea fans, for instance, celebrated one of their players during their game against Leicester City: "Álvaro, oh, Álvaro, oh. He came from Real Madrid, he hates the fucking Yids."[19]

Particularly when Spurs' supporters travel to European games outside of England, where fan cultures are expressed more visually through flags and banners, antisemitic references to the English "Jew Club" can be observed. FK Partizan Belgrade fans displayed a banner imitating the logo of the BBC show *Only Fools and Horses*. The banner declared all Spurs to be "Only Jews and Pussies."[20] It insulted Spurs as both Jewish and unmanly, referring to old antisemitic stereotypes and connections between antisemitism and sexism.[21] During their away game at the Stadio Olimpico in Rome in 2012, Lazio fans "greeted" Spurs' fans with a "Free Palestine" banner, Palestine flags, and "Juden Tottenham!" chants.[22] Using the presence of a non-Israeli and non-Jewish "Jew Club" for a "Free Palestine" demonstration—accompanied by "Juden Tottenham!" chants—seems to be an expression of anti-Israeli antisemitism, in which all Jews are attacked as representatives of the Israeli state. Curiously, the Italian ultras—who have put in some effort to create a far right image[23]—chanted "Juden" in German at the English club, thereby evoking a connection to the German history of antisemitism, Nazism, and the Holocaust and also evoking the stereotype of the "Jew" as victim. While in Rome, traveling Spurs fans were attacked in a pub by fans (most likely of Lazio), who shouted "Juden" and made Hitler salutes.[24] "Jew Clubs" evoke cultural references to the Holocaust, Israel, visual stereotypes, victimization, and gender, among other things.

Antisemitism is not limited to physical spaces such as stadiums, pubs, or public transport—it also extends to virtual spaces. The *Times of Israel* reported in 2021 that a Chelsea fan had been jailed for eight weeks after posting an image of Auschwitz together with the words "Spurs are on their way to Auschwitz" on Twitter.[25] In 2012, the *JC* reported that an Arsenal online fan forum marked users who failed to donate to the site with the Star of David, thus referring to antisemitic stereotypes linking Jews to money and trickery.[26] The act of marking people with the Star of David evokes the *Judenstern*, which Jews were forced to wear during Nazism. The forum administrators declared that they referred to Spurs and not to Jews.[27] This legitimation strategy—"they call themselves Yid, so we can address them as Jews"—points toward the complexities of the debate and signals that antisemitism is often expressed in acts of communication, regardless of someone's intention. Antisemitism is not limited to neo-Nazis. It goes beyond the racist/hooligan couplet and is sometimes "without Jews" and sometimes even "without antisemites." Antisemitic remarks, whether directed against Spurs supporters or Jews, always have an impact on Jews. And they all constantly reproduce Tottenham Hotspur's "Jew Club" image—an image that became the subject of heated debates in the early years of the twenty-first century.

HOW "YID" BECAME "THE Y-WORD" AND HOW TO STOP THE "YID ARMY"

Tottenham Hotspur, along with other institutions and individuals, began to challenge its fans' Y-identity in the early twenty-first century. Discussions arose over whether the fans' performances were anti-antisemitic, whether they triggered antisemitism, or whether the fans might be antisemitic themselves. These debates reflect how football institutions became increasingly aware of their social responsibilities, and they have affected how British society perceives racism and antisemitism. Understanding how and why the word "Yid" became a taboo provides insight into how people and institutions are dealing with antisemitism, and it reflects how Jews and antisemitism are considered in recent political developments, such as identity politics. The Y-word debates are also part of football clubs' transformation from sports clubs into global businesses.

Until the early 1990s, antisemitism, racism, and other discriminatory behavior went largely unchallenged in football.[28] The foundation of the English Premier League in 1992 transformed football into a commercial product with a promise of endless revenue. This change of culture also followed the Hillsborough stadium disaster in 1989, during which more than ninety Liverpool fans died. The causes of Hillsborough were investigated and published in what became known as the Taylor Report, which, although contested, led to drastic measures and profound transformations in English stadium culture, such as the conversion of all standing into seating areas. Fans had lost their most important social space, the standing area, and police control became part of a fan's match day experience.[29] The first initiative to challenge racism in football, Let's Kick Racism Out of Football (later shortened to Kick It Out), was founded in 1993 and initially focused on anti-Black racism. For some time, antisemitism against Spurs' fans and their Y-identity remained "alive and unchecked," as the *Guardian* described it in 2007.[30] Four years earlier, Tottenham Hotspur had conducted a poll on its website (the results of which are no longer available) asking whether "Yid" and "Yiddo" chants should be banned.[31]

During these years, "Yid" slowly became the Y-word. In 2007, representatives of the Tottenham Supporters Trust, Maccabi GB, and Kick It Out debated antisemitism directed at Spurs and their Y-identity. In this context, Simon Johnson, director of corporate affairs of the Football Association (FA), England's football governing body, said, "We have not yet made it as taboo to abuse somebody who is Jewish. . . . People do not understand that it's offensive to call someone an 'effing Yid,' or to hiss: they think it's funny. Our challenge is to make it a taboo—and I accept we've got some catching up to do."[32] After all these years, they were determined to catch up, but it took them another four years to turn "Yid" into the Y-word.

The turning point was Kick It Out's 2011 short film *The Y-Word*, which introduced writing or saying "Y-word" instead of "Yid."[33] A quick search for the Y-word in the *JC*'s online archive indicates that the Y-word (as a new alternative to "Yid") was introduced in 2009 (in a report announcing *The Y-Word* film).[34] It peaked first when the film was released in 2011 and again in 2013–14 after the arrest of three Tottenham supporters (who became known as the "Tottenham Three") for chanting "Yid" and after Tottenham Hotspur released the results of a fan consultation.

The ninety-second campaign film was intended to "raise awareness that the y-word is—and has been for many, many years—a race hate word," one of the producers—the comedian, Chelsea fan, and Jewish identity politics activist David Baddiel—said.[35] The film portrays the Y-word as equally racist as the N-word or the P-word and claims that it was used during the Holocaust as a Nazi word. The word was used by British fascists; it seems, however, unlikely that German Nazis used the term.[36] The film concludes by demanding that its audience think again before using the word. Baddiel later remembered that "for a long time it looked like the film wasn't going to get made," not least because Kick It Out was in doubt.[37] Then, "amazingly, Gary Lineker, an ex-Spurs player, agreed to take part," and the film was produced. The film turned "Yid" into the "Y-word" for four reasons: First, it shifted the debate about antisemitism in football to the word itself. Second, the film un-equivocally marked the word "Yid" as a race-hate word,[38] by comparing it with the taboo N-word and the P-word.[39] Third, it turned equal attention to Spurs' Y-identity and its rivals' antisem-itism by including Lineker in the film and by having Tottenham Hotspur endorse it publicly.[40] The film became as much about Spurs as about the antisemitism of rival fans. Fourth, Kick It Out published comprehensive educational materials aimed at raising awareness of the use of the Y-word, clearly stating that "the term is unacceptable."[41] In short, the debate increasingly shifted to a debate around the word itself.

Furthermore, the film defined antisemitism as racism. In the film, Gary Lineker claims that "Yid" is a racist word for Jews—an idea that was and still is echoed throughout the debate. For the film's coproducer, David Baddiel, the film "was not really about football," but about promoting the idea that the Y-word should perhaps "be considered as equally unmentionable as the hate words for other ethnic minorities."[42] The equation of antisemitism with racism is, however, contested. I understand antisemitism as related to racism yet also as a specific ideology characterized by a certain worldview that includes conspiracy theories about Jewish "world domination." The Y-word debate, however, drifted away from discussions about antisemitism as a certain form of ideology, with structures and specifics manifest in the "Jew" imaginary framework. Instead, the debate focused on power relations, individuals, and certain words, all within the framework of racism. In short, the problem of antisemitism shifted to a certain word that was then discussed only within a simplified framework of racism.

Thirty-three years earlier, in 1978, Spurs fans considered call-ing themselves "Yids" in response to antisemitism a good idea. Eleven years after the short film, many saw the term itself as of-fensive, as a 2022 debate in the UK parliament entitled Antisemi-tism and Other Racism in Football exemplifies. Most speakers agreed that, as one spokesperson said, the term and therefore also "its inclusion in Tottenham chants is . . . offensive in itself."[43] The complex meanings of the term "Yid" and its history as a term for Spurs fans were already abandoned when three Spurs fans were arrested in October 2013 for using the Y-word after a game between Spurs and West Ham, during which the away section engaged in typical chants about Hitler, gas chambers, and Spurs. Those arrested for "racially aggravated order offences," were, however, Spurs fans who had used the Y-word to describe themselves and not the West Ham fans who chanted about Spurs and the Holocaust.[44] They were publicly named as racists, and then the club banned them from its grounds, also withdrawing their memberships and season tickets, before the Crown Prosecution Service finally discontinued the case in 2014.[45] What remained was the notion that the Y-word is somehow illegal, something that *The Y-Word* film had already proclaimed and that the FA had repeated publicly shortly before the "Tottenham Three" were arrested.[46] The statements and arrests were intended to disassociate Tottenham Hotspur from its "Jew Club" identity. Spurs' fans, however, responded in the most curious way: they embraced their Y-identity even more. They sang "We sing what we want" and created the following chant:

> We sang it in France,
> We sang it in Spain,
> We sing in the sun and we sing in the rain,
> They've tried to stop us and look what it did,
> Cos the thing I love most is being a Yid!
> Being a Yid, Being a Yid,
> The thing I love most is being a Yid![47]

Under pressure from the authorities, the "Yid Army" became more closely knit than ever before, and the term "Yid" signified their us-against-the-world mentality that was further emboldened by attacks against Spurs fans during away games in Italy and France, during which the attacking fans also directed antisemitic slurs at them.[48] Shortly after the case against the "Tottenham Three" was discontinued, the club published the results of a 2013 consultation on the Y-word, in which a large majority of fans declared themselves to favor Spurs fans using the term "Yid."[49] The club, however, was always uncomfortable with the fans' Y-identity and concluded that the word needs to be reassessed.

Tottenham Hotspur never used the Y-word in its official merchandise products, although many of its fans embraced their Y-identity. In 2010, the club even banned a whole book from its club store because it referred to the fans' nickname "Yid Army" in a sentence.[50] Most recently, the club launched its campaign The WhY Word—Time to Think about It. After conducting a survey with more than twenty-three thousand supporters (in 2019) and holding "virtual supporter focus groups," the club launched a "hub" on its website in February 2022 presenting the results and expressing the club's position that "it is time to move on from associating this term with our Club."[51] Why now? The club introduces itself as responding to the current political shift in sport cultures toward inclusivity; think, for instance, of the taking-a-knee initiative—which became a regular fixture at game days in the English Premier League—or the renaming of sports teams, a prominent example being the Washington Commanders (formerly "Redskins").[52] Tottenham's statement begins with an appeal to fans: "We are living in times of heightened awareness of cultural appropriation and sensitivities. It is therefore crucial to the values of our Club and our fans that we are even more mindful of the controversial nature of the Y-Word."[53] The club chose its words wisely and appealed to the fans' collective identity. The club states that "the Y-word was initially taken as a positive step to deflect antisemitic abuse," which the fans "have never used . . . with any deliberate attempt to offend" and that "some fans choose to continue to chant the term now . . . to show unity and support for the team, as well as [to] each other as a defence mechanism against antisemitic

abuse that still exists." The club thus responded to earlier attempts to ban the word, which had the opposite effect: they had
reinforced the fans' Y-identity through their chanting "We sing
what we want" and "The thing I love most is being a Yid."

The club's key findings were that (some) fans feel uncomfortable with the word, that those who defended it expressed an openness to stop using the word or using it less "if it caused offence
to fellow fans," that younger fans are supposedly unaware of its
historical context, and, last of all, that "now, more than ever, is the
time to re-assess and re-consider its ongoing use."[54] The club also
suggested some further reading, namely, three articles that all ask
Spurs fans to break off from their Y-identity, thus ignoring a wide
range of differing positions published in dozens of articles on the
issue.[55] One of the articles, written by Spurs fan and former editor
of the *JC* Stephen Pollard, responds directly to the club's campaign and states, like many other articles on the campaign, that
its "results were clear" and that "Spurs fans themselves—Jewish
and non-Jewish alike—opposed its use."[56] Pollard writes that the
club's demand that fans distance themselves from the term "Yid"
was one result of the survey. But neither its design nor its results
were clear, although the club and many commentators presented
them as persuasive.

The survey's design is unknown. In 2013, the club conducted
a first consultation on the Y-word among its fans, commissioned
by a research consultancy, and, although no longer available,
made a methodology statement and detailed data available for
download. In 2022, the club published only the results, making no reference to any research consultancy, methodology, or
data. I have tried to get my hands on the questionnaire through
various means. I wrote to the club, supporter organizations,
and individual fans. No one had the survey, but its outcomes
were uncritically accepted as objective evidence by numerous
newspapers and fans alike.[57] One exception is David Newman,
a professor in Beer Sheva, Israel, who also happens to be a Jewish

Tottenham fan. He claims that the survey "was constructed poorly. Not only was it far too long, repetitive and tedious but it used every possible means of rhetoric and repetition ... to try and convince the respondent that the term was negative and should not be used."[58] Newman complained that it "included a number of quotes from prominent journalists and football fans who had previously written on the topic, but selectively used quotes which portrayed the term 'Tottenham Yids' in a negative way," thus "ignoring the equally many articles" that argue the opposite. Newman concludes that the survey "was out to engineer a result." The club's intention must remain speculative, not least because it does not answer questions and directs those interested in its campaign to its website.[59] It seems plausible, however, that the club had an idea of what it wanted to accomplish when it initiated the survey.

Shortly after the club published The WhY Word, the fan organization Tottenham Hotspur Supporters' Trust (THST) issued a statement, arguing that "Spurs fans singing the word in a footballing context isn't antisemitic" and that they "want to see action against the unambiguous antisemitism directed at us."[60] Their attempt to clearly define whether their Y-identity is antisemitic or not is typical of a common trend in public discussions about antisemitism, usually reducing the issue of antisemitism to a yes-no question, leaving no room for ambiguity or one's own involvement in antisemitic performances or the "Jew" imaginary framework. THST externalizes all antisemitism to rival supporters and claims that "any decision must come from the fans." THST, however, announced it would raise the topic in its annual End of Season Survey, conducted among its members.[61] It concluded that "opinion is clearly evenly divided among Jewish fans and non-Jewish fans, making it extremely challenging for the Trust to take a representative position. We will continue to argue for dialogue, understanding and sensitivity around this subject, while continuing to refute accusations of anti-Semitism against our fans." The issue remains contested, and the fans seem to be divided on the subject.

The club changed its strategy in 2022 and made it clear it would not ban the word, an act that had led to an increase in "Jew Club" performances in 2013. Instead, the club launched a campaign to raise awareness of hate speech and cultural appropriation amid increased warnings about rising antisemitism, and a shifting understanding of sports as being a political space after the taking-a-knee initiative, and criticism of World Cup tournaments being hosted by Russia (2018) and Qatar (2022). The club's campaign reacted to the changing cultural norms around Spurs fans' Y-identity, but how did the club become associated with Jews to begin with?

WHEN SPURS BECAME "YIDS": TALES FROM WHITE HART LANE

The "Jew Club" identity has been reproduced by several groups, individuals, and institutions. One of these institutions is the *JC*, one of the oldest continuously published Jewish newspapers in the world, which also produced hundreds of articles on Tottenham Hotspur.[62] The *JC* not only "played a fundamental role in shaping Anglo-Jewish identity" but also helped create Tottenham's Y-identity.[63] Spurs' "Jew Club" image thus derives not only from antisemitic attacks but also from British Jews and Jewish Tottenham fans. Articles claiming that Tottenham is "a team close to the heart of many Jews" are no surprise for the *JC*'s readers, as one could read in May 2019 in the lead-up to the Champions League, in which Spurs faced another English team, FC Liverpool, that was not featured similarly. The *JC*'s interest was particularly in Tottenham, and the article portrayed how "some notable Spurs fans [were] feeling" about the game.[64] They included Lord Mendelsohn, who talked about "the club's century-old close connection to the Jewish community," which, according to him, "has been about more than just its geographic proximity to the Jewish population of the East End"; rather, it has been about the club's "solidarity with the Jewish community" expressed through their "adoption of the identity as the Yid Army."[65] The JC contributed continuously to Tottenham's "Jew Club" identity. In the club's early years, articles still referred to Tottenham in passing and did not mention the club's Jewish connection (except for the 1935 friendly game between England and Germany, played at White Hart Lane). But the tone changed in the 1970s, when the JC was concerned about the club's relationship to Jewish holidays. The JC cherished Spurs' first Happy New Year (Rosh Hashanah) announcement, published in the club's game day program in 1973.[66] Although the club published Rosh Hashanah announcements in the JC,[67] Jewish holidays in the context of Tottenham remained contested: In 1981, the JC complained about Spurs playing a game on Rosh Hashanah.[68] Two years later, the newspaper grumbled because Tottenham "once again" had "to play a match on Yom Kippur."[69] Only in the 1980s did the club—finally, many Jews thought—refuse to play on Yom Kippur and thus stood up for its Jewish fans, who wanted to attend the holiday without missing a Spurs game or vice versa.

From the 1980s onward, any reader of the JC interested in football not only learned about Tottenham's relationship to Jewish holidays but also read frequent reports about the growing anti-semitism in and around English stadiums: for instance, in 1987, when Arsenal fans "jeered at the 'Tottenham Yids,'" Arsenal's Vice Chair David Dein, "a member of Hendon Reform Synagogue," as the JC noted, was upset that a previous warning to the club's fans had "not succeeded in stamping out the trouble."[70] Discrimination and violence slowly began to decrease when stadiums became all-seater and an unprecedented wave of gentrification hit football in England after the foundation of the Premier League in 1992, causing the tone to shift again. Headlines like "Soccer Hate Campaign"[71] (1980) vanished, and titles like "Tottenham Chutzpah"[72] (1991) appeared. The *JC*'s attitude was less worrisome. The bleak 1980s had passed, and football increasingly provided a space for joy and humor during leisure time. In 1996, the *JC*'s front page announced proudly that Tottenham "has been confirmed as the most popular football club among British Jews"[73] and promised unreleased findings from a recent national survey on British Jewry. The article claims that 42 percent of Jewish football fans in London support Tottenham, compared to just 26 percent who are cheering for Arsenal. It provides various details, for instance about the "unexpectedly high" 10 percent who are rooting for Millwall, which, according to the report, has to do with the club's mascot resembling the Lion of Judah.[74] Furthermore, "the survey stumbled across the case of a non-Jewish Spurs fan," who, as a "member of the Spurs fan club—popularly known as the Yids," had later become "so taken with Judaism that he decided to convert." He declared, "Once I was a Yiddo . . . Now I'm a Yid."

Although the article, published over Purim, was clearly full of irony and wit, some readers took it seriously, and a short reaction piece appeared one week later in the *JC* in which one of the article's coauthors explains that as it is Purim, he "as a Spurs fan . . . just couldn't resist a little spiel."[75] The text "was specifically aimed at Arsenal supporters," whom he "placed a poor second" in his list of clubs with the most Jewish followers, but particularly the Millwall and Chelsea supporters who had "failed to see the joke even when told that it was a joke and based on no accurate research whatsoever!" The author thus suggests that, perhaps, London's Jews are competing over whose club is "the most Jewish." (If there was any such competition, it would probably be over by now, with Spurs being the clear winner as London's "Jew Club.")[76]

Tottenham was not the only English club known for a large Jewish following. Arsenal, for instance, had "always embraced" the club's good connection to its many Jewish fans.[77] Leeds

United was similarly "known for many years as a Jewish club."[78] Numerous people gave countless reasons for how, why, and when Tottenham became the "Jew Club" it is today.[79] There is, I suppose, not one single answer to this question. Instead, I argue, Tottenham became the "Jew Club" precisely because more tales have evolved around Tottenham's Jewishness than, for instance, around Arsenal or Leeds. Furthermore, the fact that the club itself rejected—and still rejects—this image makes the "Jew Club" identity even more appealing to Spurs' fans. The making of the "Jew Club" Tottenham thus results from no single moment or story. The various origin stories all come down to one of five tales about when Spurs became the "Yids." These five tales from White Hart Lane focus on different sources: first, the Jews involved in the club, such as fans, players, and chairs; second, the Jewish area around the stadium; third, a national friendly game played between England and Nazi Germany at the Tottenham stadium in 1935; fourth, the television series *Till Death Us Do Part*; and fifth, the hooligan fan culture of the late 1960s to the 1980s.

Tale 1. Jewish Tottenham: Associating Spurs with Their Jewish Fans, Players, and Chairs

Each text on Spurs' Y-identity highlights, in one way or another, that "Tottenham's 'Jewish identity' has been perpetuated by the club historically having Jewish players, coaches, and especially owners/directors" as well as its Jewish supporter base.[80] Some even suggest that Spurs has "more Jewish fans than other English clubs."[81] Although numbers are hardly reliable when it comes to fans, some venture to suggest that between 5 percent and 10 percent of Spurs supporters are Jewish.[82] In addition to its fans, the club also had a couple of Jewish players (although hardly more than other clubs) and back-to-back Jewish chairmen since 1982, which, however, does not explain why Tottenham is known as the "Jew Club" because this image existed before the club had a Jewish chair.[83] The club's Jewish chairs were Irving Alan Scholar

(1982–91), who shared this position for a brief period with the Jew Paul Bobroff, Alan Sugar (1991–2001), and Daniel Philip Levy (since 2001).[84] Jewish players and Jewish chairs existed at other clubs as well; neither the presence of Jewish players nor chairmen alone can sufficiently explain why Tottenham Hotspur became England's "Jew Club." Perhaps even more important than the chairmen and players' identities were the club's Jewish fans.

Jewish football fans became attracted to Spurs during the interwar period for three reasons: First, the club's stadium, White Hart Lane, provided ease of access, as many Jews moved close to the stadium in the interwar period, and it was better connected to public transport than other stadiums.[85] Second, Tottenham was among the most famous and successful clubs in London.[86] Third, football attracted "second generation young men"—the increase in Jewish supporters also "reflected changes in social patterns," as for them, Saturday became a day of leisure and not (only) a day of religious obedience.[87] All three reasons are mentioned in a 1996 letter by Monty Curwen to the *JC*, which was published two weeks after the newspaper had jokingly declared that Spurs are "in the lead" among Jewish football fans in London.[88] When Curwen was a boy in the 1920s, he writes, "almost all those in the community who followed the game were Spurs supporters." At the time, he "sincerely believed that this was God's chosen Football Club," and this belief was "confirmed when Spurs won the FA Cup in 1921."[89] To Curwen, however, it was not so much because of "glory hunting"[90] but rather because games "took place on Saturday afternoons" that Jews became attracted to football.[91] It was "possible to be in synagogue until the end of *musaf* [a prayer recited on Shabbat and major Jewish holidays] to nip home for a quick plate of *lokshen* soup, and then to board a tram from Aldgate to White Hart Lane." While Curwen's letter demands nuance regarding the "glory hunting" factor, it confirms that Saturday became a day for leisure activities.[92] Furthermore, Curwen's letter suggests that accessibility was a crucial factor that favored Tottenham because "no other ground could offer such ease of access."[93] For Curwen, Spurs became attractive because the club's stadium was accessible, Spurs was successful, and the kickoff time on Saturday afternoons allowed him to observe the Sabbath and attend the football game.

Although Tottenham clearly had a Jewish component in the first half of the twentieth century, it took until the 1960s for Tottenham to become the "Yids." Brian Glanville, often called one of the greatest sports writers of all time, claims in a 1991 article in the *JC* that the "talk of Spurs as 'Tottenham Yids' was initially a disparaging reference to the Jewish hangers-on."[94] The connection between Spurs and hangers-on is documented in Hunter Davies's classic book *The Glory Game*, first published in 1972, which devotes a whole chapter to them.[95] Hangers-on are, we learn from Davies, "the ones in the expensive leather coats who look as if they've just had their hair done. They have money to burn and their ambition in life is to burn it on the players."[96] Initially, Glanville explains, "there was One-Armed Lew and there was Johnny the Stick"—both Jewish.[97] Lew's business, for instance, was tickets. "Johnny, Lew and a host of other hangers-on could be met on match days in the Spurs car park, a great, grey area which served as a kind of rendezvous. All this to say that Spurs in those days were noted for their Jewish hangers-on, which led the fans of other London clubs to call them 'Tottenham Yids.'"[98] What changed in the 1960s was that the club Tottenham Hotspur became associated with these figures, whom people met outside the stadium: the people known as hangers-on, who happened to be Jews.[99]

Two "hangers-on" (who, it seems, both felt offended by the term) are the most famous. Morris "Superfan" Keston—who features prominently in Davies's book and who was among the only fans with an autobiography (called *Superfan*)—is described in an obituary on the club's website as the club's "most ardent supporter" who, like so many other Jews (the club's website does not mention that he was Jewish), "started following Spurs in the 1940s when he regularly traveled by bus from the East End to

White Hart Lane."[100] Davies describes him as "a great fund-raiser" who "helped many charities," most often those connected to sports.[101] Keston soon became a famous superfan associated with Spurs: "Everywhere I go, people say 'There's Morris Keston of Spurs.'"[102] Keston was famous for having seen Tottenham live more than three thousand times and for being closer to the players than any other fan. In 1967, Keston celebrated Spurs' FA Cup win with a massive party at the Hilton hotel, and according to Davies, the players left the club's official celebration and attended Keston's party instead.[103] The management, Davies claims, never forgave Keston. Allegedly, there was also an anti-Jewish element that kept Keston out of the club's board of directors (he had offers from other clubs, which he declined). Keston is quoted by author Anthony Clavane, who claimed that the Tottenham board was a "closed shop" in the 1960s and 1970s. When Keston bought shares in the club, Tottenham refused to register him: "People used to say to me: 'They don't like you because you're Jewish.' They didn't want any outsiders."[104]

In addition to Keston, there was another Jew who was central to 1960s Spurs fan culture, named Aubrey Morris.[105] He was a passionate Spurs fan at a time when Spurs played in European Cups during their most successful period, and—ahead of live broadcasts and mass travel—people wanted to go and see Tottenham play. Morris, who used to be a taxi driver after helping his father with his bagel business, began organizing trips to away games. The first trip was to Sunderland in 1961. Only two years later, 2,500 people traveled with him to Rotterdam to see Spurs play in the Cup Winners' Cup final. Morris, and thus a Jew, was at the center of the emerging Spurs fan culture. It is likely that he was not the only one, as he got friends and family involved in his work with Spurs supporters. Jews like the hangers-on, Keston, and Morris became linked to Spurs as a club and White Hart Lane as a space even before the chairmen and players did. They were known and visible and became connected to what people meant when talking about Spurs.

Tale 2. The Jewish Area: Associating Spurs with Jewish London

As the club became linked to Jews, so did North London. Emma Poulton claims that Spurs' relationship with the "Jewish faith" and antisemitism "originates from Tottenham traditionally attracting Jewish fans due to its geographical location in north London, with near-by Hasidic communities who settled there in the 1930s/1940s after they fled persecution in Europe."[106] Although the areas close to White Hart Lane are partly Jewish, very few Hasidic Jews, if any, attend Spurs games. Despite Spurs becoming popular among "anglicized" Jews from the area, Jews also came from other parts of the capital, even before the 1930s and 1940s.[107] Tottenham's proximity to Hasidic communities, and thus to Jews who are easily recognizable as such, exemplifies the connection of Spurs' "Jew Club" identity to space. The connection between the stadium and Jewish space makes Tottenham unique in England, and it may attract banter and discrimination from rival fans. European football fans identify with the local identities of their clubs, and they construct their collective local identities in opposition to the local identities of their rivals. For Spurs, this often meant opposition to a space perceived as "Jewish."

Whoever travels North toward White Hart Lane from central London will pass through one of the largest Hasidic communities in the world. Away fans frequently encounter Jews on their way to White Hart Lane when passing through Stamford Hill, which is home to Europe's largest ultra-Orthodox Jewish community, with about twenty thousand Haredim and over fifty synagogues.[108] John Efron notes in his discussion of "Yiddo culture" that North London "is home to the majority of London's Jewish population of approximately two hundred thousand."[109] Linking the perception of Jews as Other to space is not new. The historian

Hannah Ewence's work shows how the "figure of the alien Jew" has been part of the British imagination since the nineteenth century.[110] In London, this figure was long tied to the East End, where many Jewish immigrants used to live.[111] In the East End, the family of Spurs fan Aubrey Morris had a bakery shop, and Morris Keston ran a business for women's clothing.[112] That most Jews left the East End in the first half of the twentieth century is usually understood as the result of upward mobility. Ewence shows, however, that many Jews also left the East End because it had become a cultural code for antisemites.[113] The figure of the alien Jew and the East End had become intertwined. While the East End as a supposedly Jewish space lives on in collective memories, the connection between space and the alien Jew has moved: The alien Jew of the past stays in the East End; the alien Jew of the present, however, has found a new home in the "Jew Club" Tottenham Hotspur.

Tale 3. England versus Germany: When the
Swastika Flew above White Hart Lane

White Hart Lane embodies the connection between Spurs and Jews. Some even describe the stadium as "a second home to many north London Jewish fans."[114] Public memory connects the stadium to the hangers-on, the fans' Y-identity, local Jewish life, and an event that took place almost a hundred years ago but that is well remembered, even in the present: It was here that England's national team played an international friendly game against Nazi Germany in December 1935 in front of seventy-five thousand spectators, about ten thousand of whom had traveled from Germany to represent a country that would host the Olympic Games and that had just enacted the Nuremberg Race Laws. At this time, a sense that Jews favored Spurs had already taken shape, and the game's location was discussed as an affront to Jews, many of whom protested the game alongside trade unions, communists, and others.[115]

England discussed the game's implications publicly once it was announced in October 1935. The football and political authorities, however, "failed to perceive both the symbolic and actual power" it represented.[116] White Hart Lane was not selected deliberately—"it was simply Spurs' turn," as England games were played at changing league grounds.[117] In contrast to the British sport and political authorities, the location mattered for London's Jews, and many of them considered it problematic that the game took place at White Hart Lane, a stadium that represented acceptance and belonging to Spurs' many Jewish supporters. Discussions arose, and the Board of Jewish Deputies even feared that "a potential Jewish presence outside the Spurs stadium" would serve the Nazi propaganda; the JC warned that any disturbance would only "bring discredit on the Jews."[118] Briefly after the game was announced, around fifty protest letters were sent to Spurs by Jewish individuals and Jewish organizations, which Spurs forwarded to the FA, which had organized the game.[119] Nonetheless, readers of the JC were concerned; "Will They Play at the 'Spurs'?," one letter to the editor was headed. In it, the author complained about the "strange irony of faith" that the game was scheduled at Tottenham, although it would be "common knowledge" that this club had "a bigger Jewish following" than any other team.[120] The author claimed that Spurs' directors should approach the FA "with a view to transferring the match to a ground where Jews do not usually congregate if, indeed, the match must take place at all." While the game was an important propaganda tool for the Germans before the Olympic Games, the English authorities did not care much about it. Local Jews, however, were alarmed and protested Nazism before, during, and after the game.

Antisemites also took notice of the game. Newspapers received numerous letters arguing against any protests whatsoever, and some letters were blatantly antisemitic. One letter, written by "one of the oldest season ticket holders of the Spurs," responded to the publicly discussed idea that "6,000 Jews would walk out of the ground" during a Spurs game to protest the planned national friendly.[121] The author declared himself to be "in every way with them that they should walk out" although "with a one way ticket and not come back." The author was not alone in dreaming of a Spurs stadium "cleansed" of Jews. Sport was also a prominent topic in the main publications of the British Union of Fascists (BUF), *The Blackshirt* and *Action*.[122] Shortly after the game took place, *The Blackshirt* claimed that Jews had conspired to try to prevent the game from happening.[123] A few months later, *Action* took up this notion in an article titled "Sport and Race." The author understood the "trouble" around the national friendly as the "logical sequel to the permeation of the sport of Nordic peoples by races foreign to them."[124] According to this author, the blame lay in "an increasing number of Jewish spectators [who] have 'attached' themselves to this well-known club." The author, a self-declared Spurs fan "since the day [he] was able to understand football," claimed that "'Spurs' ground would become a far, far better place" without Jews.[125] These articles suggest that British fascists experienced the national friendly as supportive of their cause. Furthermore, with their repeated discussions about the connection between Jews and Spurs, fascist newspapers contributed to the idea that Tottenham was a "Jew Club" from an antisemitic perspective.[126]

On game day, ten thousand Germans arrived in the morning in London.[127] Although the police were present in strong force, protests occurred around the stadium: dozens of protesters presented large signs that read, "Stop The Nazi Match." Thousands of leaflets were distributed, and demonstrators marched from different tube stations toward the stadium.[128] The area was filled with posters reading, "Fascist Sport Is Jew Baiting"; "Our Goal, Peace: Hitler's Goal, War"; "Hitler Hits Below the Belt"; and "Keep Sport Clean, Fight Fascism."[129] Inside the stadium, the German players performed the Nazi salute before kickoff and the swastika flag was waving above the ground. Whether it was "midway through the second half,"[130] or "during the half time break,"[131] the 1935 game is unforgettable to many Spurs supporters because it was one of them, a Spurs fan, who climbed on the stadium roof and tore down the Nazi flag, although the flag was soon back in its original place and the fan arrested.[132] The incident went unreported by most contemporary newspapers, such as the JC, which reported instead about "the foreign Jews who had acted as guides to the visiting party."[133] Nonetheless, this act of resistance is now "an important element of memory shared by the fans."[134] The game is important today for the "Jew Club" notion because it imagines Spurs' club identity as opposed to Nazism.

Tale 4. Till Death Us Do Part: *How a Television Series Popularized Associating Spurs with "Yids"*

The superfan Keston, travel agent Morris, and a couple of hangers-on shaped the "Jew Club" image of Tottenham Hotspur, but were they enough to perpetuate it in the public consciousness? Perhaps, but the idea was also amplified by popular cultural products, such as the sitcom *Till Death Us Do Part*, which aired on BBC1 from 1965 to 1975. Allegedly, it was the show's resentful antihero, Alf Garnett, who popularized the term when ranting about those Tottenham "Yids" while wearing a scarf of Spurs' local rival West Ham.[135] For Efron, "this is the likely origin of the association of Tottenham as Yids."[136] According to Spurs fan and author Alan Fisher, some "blamed Alf Garnett for popularising the term," but, Fisher suspects, the scene could have derived "from actor Warren Mitchell, who would have heard it regularly when he came to the Lane as a fervent Tottenham fan."[137]

One may think that actor Warren Mitchell was not particularly welcomed at White Hart Lane, as the character Alf Garnett had supposedly triggered the antisemitic banter that haunted Spurs for years to come, but he was beloved by both the club and its fans. After his death in 2015, the club declared it was "saddened" by Warren's passing, and users of the fan forum Spurs Community unanimously praised him.[138] One user wrote: "Yiddo Yiddo Yiddo Yiddo! RIP," thus using the term "Yiddo" to express Warren's belonging to the Spurs collective. Warren was, in fact, a Spurs fan and a Jew, and some Spurs fanzines even speculated that Warren, who allegedly attended every home game, "used to be the recipient of two free tickets for putting on the Alf Garnett routine in the VIP lounge before games."[139]

Tale 5. Fan Culture and Hooliganism from the 1960s to the 1980s

The television series *Till Death Us Do Part* displayed an East End family, and its often-racist main character Alf Garnett parodied the post–World War II cliché of the East End being England's "power base for fascism and racism"[140]—a public image the area, which in the past was associated with Jews, shared with its local club West Ham United, of which Garnett wore a fan scarf while ranting about the Tottenham "Yids." The series was one catalyst for associating Tottenham with a "Jew Club" identity, while the developing fan cultures on the English terraces was a second catalyst. In the 1960s, West Ham United, like other clubs, increasingly attracted younger fans who gathered at a particular area in the stadium and created a new fan culture by converting popular music tunes into fan chants,[141] and some of them also sought out physical fights with rival fans.[142] It was in the context of this playful yet violent and often racist fan culture, accompanied by significantly greater media attention, that Spurs' "Jew Club" image became a constant and popular part of English football.

As in the Netherlands, the long 1970s in the UK were the backdrop to increasing antisemitism against Spurs, and their response was to name themselves "Yid Army." Increased Holocaust awareness, new forms of antisemitism, emerging subcultures, and carnivalesque and hooligan fan cultures coincided with the economic crisis and the later financialization of both the sport and the nation; England's deindustrialization in the early 1970s was accompanied by football's "declining attractiveness, violence, poor finance and lack of investment."[143] As in other nations, the UK's answer, and that of its football clubs, was financialization: the transformation to privatization and a free market economy. English hooliganism peaked in this climate, and racism in football became a public concern as far right groups such as the National Front influenced the hooligan subculture.[144]

Every football fan from this period has a theory about when the antisemitic chants directed at Spurs started. Some recall "standing at White Hart Lane in the 1970s and 80s while rival supporters especially from London Clubs chanted anti-Semitic songs."[145] Lord John Mann, Leeds United fan and adviser on antisemitism to the government, says that they really took off in 1981 when Manchester City played Tottenham in the FA Cup final at Wembley Stadium in London.[146] Manchester City fans, Mann remembers, changed the lyrics of the Spurs hymn "Spurs are on their way to Wembley," composed for the 1981 FA Cup final, to "Spurs are on their way to Auschwitz." There was hardly anything similar before that game, Mann claims, saying, "It needed a tune."[147] Others claim the antisemitic chants really became prevalent from around 1974–75 onward.[148] While the exact date remains unknown, the "Jew Club" association was articulated in the 1960s and 1970s with the invention of a new fan folklore.

Antisemitic abuse against Spurs became commonplace from the 1970s onward.[149] In the 1980s, the *JC* reported on several incidents. In April 1985, the *JC* wrote that Chelsea warned its supporters to refuse entrance to the stadium if wearing a T-shirt with the slogan "Chelsea Yidbusters coming soon to rid the world."[150] A seventeen-year-old Chelsea fan who had been fined one hundred pounds for wearing the T-shirt, explained that these T-shirts were "as common as Chelsea shirts" and were supposedly "flooding the market around the ground." Whether this was a strategy to downplay his action and avoid punishment or not, the excuse indicates that widespread antisemitism was perceived as a reasonable excuse for young fans in the 1980s. Another article in the

JC detailed Arsenal's Jewish supporters who expressed disgust about Spurs fans waving Israeli flags.[151] One Arsenal fan stated that he did not want to see the flag "abused by non-Jews who don't understand what it represents," and Arsenal's managing director said, "I am distressed that this wasn't reported to us on Sunday, when we could have stopped this offensive behaviour." Furthermore, Chelsea informed its fans before playing against Spurs in 1988 that the police will not hesitate to arrest those who utter "racial chants of any kinds."[152] Additionally, Chelsea forbade Tottenham fans from flying flags with the word "Yid" or a Star of David. As early as in the 1980s, Chelsea was thus concerned with Chelsea fans' antisemitism and the Spurs fans' Y-identity. Today, Chelsea FC has become a role model for anti-antisemitism in football since the club launched its No to Antisemitism campaign in January 2018, with workshops, exhibitions, events, statements, murals, and more.[153] Watford FC, Arsenal FC, and Chelsea FC even launched Jewish fan clubs, aimed at bringing fans together; Chelsea FC announced that the creation of its Jewish fan club was "to celebrate Jewish culture and identity, and [it aimed to] work closely with the club on initiatives and campaigns to help ensure Chelsea FC is a welcoming and inclusive environment for everyone."[154]

These five tales collectively contributed to the formation of Tottenham Hotspur's "Jew Club" identity, which does not stem from a single origin story. This identity is rooted in the presence of Jewish people in and around the club, the intersection of local spaces with football and Jewish life, and the memory of the 1935 game. Additionally, pop-cultural influences, such as the TV show *Till Death Us Do Part*, and the rise of emerging fan cultures played a significant role in shaping the association of Spurs and "Jews." Having explored how Spurs came to be identified as Britain's "Jew Club," I now turn to examine how Tottenham fans embraced this identity, focusing on the "Yid Army" and its expressions of Y-identity.

Y-IDENTITY

Fans express their Y-identity through flags, banners, scarves, and chants (see figs. 4.1 and 4.2). The episode discussed at the beginning of this chapter suggests that Spurs fans developed their Y-identity in 1978. Even if no second source confirms this, the story seems plausible. Those commenting under the blog entry agree with the author, and others who discussed the origin of Y-identity point more or less to the same period. One fan, interviewed by Efron, claims that if he "had to put a date" on the Y-identity's origin, it would be April 3, 1976, when Spurs fans, who had just "taken" Arsenal's fan section (the North Bank), had to endure "Yiddos, Yiddos" chants. In response, they began cheering "Yiddos took the North Bank."[155] Others told Efron that the chanting of Yiddos did not get going in large numbers until 1980–81.[156] Whatever happened exactly, Spurs fans appropriated a term that had been thrown at them for years, and it soon became the core of their collective identity. As Cloake and Fisher remember, "Supporters wore skullcaps to games. The Israeli flag flew from the terraces. The Star of David was incorporated into home-made banners or the decorated white butchers' coats that were popular at the time."[157] When I went to see this for myself in 2022, I did not see any kippot, Israeli flags, or the Star of David inside the stadium. I did, however, buy a couple of pins displaying the term "Yid" from an unofficial seller near the stadium. And I heard the term hundreds of times in and outside the stadium. Witnessing Spurs' Y-identity firsthand was both fascinating and educational. Here is an account of my visit to White Hart Lane on August 6, 2022, where Tottenham Hotspur played against Southampton FC (see fig. 4.3):

> Up North to White Hart Lane, I take the 149 bus. From my window, I spot Hasidim walking hastily through the streets. I get out of the bus at Seven Sisters station. I encounter an uplifted and increasingly gentrified area largely inhabited by migrants, most

Figure 4.1. A flag displaying the Star of David and Tottenham's club symbol. Courtesy Jewish Museum Vienna (Photo: Tobias de St. Julien).

Figure 4.2. A "Yid Army" scarf. Courtesy Jewish Museum Vienna (Photo: Tobias de St. Julien).

Figure 4.3. White Hart Lane. Photo by author.

of whom will not attend the game. Spurs' fans of today come almost exclusively from other areas of town, and like me, they walk from the bus and tube stations toward the arena. Individuals become one large crowd, and I begin hearing the chant I had expected: "Yid Army!" Somewhere in the crowd, I hear the chant. A first time, then a second and a third. Somewhere to the right, now behind and in front of me. It sounds like a battle cry. It is a ritual that says, "Here we are" and "Today we become one Tottenham Hotspur family." The eleven players on the field are supposed to be one unit; so are the fans, who are often described as "the twelfth player." To become the twelfth player, they need to be one unit, one "Yid Army." The chants help them to accomplish this.

The Jewish symbols have disappeared, but the battle cry remains. In the stadium, I try to count how often they chant "Yid Army" and "Yiddo," but I soon give up. It is countless and in every section of the stadium. The club does not react. The fans celebrate every corner kick with a "Yid Army" clap, clap, "Yid Army" clap, clap, chant. The whole stadium joins in. I am sitting next to a boy, perhaps thirteen years old, who came with his father. Both join in regularly. Like most others do. The father sometimes chants it to his son endearingly. Spurs fans pass their Y-identity from one generation to the next. I wonder how the term's meaning changes over time. The fans celebrate each of the four goals with the chant "Yiddo Yiddo." It seems as if the chant takes on a different meaning in the stadium context. During the game's ninety minutes, winning or losing is all that matters. All that counts is the support of the team. The history, the problem, the debate—all must wait outside. Tottenham wins.[158]

The fans call themselves "Yids," "Yiddos," and "Yid Army." But what does it mean? An in-group uses specific terms to express intimacy, and these terms mark the boundary with out-groups. The "Yid Army" exists only here and only to support Tottenham Hotspur. It is a term of belonging, and during the chants, individual bodies merge into one large mass of fans.[159] The mass makes its way to White Hart Lane, "Yid Army" expresses that they have arrived and are ready to support their team and defend their club colors.[160] The term, as Bogna Wilczyńska notes, "bonds supporters from different backgrounds together."[161] In this sense, Spurs fans are no different from fans of other clubs, as Gerald Jacobs comments in the *JC*: "the 'Yids' are no different to the Arsenal 'Gooners' or Man U 'Reds.' All three labels are worn with pride, not shame."[162] Many Spurs fans argue that context is key in determining whether the word "Yid" is antisemitic or not. "When used by Spurs fans," one fan argues, "the term 'Yid' is a sign of respect saying 'you're one of us.'" To this fan, it does not matter that most fans are not Jewish, "because the word is not being used literally."[163] Instead, the fans see the word "Yid" as a symbolic performance of their collective identity. But why is it, then, that the word became so contested?

"Yid"—What's in a Word?

At the center of the performances and debates is one term: "Yid." As a performative term for Spurs fans, the word was a response to antisemitism and has become a symbol meant to unify them as one "Yid Army." Yet the fans and the public are utterly divided over its meaning and whether it should be used at all. In 2020, the Y-word made global headlines when the *Oxford English Dictionary* (*OED*) changed its entry on "Yid" and "Yiddo," now stating that "in extended use," the words also describe "a supporter of or player for Tottenham Hotspur Football Club (traditionally associated with the Jewish community in north and east London). Originally and frequently derogatory and offensive, though later also often as a self-designation."[164] Within days, a website mentioned the new entry,[165] and the BBC, the *Guardian*, the *Times of Israel*, ESPN, and Hawaiʻi Public Radio, among many others, reported that the *OED* entry now included Spurs fans. Most of them also incorporated a statement by Spurs: "As a club, we have never accommodated the use of the Y word on any club channels or in club stores and have always been clear that our fans (both Jewish and gentile) have never used the term with any intent to cause offense."[166] Jewish Chelsea fan David Baddiel also joined in the debate. He criticized the new entry, stating that it "will weirdly give succour to . . . the sense that Tottenham fans, rather than Jews, 'own' this race-hate word for Jews."[167] The *OED* itself justified its entry: "We reflect, rather than dictate, how language is used which means we include words which may be considered sensitive and derogatory. These are always labelled as such."[168] To explain the word's offensiveness, Baddiel refers to an experience he had in 2008 at Stamford Bridge together with his brother, Ivor: "On this particular afternoon, the chanting of the word 'Yiddo' was joined by one particular fan about ten rows behind us deciding to shout, repeatedly, 'Fuck the fucking Yids! Fuck the fucking Yids!' And then, just to make clear that, by Yids, he didn't just mean 'Spurs fans,' that became 'Fuck the fucking Jews! Fuck the fucking Jews!' . . . By the time this happened, we had sat well, stood and then sat—listening to this stuff at Stamford Bridge for thirty years."[169] In this case, the words "Yids" and "Jews" are both used as slurs associated with Chelsea's hated rival club Tottenham. The prerequisite for insulting Spurs in this way is that

Jews are seen as a despicable other—as the "alien Jew." The words are experienced as hurtful; they function as a "psychic blow."[170] According to a Spurs supporter quoted on the club's website, the Y-word can be painful: "I'm Jewish and I feel strongly that the word is a pejorative word. My parents were both refugees from Germany and Austria in the Second World War and came to England. They would have felt very strongly at description of it as simply *Jude* which if my parents were alive, possibly the most offensive term they could ever hear."[171]

This fan's expression illustrates how specific words may evoke transgenerational trauma.[172] Cynthia M. Baker, author of the 2017 book *Jew*, highlights how even the question "Jew?" can function as a "psychic blow." Franz Kafka expresses this, for instance, in a 1920 letter in which he reflects on the question "jste žid?" ("Are you a Jew?"): "Don't you see how the fist is pulled back in the word *jste*, so as to gain muscle power? And then the word *žid* the happy blow, flying unerringly forward?"[173] Spurs fans do not call themselves "Jews" but "Yids." Although the terms are related—they are sometimes used synonymously and almost all dictionaries translate "Yid" to "Jew"—more nuance is required. In contrast to the Spurs fan who perceives both "Jude" and "Yid" as equally hurtful, another fan stated that they have no problem with the word "Yid":

> I'm Jewish; I'm quite observant. I pray every day, and I've got no problem using the word. In fact, I actually use the word when I study. I study in Yiddish and the rabbis that I study with will regularly be using the word either in short or in full, the Yidden, and this is what we are, and I have no problem because I understand the idea about the context. I have been called dirty Jew; I have not been called dirty Y*d, except outside White Hart Lane by opposing fans. So, in the end, it's down to the context.[174]

A distinction is made between *Yid* as a Yiddish term for the individual self during prayer and *Yid* as an English term for a social Other, used as an epithet by rival fans. *Yid* in Yiddish has a different meaning to *Yid* in English, where, as Leo Rosten writes in

The Joys of Yinglish, "Yid" is "an offensive, demeaning, disagreeable way of referring to a Jew" when pronounced "to rhyme with 'kid,' instead of YEED, to rhyme with 'deed.'"[175] Baker notes that the comparison is between the "Jew as self ('Yeed') versus Jew as other ('Yid')."[176] In Yiddish, the word is not only used in a religious service but also as a common way to address adult males. The question "Vos macht a Yid?" (How is a Yid?), Efron notes, is "considered warmer and more intimate than the mere use of the person's name to ask after their well-being."[177] Baker argues that "*Der yid*, as a polite or intimate term of address, is a peculiarity of Yiddish linguistic culture."[178] Meanwhile, the term *Jew*, in contrast, "can never function this way."[179] In sum, the meanings differ between *Jew* and the English or Yiddish *Yid*, but they are connected by the "Jew" imaginary framework.

The debates over "Yid" in football seem to be a fairly new phenomenon, but the word *Jew* has, in fact, a similarly contested recent history and present. Historically, Jews have avoided the term for centuries. The word *Jew* features far less in the Hebrew Bible (Old Testament) than in the New Testament, where it is a Christian term for an Other "against which the Christian *self* was and is constituted."[180] Jews have, Baker writes, neither "owned the word Jew" nor used it often during "the past two thousand years"—in contrast to the Yiddish term *Yid*, which Jews actually used as a term for "the Self."[181] Jews strategically exchanged the word *Jew* for terms like *Yid* and *Hebrew*. The appropriation of the word *Jew* by Jews is a historically recent phenomenon and the result of a century-long process.[182] Today, *Jew* functions simultaneously as a slur word and a term for the Self. David Baddiel, for instance, now proudly describes himself on his X (Twitter) bio with one single word: "Jew." He remarked, "Only I have made being Jewish part of my public identity."[183] The shift to Jewish identity politics is also the result of a long historical process.

Many critics of the Y-word imply that *Jew* is more neutral than the English word *Yid*, often ignoring how contested the term *Jew* still is. Baker's book *Jew* asks significant questions that are also at stake in the Y-word debates: "Who decides what the word *Jew* means and connotes? Who gets to 'own' it?"[184] Robert Burchfield, editor of the *OED* for thirty years, recalls that the dictionary's description of the term *Jew* became a "public controversy" in the early 1970s, when criticism arose that the "definitions of Jew were 'abusive and insulting and reflected a deplorable attitude towards Jewry.'"[185] Dictionaries have been perceived as authoritative, and their entries tend to be used as "definitions" and not merely as "explanations." Minority groups have fought against discrimination by challenging dictionary entries for at least a century. In the 1920s, the *JC* noted that the explanation of Jews as "unscrupulous usurer or bargainer" was unbearable. Consequently, the respective dictionaries altered their entries, describing such perceptions of Jews as discriminating.[186] At the same time, protest movements in the United States demanded that dictionaries capitalize the initial letter of the word *Negro* and abandon the word *nigger*.[187] Lexicographers stated that if an initial capital for *Negro* became widely used, they would incorporate it in dictionaries.[188] Attempts to alter dictionary entries intend to change how these words are used and defined. Today, it is hard to imagine a dictionary that does not describe the N-word as offensive. Dictionaries do not merely describe how a word is used, as Burchfield believes, but also influence a word's meaning. To contest a dictionary entry is to take part in a struggle about hegemony, power, and meaning making. For minorities, dictionaries consequently offer a possibility for political action and agency. Baddiel and others challenged the *OED* for defining *Yid* as a Spurs fan or player, perhaps not so much because it is, in fact, one meaning of the word, but because, in their view, the word should not be used to describe Spurs fans. Their critique was also a means to amplify Jewish perspectives amid the fans' linguistic appropriation (see chap. 3), which encompasses the directing group (rival fans), the receiving group (Ajax or Spurs fans), and the targeted group (Jews), who may belong to both the directing and the responding group or none of the two. The vicious circle between two fan collectives subject Jews to a third position that is paradoxically not only one of being victimized but also of being forced to be a bystander of their own discrimination. Perspectives on the Y-identity thus differ depending on the perspective holder's position within the triangular framework of linguistic appropriation.

PARTIAL SOLIDARITY: THE INCLUSION
AND EXCLUSION OF THE "YID ARMY"

Fans hold diverse perspectives on the appropriation of the term *Yid*. Although any categorization of the eclectic positions on the topic risks generalization, I suggest the following general overview of perspectives:

1. *Jewish Spurs fans who favor the term* Yid
    Various Jewish Spurs fans experienced the appropriation as a form of solidarity and empowerment. For some of them, the term has a double meaning.[189] For them, a Y-identity entails "a beautiful collision" of their identities as Spurs fans and as Jews.[190] Jewish Ajax supporters have described similar emotions. Others explain how these chants make them feel "comfortable" and "welcomed."[191] They are not willing to stop chanting "Yid," they claim, because of other clubs' inability to control their racist fans.[192]

2. *Jewish Spurs fans who are against the Y-word*
    Other Jewish Spurs fans experience the Y-word as offensive.[193] Some argue that the term is anachronistic and no longer anti-antisemitic. Others who used to defend the word changed their mind because "our use of the Y Word gave license to their [rival clubs' fans] antisemites to use it."[194] Similarly, calls to discontinue the "Jew Club" as fan performance have also been raised by Jewish representatives of Ajax Amsterdam.

3. *Jewish Spurs fans who do not mind*
   Many Jewish Spurs fans state that they do not chant "Yid,"
   although they do not mind if others do—often with a certain
   undertone of pride.

4. *Jews who are not Spurs fans and who are against the Y-word*
   Some, like the Jewish Chelsea fans David and Ivor Baddiel,
   take a strong position that the word is always inappropriate and
   that Spurs fans should not be using it. In 2019, the World Jewish
   Congress and the Board of Deputies of British Jews issued a
   statement declaring that "there is no grey area" and its "use by
   fans in the stands, either as a self-designated nickname or as a
   slogan against rivals must not be tolerated in any way."[195]

5. *Jews who are not Spurs fans and are in favor of the Y-identity*
   When Tottenham played against RB Leipzig in the Champions League in 2020, Ayala Goldmann wrote in the German
   newspaper *Jüdische Allgemeine* that she would, although
   disinterested in football, cheer for Spurs particularly because
   of their Y-identity.[196] In 1989, Arsenal fan Paul Levene wrote
   a letter to the *JC* demanding that "credit should be given
   to Tottenham Hotspur supporters for helping to defuse
   antisemitism on the terraces" instead of criticizing them "for
   supposedly provoking it."[197] For ten years, he explained, "I
   have had to endure the offensive chanting from my fellow
   fans," until "Tottenham fans turned the jibe around by calling
   themselves 'Yiddos.'" After this, Arsenal fans would "rarely
   use the antisemitic chant."

6. *Non-Jews against the Y-word*
   Non-Jewish fans supporting Spurs who agree that the word
   is offensive declared their willingness to discontinue using it.
   Some declared they would do so because Jews feel offended
   by it or because they perceive it as triggering antisemitism by
   rival fans.

7. *Non-Jews in favor of* Yid
   Emma Poulton argues that Tottenham fans either use the
   term with "positive intent" or because the word is, for them,
   "simply synonymous with Tottenham."[198] Besides intent,
   those in favor of the word frequently also refer to context
   as a key factor. The Tottenham Hotspur Supporters' Trust
   (THST), which represents Jewish and non-Jewish Spurs fans,

argues that "the word in a football context is not an expression of hatred against Jewish people."[199] Instead, many Jews "found this positive assertion of identity empowering and emboldening" and the word has become a "badge of honour and a source of fierce pride." Any attempt to portray Spurs fans' use of the word as antisemitic is part of the problem, THST claims.

Some perceive Spurs fans' appropriation of the term *Yid* as a form of solidarity, while others criticize it as offensive. Despite the deep divide on how to interpret the contested performances, almost all commentators agree that its use is always antisemitic when it occurs outside the context of football. In total, 88 percent of those who responded to the club's WhY Word campaign survey said that "they do not use the word outside of a footballing context, more than half reasoned it was inappropriate (66%)."[200] A Jewish Spurs fan claims, according to one of the focus group excerpts, that "everyone agrees" the term is "offensive" outside the stadium, "maybe unless it's just among Jews."[201] Another (non-Jewish) fan states that the "implication of children using the Y-word is huge" and wonders what would happen if a child used the word in the park or at school.[202] Indeed, it appears to me that the vast majority of those involved in the debate agreed that the term can, if at all, be used only inside the stadium or as a term for Self by Jews.[203] What kind of image do Tottenham fans have of Jews? And how do they behave toward Jews outside the stadium?

Spurs fans are not free of stereotypes about Jews. They chant "Yids" with Jews, but they also evoke stereotypical imagery when declaring themselves to be the "Yid Army." Wilczyńska argues that gentile Spurs fans associate real Jews primarily with the "figure of a traditional religious Jew."[204] Indeed, Spurs fans have used such images on various occasions; some even came to the stadium dressed as "rabbis" or wearing *payots* [sidelocks], while others greeted Orthodox Jews near the stadium.[205] Addressing Orthodox Jews in the streets as "one of them" is a continuation of a praxis used by Spurs' fans in the stadium. Whenever they are impressed by a particular player, they devote a chant to him that crowns him a "Yid." In the most curious play with identities, they even praised their beloved German striker Jürgen Klinsmann with the following chant:

> Chim chiminee, chim chiminee
> Chim Chim churoo
> Jürgen was a German
> But now he's a Jew![206]

Klinsmann, a former world-class striker, played for Tottenham in the 1990s.[207] Klinsmann's episode at Tottenham is well-known because the English public was highly critical of Klinsmann's behavior. He was known as a "diver," as he would fall to the ground to trick the referee into calling a foul. That Jürgen was a German may have contributed to the skepticism. However, he became immediately loved for ironically diving to the ground after his first goal, which he scored during his debut for Spurs. "Klinsmannia was born."[208] Spurs fanzines called him "the sublime Aryan," "everybody's favourite German," "the blond bomber," or "the person who has done more for Germany than the combined Allied forces."[209] Whole magazines were published about him, greeting readers in German with "Guten Tag."[210] The fans' carnivalesque playfulness was not only directed at Orthodox Jews in the streets of Tottenham, but also toward Klinsmann, whom the fans declared a "Jew."[211] They chose *Jew* instead of *Yid* perhaps because it fits the song's rhyme scheme. Additionally, the choice of words makes the play with identities even more explicit. It suggests that a German, who has established himself by playing successfully, is not part of the Germans, understood as a perpetrator collective, but rather part of the "Yid Army."[212] Other songs, however, suggest that their choosing the label "Jew" instead of "Yid" was neither an exception nor (only) due to rhyme, rhythm, and flow: Spurs' fans similarly incorporated the French superstar David Ginola in a chant, calling him "our French Jew":

Plays down the wing (Plays down the wing)
Crosses it over (ahhh, ahhh, ahhh)
His name's Ginola (ahhh, ahhh)
He's our French Jew[213]

In contrast to other fan collectives, Spurs fans celebrate these labels rather than attack them. In the stadium, Spurs fans praise Jürgen Klinsmann and David Ginola. Outside, they celebrate Orthodox Jews. In this triangular and nonlinear process of linguistic appropriation, the fans' Y-identity allows for a playful engagement with collective identities that, within the limits of football culture and the "Jew" imaginary framework, can flip binaries and norms between Jews and non-Jews. In general, "visibly orthodox Jews" are "far more likely" to experience antisemitism.[214] When Orthodox Jews are addressed by non-Jews in the streets, this is often antisemitic, aggressive, and intended as a "psychic blow." In the case of Spurs fans, however, the message is more philosemitic than antisemitic: "Hey, Jew/Yid, you are one of us!" instead of "Hey, Jew, [insert slur here]." These elusive moments seem to flip what is normative. Instead of marking Jews as Other, they are addressed as fellow "Yids."

This "friendly" addressing of Orthodox Jews, however, is still based on the notion that Jews are different. Whether fans are addressing players as "Jews" on the pitch or as actual Jews in the streets, the relationship between fans and real or imagined Jews is not mutual. In these cases, it is the Tottenham fans who decide whether, when, and how to address someone using these labels and when and how to perform the "Jew Club" identity. As mostly non-Jewish "Yids," they have a certain power that actual Jews do not have. By playacting a "Jew Club" identity, they cement the order of Jew / non-Jew binary so deeply engrained in the hierarchical concept of Jewish difference[215] and the stereotypes embedded in the "Jew" imaginary framework. Solidarity regarding the "Jew Club" performances remains partial and within the boundaries of Jewish difference and the "Jew" imaginary framework.

"If One Is Attacked as a Jew, One Must Defend
Oneself as a Jew": Agency and the Y-Word

Hannah Arendt demanded that "if one is attacked as a Jew, one must defend oneself as a Jew."[216] Defending oneself as a Jew, however, is complicated if one is not directly attacked as a Jew, for instance, because antisemitic football chants are directed at Spurs. Consequently, Jews may find themselves subjected to the position of observers witnessing their own discrimination. For Jewish football fans, who are either subordinated to or excluded from the responding group, depending on whom they support, gaining agency in this situation is particularly complex. Some practice agency by chanting "Yid Army," while others acquire agency by opposing the Y-word from an explicitly Jewish position. Both are anti-antisemitic strategies. They share an understanding of antisemitism as a problem that demands a (Jewish) response, and they both aim to make Jews "count."

Several Jewish Spurs fans explain how the Y-identity empowers them. Jewish Spurs fan Alan Fisher describes most clearly how powerfully he experienced the appropriation of *Yid* in the late 1970s: "Jews have a long history of exclusion, except here, it became a powerful form of inclusion. Going home and away in the seventies, often on my own, this truly meant something. Spurs fans did not join in the abuse. This is fundamental to my formative experience as Spurs fan and of the Y word. I was there, I felt it, and if it looked ridiculous to see gentiles wearing a kippah and prayer shawl, or carrying an Israeli flag, it was part of the celebratory carnival culture of being a Spurs fan."[217] To Jewish Spurs fans like Fisher, Spurs became a space like no other in society. These fans faced exclusion throughout their lives, "except here." In football, the response to antisemitism was collective, visible, and loud and thus experienced as "powerful." Shaul Behr's article "I'm a Jewish Football Fan and I Have Never Been Prouder to Support Spurs" makes a similar argument.[218] Published just one day after the club launched its WhY Word campaign, the Israel-based Orthodox rabbi Behr describes how he was initially "a little alarmed" by the "Yid Army" chants but that, after learning about the historical background, he changed his position: "These fans were actually expressing a kind of love and solidarity with me and my people. Tens of thousands of non-Jews, all effectively telling me, 'We've got your back, mate. We're all Jews here.' In that moment, I have never felt prouder to be a Spurs supporter. So, I am not in the least offended by the 'Yid Army' chants. On the contrary—I love them." Behr responds directly to calls for discontinuing their use of "Yid." For him, it is "not the word that's offensive," as Jews have been using the term "for centuries." Preventing Spurs fans from using the term will not make antisemitism "go away" just as wearing "baseball caps rather than yarmulkes" would not. Instead, Jews would "feel less supported." Fisher and Behr both suggest that, from their perspective as Jewish Spurs fans, the solidarity they experience when Spurs fans shout "Yid" is incomparably empowering.

Spurs games allow for anti-antisemitic agency. The Jewish American author Izzy Wasserstein writes: "In the Yid Army, I found a direct refutation of the ugliest aspects of humanity. Tottenham's support had reclaimed the word and made it their own. And that's what Yid means to me, whenever I hear or see it in the context of Spurs. It isn't just a name, and it certainly isn't hate speech. It's a show of unity and solidarity."[219] As another fan explains: "I feel empowered to be amongst non-Jews at Spurs and to sing the songs."[220] No other social spaces exist where thousands of people loudly proclaim that they are proud Yids. Likewise, however, there are few spaces where antisemitism is as public and blatant as it is at Spurs games. Antisemitism after the Holocaust is often veiled, latent, and expressed in coded language.[221] Here, in the stadium, antisemitic chants are openly expressed in front of a large audience. Usually, antisemitism is hard to confront because it is coded. Rare are the places where direct collective responses to antisemitism are possible. Chanting "Yid Army" back at the antisemitic slurs of rival fans is a meaningful collective experience that is impossible in most other social spaces.

The Y-identity performances are experienced as strong moments of solidarity, fellowship, and empowerment by many Jewish Spurs fans. The Israeli professor David Newman describes how he engages publicly with his network of fellow Jewish supporters, expressing holiday greetings or holding a Maariv minyan at the stadium so that someone could say the Mourner's Kaddish (a prayer recited in honor of deceased loved ones).[222] The Y-identity creates a public space without a need to hide one's kippah.[223] Fans even wear kippot with the symbol of Tottenham Hotspur on it—thereby connecting their Jewish identity with their fan identity (see fig. 4.4). Newman declares, "We are proud Tottenham Yids."[224] He argues that antisemitism should be "combatted wherever it is to be found" instead of making Spurs fans "feel guilty." Alan Fisher argues similarly that the Y-identity's inclusiveness is "acknowledged but too readily dismissed."[225] For these fans, the Y-identity is not offensive, but empowering. The feeling of opposition to other clubs can collide with a sense of opposition to antisemitism. The identification of Jewish Spurs fans with their collective club identity can be a double one.

The "Jew Club" narrative can be experienced by Jews as inclusive and empowering, while also intensifying the opposition on both sides and reinforcing football as a masculine space. John Efron quotes a Spurs fan who describes a scene that occurred during an away game: "There is only a thin wire fence separating us from the City supporters and a large group of them are singing the 'We've got foreskins, we've got foreskins, you ain't' song. Nothing nasty, just some mild abuse. Large group of well-known Jewish Spurs supporters comes along, drop their trousers en masse and then wave their circumcised members at the City supporters. Supporters on both sides of the fence collapse into

Figure 4.4. Tottenham kippah. Courtesy Jewish Museum Vienna (Photo: Tobias de St. Julien).

laughter—the City fans even applaud."[226] This episode from a game in the 1980s vividly exemplifies how the appropriation of "Yid" can create a space that allows for agency and empowerment. This space is, however, created by Spurs fans for Spurs fans and thus excludes numerous Jewish football fans—all those who do not support Spurs, to be precise. The appropriation results in the inclusion and exclusion of Jewish football fans, and the solidarity with Jews thus remains partial. The empowerment is, likewise, a partial empowerment. Gaining agency in the debate is thus particularly challenging and complex for Jews. Likewise, this episode strengthens football culture's masculine grammar: it relies on mutual recognition between the two fan collectives and the reciprocal perception as competitive, masculine, and physically strong—in other words, as "real" fans. "Jew Club" performances thus can be simultaneously inclusive toward masculine Jewish Spurs fans and exclusive toward nonmasculine non-Jewish fans.

Younger Jewish Spurs fans seem to feel more comfortable with Y-identity than older fans. Generations of British Jews were socialized in families whose strategy was "radical assimilation."[227] Some of them felt uncomfortable shouting "Yids" loudly in the stadium. For instance, there are those who state they "do not mind" but who do not participate in the chants. Others experienced proud self-identification as "Yids" as a "liberating act of great license," which, as Efron argues, marked "a significant shift away from traditional Anglo-Jewish reticence about public proclamations about one's Jewish identity."[228] In the 1950s, the Jewish Spurs player Micky Dulin recalls, no one at Spurs knew he was Jewish: "They thought I was Turkish or Greek. You could be all things to all people. I was dark-skinned. With Jews, we don't go out of our way to broadcast. We keep quiet."[229] Players and fans—like most Jews who attempted to assimilate—used to hide their Jewish identity. It has, as Baddiel writes in *Jews Don't Count*, "never been cool" to be Jewish in the UK, where "some shame" is connected to a person's Jewish identity.[230] Philip Spencer, Spurs fan and professor of Holocaust studies, explains: "When you grew up in North-West London in the 1950s, an Anglo-Jewry being . . . relieved to be here; what you were taught really is not to be open about it. Not hide it, but certainly not draw attention to it."[231] Spencer's first reaction to hearing Spurs fans chanting "Yid Army" was that these chants were antisemitic. Then his niece explained the context: "No, Uncle, they are Spurs fans." Spencer's second reaction was: "We do not want this because it draws attention to us." His niece responded, "No, no, it is not like this anymore." This episode between Philip Spencer and his niece suggests that the Y-identity is experienced differently by older and younger Jewish Spurs fans. Philip Spencer has come to appreciate the Y-identity, but many Jews, particularly those of an older generation, felt and still feel uncomfortable with the chants, not least because they draw attention to Jews and Judaism.

The empowerment experienced by some Jewish Spurs fans evokes collective memories. Jewish Spurs fan and human rights lawyer Daniel Merriman had intended to travel to Germany for some time to explore his "roots," a family history connected to Nazi persecution, but "the far right surge there had put me off," Merriman writes.[232] When Spurs played a Champions League game in Leipzig in 2021, Merriman finally used the game as an opportunity and, together with his mother, went on a packed itinerary of six stops in five days. Then, in Leipzig's stadium, "after visiting various sites where the family had suffered" from Nazi terror, his mother "joined in with screams of 'Yid Army.'" She did so from "the top of her lungs" and "with a zeal in her eyes [he] had never seen before. There was a bit more to it this time." The Y-identity chants, performed on German soil by fans of an English team, were particularly meaningful on this day. For Merriman and his mother, the "Yid Army" was connected to Jewish suffering in Germany but also to strength, pride, and survival, as the English army had beaten Nazi Germany in World War II— and many Jews had fought with them. The empowerment some Jewish Spurs fans experience in these chants may have supported his decision to go on this difficult journey. Merriman's trip and encounter at the Spurs game exemplifies how, as Fisher notes, the experiences of those who feel empowered are "significant rather than trivial" for any discussion of the Y-word.[233] Personal accounts like that of Merriman, who was reluctant to travel to Saxony until Spurs played there, show how empowering the club's Y-identity can be for its Jewish fans.[234]

Collective memories are central for collective identities. In the case of Spurs, Jewish fans not only link the Y-identity to histories of persecution in Germany, like Merriman, but also, and more often, to resistance and solidarity. The Battle of Cable Street, during which protesters prevented the British Union of Fascists (BUF) and its leader Oswald Mosley from marching through London's

East End, is frequently cited. In October 1936, between two thousand and five thousand fascists came dressed in their black shirts to the East End but were expected by counterdemonstrators, the estimates range between one hundred thousand and three hundred thousand of them. Barricades were built on Cable Street and the police, given the massive protests, directed the fascists out of the East End. The Battle of Cable Street has come to embody Jewish and non-Jewish resistance to fascism, and it is a key event in Jewish and antifascist collective memories in Britain. In 2011, when "Yid" became the "Y-word," London commemorated the seventy-fifth anniversary of the Battle of Cable Street. It became an important focus point for public memory in the context of rising far right populist parties and antisemitism allegations against the Labour politician Jeremy Corbyn, who referred to the Battle of Cable Street to show he is not antisemitic: "My mother stood in Cable Street alongside the Jewish people and the Irish people."[235] In the context of Spurs, people refer to the Battle of Cable Street in two ways: as a moment of agency, solidarity, and empowerment or as a moment of antisemitism that shows how "Yid" is a race-hate word.

The East End memories serve as a celebration of resistance and, likewise, refer to the hurtfulness transmitted in the word "Yid." People refer to the Battle of Cable Street to defend and criticize Spurs fans' Y-identity. A Jewish Spurs fan states that he "particularly love[s] it that non-Jewish people celebrate us being the Y*d Army," because it takes him back "to when the dockers stood shoulder to shoulder with the Jews of the East End in the 1930s facing the fascists of Mosley, it evokes that kind of spirit for me."[236] Furthermore, the Battle of Cable Street is also linked to important Spurs fans like travel agent Aubrey Morris, who "fought Mosley's fascist blackshirts on Cable Street."[237] Some thus feel that the empowerment they experience when Spurs fans chant "Yid" is similar to that of the memory of the Battle of Cable Street.

Others refer to the East End to highlight the Y-word's offensiveness: A Jewish fan states, for instance, that his "grandmother was at Cable Street" when the fascists chanted "get the f**cking Y*ds" and that he does not want Spurs fans "to use a racist term."[238] Another Jewish fan claims that his father "was fighting in those streets against Mosley," and that he understands and respects the history, but that he wants to leave the "anachronistic" term behind.[239] Newspapers also refer to the BUF's use of the Y-word to explain why it is problematic. *The Athletic* explains, for instance: "For those unaware, Y*d is a racial slur aimed at the Jewish community—one that was used by the fascist Oswald Mosley and his disciples, and daubed on the walls of London's East End in the 1930s."[240] *The Athletic*, Baddiel, and others repeatedly refer to the East End and Mosley to prove their point that "Yid" is a race-hate word.[241] The memories that the Y-word evokes for them are not those of solidarity and counterdemonstrators but of fascism and exclusion. For them, the Y-word does not signify a defense against antisemitism but an attack against Jews. As a result, defending oneself as a Jew means attacking the Y-word.

CONCLUSION

No "Jew Club" identity is debated as much as Tottenham Hotspur's. Spurs fans have proudly branded themselves as "Yids" in reaction to antisemitic taunts by rival supporters since 1978. At the time, people saw the egregious antisemitic chanting against Tottenham as a main problem. After the gentrification of football and the transformation of British fan culture in the 1990s, the debate increasingly focused on Spurs fans' Y-identity. The campaign film *The Y-Word*, released in 2011, shifted the focus to the word "Yid" itself and framed the problem of antisemitism within the vocabulary of racism. In 2011, "Yid" became the Y-word.

Spurs fans' Y-identity, however, intensified after three fans were arrested in 2013 for using the word "Yid" when supporting their team. The club Tottenham Hotspur, in contrast to its fans, never used "Yid" in any of its products and never endorsed the fans' Y-identity. When football clubs became global businesses in the late twentieth century, they attempted to disassociate the sport from hooliganism and discrimination. In the case of Tottenham Hotspur, this meant abandoning the "Yid Army": in 2022, the club began a campaign urging Spurs fans to leave the term behind.

The making of the "Jew Club" Tottenham Hotspur does not have a single genesis but is rather constantly reproduced in five stories. Combined, these stories explain why Tottenham in particular is known as Britain's "Jew Club." The first tale is about people—it is about the club's Jewish fans, players, and the officials who contributed to Tottenham's "Jew Club" identity. The second tale concerns space, as Spurs became identified with Jews due to the club's proximity to Hasidic neighborhoods. The third tale is about a single game, the 1935 friendly between England and Nazi Germany, which took place at White Hart Lane. The fourth story developed around the well-known TV show *Till Death Us Do Part* (1965–75), in which the main character Alf Garnett rants about "Tottenham Yids," thus bringing the link between Spurs and "Yids" to a broad audience. The fifth tale is about the vocal fan cultures that adapted popular music melodies. While they frequently supported their own clubs, they also chanted about gas chambers and "Yids" whenever Tottenham played. Together, these five tales all contributed to the making of the "Jew Club" Tottenham Hotspur.

Furthermore, this chapter poses the question: What's in a word? "Yid" is a different word than "Jew." *Jew* is used as both a term for the Other and a term for the Self, although its use for the Self is a rather recent phenomenon. The meaning of "Yid" differs based on context. In Yiddish, Jews view it as a polite address for other Jews. Yet the same term is an epithet in English. The 2020 discussion over the *OED* article for "Yid," which claims that the term can also refer to a Tottenham player or supporter, exemplifies the importance of dictionaries in discussions about antisemitism and minority subjectivity.

I make the case that this linguistic appropriation is a form of partial solidarity. While many Jewish Spurs fans experience a Y-identity as empowering, Jewish fans of rival clubs find themselves excluded from the "Yid Army." Despite being exclusive, Spurs fans' Y-identity allows for anti-antisemitic performances; in the specific context of football fan cultures, Spurs fans' performances turn the normative relationship between Jews and non-Jews on its head. This play with collective identities provides a liminal space of agency and empowerment. This "Jew Club" space allows for direct collective action against antisemitism, for instance by chanting back when antisemitic songs occur in the stadium. In essence, the "Jew Club" as problem points to the dual potential of philosemitic expressions: on the one hand, philosemitism perpetuates images of the "alien Jew" and excludes certain Jewish perspectives. On the other hand, philosemitism provides an opportunity for empathy, empowerment, and (Jewish) agency, albeit within the limits of the "Jew" imaginary framework.

CONCLUSION

THIS BOOK SET OUT TO understand the "Jew Club" conundrum. While memory culture is often associated with institutionalized rituals and state memorials, this study of football
culture demonstrates how societal groups are coping with the
still unmastered consequences of the Holocaust. This study can
lead to a more thorough understanding of football cultures, of
the link between memory cultures and collective identities, and
the spaces that Jews (as Self) and "Jews" (as Other) occupy in
contemporary European societies. This book argues that *working
through* the past is still an ongoing process, while *working off* the
Nazi past remains impossible. In summary, the analysis of "Jew
Clubs" shows how the consequences of the Holocaust affect the
present in conscious and unconscious ways.

At least since the 1970s, European football clubs have become
a significant cultural space for identity collectives to engage with
memory cultures and the "Jew" imaginary framework, with ideas
and representations of "Jews," and with underlying, linked components of antisemitism and philosemitism. This study appears
to be the first to examine the "Jew Club" phenomenon from a
transnational perspective. I have examined four different ways
of acting out the unmastered past: I analyzed the "Jew Club" as

memory culture, as cultural code, as fan performance, and as problem.

Chapter 1 explores the "Jew Club" as memory culture through the case study of FC Bayern Munich. It reveals how the "Jew Club" identity developed in two historical moments, namely, (1) the "Jew Club" as denazification and (2) the "Jew Club" as memory culture. First, I argue that FC Bayern's "Jew Club" narrative appeared initially during denazification, that is, at a moment in which the narrative could portray the club and its protagonists as favorable toward the authorities. This narrative seemed, however, plausible because the club was associated with Jews before 1933. Second, the club made a turn to commemorate its German Jewish president Kurt Landauer in 2009. This memory boom was accompanied by the portrayal of FC Bayern as a former "Jew Club" that was supposedly discriminated against by the Nazi regime. I argue that the turn to Landauer occurred amid a memory culture that identifies with the victim and therefore risks forgetting the perpetrators. Furthermore, I analyze two memory regimes: I make the case that as the club grows more and more international, the new club icon, Landauer, aids the club in maintaining its sense of local identity. The fans, in contrast, developed a form of working through the present, that is, a wide range of antidiscriminatory activities, for which they used Landauer as a "vehicle." Ultimately, the club made a turn to history that challenges the "Jew Club" identity and also highlights the club's active role in excluding its Jewish members during Nazism.

In chapter 2, I explore the "Jew Club" as "cultural code," analyzing the case of FK Austria Vienna (FAK). I demonstrate how, during the interwar years, stereotypically Jewish characteristics like cosmopolitanism, modernity, and rootlessness came to be linked to the club. Today, FAK is struggling with neo-Nazis among its fan base and, therefore, is reluctantly establishing the "Jew Club" as a new cultural code against Nazism. At the same time, the fans are reinventing the club's traditions: what was once considered "Jewish," modern, and rootless—such as the club's technical style of playing football—is now perceived as the core of FAK's collective local identity as a traditional club. It has largely disassociated from being identified as "Jewish," although individuals at the margins of the fan scene are slowly beginning to add Jewish symbols to the symbolic landscape of FAK's collective identity.

The "Jew Club" as fan performance is examined in the third chapter on Ajax Amsterdam. Ajax's fans, who are largely not Jewish, developed their collective identity as "Super Jews" after opposing supporters labeled them as "Jewish" in antisemitic chants like "Jew to the gas." This chapter examines the performative culture of the football stadium in which these performances take place, and the distinctive Dutch memory culture that developed around the "founding myth" of Dutch resistance. Performing Jewishness and antisemitism became particularly attractive in the 1970s when it offered an opportunity to engage with shifting perceptions of the Holocaust.

Chapter 3 furthermore proposes a model of linguistic appropriation to understand how fans appropriate the "Jew Club" identity. This model differs significantly from existing theories of linguistic reclamation because, in this case, it is not the targeted group (Jews) that is reclaiming the word but Ajax and, as examined in chapter 4, Spurs fans. This model of linguistic appropriation is triangular instead of dual because this case involves three groups instead of two. It goes beyond the framework of "perpetrator" (rival fans) and "victim" (Ajax or Spurs fans) and it makes the case that Jews must be considered important actors. Furthermore, linguistic appropriation is nonlinear. Usually, a term that is (1) a slur, is (2) reclaimed by the targeted group, and this reappropriation leads to (3) a semantic change as has been the case with words like *gay* and *queer*. Potentially, the term (4) may be appropriated again to be used by out-groups after the meaning has changed (e.g., *gay* or *queer*) or not (e.g., the N-word).

Nonlinear appropriation, however, is more circular. Here, the meaning changed for Ajax or Spurs fans, who experienced the appropriation as a positive change in meaning, while Jewish supporters of other clubs argued that the appropriation of a race-hate word is discriminatory. Ultimately, the term "Yid" ended up being perceived as more problematic and the word *Joden* is seen as more negative than before.

Finally, chapter 4, on Tottenham Hotspur, analyzes problematizing the "Jew Club"; in London, the "Jew Club" identity has been debated and problematized like nowhere else. In the 1970s, antisemitism and racism were rampant in the football stadiums, but the mostly non-Jewish Tottenham fans responded by turning the slur "Yid" into a term for themselves. Amid an emerging identity politics and growing cultural sensitivities, the perception of the problem increasingly shifted from antisemitism against Spurs to the word itself and thus the Spurs fans performing this linguistic appropriation in their fan performances. Perspectives differ: while the fans' Y-identity is a form of antisemitic exclusion for some, some Jewish Spurs fans have experienced the appropriation as a form of solidarity that opened a space for Jewish agency.

All four case studies show that "Jew Clubs" differ from actually Jewish clubs. A "Jew Club" is not Jewish in the sense that it uses Jewish symbols, celebrates Jewish holidays, or consists of predominantly Jewish members, players, or fans. How then, can we understand what a "Jew Club" is? What are the common features, and what are the differences between the four clubs studied?

WHAT IS A "JEW CLUB"?

The four "Jew Clubs" indicate the importance of memory cultures for collective identities. All four "Jew Clubs" are built on "invented traditions." In Munich and Vienna, the "Jew Club" predominantly developed as a historical category that overshadowed how the

clubs participated in Nazism and allowed for a self-portrayal as resistant victims. The historical misconceptions result from a separation of football from society, a notion that this book challenges.
Because of the idea of an "unpolitical sport," the turn to memory
in both cases occurred even later than in their respective societies, indicating that football clubs are still hesitant to acknowledge
their societal significance. In Amsterdam and London, fans understand the "Jew Club" identity as more contemporary, although
their collective identities rely on invented traditions such as the
story about a Tottenham fan who took down a swastika flag during the 1935 England-Germany football game at White Hart Lane.
In the football stadiums of England and the Netherlands, fans are
performing Jewishness and antisemitism in the present, suggesting that both the words *Jew* and *Joden* as well as antisemitic expressions are less taboo than in Germany and Austria. Nonetheless, all
"Jew Clubs" have in common that the memory of the Holocaust
is essential for their collective identities.

The memory of football clubs develops in dialectical relationship with other memorial landscapes. A club's memory culture
is influenced by and influences the memorial landscapes of the
nation, the city, and the sporting community. The collective
memories of all football clubs are stitched together by (at least)
two memory regimes: those of the fans and those of the club. In
Munich, for instance, the club is leaning more toward Vergangenheitsbewältigung (working off the past), while the fans are
invested in Gegenwartsbewältigung (working through the present). The former uses the turn to Landauer to navigate its glocal
ambitions, while the latter uses memory culture as an inspiration
for subversive actions in the present. A club can be identified as
a "Jew Club" even if one of the two memory regimes resists the
"Jew Club" notion: Ajax and Tottenham are "Jew Clubs" although
both clubs reject the fans' "Jew Club" identities. In Vienna, it is
the club that embraces the "Jew Club" identity even though (or
better still: because) parts of its fan base lean toward neo-Nazism.

In essence, a "Jew Club" identity requires that at least one of the two memory regimes embraces it.

The club and fan cultures dramatize Jewishness and antisemitism in different ways. In Germany, it is considered inappropriate to tattoo oneself with the Star of David together with the club symbol—something regarded positively by some fans in Amsterdam and London. In Vienna, Jewish FAK fans look with admiration at performances of Jewishness at Ajax and Tottenham, while other FAK fans reframe the "Jew Club" as a traditional club. They all share a sense of tradition and local identity. This has significant implications for understanding how the Holocaust is remembered. Holocaust memory always has localized forms with regional specifics: It is more accurately described as glocal than global.

The concept of "Jew Clubs" is more myth than fact. In other words, a "Jew Club" consists of the ideas and images told about it, not an empirical Jewish core. The "Jew Club" is a cultural code, to use Shulamit Volkov's concept, that develops in contrast to other clubs and that serves as a marker of distinction. As an expression of the notions of the "Jew" imaginary framework, "Jew Clubs" evoke a line of association with concepts perceived as linked to "Jews" and "Jewishness," for instance cosmopolitanism, modernity, commerce, a technical style of football, the bourgeoisie, and urbanism. Another key component of the "Jew Club" is that the clubs are linked to spaces that have a certain position in the "Jew" imaginary framework: FC Bayern and FAK are both linked to the coffeehouse; Ajax and Tottenham are associated with "Jewish" neighborhoods. Like antisemitism, the "Jew Club" concept can be contradictory: while most clubs are linked to specific areas (FC Bayern, for instance, represents Schwabing), FAK was long imagined as "rootless in the city" because the club's main office was a coffeehouse in central Vienna while the club had no home stadium.

The making of "Jew Clubs" always occurs in contrast to other clubs. FAK is, for instance, associated with both the metropolis and rootlessness, in a conceptual opposition with FAK's local rival, Rapid Vienna, which appears to represent nature and Bodenständigkeit. In the same way, FC Bayern's "Jew Club" image relies on its opposite, the alleged "Nazi club" 1860 Munich. Equally important, Ajax represents Amsterdam and thus a city long perceived as one of Europe's "most Jewish" cities. Today, Amsterdam represents intellectualism and coffeehouse culture. Feyenoord, in contrast, represents a working-class style of football associated with Rotterdam, the city of the dockworkers. Finally, Tottenham's Y-identity developed in direct interaction with rival fans from clubs like Chelsea and West Ham, who directed antisemitic chants against Spurs. The "Jew Club" framework acts as a marker of identity for different fan collectives: opposing fans can project everything onto the "Jew Club," which is supposed to be "not Self," while the supporters of "Jew Clubs" use this concept as a marker of distinction. In simpler terms, the "Jew Club" concept enables identity collectives to negotiate their ideas about themselves and others.

The different memory cultures also result in different ways of performing the "Jew Club" identities. In Munich and Austria, the "Jew Club" is externalized as a historical phenomenon remembered in the present to establish a certain identity ("not Nazi"). In Amsterdam and London, the "Jew Club" identity is based on more recent developments and, although fueled by memory cultures, refers less to club histories. The fans of Ajax and Tottenham frequently call themselves "Super Joden" or "Yid Army"; their performances transform the stadium into a virtually Jewish arena, while FC Bayern and FAK turn their museums into spaces that nostalgically celebrate a lost German-Jewish symbiosis.

Finally, all case studies reveal different understandings of the "Jew Club" as problem. The club Tottenham Hotspur launched a campaign to stop the club's fans from using the word "Yid" as a term for themselves. Ajax Amsterdam has long propagated that the club has no ties to being Jewish whatsoever and is now mostly ignoring the fans' performances of Jewishness. FAK reluctantly began to embrace its "Jew Club" identity because it wishes to establish it as a new cultural code directed against the club's neo-Nazi fans. FC Bayern joined the turn to Landauer after their fans and historians had rewritten the club's former president into its history. Today, the club benefits from the space Landauer occupies in the club's collective identity because it helps navigate the club's glocal identity. In essence, the clubs' approaches differ, and they reflect various understandings about what seems socially acceptable and admirable in society, something the "Jew Clubs" also shape in return.

RECONSIDERING THE (NEGATIVE) GERMAN-JEWISH SYMBIOSIS

"Jew Clubs" tell us a great deal about memory cultures, collective identities, and gentile-Jewish relationships more broadly. The findings of this study allow us to reconsider one of the scholarly frameworks that has significantly influenced how scholars understand the consequences of the Holocaust for the present—Dan Diner's thesis of a (negative) German-Jewish symbiosis.

The 2014 feature film *Landauer—Gefeiert, Verbannt, Vergessen* (*Landauer—Celebrated, Banned, Forgotten*) displays FC Bayern's German Jewish president, Kurt Landauer, walking through the ruins of Munich after his return in 1947. Only two years after Landauer returned to Munich, Hannah Arendt traveled to Germany, where she was "watching the Germans busily stumble through the ruins of a thousand years of their own history."[1] Arendt sharply observed how Germans were "shrugging their shoulders at the destroyed landmarks or resentful when reminded of the deeds of horror that haunt the whole surrounding world." For Germans, busyness had become "their chief defense against reality."[2] They were characterized by "the inability to mourn."[3] As early as in 1946, Arendt had written a letter to Karl Jaspers that later inspired

Figure Conc.1. The *Kurt Landauer* statue (3). Photo by author.

Dan Diner to write his famous essay about the negative symbiosis that binds Germans and Jews after Auschwitz; Arendt argued, "We are simply not equipped to deal, on a human, political level, with a guilt that is beyond crime and an innocence, that is beyond goodness or virtue. This is the abyss that opened up before us . . . and into which we have finally stumbled."[4] For Arendt, "something happened there to which we cannot reconcile ourselves. None of us ever can."[5]

Only a few decades later, all of Munich's ruins have been replaced with new buildings. The "busy" local population had constructed a city that today appears as rooted in tradition but that overshadows its past as "Nazism's capital."[6] The city's memorial landscape developed further and is now also marked by memorials for Jews like Landauer, who is commemorated in the form of a statue at FC Bayern's practice facility. The statue consists of a crevice, an abyss that symbolizes the "rupture of civilization" that was the Holocaust (see figs. concl.1 and concl.2).[7]

Figure Conc.2. The *Kurt Landauer* statue (4). Photo by author.

The monument paradoxically thematizes yet rejects the consequences of Nazism. It rejects the continuities between Nazism
and its aftermath and instead presents the links between Weimar and post–World War II Germany as one continuum. The
crevice is small, and the concrete is smooth on both sites of the
abyss, as if the rupture had left no marks on what came after it.
The gap is only a tiny detail in a monument that places the onlooker within the supposed continuity between the pre-Nazi and
post-Nazi era. The monument invites its spectators to sit next to

Landauer—either to his left (pre-1933) or to his right (post-1945). The abyss that symbolizes Nazism appears and disappears suddenly. Nothing before or after it suggests it had even been there. The abyss is buried under Landauer and is thus inaccessible. Landauer, however, effortlessly reaches his hand to the other side. The monument manages to rewrite one of the club's most significant Jews into FC Bayern's collective memory. At the same time, however, it turns Landauer into a symbol of reconciliation, redemption, and continuity. Memory is always also a form of forgetting. Hannah Arendt had still questioned whether "we will ever get out of the abyss";[8] it now seems as if the Germans have been busy constructing new monuments and new buildings on top of it. This is not only the case in Germany—the new memorial landscapes are bridges of continuity, reaching from one side of the rift to the other. The "busyness" has turned into compulsive remembering, but it has also left the bottom of the crater intact. We have overbuilt, not overcome, the past.

Despite all the memorial sites and commemoration activities, something at the bottom seems to be left untouched. In 1986, Dan Diner published *Negative Symbiosis—Germans and Jews after Auschwitz*.[9] According to Diner, the aftermath of the Holocaust became the starting point for self-understanding for both Jews and Germans, who now share "a communality of opposites."[10] Following Arendt, Diner doubted whether the past could be worked off. More precisely, Diner argued that "the monstrosity of the crime makes overcoming impossible," and all intense efforts would only "prove to be at best hopeless attempts to free oneself from the burden of the past."[11] The consequence is "a culture deeply marked by guilt over Auschwitz and constantly in search of relief."

Diner sharply criticized the notion of a German-Jewish symbiosis as a distortion because it suggests that "the limited, idealized period between the emancipation of the Jews and National Socialist barbarism, which lasted only two generations, was the rule rather than the exception."[12] In football, the celebration of "Jews" as "lost heroes" refers to the currency of Diner's intervention against the nostalgia that idealized the German-Jewish symbiosis as actually a "deplorable loss."[13] Diner's main argument is that "after Auschwitz it is actually possible—what a sad irony—to speak of a 'German–Jewish symbiosis,' albeit a negative one."[14] Auschwitz, Diner argued, will remain part of the unconscious in two ways.[15] First, "as something unconscious that was realized in a collective act, and as a continuing, collective sense of guilt caused by the act." Second, there are various possible ways of reacting to the "sense of collective guilt." Germany has changed since Arendt and Diner discussed the "negative symbiosis," and so has the historical discourse. In May 2000, a conference was held at the University of Minnesota titled Unlikely History: The Changing German-Jewish Symbiosis, 1945–2000, because, the organizers argued, the "emphasis on the Holocaust often conceals the astonishing transformation of the relations between Germans and Jews since 1945."[16] The conference identified two major shifts: the "renascence of Jewish culture in Germany" and the "tendency toward nostalgic memorialization of past Jewish life, of Jewish absence."[17] The "Jew Club" phenomenon clarifies both of these transformations: the celebration of a new Jewish presence and the nostalgia for Jewish absence.

As the introductory chapter to the conference volume states, "it seems that Dan Diner's declaration of a negative symbiosis between Germans and Jews . . . may no longer be true."[18] While German-Jewish relations are, in fact, shifting, the negative symbiosis continues into the present, at least in the unconscious. Katja Behrens, keynote speaker at the conference, talked about an "uncanny secret continuity" from Nazism into the post-1945 period:[19] "Every Jew in Germany knows it, that treading-on-thin-ice and asking: Will it hold? And what's underneath?"[20] Looking at the fans' performances of antisemitism, chants like "Jews to the gas" appear to be what lies down there in the abyss. Even despite all

the commemoration activities, "repression and denial are still pre-
dominant."[21] In this context, Behrens asserts a long continuity of
attempts to ward off guilt, a "complicity of the generations," that
is predominantly active "in the realm of the unconscious, and
that makes it so hard to get hold of."[22] This raises the question
of whether the compulsive remembering activities are a kind of
thin ice or, as Dan Diner claims, "covering memories" (*Deckerin-
nerungen*), that is, "a new historical assiduity that brings one closer
to the events of 1933–45, yet at the same time leaves out the source
of one's own unease."[23]

The football cultures discussed in this study are, I argue, a
space where we can get hold of expressions of the unconscious for
which the "negative symbiosis" is a central operator. The "unmastered" past is acted out in chants like "Jews to the gas." Such expressions are only understandable in the context of the Holocaust,
but as celebratory and carnivalesque performances between football fans, they testify to the actuality of Diner's observation that
"an understanding formed by secular patterns of thought cannot
integrate such an action [the Holocaust]—at least not without
splitting apart."[24] The "Jew Club" phenomenon expresses this
split in different forms: as memory culture, as (the nostalgia for
a) cultural code, as fan performances, and as problem.

I argue that the performances of Jewishness and antisemitism
in European football and fan cultures advance the concept of a
"negative symbiosis" in two directions. First, I make the case that
the (negative) German-Jewish symbiosis is not limited to Germany. It is more accurate to speak of a (negative) gentile-Jewish
symbiosis that is shaped by the "Jew" imaginary framework in its
local and global contexts. The (negative) gentile-Jewish symbiosis is thus glocal. Second, this (negative) gentile-Jewish symbiosis
is still significant, but it does not determine the subjectivities of
Jewish and non-Jewish football fans. The "Jew Clubs" disclose
hateful antisemitism, but they also reveal the potential for agency.
In Munich, FC Bayern's fans created their own subversive ways of

working through the present while some of Tottenham's supporters found the courage to visit the former sites of Nazi atrocities
against their ancestors because of the empowerment they felt
from being part of an identity collective that proudly calls itself
the "Yid Army."

"Jew Clubs" remain a paradoxical phenomenon. They bring the
consequences of the Holocaust to the surface and are a constant
reminder of the relevance of working through the past. They lay
bare the most egregious antisemitism while offering a space for
anti-antisemitism, agency, and belonging. The negative symbiosis
does not determine minority subjectivities. In Munich, Vienna,
Amsterdam, and London, Jewish fans both reject and embrace
"Jew Club" identities, thereby testifying to the wide spectrum of
strategies used to navigate the "Jew" imaginary framework: Jews
do not experience "Jew Clubs" in the zero-sum logic of either antisemitism or anti-antisemitism. Ultimately, the "Jew Clubs" are
ambiguous spaces of both exclusion and inclusion and their social
relevance reaches far beyond the gates of the football stadium.

AFTERWORD

The "Jew Clubs" after October 7

WHEN THREE THOUSAND FANS OF the Israeli football club Maccabi Tel Aviv traveled to Amsterdam in November 2024, they anticipated a warm welcome, similar to what they had received on many previous visits to their counterparts, the supporters of the Dutch "Jew Club," Ajax. Instead, the streets of Amsterdam were marred by scenes of violent unrest, with images of chaos quickly spreading across social media and news outlets worldwide. Israelis and Jews in the city were advised to lock their doors, and the Israeli government dispatched two planes to evacuate the visiting supporters.

Given Europe's long history of far right football hooliganism, many wondered whether the attackers were Ajax hooligans—unaware of the actual friendship between Ajax and Maccabi Tel Aviv fans. Instead, videos circulating online offered clues into the complex dynamics of the events that unfolded that day: antisemitism, racism, football fan dynamics, and collective traumas overlapped and spilled over into the chaotic scenes that played out in Amsterdam's streets and into how these scenes were perceived.

While the extent of the violence against Maccabi supporters was a surprise, the anti-Israeli sentiment was not unexpected. An anti-Israel demonstration had been planned at the stadium, but Amsterdam's mayor had ordered that it take place elsewhere. Chat groups reacted to the videos of Maccabi fans and also discussed how some of them had attacked a cab driver, resulting in their mobilizing for more direct action. Footage showed Maccabi fans chanting in support of the Israel Defense Forces (IDF) and celebrating the destruction of "the Arabs." Others climbed a building to tear down a Palestinian flag, actions seemingly undertaken with a sense of impunity. For the Maccabi fans, the streets of Amsterdam represented a safe environment—a reflection of their long-standing camaraderie with Ajax supporters. Yet this sense of safety shattered when they arrived back in the city center late at night after the game: small, mobile groups of attackers descended on Maccabi fans. These groups, armed and on scooters and bikes, hunted their targets, interrogating strangers to determine whether they were Israeli or Jewish. They unleashed brutal violence, continuing to attack even as victims lay on the ground.

The attackers were not confronting those fans who chanted about the IDF or who took down the Palestinian flag. Nor were they using the opportunity of many Israelis traveling to Amsterdam to discuss whether those fans attending were involved in the antiwar protests occurring daily on Israeli streets that seek to liberate the hostages and end the war. Instead, the circulating videos seemed to confirm what the attackers already knew: that Israelis lay within the "Jew" imaginary framework and are complicit with, if not responsible for, all evil that occurs in the world. From this perspective, a "Jew hunt"—as some attackers self-described their actions—seemed perfectly fine and morally justified. Within this framework, there was no room for nuance. There was no consideration of the antiwar protests so widespread in Israel, nor was any effort made to discern individuals or their fan collective from the politics of the Israeli government.

While history does not repeat itself, we often reflect on it, relate it to the present, and find meaning in today's world through yesterday's events. After the Amsterdam attacks, many commentators noted the bitter irony of the timing: November 7, a date close to the commemoration of the infamous anti-Jewish pogroms of 1938, also known as "Kristallnacht." The distressing images of a modern-day "Jew hunt" unfolding in a European capital restored these haunting memories from a past that—as I argue throughout this book—still needs to be worked through and cannot be worked off.

I completed the research and writing of this book during the COVID-19 pandemic, a time when the climate crisis and other catastrophes took on renewed urgency, but I wrote it before October 7, 2023. Since then, a global surge in ressentiment and antisemitism have created a different sense of being in the world for Jews, Muslims, and others who felt personally affected by October 7 and everything that followed. This shift has inevitably left its mark on the "Jew Clubs" examined in this book, including Ajax's supporters.

Although the violence in Amsterdam had little to do with Ajax's "Jew Club" identity directly, the events of October 7 also affected the Ajax fan scene. Shortly after October 7, a small group displayed Palestinian flags on the outmost corner of Ajax's supporter section, yet still within it.[1] This act, perceived as a direct challenge to the fan base's long-standing identification as a "Jew Club" and to the established hierarchy within the fan scene, provoked immediate conflict. An Ajax fan organization named the AFCA Supportersclub issued a statement calling for unity, asking fans to bring Ajax flags instead of making political statements by bringing the flags of countries to the stadium.[2] The statement was reiterated ahead of the game against Maccabi Tel Aviv. Inside the stadium, no Israeli or Palestinian flags were visible, but the iconic chant celebrating Ajax's "Super Jews" echoed proudly from every corner—including from the Maccabi Tel Aviv section. Despite these efforts to maintain unity, the aftermath of October 7 has exposed new fissures within Ajax's fan base. Yet

some things remain unchanged: The "Super Jews" chants continue to resound, a symbol of pride, while Ajax remains a central
target of antisemitic chants in Dutch football—not least chants
like "we are going on a 'Jew hunt'" or "Hamas, Hamas, Jews to the
gas," which, from today's perspective, also transmit the memory
of October 7 and of the scenes from Amsterdam's streets after
the Maccabi game.

Other than Ajax Amsterdam, Tottenham Hotspur issued an
official statement addressing the October 7 attacks, declaring that
the club was "saddened by the escalating crisis in Israel and Gaza,
and strongly condemns the horrific and brutal acts of violence
against innocent civilians."[3] However, the timing of the statement, published on October 12, drew significant criticism, as the
club had waited several days and, more importantly, until after
both the Football Association and the Premier League had issued
similar declarations. This perceived delay prompted a backlash,
including the resignation of Tottenham's charity chair, who cited
the club's "lack of moral clarity" and insufficiently forceful condemnation of the atrocities committed against Israeli civilians on
October 7 as reasons for his departure.[4]

The club's carefully worded yet vague statement reflects its
broader strategy of managing its corporate identity. This approach can also be interpreted as an attempt to distance itself
from its long-standing reputation as a "Jew Club." Seeking to
avoid controversy, Tottenham adhered to Premier League guidance by banning all Israeli and Palestinian flags from its stadium.
Yet the official stance stood in stark contrast to the actions of its
supporters, highlighting a persistent difference between the club
and its fan base.

During a minute of silence observed across Premier League
stadiums in late October, Tottenham fans displayed several Israeli
flags in defiance of the ban. Some supporters took their expressions further, gathering within the stadium to recite Kaddish, the
Jewish prayer for the deceased, in memory of the victims. Later,

chants and banners emerged demanding the release of a Spurs supporter who had been taken hostage in Gaza on October 7.

While my previous analysis discusses the fans' Y-identity as a form of philosemitism that contributes to the "Jew" imaginary framework, I also emphasize how the "Jew Club" identity creates a space for liminal agency and expressions of solidarity. This was evident in the fans' response to the October 7 attacks. To my knowledge, Tottenham stands out as the only European football club where fans organized a Jewish mourning prayer in the stadium. The divergent responses after October 7 not only illustrate the complexities of Tottenham's "Jew Club" identity but also highlight the specific potential for Jewish agency they can create in European public spaces.

FK Austria Vienna (FAK) pursued a distinct path that maintained its ties to memory. While fans largely refrained from engaging with any politics, the club was the only Austrian one that issued a social media statement.[5] It expressed solidarity with the victims of the terrorist attack on Israel and reiterated its commitment to tolerance and opposition to antisemitism. The statement was posted along with a photo displaying a Star of David at the Judenplatz memorial surrounded by four purple stones; these symbolized FAK's club color and the act of mourning. The photo had been used before to illustrate the club's commemorative gatherings at Judenplatz—its use on October 7 thus builds a visual connection between commemorating the Holocaust and the victims of October 7. It connects FAK's memory culture and the club's identity in the present.

At the same time, FAK remains a target of antisemitism. The fact that it is still targeted is a reminder of the challenges that accompany its "Jew Club" association and why FAK originally chose to embrace it to overcome such adversity. In March 2024, a piece of FAK graffiti was defaced with green paint—the color of the rival club Rapid Vienna—and included the word "Juden," a slur aimed at reinforcing the stigmatization of FAK as the "Jewish

Other."[6] Such acts exemplify how the "Jew" imaginary frame-work remains a constant potential resource that some people use and direct to discriminate against any of the "Jew Clubs." FAK's response to such hostility remains rooted in remembrance.

In Germany, antisemitism in football almost exclusively targets the Jewish Makkabi clubs but has otherwise remained subdued amid the rising hostility and threats against Jews and Israelis after October 7 in all areas of society.[7] Despite football's continued potential for antisemitic hostility—especially due to its inherent "us versus them" dynamics combined with localism and traditionalism—many German clubs and fans, including Germany's "Jew Club" FC Bayern Munich, did not engage in antisemitism but instead demonstrated solidarity with the victims of the Hamas attacks. Bayern's actions, however, were seen as more nuanced and, at times, controversial compared to other clubs.

FC Bayern has taken a stand against antisemitism in many ways: for instance, in November 2023, FC Bayern invited ten family members of Israelis kidnapped by Hamas to attend a home game, signaling a public gesture of solidarity.[8] In October 2024, the club issued a formal statement denouncing antisemitism and participated in a large public demonstration in Munich with thousands of demonstrators.[9] Yet the club was also surrounded by controversy when the Moroccan player Noussair Mazraoui shared a video after the October 7 attack, calling for the victory of his "Palestinian brothers"—an expression of solidarity with the perpetrators that could hardly be understood as anything but a call for a violent end to the existence of Israel and more deadly violence.

After a significant backlash, including condemnation from Jewish organizations such as Makkabi and the Central Council of Jews in Germany who highlighted the relevance and potential impact of political statements coming from celebrities like football players, FC Bayern issued a statement detailing a "clarifying conversation" with Mazraoui, during which, according to the statement, the player expressed regret and stated his opposition to terror and war.[10] Furthermore, Mazraoui also met with the Israelitische Kultusgemeinde München. Critics argued that Bayern's decision not to suspend or terminate Mazraoui's contract, as happened in similar cases at other clubs, failed to demonstrate a clear response. This was further complicated by the presence of Daniel Peretz in the same locker room, an Israeli goalkeeper signed by the club. Peretz publicly expressed his shock over the October 7 attacks and posted a statement in support of Israel, signaling contrasting responses within the club.

Perhaps because diverging positions on the Israel-Palestine situation not only existed within the club but also among its fans, Bayern's fan base largely refrained from direct political engagement although FC Bayern fan groups remained vocal about other political issues. Meanwhile, fan groups linked to other German clubs displayed dozens of banners calling for the release of hostages or condemning antisemitism. Instead, Bayern fans continued with their traditional focus on memory activism and resistance to contemporary far right politics. On November 9, 2024, fans commemorated the November pogroms. Club representatives and fans gathered for a public unveiling of a new plaque honoring the former club president Kurt Landauer at his birthplace on what would have been his 140th birthday.[11] Yet these initiatives seemed curiously detached from contemporary events; neither the celebrated Kurt Landauer Foundation nor its prominent Facebook page made any direct mention of the October 7 attacks or their aftermath, underscoring a deliberate separation between historical commemoration and contemporary anti-antisemitism. In 2009, the fans convinced the club to engage in memory politics around Kurt Landauer. Fifteen years later, the club was more engaged in anti-antisemitism than its fan groups: they announced and participated in demonstrations and invited families of hostages, and in November 2024, the club cooperated again with Munich's Jewish community by cohosting events such as joint Shabbat gatherings and synagogue tours as well as city tours to educate people about Munich's Jewish history during the Nazi era.

Ajax Amsterdam, deeply affected by the aftershocks of October 7, faced internal tensions as its fans struggled over hegemonic positions in the fan scene as well as diverging associations with Israel and Palestine. While the whole stadium still chants about the "Super Jews" from Amsterdam, the calls for depoliticization and fractions among the supporters became increasingly visible as European societies struggled to cope with the October 7 attacks, the subsequent Israeli military response, and the rise in antisemitism. Perhaps, the fans will maintain a "Jew Club" identity that increasingly disassociates itself from any relationship with Israel and its symbols. Yet in contrast to Amsterdam, Tottenham's "Yid Army" seems to be more unified after they took increasingly diverse positions on the "Jew Club" identity after the club's WhY Word campaign attempted to disassociate the club from it. Some fans uniquely expressed their Y-identity by holding a Kaddish in solidarity with Israeli victims, and some displayed Israeli flags despite them being banned by a club leadership that kept its statements vague and continued its attempts to distance itself from the "Jew Club" identity. FK Austria Vienna and FC Bayern Munich, in contrast, leaned heavily into memory activism.

The diverse responses of these "Jew Clubs" to October 7 caused public controversies, visible in trending hashtags on social media, and in major newspapers and TV shows covering the topic. This all demonstrates the impressive symbolic position of these clubs in European societies and the ongoing struggles over memories and identities. The clubs have become signifiers through which contemporary fan collectives—and not only them—attempt to make sense of the present by referring to the past.

This afterword is not merely a postscript but an invitation for readers to consider how the dynamics between memory cultures and collective identities as well as the "Jew" imaginary framework explored in these pages continue to evolve. Football, as this book demonstrates, is not just a game—it is a microcosm and motor of broader societal tensions, memories, and collective identities. As the world grapples with these latest upheavals, the "Jew Clubs" are a constant reminder of the continuing presence of the "Jew" imaginary framework and the impossibility of working off the past.

APPENDIX: ARCHIVES, MONUMENTS, AND MUSEUMS

ARCHIVES

Ajax Archief (https://archief.ajax.nl/)
Archiv der Jugendkulturen e.V.
Archiv der Arbeiterjugend
British Library
British Online Archive
FC Bayern Munich Club Archive
Österreichische Nationalbibliothek
Stadtarchiv München
Staatsarchiv München
Jewish Chronicle

MONUMENTS

Deaf Memorial, Amsterdam
De Dokwerker, Amsterdam
Holocaust Memorial, Amsterdam
Honorary Grave Matthias Sindelar, Vienna
Judenplatz Holocaust Memorial ("Nameless Library"), Vienna
Namenmonument (Dutch Holocaust Memorial of Names), Amsterdam
Kurt-Landauer-Weg, Munich
Memorial to the Victims of Auschwitz, Amsterdam
Monument to Jewish Resistance, Amsterdam
Plaque, Kurt Landauer, Munich

Statue, *Dionys "Mister Rapid" Schönecker*, Vienna
Statue, *Kurt Landauer*, Munich
Stumbling Stone, Edward Hamel, Amsterdam

MUSEUMS

Ajax Amsterdam Museum, Amsterdam
Anne Frank House, Amsterdam
Dutch Resistance Museum, Amsterdam
FC Bayern Museum, Munich
FK Austria Vienna Museum, Vienna
Jewish Museum, Amsterdam
Jewish Museum, Munich
"Rapideum," SK Rapid Vienna Museum, Vienna

NOTES

INTRODUCTION

1. Nirit Peled, dir., *Superjews* (NTR / Viewpoint Productions, 2013).
2. Walter Benjamin, "Über den Begriff der Geschichte," in *Walter Benjamin—Gesammelte Schriften, Band 1.2.,* ed. Rolf Tiedemann and Hermann Schweppenhäuser (Frankfurt: Suhrkamp, 1991), 691–706.
3. Walter Benjamin, "Über den Begriff der Geschichte—Anmerkungen," in Tiedemann and Schweppenhäuser, *Walter Benjamin—Gesammelte Schriften,* 1232. "Marx sagt, die Revolutionen sind die Lokomotive der Weltgeschichte. Aber vielleicht ist dem gänzlich anders. Vielleicht sind die Revolutionen der Griff des in diesem Zuge reisenden Menschengeschlechts nach der Notbremse" (my translation).
4. Theodor W. Adorno, "The Meaning of Working through the Past," in *Critical Models: Interventions and Catchwords,* by Theodor W. Adorno (New York: Columbia University Press, 1959), 89–103.
5. Adorno, 96.
6. Susan Neiman, *Learning from the Germans: Race and the Memory of Evil* (New York: Farrar, Straus and Giroux, 2019).
7. The conference took place on June 11 and June 12, 2015, in the Amsterdam ArenA. The author attended the conference, of which a conference report is available online: Joram Verhoeven, "Football-Related Anti-Semitism Compared: Report on the International Conference on Anti-Semitism in Professional Football" (Anne Frank House, 2015), https://www.annefrank.org/en/downloads/filer_public

/db/2d/db2d8481-5a32-4d4b-b695-498849e71d1e/football-related-anti
-semitism-compared_2016.pdf.

8. I use *antisemitism* (without a hyphen) instead of *anti-Semitism* because there is no "Semitism" that antisemites oppose.

9. On archaeology as a methodological approach see Knut Ebeling, "The Art of Searching: On 'Wild Archaeologies' from Kant to Kittler," *Nordic Journal of Aesthetics* 25, no. 51 (January 10, 2017): 7–18, https://doi
.org/10.7146/nja.v25i51.25152.

10. Shulamit Volkov, "Antisemitism as a Cultural Code: Reflections on the History and Historiography of Antisemitism in Imperial Germany," *Leo Baeck Institute Yearbook* 23, no. 1 (1978): 25–46.

11. Pavel Brunssen and Stefanie Schüler-Springorum, introduction to *Discrimination in Football: Antisemitism and Beyond*, ed. Pavel Brunssen and Stefanie Schüler-Springorum, Critical Research in Football (Abingdon, UK: Routledge, 2021), 1–7.

12. Michael Cole, "Holy War in the City of Knives: Anti-Semitism and Football on the Streets of Krakow," openDemocracy, November 17, 2020, https://www.opendemocracy.net/en/countering-radical-right/holy-war
-city-knives-anti-semitism-and-football-streets-krakow/; Michael G. Esch, *Die Stadt als Spielfeld: Raumbegriffe, Raumnutzungen, Raumdeutungen polnischer Hooligans* (Göttingen, Germany: Wallstein, 2016); Britta Lenz, "Wisła und Cracovia im 'Heiligen Krieg' Die Anfänge eines polnischen Traditionsderbys 1906–1927," in *Überall ist der Ball rund: Zur Geschichte und Gegenwart des Fußballs in Ost- und Südosteuropa—Die zweite Halbzeit*, ed. Dittmar Dahlmann, Anke Hilbrenner, and Britta Lenz (Essen, Germany: Klartext, 2008), 89–114; Bogna Wilczyńska, "Żydzi i Polacy na boiskach międzywojennego Krakowa, czyli co piłka nożna może powiedzieć o społeczeństwie / Polish-Jewish interwar Kraków from the perspective of football," *Studia Judaica* 2, no. 36 (March 31, 2016): 293–319; Bogna Wilczyńska, "Makkabi, Jutrzenka, Wisla and Cracovia: Polish-Jewish Krakow from the Perspective of Football," *Aschkenas* 27, no. 1 (January 27, 2017), https://doi.org/10.1515/asch-2017-0007.

13. Yossi Lempkowicz, "'Our Parents Were Burning Jews,' Chanted Fans of a Belgian Football Club in an Antisemitic Video," *EJP*, December 21, 2018, https://ejpress.org/our-parents-were-burning-jews-chanted
-fans-of-a-belgian-football-club-in-an-antisemitic-video/; Cnaan Liphshiz, "Belgian Soccer Fans Filmed Giving Nazi Salutes, Singing 'Jews to the Gas,'" *Times of Israel*, December 30, 2021, https://www.timesofisrael.com
/belgian-soccer-fans-filmed-giving-nazi-salutes-singing-jews-to-the-gas/;

Benjamin Weinthal, "Belgian Jews Demand Soccer Club Stop Antisemitic Chants in the Stands," *Jerusalem Post*, December 17, 2017, https://www .jpost.com/diaspora/belgian-jews-demand-soccer-club-stop-antisemitic -chants-in-the-stands-518330.

14. Raanan Rein, "Struggling to Belong in the Face of Otherness: The Atlanta Fútbol Club of Buenos Aires," in *Football and Discrimination: Antisemitism and Beyond*, ed. Pavel Brunssen and Stefanie Schüler-Springorum, Critical Research in Football (Abingdon, UK: Routledge, 2021), 127–37.

15. Róbert Győri Szabó, "Football and Politics in Twentieth-Century Hungary," *International Journal of the History of Sport* 36, no. 2–3 (February 11, 2019): 131–48, https://doi.org/10.1080/09523367.2019.1629583; Victor Karady and Miklós Hadas, "Soccer and Antisemitism in Hungary," in *Emancipation through Muscles: Jews and Sports in Europe*, ed. Michael Brenner and Gideon Reuveni (Lincoln: University of Nebraska Press, 2006), 213–34; Dietrich Schulze-Marmeling, "Die gescheiterte Assimilation: Juden und Fußball in Budapest," in *Davidstern und Lederball: Die Geschichte der Juden im deutschen und internationalen Fussball*, ed. Dietrich Schulze-Marmeling (Göttingen, Germany: Die Werkstatt, 2003), 319–46.

16. Cynthia M. Baker, *Jew*, Key Words in Jewish Studies (New Brunswick, NJ: Rutgers University Press, 2017).

17. Baker, 2.

18. Maurice Samuels, "Philosemitism," in *Key Concepts in the Study of Antisemitism*, ed. Sol Goldberg, Scott Ury, and Kalman Weiser (Cham, Switzerland: Palgrave Macmillan, 2021), 201, https://doi.org/10.1007 /978-3-030-51658-1.

19. Samuels, 201.

20. Samuels, 202.

21. Dara Horn, "Auschwitz Is Not a Metaphor," *Atlantic*, June 6, 2019, https://www.theatlantic.com/ideas/archive/2019/06/auschwitz-not -long-ago-not-far-away/591082/.

22. Bernd Marin, *Antisemitismus ohne Antisemiten: Autoritäre Vorurteile und Feindbilder*, unveränderte Neuauflage früher Analysen 1974–1979 und Umfragen 1946–1991 (Frankfurt: Campus, 2000).

23. "Bestuur supportersvereniging De Feijenoorder verdeeld over anti-semitische muurtekening," Rijnmond, July 27, 2021, https://www.rijnmond.nl /nieuws/1294346/Bestuur-supportersvereniging-De-Feijenoorder-verdeeld -over-antisemitische-muurtekening. "Het is niet zo dat iedereen denkt dat

joden vergast moeten worden. We praten altijd over 'voetbaljoden'" (my translation).

24. Dov Waxman, David Schraub, and Adam Hosein, "Arguing about Antisemitism: Why We Disagree about Antisemitism, and What We Can Do about It," *Ethnic and Racial Studies*, August 13, 2021, 1–22, https://doi.org /10.1080/01419870.2021.1960407.

25. Pavel Brunssen, "Hitler's American Countermodel: The United States and the Making of Nazi Ideology," *German Politics and Society* 41, no. 3 (Autumn 2023).

26. Reinhard Rürup, *Emanzipation und Antisemitismus: Studien zur "Judenfrage" der bürgerlichen Gesellschaft* (Göttingen, Germany: Vandenhoeck & Ruprecht, 1975).

27. Moishe Postone, "Anti-Semitism and National Socialism," in *Germans and Jews since the Holocaust: The Changing Situation in West Germany*, ed. Anson Rabinbach and Jack Zipes (New York: Holmes & Meier, 1986), 302–14.

28. Jean-Paul Sartre, *Anti-Semite and Jew: An Exploration of the Etiology of Hate*, trans. George J. Becker (New York: Schocken Books, 1944).

29. Emma Poulton and Oliver Durell argue that the meaning of a word like "Yid" is "dependent on *cultural context* and the *intent* behind the use of language." They take the side of those Spurs supporters who justify the chants: "Tottenham fans are justified in their appropriation and continued use of 'Yid' as an expression of their fandom. . . . We recommend that future policies to combat antisemitism in football focus upon the *real* perpetrators of antisemitic discourse and behaviour, not Tottenham fans, who are the victims" ("Uses and Meanings of 'Yid' in English Football Fandom: A Case Study of Tottenham Hotspur Football Club," *International Review for the Sociology of Sport* 51, no. 6 [September 2016]: 731, https://doi .org/10.1177/1012690214554844).

30. Zygmunt Baumann believes the concept of antisemitism is too narrow because of its focus on hostility, which aligns with my critique of focusing on intentions alone. Baumann coined the term *allosemitism* to challenge the idea that antisemitism is a fixed and unchanging concept. Allosemitism, which distinguishes Jews as "different" from others, is linked but not restricted to antisemitism ("Allosemitism: Premodern, Modern, Postmodern," in *Modernity, Culture, and "the Jew*," ed. Bryan Cheyette and Laura Marcus [Cambridge: Polity Press, 1998], 153–56).

31. Lisa Silverman, "Rethinking Jews, Antisemitism, and Jewish Difference in Postwar Germany," in *The Future of the German-Jewish Past: Memory and the Question of Antisemitism*, ed. Gideon Reuveni and Diana Franklin (West Lafayette, IN: Purdue University Press, 2021), 136.

32. Pavel Brunssen, "Antisemitic Ressentiment-Communication Directed at RB Leipzig in German Football Fan Culture: The Third Other," in Brunssen and Schüler-Springorum, *Football and Discrimination*, 81–94.

33. Klaus Holz, *Nationaler Antisemitismus: Wissenssoziologie einer Weltanschauung* (Hamburg, Germany: Hamburger Edition, 2001).

34. Lisa Silverman, *Becoming Austrians: Jews and Culture between the World Wars* (Oxford: Oxford University Press, 2012), 7.

35. Silverman, "Rethinking Jews," 138.

36. Karin Stögner, "New Challenges in Feminism: Intersectionality, Critical Theory, and Anti-Zionism," in *Anti-Zionism and Antisemitism: The Dynamics of Delegitimization*, ed. Alvin H. Rosenfeld, Studies in Antisemitism (Bloomington: Indiana University Press, 2019), 84–111.

37. Jean Améry, *Essays on Antisemitism, Anti-Zionism, and the Left*, ed. Marlene Gallner, trans. Lars Fischer, Studies in Antisemitism (Bloomington: Indiana University Press, 2021), 11.

38. Elad Lapidot, *Jews Out of the Question: A Critique of Anti-Anti-Semitism*, Suny Series, Philosophy and Race (Albany: State University of New York, 2020).

39. The psychoanalyst Jacques Lacan understood the imaginary as the formation of the ego, a sense of self achieved through a person's identification with images of themself. Lacan introduced the "mirror stage" concept to elucidate the formation of the imaginary. For Lacan, this process occurs during infancy. He proposed that when infants first see their reflection in a mirror, they experience a sense of unity and coherence in their fragmented self. This momentary identification with the idealized image in the mirror contributes to the formation of the ego and of a cohesive self, despite it being an illusion.

40. Michael Brenner and Gideon Reuveni, "Introduction: Why Jews and Sports," in Brenner and Reuveni, *Emancipation through Muscles*, 9.

41. Brenner and Reuveni, 8.

42. Jonathan M. Hess, *Germans, Jews, and the Claims of Modernity* (New Haven, CT: Yale University Press, 2002); George L. Mosse, *German Jews beyond Judaism* (Bloomington: Indiana University Press; Cincinnati: Hebrew Union College Press, 1985).

43. Mosse, *German Jews beyond Judaism*, 24.

44. Marline Otte, *Jewish Identities in German Popular Entertainment, 1890–1933* (Cambridge: Cambridge University Press, 2006), 16.

45. Otte, 16.

46. Ezra Mendelsohn, preface to *Jews and the Sporting Life*, ed. Ezra Mendelsohn, Studies in Contemporary Jewry 23 (Oxford: Oxford University Press, 2008), viii.

47. Max Nordau, "Muskeljudentum," in *Reden und Schriften zum Zionismus* (Boston, MA: De Gruyter, 1900), 136–37.

48. Klaus Hödl, "Jewish Studies without the 'Other,'" in Reuveni and Franklin, *Future of the German-Jewish Past*, 125.

49. Hödl, 128.

50. Brenner and Reuveni, introduction, 4; see also Susanne Helene Betz et al., "Jüdischer Sport in Metropolen: Einleitende Bemerkungen," *Aschkenas* 27, no. 1 (January 27, 2017): 1, https://doi.org/10.1515/asch-2017-0001; Dietrich Schulze-Marmeling, "Einführung," in Schulze-Marmeling, *Davidstern und Lederball*, 14.

51. Brenner and Reuveni, introduction, 2.

52. Silverman, *Becoming Austrians*, 4.

53. Silverman, 4.

54. Silverman, 17.

55. German football clubs and sport organizations quickly acted to expel Jews long before any such measure was required by the Nazi government. On April 9, 1933, the biggest clubs of the South German sports association Süddeutscher Fußball- und Leichtathletikverband (SFLV), among them FC Bayern, issued the following statement: "The undersigned clubs of the South German Football and Athletics Association, present in Stuttgart on April 9, 1933, and participating in the finals of the German football championship, happily and decisively make themselves available to the national government in the area of physical training and are prepared to cooperate with all their strength. They are willing to draw all conclusions from this cooperation, especially with regard to the removal of Jews from sports clubs" ("Die unterzeichneten, am 9. April 1933 in Stuttgart anwesenden, an den Endspielen um die deutsche Fußballmeisterschaft beteiligten Vereine des Süddeutschen Fußball- und Leichtathletikverbandes stellen sich freudig und entschieden den von der nationalen Regierung auf dem Gebiet der körperlichen Ertüchtigung verfolgten Besprechungen zur Verfügung und sind bereit, mit allen Kräften daran mitzuarbeiten. Sie sind gewillt, in Fülle dieser Mitarbeit alle Folgerungen, insbesondere in

der Frage der Entfernung der Juden aus den Sportvereinen zu ziehen") (my translation; quoted in Dietrich Schulze-Marmeling, *Der FC Bayern, seine Juden und die Nazis*, 3., erweiterte Auflage [Göttingen, Germany: Die Werkstatt, 2017], 135). Ten days later, the German Football association Deutscher Fußball-Bund and the Deutsche Sportbehörde issued another statement, asking for the immediate removal of Jews from German sport clubs.

56. Lorenz Peiffer and Henry Wahlig, *Jüdische Fussballvereine im nationalsozialistischen Deutschland: Eine Spurensuche* (Göttingen, Germany: Die Werkstatt, 2015); Henry Wahlig, *Sport im Abseits: Die Geschichte der jüdischen Sportbewegung im nationalsozialistischen Deutschland* (Göttingen, Germany: Wallstein, 2015).

57. As of January 2025, the website has entries for more than one thousand sporting statues (Sporting Statues Project official website, accessed July 2, 2024, http://offbeat.group.shef.ac.uk/statues/).

58. Julijana Ranc, *"Eventuell nichtgewollter Antisemitismus": Zur Kommunikation antijüdischer Ressentiments unter deutschen Durchschnittsbürgern* (Münster, Germany: Westfälisches Dampfboot, 2016).

59. Pavel Brunssen, *Antisemitismus in Fußball-Fankulturen: Der Fall RB Leipzig* (Weinheim, Germany: Beltz Juventa, 2021); Brunssen, "Antisemitic Ressentiment-Communication Directed at RB Leipzig in German Football Fan Culture: The Third Other"; Pavel Brunssen, "Antisemitic Metaphors in German Soccer Fan Culture Directed at RB Leipzig," in *Football Nation: The Playing Fields of German Culture, History, and Society*, ed. Rebeccah Dawson et al., Spektrum: Publications of the German Studies Association 25 (New York: Berghahn Books, 2022), 218–39.

60. AG Fankultur, "Vor Leipzig. Erklärung der AG Fankultur," 2016, https://fc.de/fc-info/news/detailseite/details/erklaerung-der-ag-fankultur/. "Deshalb erkennt jeder Fußballfan einen Traditionsverein auf Anhieb" (my translation).

61. Eric J. Hobsbawm, "Introduction: Inventing Traditions," in *The Invention of Tradition*, eds. Eric J. Hobsbawm and Terence Ranger (Cambridge: Cambridge University Press, 2015), 4.

62. Hobsbawm, 10.

63. Jeffrey K. Olick, Vered Vinitzky-Seroussi, and Daniel Levy, eds., *The Collective Memory Reader* (New York: Oxford University Press, 2011), 19.

64. Andrei S. Markovits and Simon Reich, *The German Predicament: Memory and Power in the New Europe* (Ithaca, NY: Cornell University Press, 1997), 12.

65. Pavel Brunssen and Andrei S. Markovits, "Soccer in America: From Pele's Periphery to Messi's Semi-Periphery! But Will There Be an Entry into Football's Core?" *Soziopolis* (blog), June 12, 2024, https://www.soziopolis .de/soccer-in-america-from-peles-periphery-to-messis-semi-periphery -but-will-there-be-an-entry-into-footballs-core.html; Stefan Szymanski and Silke-Maria Weineck, *It's Football, Not Soccer (and Vice Versa): On the History, Emotion, and Ideology behind One of the Internet's Most Ferocious Debates* (independently published, 2018).

66. Norbert Elias, introduction to *Quest for Excitement: Sport and Leisure in the Civilizing Process*, by Norbert Elias and Eric Dunning (Oxford: Basil Blackwell, 1986), 26.

67. Brunssen and Schüler-Springorum, introduction, 2.

68. Andrei Markovits and Lars Rensmann write that to them, "each sport has a distinctive symbolic and normative framework comprised of formal rules and informal codes, which in turn generate a penumbra of meaningful practices, symbols, and evaluations. We see these analogous to languages or idioms. In no way do we mean to imply that each sport is a language. Rather, we see each sport as having a distinctive (normative, symbolic, conceptual, and terminological) language associated with it, which constitutes part of that sport's singular culture" (*Gaming the World: How Sports Are Reshaping Global Politics and Culture* [Princeton, NJ: Princeton University Press, 2010], 17).

69. Richard Giulianotti, ed., *Routledge Handbook of the Sociology of Sport* (London: Routledge, 2015), xix.

70. Markovits and Rensmann, *Gaming the World*, 13.

71. Ramón Spaaij et al., "Football and Politics: Between the Local and the Global," in *The Palgrave International Handbook of Football and Politics*, ed. Jean-Michel De Waele et al. (Cham, Switzerland: Palgrave Macmillan, 2018), 13.

72. Martin Cloake and Alan Fisher, *A People's History of Tottenham Hotspur Football Club: How Spurs Fans Shaped the Identity of One of the World's Most Famous Clubs* (Seaford, UK: Pitch, 2016), 44.

73. Cloake and Fisher, 209.

74. Richard Giulianotti and Roland Robertson, *Globalization and Football* (Los Angeles: SAGE, 2009).

75. Jacob S. Eder, Philipp Gassert, and Alan E. Steinweis, eds., *Holocaust Memory in a Globalizing World*, Beiträge zur Geschichte des 20. Jahrhunderts 22 (Göttingen, Germany: Wallstein, 2017).

76. Mark Doidge, Radosław Kossakowski, and Svenja Mintert, *Ultras: The Passion and Performance of Contemporary Football Fandom* (Manchester, UK: Manchester University Press, 2020), 2.

77. Doidge, Kossakowski, and Mintert, 12.

78. Mikita Hoy, "Joyful Mayhem: Bakhtin, Football Songs, and the Carnivalesque," *Text and Performance Quarterly* 14, no. 4 (October 1994): 292, https://doi.org/10.1080/10462939409366091.

79. Les Back, "Sounds in the Crowd," in *The Auditory Culture Reader*, ed. Michael Bull and Les Back, Sensory Formations Series (Oxford: Berg, 2006), 320.

80. Back, 323–325.

81. Doidge, Kossakowski, and Mintert, *Ultras*, 13.

82. Maurice Halbwachs, *The Collective Memory*, trans. Francis J. Ditter and Vida Yazdi Ditter, Harper Colophon Books, CN/800 (New York: Harper & Row, 1980), 86.

83. Adorno, "Meaning of Working Through," 90.

84. Robert Claus, Cristin Gießler, and Franciska Wölki-Schumacher, "Geschlechterverhältnisse in Fußballfanszenen," 2016, 86. https://www.vielfalt-mediathek.de/material/homo-trans-und-interfeindlichkeit/geschlechterverhaeltnisse-in-fussballszenen-eine-expertise-der-kofas.

85. Carrie Dunn argues that "female fans choose to perform their fandom in a way that is not marked as feminine; rather, they perform fandom in an unmarked, that is, 'normal', that is, 'authentic', that is, 'typically male' way" (*Female Football Fans: Community, Identity and Sexism* [Basingstoke, UK: Houndmills: Palgrave Macmillan, 2014], 106).

86. Dunn, *Female Football Fans*.

87. Anne Coddington, *One of the Lads: Women Who Follow Football* (London: HarperCollins, 1997); Dunn, *Female Football Fans*; Honorata Jakubowska, Dominik Antonowicz, and Radosław Kossakowski, *Female Fans, Gender Relations and Football Fandom: Challenging the Brotherhood Culture*, Routledge Research in Sport, Culture and Society (London: Routledge, 2021); Andrei S. Markovits and Emily K. Albertson, *Sportista: Female Fandom in the United States*, Politics, History and Social Change (Philadelphia: Temple University Press, 2012); Gertrud Pfister and Stacey Pope, eds., *Female Football Players and Fans: Intruding into a Man's World* (London: Palgrave Macmillan UK, 2018); Stacey Pope, *The Feminization of Sports Fandom: A Sociological Study*, Routledge Research

in Sport, Culture and Society 81 (New York: Routledge, 2017); Nicole Selmer, *Watching the Boys Play: Frauen als Fußballfans* (Kassel, Germany: Agon, 2004); Kim Toffoletti, *Women Sport Fans: Identification, Participation, Representation,* Routledge Research in Sport, Culture and Society (New York: Routledge, Taylor and Francis Group, 2017).

88. Nina Degele, *Fussball verbindet—durch Ausgrenzung* (Wiesbaden, Germany: Springer VS, 2013), 76.

89. Jochen Roose, Mike S. Schäfer, and Thomas Schmidt-Lux, "Fans in theoretischer Perspektive," in *Fans: Soziologische Perspektiven,* ed. Jochen Roose, Mike S. Schäfer, and Thomas Schmidt-Lux, 2nd ed. (Wiesbaden, Germany: Springer VS, 2017), 22.

90. Almut Sülzle, *Fussball, Frauen, Männlichkeiten: Eine Ethnographische Studie im Fanblock* (Frankfurt: Campus, 2011), 222.

91. Nina Degele and Caroline Janz, "Homosexualität im Fußball—Zur Konstruktion von Normalität und Abweichung," in *Spielen Frauen ein anderes Spiel?* ed. Gabriele Sobiech and Andrea Ochsner (Wiesbaden, Germany: VS Verlag für Sozialwissenschaften, 2012), 198.

92. Dunn, *Female Football Fans,* 64–67.

93. Philip Joseph Deloria, *Playing Indian,* Yale Historical Publications (New Haven, CT: Yale University Press, 1998); Jennifer Guiliano, *Indian Spectacle: College Mascots and the Anxiety of Modern America,* Critical Issues in Sport and Society (New Brunswick, NJ: Rutgers University Press, 2015).

94. Renato Rosaldo, "Imperialist Nostalgia," *Representations.* Special Issue: Memory and Counter-Memory, no. 26 (Spring 1989): 107–22.

95. C. Richard King, *Redskins: Insult and Brand* (Lincoln: University of Nebraska Press, 2016), 4.

96. Andrew Keh, "Tomahawk Chops and Native American Mascots: In Europe, Teams Don't See a Problem," *New York Times,* May 7, 2018, sec. Sports, https://www.nytimes.com/2018/05/07/sports/native-american -mascots-europe.html.

97. Benedict Anderson, *Imagined Communities: Reflections on the Origin and Spread of Nationalism,* rev. ed. (London: Verso, 2006), 6.

98. Back, "Sounds," 312.

99. Pierre Nora, ed., *Les Lieux de Mémoire* (Paris: Gallimard, 1984).

100. Y. Michal Bodemann, *Gedächtnistheater: Die jüdische Gemeinschaft und ihre deutsche Erfindung* (Hamburg, Germany: Rotbuch, 1996).

101. Bodemann, 84. "Gedenken findet . . . immer in theaterartigen Kontexten statt: Mit Bühne, Zuschauern, Schauspielern, Bühnenbildern, dem Drama und seiner Inszenierung selbst" (my translation).

102. Knut Ebeling, "Die Flut des Raums: Eine Archäologie der Masse," in *Stadien: Eine künstlerisch-wissenschaftliche Raumforschung*, ed. Knut Ebeling and Kai Schiemenz (Berlin: Kadmos, 2008), 121. They are "Architekturen der Blicklenkung und Augensteuerung" (my translation).

103. Johann Wolfgang von Goethe, *Italian Journey [1786–1788]*, trans. Wystan H. Auden and Elizabeth Mayer, Penguin Classics (San Francisco: North Point Press, 1982), 35.

104. Goethe, 36.

105. Georg Simmel, "Exkurs über den Fremden," in *Soziologie: Untersuchungen über die Formen der Vergesellschaftung*, by Georg Simmel (Berlin: Duncker & Humblot, 1908), 509–12.

106. Ruth Ellen Gruber, *Virtually Jewish: Reinventing Jewish Culture in Europe*, S. Mark Taper Foundation Imprint in Jewish Studies (Berkeley: University of California Press, 2002), 4.

107. Gruber, 21.

108. Gruber, 27.

109. Poulton and Durell, "Uses and Meanings," 728.

110. Scott Spector, "Forget Assimilation: Introducing Subjectivity to German-Jewish History," *Jewish History* 20, no. 3–4 (December 27, 2006): 351, https://doi.org/10.1007/s10835-006-9015-2.

111. Spector defines subjectivity as follows: "Subjectivity refers to the intricate, complex, and self-contradictory ways in which historical actors experience their place in the world, in contrast to how they are perceived by others, or how they are ordered within relatively rigid external systems" (358).

112. Spector, 352.

113. Paul Lendvai, *Antisemitismus ohne Juden: Entwicklungen und Tendenzen in Osteuropa* (Vienna: Europaverlag, 1972).

114. Gruber, *Virtually Jewish*, 9.

115. Diana Pinto, "A New Jewish Identity for Post-1989 Europe," *JPR / Policy Paper*, no. 1 (1996): 7.

116. Gruber, *Virtually Jewish*, 11.

117. Dan Diner, "Negative Symbiose—Deutsche und Juden nach Auschwitz," in *Jüdisches Leben in Deutschland nach 1945*, ed. Micha Brumlik et al. (Frankfurt: Jüdischer Verlag bei Athenäum, 1986), 243–57; Dan Diner, "Negative Symbiosis: Germans and Jews after Auschwitz," in *The Holocaust: Theoretical Readings*, ed. Neil Levi and Michael Rothberg (Edinburgh: Edinburgh University Press, 2003), 423–30.

118. Diner, "Negative Symbiosis," 424.

119. Ulrike Jureit and Christian Schneider, *Gefühlte Opfer: Illusionen der Vergangenheitsbewältigung* (Stuttgart, Germany: Klett-Cotta, 2010).

1. FC BAYERN MUNICH

1. FC Bayern München, *Our Club. Our History. Since 1900* (Munich: FC Bayern München, 2022), 13–21.

2. Gregor Hofmann, *Mitspieler der "Volksgemeinschaft": Der FC Bayern und der Nationalsozialismus* (Göttingen, Germany: Wallstein, 2022).

3. FC Bayern München, "FC Bayern Museum," visited January 23, 2022.

4. Kurt Landauer was born in 1884 as the son of Jewish merchants in Planegg, not far from Munich. In 1901, aged seventeen, the young Landauer became a member of FC Bayern for the first time when he acted as the club's reserve-team goalkeeper. Landauer was more talented off the football field, however. In 1913, the twenty-nine-year-old Landauer became the president of FC Bayern, which had been founded just thirteen years before. After fighting for Germany in World War I—Landauer had received the Verdienstorden 4. Klasse and reached the rank of *Vizefeldwebel* and *stellvertretender Offizier*—Landauer became the club's president in 1919 for a second time. Germany's contemporary record champion finally won his very first national championship under Landauer's leadership in 1932. Just one year later, Landauer resigned from the club presidency on March 22, 1933. Five years later, Nazis arrested Landauer at his workplace on November 10, 1938. In May 1939, after spending thirty-three days in Dachau concentration camp, Landauer barely escaped to Switzerland, where he was forced to stay until the end of Nazism. The Nazis killed many of his family members. In 1947, Landauer returned to Munich, where he became the club's president once more. Landauer died in Schwabing, Munich, on December 21, 1961. After having forgotten him for many years, the club retrospectively awarded Landauer an honorary presidency in 2013.

5. Anton Löffelmeier, "Grandioser Aufschwung und Krise: Der Münchner Fußball von 1919 bis 1945," in *München und der Fußball: von den Anfängen 1896 bis zur Gegenwart*, by Stadtarchiv München (Munich: Buchendorfer, 1997), 51–96; Dietrich Schulze-Marmeling, *Die Bayern: Vom Klub zum Konzern; Die Geschichte eines Rekordmeisters* (Göttingen, Germany: Die Werkstatt, 1997), 67–79.

6. Andreas Meyhoff and Gerhard Pfeil, "Münchner Protokolle," *Der Spiegel*, May 20, 2016, https://www.spiegel.de/sport/muenchner-protokolle -a-74482b35-0002-0001-0000-000144886593.

7. "Warum es doch einen Grund gibt, den FC Bayern zu lieben: Die Geschichte eines Clubs, der zu seinem jüdischen Präsidenten hielt" (Heike Faller, "Onkel Kurt und die Bayern," *Die Zeit*, May 28, 2003, https://www .zeit.de/2003/23/Sport_2flandauer).

8. Dominik Fürst, "Streit um Nazi-Vergangenheit des FC Bayern," *Süddeutsche Zeitung*, May 24, 2016, https://www.sueddeutsche.de /sport/muenchen-streit-um-nazi-vergangenheit-des-fc-bayern-1 .3004904; Markwart Herzog, "Die drei 'Arierparagrafen' des FC Bayern München: Opportunismus und Antisemitismus in den Satzungen des bayerischen Traditionsvereins," in *Die "Gleichschaltung" des Fussball-sports im nationalsozialistischen Deutschland*, ed. Markwart Herzog and Berno Bahro, 1. Auflage, Irseer Dialoge 20 (Stuttgart, Germany: W. Kohlhammer, 2016), 75–113; Markwart Herzog, "Das Selbstbild des FC Bayern als 'Opfer' des Nationalsozialismus: Ein Beitrag zum Einfluss der Medien auf Konstruktion und Widerlegung eines populären Geschichtsmythos," in *Zwischenräume: Macht, Ausgrenzung und Inklusion im Fußball*, ed. Siegfried Göllner et al., Beiträge zur 2. Salzburger Fußballtagung (Göttingen, Germany: Die Werkstatt, 2019), 228–38; Dirk Kämper, "Geschichte als dritte Halbzeit—Eine Replik auf Markwart Herzog," Verlag Die Werkstatt, May 24, 2016, https:// www.werkstatt-verlag.de/node/223; Dirk Kämper and Dietrich Schulze-Marmeling, "Der FC Bayern, die Nazis und Herr Herzog," Dietrich Schulze-Marmeling official website, accessed January 25, 2023, https:// www.schulze-marmeling.com/artikel/der-fc-bayern-die-nazis-und -herr-herzog; Andreas Meyhoff and Gerhard Pfeil, "Fußball: Expertenstreit um FC Bayern zur NS-Zeit," *Der Spiegel*, May 24, 2016, https:// www.spiegel.de/spiegel/spiegelblog/fussball-expertenstreit-um-fc -bayern-zur-ns-zeit-a-1093975.html; Dietrich Schulze-Marmeling, "Der FC Bayern München in der NS-Zeit: Eine Enthüllung, die keine ist," *Der Tagesspiegel*, May 25, 2016, https://www.tagesspiegel.de/sport/eine -enthullung-die-keine-ist-4884679.html; Dietrich Schulze-Marmeling, "Herzog, der 'Spiegel' und die 'Erinnerungskultur,'" in Göllner et al., *Zwischenräume*, 239–51.

9. Dietrich Schulze-Marmeling, *Die Bayern: Die Geschichte des deutschen Rekordmeisters* (Göttingen, Germany: Die Werkstatt, 2007), 65. "Showdown zweier 'Juden-Klubs'" (my translation).

10. On Eintracht Frankfurt, see Matthias Thoma, *"Wir waren die Jud-debube": Eintracht Frankfurt in der NS-Zeit* (Göttingen, Germany: Die Werkstatt, 2007); Matthias Thoma and Martin Liepach, "Eintracht Frankfurt Fans and the Museum: Football History, Remembrance Culture, and the Fight against Antisemitism," in Brunssen and Schüler-Springorum, *Football and Discrimination*, 152–65.

11. FC Bayern München, "FC Bayern Museum."

12. Schickeria München, "Erinnerungen, Erzählungen, Anekdoten zur Deutschen Meisterschaft 1932," *Gegen den Strom*, November 2010, Archiv der Jugendkulturen.

13. FC Bayern München, "FC Bayern Museum." For a critical discussion of the symbolic space the 1932 championship became, see Hofmann, *Mitspieler der "Volksgemeinschaft,"* 48–53.

14. Philipp Lahm, "Vorwort," in *Kurt Landauer: Der Mann, der den FC Bayern erfand*, by Dirk Kämper (Zürich: Orell Füssli, 2014), 7.

15. Hofmann, *Mitspieler der "Volksgemeinschaft."*

16. Hofmann, 402.

17. Hofmann, 91–94.

18. Anton Löffelmeier, *Die "Löwen" unterm Hakenkreuz: der TSV München von 1860 im Nationalsozialismus* (Göttingen, Germany: Die Werkstatt, 2009).

19. FC Bayern München, "Neue Seiten der Erinnerung," *51—Das FC Bayern Magazin*, January 2023, 77.

20. Hofmann, *Mitspieler der "Volksgemeinschaft,"* 209–217. No Arierparagraph was required of German sports clubs before 1940.

21. The 1997 book by Schulze-Marmeling discusses Kurt Landauer in detail for the first time (Schulze-Marmeling, *Die Bayern: Vom Klub zum Konzern*, 67–79). The subtitle to Löffelmeier's chapter is "'Judenverein' und Parteigeklüngel: Die Vereinsführung des FC Bayern und der TSV 1860 in der NS-Zeit" ["Jew Club" and Party Cronyism: The Club Management of FC Bayern and TSV 1860 in the Nazi Era] (Löffelmeier, "Grandioser Aufschwung," 65).

22. The note at the Munich city archive reads: "The letter of 6.3.44 was returned on 13.4.44, by Director Obermaier with the addition that the circumstances have shifted to the disadvantage of such honors, that 1860 has other relations with the city through the councilors Gleixner and Dr. Ketterer, that FC Bayern was led by a Jew until the seizure of power, and that FC Bayern's role toward 1860, enacted through its member Harlacher, was very unpleasant" ("Das Schreiben vom 6.3.44 wurde am 13.4.44 von

Direktor Obermaier zurückgegeben mit dem Beifügen, daß die Verhältnisse sich zu ungunsten solcher Ehrungen verschoben haben, daß bei 1860 andere Beziehungen zur Stadt bestehen durch die Ratsherrn Gleixner und Dr. Ketterer, daß der FC. Bayern bis zur Machtübernahme von einem Juden geführt worden ist und daß der FC. Bayern durch ein Mitglied Harlacher eine sehr unerfreuliche Rolle gegenüber 1860 gespielt hat") (my translation; Stadtamt für Leibesübungen, March 14, 1944, Amt für Leibesübungen [AfL] 151, Stadtarchiv München).

23. Löffelmeier, "Grandioser Aufschwung," 69.

24. Hofmann, Mitspieler der "Volksgemeinschaft," 198.

25. The phrase "Jew Club" appears neither in the club's magazine Clubnachrichten nor in newspapers during the twentieth century. See also Hofmann, 405.

26. "Wir sind auch überall als 'Judenverein und Judenclub' geschimpft worden und hatten sehr die 12 Jahre hindurch zu leiden" ("We were also called a 'Jewish club' and 'Jew Club' everywhere, and we suffered immensely over the 12 years") (Spruchkammer München I, "Protokoll der öffentlichen Sitzung am 28. November 1946 14 Uhr," November 28, 1946, SpK K 1000, Staatsarchiv München; see also Hofmann, Mitspieler der "Volksgemeinschaft," 199).

27. The German civilian court handling denazification.

28. Spruchkammer München I, "Spruch I-410/46," November 28, 1946, SpK K 1000, Staatsarchiv München. "Der FC-Bayern war während der Nazizeit als Judenclub bezeichnet, weil der s.Zt.Vereinsvorsitzende, Landauer, Jude war" (my translation).

29. FC Bayern München, "FC Bayern to Oberbürgermeister," May 15, 1944, Amt für Leibesübungen [AfL] 151, Stadtarchiv München. "Wir sind bereit, Ihnen bedingungslos und treu Gefolgschaft zu leisten, hat doch mit Ihrer Amtsübernahme auch für uns 'Bayern' wieder eine Zeit neuen Aufbau's begonnen, nachdem wir bisher als 'Juden-Club', der es ablehnte sich eine nat.soz. Vereinsführung aufzwingen zu lassen, mit allen Mitteln gedrückt wurden" (my translation).

30. Siegfried Herrmann, "Herrmann to Jutzi," August 7, 1946, Karton Mitgliederverwaltung ~ 1950 (ausgeschieden) Ginbart-Jutzi, FC Bayern Munich Club Archive. "Jedenfalls muß der in München so verschrieene 'Judenverein' um sein Dasein in der neuen Demokratie kämpfen" (my translation).

31. Quoted in Schulze-Marmeling, Der FC Bayern, seine Juden und die Nazis, 151–52. "Selbst in meinen jungen Jahren war es für mich nie ein

Geheimnis, dass mein Großvater immer stolz darauf war, gerade in dem 'Juden-Verein' und in keinem anderen Aufnahme gefunden zu haben. Und ihm anzugehören. Der Grund dafür waren der liberale, intellektuelle und künstlerische (neben der sportlichen) Anspruch und das Umfeld der Mitglieder dort."

32. Bayerischer Rundfunk, "Alpha-Forum: Uri Siegel im Gespräch mit Sybille Krafft," June 16, 2014, https://www.br.de/fernsehen/ard-alpha /sendungen/alpha-forum/uri-siegel-gespraech-100.html. "Aber das war eigentlich eher spöttisch-liebevoll gemeint, da hat sich niemand etwas dabei gedacht."

33. The *Dietwart* position became mandatory for clubs under Nazi rule in August 1934. This person's task was to bring Nazi ideology to the club members.

34. Quoted in Hofmann, *Mitspieler der "Volksgemeinschaft,"* 199. "Aus früheren Zeiten der Club nicht gerade als auf rein völkischer Grundlage aufgebaut gilt" (my translation).

35. Because of the long history of nationalism, racism, antisemitism, and Nazism that has shaped the German term *Volk*, the word's adjective form *völkisch* cannot be directly translated as "people" or as any other English word.

36. The description of Kurt Landauer as a Jew or as German Jewish needs qualification. Today, Kurt Landauer is remembered as a Jew, although it is often overlooked that his primary identification was probably Bavarian. Landauer was a secular Jew. He was neither religious nor Zionist. His family had assimilated more and more into Bavarian culture: Kurt's father, Otto Nathan—his middle name was known only within the family—and his mother, Hulda Bernheimer, named their first son Leo, in reference to the grandfather Leopold "Loeb" Landauer, a name associated with Judaism. Their second son was named Paul Gabriel—in reference to the angel Gabriel. With the birth of the third son, Franz, the children's first names became more and more secular. Kurt and Alfons, finally, were named in the spirit of neither Judaism nor Catholicism but as Bavarian citizens. Kurt Landauer was, furthermore, a patriot who volunteered to fight in World War I. The conflation of Landauer with progressive politics is thus also questionable.

37. Volkov, "Antisemitism as a Cultural Code."

38. Rudolf Oswald, "Mythos 'Judenklub'—Feindbildkonstruktionen im mitteleuropäischen Fußball der Zwischenkriegszeit," *Aschkenas* 27, no. 1 (January 27, 2017): 158, https://doi.org/10.1515/asch-2017-0010.

"Schwabing, das für Bohème und künstlerische Avantgarde stand, in einem Viertel somit, das aus der Perspektive eines Konservativen Revolutionärs, eines völkisch denkenden Zeitgenossen der 1920er nichts anderes als 'jüdisch' war."

39. Herbert Moll, "'Der Sport hat alles überdeckt . . . ,'" in Stadtarchiv München, *München und der Fußball*, 9. "Es war doch so, daß damals Bayern und 60 viertelbezogen war: also Bayern war Schwabing" (my translation).

40. FC Bayern München, "FC Bayern Museum."

41. Schulze-Marmeling, *Die Bayern: Vom Klub zum Konzern*, 26. "Künstler- und Intelektuellen-Zentrum" (my translation).

42. The neighborhoods Schwabing and Maxvorstadt built one cultural center in the early twentieth century: The area was known as the town's literary and artists' quarter and was even praised as the most liberal place in Germany—artists and intellectuals such as Paul Klee, Wassily Kandinski, and Gabriele Münter, all part of the artists' group Der Blaue Reiter, as well as Heinrich Mann, Thomas Mann, Rainer Maria Rilke, Christian Morgenstern, Lion Feuchtwanger, Joachim Ringelnatz, and many others had worked and lived there; so did some of the founders of FC Bayern (Schulze-Marmeling, *Der FC Bayern, seine Juden und die Nazis*, 33–35).

43. A picture of players with large straw hats is displayed in the FC Bayern Museum (FC Bayern München, "FC Bayern Museum").

44. Michael Lenhard, *Fußballheimat München und Südbayern: 100 Orte der Erinnerung* (Hildesheim, Germany: Arete, 2018), 84.

45. Jutta Fleckenstein and Rachel Salamander, *Kurt Landauer—Der Präsident des FC Bayern Lebensbericht und Briefwechsel mit Maria Baumann* (Berlin: Insel, 2021), 10.

46. Schulze-Marmeling, *Der FC Bayern, seine Juden und die Nazis*, 35.

47. For a detailed discussion of the connection between the concepts of the coffeehouse club and the "Jew Club," see chapter 2.

48. The university, located in Maxvorstadt, became a hotspot for anti-semitism in the 1920s. Soon, many of the intellectuals began to leave Munich for Berlin (Bertolt Brecht in 1925 was followed by Lion Feuchtwanger and Heinrich Mann in 1928) or other places. In the mid-1920s, the NSDAP in Schwabing was the strongest NSDAP section in the city, and it was in Maxvorstadt that Adolf Hitler opened his party headquarters, Das Braune Haus, in 1930. The building was destroyed in World War II, and the ruins were demolished in 1947. Since 2015, the NS-Dokumentationszentrum has stood at this location. In these years, Munich really "earned" its 1935

"honorary title" as capital of the Nazi movement: On February 24, 1920, the NSDAP was founded at the Münchner Hofbräuhaus. In January 1923, the party held its Reichsparteitag at Münchner Löwenbräukeller, and in November 1923, Hitler's putsch attempt started in Munich.

49. Hofmann, *Mitspieler der "Volksgemeinschaft,"* 54, 32.

50. Heiner Gillmeister, "The Tale of Little Franz and Big Franz: The Foundation of Bayern Munich FC," *Soccer & Society* 1, no. 2 (June 2000): 80–106, https://doi.org/10.1080/14660970008721266.

51. Schulze-Marmeling, *Der FC Bayern, seine Juden und die Nazis*, 12.

52. Schulze-Marmeling, 14. A "weltoffener und liberaler Klub, in dem auch Juden eine Heimat fanden. Religiöse und nationale Zugehörigkeit spielten in seinen Reihen keine Rolle" (my translation).

53. Hofmann, *Mitspieler der "Volksgemeinschaft,"* 15, 87–88; Schulze-Marmeling, *Der FC Bayern, seine Juden und die Nazis*, 14–15.

54. Hofmann, *Mitspieler der "Volksgemeinschaft,"* 51–53.

55. Schulze-Marmeling, *Der FC Bayern, seine Juden und die Nazis*, 65. "Pioniere der Moderne" (my translation).

56. In 1919, Landauer invited the world-famous "Jew Club" MTK Budapest to Munich. The friendly game attracted a record crowd of about ten thousand spectators and resulted in numerous and laudatory newspaper articles. Soon, FC Bayern aimed to copy "Donau football" (Donaufußball)—a modern way of playing the game that differed immensely from how football had previously been played in Germany.

57. Schulze-Marmeling, *Der FC Bayern, seine Juden und die Nazis*, 69.

58. Bernd Beyer, *Der Mann, der den Fußball nach Deutschland brachte: Das Leben des Walther Bensemann; ein biografischer Roman*, Erweiterte Neuausgabe (Göttingen, Germany: Die Werkstatt, 2014). Landauer developed his modern cosmopolitanism in Switzerland, where he lived from July 1901 to September 1903 to be educated as a banker. Yet it was in Switzerland where his son not only met people from half of Europe but also established contacts with English students, from whom Landauer learned about the organization and the professionalization of football in England (Kämper, *Kurt Landauer*, 36–43).

59. Of the 361 football games FC Bayern played before World War I, 50 were international friendly games. Between June 1919 and June 1933, FC Bayern played 56 international friendly games, including against teams from Vienna, Prague, and Budapest (Schulze-Marmeling, *Der FC Bayern, seine Juden und die Nazis*, 43, 74).

60. For instance, Landauer granted accident insurance to the club's players in 1920—a revolutionary invention at the time (Schulze-Marmeling, 69).

61. Volkov, "Antisemitism as a Cultural Code."

62. The film's impact on the club's collective memory is hard to measure empirically, but I assert that its relevance can hardly be over-estimated. The film was accompanied by a documentary and the launch of the website www.kurtlandauer.de, consisting of further resources such as an augmented reality app and "the making of" videos. The German media devoted much attention to it. *Landauer—Der Präsident* aired on the largest public broadcaster network globally: ARD (Arbeitsgemein-schaft der öffentlich-rechtlichen Rundfunkanstalten der Bundesrepublik Deutschland).

63. *Landauer—Der Präsident,* feature film (ARD, 2014).

64. Julia Hell, *The Conquest of Ruins: The Third Reich and the Fall of Rome* (University of Chicago Press, 2019), 13; Julia Hell and Andreas Schönle, introduction to *Ruins of Modernity,* ed. Julia Hell and Andreas Schönle, Politics, History, and Culture (Durham, NC: Duke University Press, 2010), 1.

65. Johannes von Moltke, "Ruin Cinema," in Hell and Schönle, *Ruins of Modernity,* 396.

66. Amir Eshel, "Layered Time: Ruins as Shattered Past, Ruins as Hope in Israeli and German Landscapes and Literature," in Hell and Schönle, *Ruins of Modernity,* 147.

67. Eshel, 147.

68. FC Bayern München, "FC Bayern Museum."

69. FC Bayern München.

70. FC Bayern München. According to Hofmann, Landauer indeed played a role in the club's acquisition of the facilities at Säbener Straße, al-though his role was probably overstated by the club museum and the film, among others (Hofmann, *Mitspieler der "Volksgemeinschaft,"* 359–60).

71. Fleckenstein and Salamander, *Kurt Landauer,* 143. "Aber der Bayern wegen komme ich ja nicht, da ist schon ein ganz ganz anderer Anziehungs-punkt!" (my translation).

72. This notion of reconstruction is also expressed in the club's mu-seum: It displays Nazism as part of what it describes as the "bitter years, hard times"—namely, the period between 1933 and 1965, beginning with Nazism's seizure of power and ending with the club's promotion to the first

league in 1965. This periodization connects the club's supposed suffering under Nazism to the club's meager sporting successes.

73. Schulze-Marmeling, *Der FC Bayern, seine Juden und die Nazis*, 277. "Wir wollen die letzten Jahre vergessen und Gnade walten lassen" (my translation).

74. "Ich verzichte gerne auf die Ehre mit solch politisch Verblendeten von damals, von denen es heute bereits wieder in Deutschland genug Fanatiker gibt, einen Tisch zu teilen" (my translation; FC Bayern München, "Hans Bermühler to Kurt Landauer," June 1950, MG Karton 4 5 9, Landauer 1955 Liste, Hecker Julius, Bermühler Hans, John Franz, 1947–1952, FC Bayern Munich Club Archive).

75. FC Bayern München, "FC Bayern to Hans Bermühler," June 16, 1950, MG Karton 4 5 9, Landauer 1955 Liste, Hecker Julius, Bermühler Hans, John Franz, 1947–1952, FC Bayern Munich Club Archive. "Gerade dieser Jubeltag war vielleicht wie kein anderer Zeitpunkt so geeignet manchem irregeleiteten Bayernmitglied aus der Nazizeit versöhnend die Hand zu reichen" (my translation).

76. FC Bayern München, "FC Bayern to Hans Bermühler," March 2, 1953, MG Karton 4 5 9, Landauer 1955 Liste, Hecker Julius, Bermühler Hans, John Franz, 1947–1952, FC Bayern Munich Club Archive. "Im Auftrage der Klubleitung habe ich es damals unternommen Ihnen klarzumachen, daß der Klub nicht für alle Ewigkeit gegenüber allen ehemaligen Nazis im Verein den Bannstrahl aufrecht erhalten kann. Sie dürften doch wissen, daß viele alte und wirklich tadellose Bayern Nationalsozialisten waren und es würde mir nicht schwerfallen, Ihnen viele Dutzend von Namen zu sagen. Der Klub hat zwar nicht alle, aber doch sehr viele davon wieder in seinen Reihen als Mitglieder aufgenommen und all das Geschehene einen dicken Strich gemacht" (my translation).

77. "Mit altem, getreuen Bayerngruß!" (my translation).

78. Hofmann, *Mitspieler der "Volksgemeinschaft,"* 371.

79. *Persilschein* is a German idiom for denazification certificates. It refers to Persil, a laundry detergent brand. If someone received a *Persilschein*, it meant they had a clean political history during Nazism. During denazification, statements from others helped suspected Nazi offenders. Ideally, these statements came from victims or enemies of the Nazi regime.

80. FC Bayern München, *50 Jahre F.C. Bayern München e.V.* (Munich, 1950), 104. "Die Machtübernahme Hitlers bedeutete für den F. C. Bayern einen ganz gewaltigen Eingriff in sein innerstes Gefüge. Die Parteipolitik und der wie Gift ausgestreute Rassenhaß machte auch vor der sportlichen

Kameradschaft nicht Halt. Immer schon hatte man im Club die Anschau-
ung vertreten, daß jeder anständige Mensch, gleichwie welcher Rasse oder
Religion, Platz beim Sport finden könnte" (my translation).

81. FC Bayern München, 109. "Trotz vieler Schwierigkeiten versuchte
die Clubführung vor allem die innere Geschlossenheit im Verein zu
wahren" (my translation).

82. FC Bayern München, 121. "Wer diese Zeiten selbst nicht mitgemacht
hat, der hat keinen Anspruch darauf zu rechten, was dabei richtig war
oder besser gemacht hätte werden können. Es ging um das Leben und die
Existenz des F. C. Bayern" (my translation).

83. Adorno, "Meaning of Working Through," 89.

84. Markovits and Reich, *German Predicament*, 15.

85. Barbara A. Misztal, *Theories of Social Remembering*, Theorizing Society (Maidenhead, UK: Open University Press, 2003), 93.

86. Astrid Erll, *Memory in Culture* (London: Palgrave Macmillan UK,
2011), 9, https://doi.org/10.1057/9780230321670.

87. James E. Young, *The Texture of Memory: Holocaust Memorials and
Meaning* (New Haven, CT: Yale University Press, 1993), 5.

88. The Kurt Landauer Stiftung was founded by active fans after they
received the Julius Hirsch Prize.

89. When I visited the statue in January 2023, I had to ask for an ap-
pointment to see it.

90. Kurt Landauer Stiftung e.V., "Welcome Back, Kurt Landauer!," Kurt
Landauer Stiftung, accessed January 29, 2023, https://www.kurt-landauer
-stiftung.de/kurt?lang=en; FC Bayern München, "Von der Idee zum Kurt-
Landauer-Denkmal," FC Bayern München, May 22, 2019, https://fcbayern
.com/de/news/2019/05/entstehungsgeschichte-von-der-idee-zum-kurt
-landauer-denkmal.

91. FC Bayern München, "Von der Idee zum Kurt-Landauer-Denkmal."

92. Kurt Landauer Stiftung e.V., "Welcome Back, Kurt Landauer!"

93. Dan Diner, ed., *Zivilisationsbruch: Denken nach Auschwitz* (Frankfurt: Fischer Taschenbuch, 1988).

94. Schulze-Marmeling, *Der FC Bayern, seine Juden und die Nazis*, 325.

95. "Der FC Bayern war sein Leben—Nichts und Niemand konnte das
ändern: 125 Jahre Kurt Landauer" (my translation).

96. Uri Siegel, Kurt Landauer's nephew, was born in Munich on February 2, 1922. He escaped with his family in 1934 and joined the British army
at age nineteen. Later, he fought for Zahal in the Israeli War of Independence. In the 1950s, he returned to Munich, where he became a German

citizen in 1956. In 1957, he began working as a lawyer for an Israeli repara-
tion office. After his return to Munich, he developed an interest in Jewish
religion and served as the director of Munich's Israelitische Kultusgemeinde for seventeen years (Schulze-Marmeling, *Der FC Bayern, seine
Juden und die Nazis*, 288–90).

97. "Jetzt sitzt Kurt Landauer wieder hier, lebensgroß, und blickt auf
seinen FC Bayern. Willkommen zurück, Kurt!" (my translation; FC Bayern München, "FC Bayern enthüllt Kurt-Landauer-Statue an der Säbener
Straße," May 22, 2019, https://fcbayern.com/de/news/2019/05/enthuellung
-kurt-landauer-denkmal-an-der-saebener-strasse).

98. Christoph Leischwitz, "Ein Weg, sich zu erinnern," *Süddeutsche Zeitung*, February 26, 2020, https://www.sueddeutsche.de/muenchen/sport
/kurt-landauer-weg-ein-weg-sich-zu-erinnern-1.4822515.

99. "Die Machtübernahme der Nationalsozialisten wirkte sich auch auf
den FC Bayern aus, dessen erster Vorsitzender Kurt Landauer die Leitung
des Clubs abgab" ("The National Socialist assumption of power had an
influence on FC Bayern, whose first chairman Kurt Landauer surrendered
control of the club") (my translation; quoted in Schulze-Marmeling, *Der
FC Bayern, seine Juden und die Nazis*, 322).

100. "Unter dem nationalsozialistischen Regime geriet auch das Vereins-
leben ins Stocken. Kurt Landauer musste aus 'rassenpolitischen' Gründen
in die Schweiz emigrieren" ("Under the National Socialist dictatorship,
club life also came to a halt. Kurt Landauer was forced to relocate to Switzerland for 'racial policy' reasons") (my translation; quoted in Schulze-
Marmeling, 322).

101. "Am 30. Januar 1933 übernimmt Adolf Hitler die Macht. In den
folgenden Monaten wird nicht nur sportlich alles auf den Kopf gestellt.
Präsident Landauer, der jüdischer Abstammung ist, tritt am 22. März 1933
zurück. Die Vereinsführung versucht noch eine Weile, sich den neuen
Begebenheiten entgegenzustellen, da der FC Bayern sehr viele jüdische
Mitglieder hat. Dies bringt dem Verein in der Folgezeit noch viel Ärger
ein" ("Adolf Hitler is elected chancellor on January 30, 1933. Everything
is turned upside down in the months that follow, and not just in sports.
On March 22, 1933, President Landauer, who is of Jewish heritage, resigns.
As FC Bayern has a considerable number of Jewish members, the club
management initially tries to oppose the new events. This caused the club
a lot of problems in the years that followed") (my translation; quoted in
Schulze-Marmeling, 323).

102. Schulze-Marmeling, 325. The filmmaker Michael Verhoeven had a similar experience while working on his 2008 documentary *Menschliches Versagen* (Human failure), which thematizes "Aryanization" and also deals with Landauer. Verhoeven, who had played in Munich's youth teams under President Landauer after World War II, attempted unsuccessfully to speak with a club representative (Heike Mund, "Verhoeven: 'Landauer war mein FC Bayern-Präsident,'" Deutsche Welle, October 15, 2014, https://www.dw.com/de/verhoeven-landauer -war-mein-fc-bayern-pr%C3%A4sident/a-17997537).

103. Schulze-Marmeling, *Der FC Bayern, seine Juden und die Nazis,* 332, 335–36.

104. The sports ground was funded by FC Bayern with €25,000; Sparkasse Munich, €40,000; the DFB, €10,000; and the city, €100,000 (Schulze-Marmeling, 339).

105. The football field was opened on October 15, 2020, on the roof of the Bellevue di Monaco building—which offers apartments for refugees and functions as a cultural center.

106. "Der FC Bayern hat eine jüdische Vergangenheit, eine sehr reiche und erfolgreiche. Wir sind stolz auf diese jüdische Vergangenheit, und gemeinsam mit unseren jüdischen Freunden werden wir auch eine stolze Zukunft haben" (Christian Krügel, "Stolz auf die jüdische Vergangenheit," *Süddeutsche Zeitung,* May 26, 2011. https://www.sueddeutsche.de /muenchen/fc-bayern-muenchen-stolz-auf-die-juedische-vergangenheit -1.1101845).

107. Fleckenstein and Salamander, *Kurt Landauer;* Kämper, *Kurt Landauer;* Dietrich Schulze-Marmeling, *Der FC Bayern und seine Juden: Aufstieg und Zerschlagung einer liberalen Fußballkultur,* 2nd erweiterte Auflage (Göttingen, Germany: Die Werkstatt, 2013); Schulze-Marmeling, *Der FC Bayern, seine Juden und die Nazis;* Dietrich Schulze-Marmeling, *Kurt Landauer: Der Vater des modernen FC Bayern,* Jüdische Miniaturen 189 (Berlin: Hentrich and Hentrich, 2018).

108. *"Kick It like Kurt": Eine Erinnerung an den legendären Fußballfunktionär Kurt Landauer,* 2010. Regie: Nadine Filler, Avraham Bador. Germany: Kreisjugendring München-Stadt.

109. Bayerischer Rundfunk, "LandauerWalk: Auf den Spuren von Kurt Landauer," September 23, 2014, https://www.br.de/fernsehen/das-erste /sendungen/kurt-landauer-der-film/die-app100.html; Nick Golüke and Michael Müller, *Landauer: Gefeiert, verbannt, vergessen,* documentary film,

2014; Robert Schöffel and Uli Köppen, "LandauerWalk: Das Making-Of zur Augmented-Reality-App," Das Erste, September 19, 2014, https:// www.br.de/fernsehen/das-erste/sendungen/kurt-landauer-der-film/die -app-making-of-100.html. Air date: 2024, channel: Bayerischer Rundfunk. Germany: ZeitSprung pictures gmbh; *Landauer—Der Präsident*.

110. Sightseeing Munich, "FC Bayern—Humble Beginnings Tour in Munich," *Sightseeing-Touren Durch München* (blog), accessed February 5, 2023, https://sightseeing-munich.tours/en/fc-bayern-bescheidene -anfaenge/.

111. Bodemann, *Gedächtnistheater*.

112. "Gedenken findet . . . immer in theaterartigen Kontexten statt: mit Bühne, Zuschauern, Schauspielern, Bühnenbildern, dem Drama und seiner Inszenierung selbst. Charakteristisch für das Theater ist, daß es sich aus der alltäglichen Praxis heraushebt, daß es zunächst außerhalb des 'Stroms der Geschichte' zu stehen scheint" (my translation; Bodemann, 84).

113. Bodemann, 83.

114. Bodemann, 82. Plato: "Let us, then, say that this is the gift of Memory, the mother of the Muses, and that whenever we wish to remember anything we see or hear or think of in our own minds, we hold this wax under the perceptions and thoughts and imprint them upon it, just as we make impressions from seal rings; and whatever is imprinted we remember and know as long as its image lasts, but whatever is rubbed out or cannot be imprinted we forget and do not know" (*Theaetetus. Sophist*, trans. Harold North Fowler, Loeb Classical Library 123 [Cambridge, MA: Harvard University Press, 1921], 185–87).

115. The German phrase in the title of this section was the official slogan of the FIFA World Cup 2006 in Germany. It literally translates as: "The world welcomed by friends." The official English motto was "A time to make friends."

116. Carl Koppehel, *Geschichte des deutschen Fussballsports. Herausgegeben in Zusammenarbeit mit dem Deutschen Fussballbund* (Frankfurt: W. Limpert, 1954). Koppehel was the DFB's press secretary from 1937 to 1945 and again from 1951 to 1958; in 1951, the DFB named its media department Amt für Presse und Propaganda (Department for Press and Propaganda).

117. Schulze-Marmeling, *Der FC Bayern, seine Juden und die Nazis*, 319.

118. Hajo Bernett, *Nationalsozialistische Leibeserziehung: Eine Dokumentation ihrer Theorie und Organisation* (Schorndorf, Germany: Hofmann, 1966); Hajo Bernett, *Sportpolitik im Dritten Reich* (Schorndorf, Germany: Hofmann, 1971); Hajo Bernett, *Der jüdische Sport im nationalsozialistischen*

Deutschland 1933–1938 (Schorndorf: Hofmann, 1978); Hajo Bernett, *Der Weg des Sports in die nationalsozialistische Diktatur* (Schorndorf, Germany: Hofmann, 1983).

119. Gerhard Fischer and Ulrich Lindner, *Stürmer für Hitler: Vom Zusammenspiel zwischen Fussball und Nationalsozialismus* (Göttingen, Germany: Die Werkstatt, 1999); Arthur Heinrich, *Der Deutsche Fussballbund: Eine Politische Geschichte* (Cologne, Germany: PapyRossa, 2000).

120. Nils Havemann, *Fussball unterm Hakenkreuz: der DFB zwischen Sport, Politik und Kommerz* (Frankfurt: Campus, 2005).

121. "Ein 473 Seiten dicker Schlussstrich" (my translation); Detlev Claussen, "Fussball mit dem Hitlergruss," *indirekter freistoss* [blog], October 24, 2005, https://www.indirekter-freistoss.de/2005/10/24/nachschuss/.

122. Lorenz Peiffer and Henry Wahlig, *Jüdischer Sport und Sport der Juden in Deutschland: Eine kommentierte Bibliografie* (Göttingen, Germany: Die Werkstatt, 2009).

123. Deutscher Fußball-Bund, "Julius Hirsch Preis," accessed January 6, 2025, https://www.dfb.de/nachhaltigkeit-2/julius-hirsch-preis; DFB-Kulturstiftung. 'Auf den Spuren von Julius Hirsch: Die Deportation nach Auschwitz im März 1943.' DFB-Kulturstiftung, January 27, 2021. https://www.dfb.de/fileadmin/_dfbdam/234034-Auf_den_Spuren_von_Julius_Hirsch_einz.pdf; Werner Skrentny, *Julius Hirsch—Nationalspieler—Ermordet: Biografie eines jüdischen Fussballers* (Göttingen, Germany: Die Werkstatt, 2012).

124. Pavel Brunssen and Peter Römer, "Erinnern, um nicht zu vergessen," *Transparent—Magazin für Fußball und Fankultur*, no. 8 (2014): 10–16. Jenő Konrád was the club's coach when Nuremberg lost to FC Bayern in 1932, which cost them the North Bavarian championship. The antisemitic pamphlet *Der Stürmer* commented on the loss with a title page reading, "The 1. FCN perishes because of its Jews" [Der 1. FCN geht am Juden zugrunde]. Shortly after, Konrád left Germany together with his family (1. FC Nürnberg, "Nürnberger Ultras erinnern an Jenö Konrad," fcn.de, November 19, 2012, https://www.fcn.de/news/artikel/nuernberger-ultras-erinnern-an-jenoe-konrad).

125. 11 Freunde, "Verlorene Helden," 2014, https://11freunde.de/assets/downloads/13724-11F_148_beilage_gesamt.komprimiert.pdf.

126. Google Maps, "Erinnerung-Fußball," Google My Maps, November 12, 2021, https://www.google.com/maps/d/viewer?mid=1iWZWV6xarJ9z5_lu_sryKca3aLOk67QX.

127. Gavriel David Rosenfeld, *Munich and Memory: Architecture, Monuments, and the Legacy of the Third Reich,* Weimar and Now 22 (Berkeley: University of California Press, 2000), 15.

128. Leland M. Roth, *Understanding Architecture: Its Elements, History, and Meaning,* 3rd ed. (London: Routledge, 2018), 154; Rosenfeld, *Munich and Memory,* 5. According to Roth, "on a deep psychological level, our architecture is our built memory; it is a legacy, both the acclaimed architecture and the anonymous building. When we remove any element, we erase part of that memory, performing an incremental cultural lobotomy" (*Understanding Architecture,* 154).

129. Rosenfeld, *Munich and Memory,* 11–12.

130. Rosenfeld, 124.

131. Erwin Schleich and Eva Dietrich, *Die zweite Zerstörung Münchens,* Neue Schriftenreihe des Stadtarchivs München 100 (Stuttgart, Germany: Steinkopf, 1981).

132. Rosenfeld, *Munich and Memory,* 143–145.

133. Gavriel David Rosenfeld, *Architektur und Gedächtnis: München und Nationalsozialismus. Strategien des Vergessens,* trans. Uli Nickel and Bernadette Ott (Munich: Dölling und Galitz, 2004), 378.

134. Rosenfeld, *Munich and Memory,* 230.

135. Winfried Nerdinger, "München—Hauptstadt der Verdrängung: Gedenken auf Sparflamme: Wie in der bayerischen Landeshauptstadt mit den Bauten aus der Zeit des Nationalsozialismus umgegangen wird," *Süddeutsche Zeitung,* November 17, 2001.

136. "Ever since 1945, the members of the German resistance who were killed fighting the Nazis had been given considerable commemorative attention in Munich as a means of redefining the former *Hauptstadt der Bewegung* as the '*Hauptstadt der Gegenbewegung,*' the City of the Countermovement, or resistance" (Rosenfeld, *Munich and Memory,* 284). Most of the memorials for Jewish victims of Nazism were placed at the sites of historical events. Although well-intended, this "paradoxically promoted the Nazis' attempts to remove the Jews from German public life" (Rosenfeld, 299).

137. Ulrike Jureit and Christian Schneider, *Gefühlte Opfer: Illusionen der Vergangenheitsbewältigung* (Stuttgart, Germany: Klett-Cotta, 2010), 10–11.

138. "Sechs Millionen Juden werden . . . nicht als Opfer des von Deutschen verübten Massenmordes erinnert, sondern als eigene Tote rituell vereinnahmt" (my translation); Jureit and Schneider, 50.

139. Jureit and Schneider, 29.

140. Jureit and Schneider, 30, 52.

141. Jureit and Schneider, 36.

142. "Memory is not per se a precious commodity, and memory's antonym is not forgetting. A collective memory is not like an identity engine that one only needs to keep running to know who one is" ("Erinnerung stellt nicht per se ein kostbares Gut dar, und ihr Gegenbegriff ist auch nicht das Vergessen, und ein kollektives Gedächtnis gleich auch keinem Identitätsmotor, den man nur am Laufen halten muss, um zu erfahren, wer man ist") (my translation; Jureit and Schneider, 53).

143. I am referencing the title of an article I coauthored in 2014 to critically comment on and revise some of my earlier arguments (Brunssen and Römer, "Erinnern," 2014).

144. "Der 'Judenclub' Der Hass der Nazis auf den FC Bayern" (Rüdiger Liedtke, *111 Orte in München auf den Spuren der Nazi-Zeit* [Cologne, Germany: Emons, 2018], 116). Leading local broadcasters like Bayerischer Rundfunk also use the concept to describe the club: it claims in a headline that Nazism meant "Hard Times for the 'Jew Club'" (Bayerischer Rundfunk, "Die Bayern in der NS-Zeit: Schwere Zeiten für den 'Judenklub,'" August 12, 2015, https://www.br.de/themen/sport/inhalt/fussball /bundesliga/fc-bayern-muenchen/fc-bayern-muenchen136.html).

145. FC Bayern Museum, "Venerated—Persecuted—Forgotten," March 18, 2016, https://fcbayern.com/museum/en/the-exhibition/touring -exhibition.

146. Markwart Herzog, "FC Bayern Munich as a 'Victim' of National Socialism? Construction and Critique of a 'Heroic Myth,'" *Sport in History* 41, no. 1 (January 2, 2021): 131–52, https://doi.org/10.1080/17460263.2020 .1766548; Stephen Smith, "The Incredible Story of a Munich Soccer Team during the Holocaust Offers a Lesson," Jewish Journal, July 16, 2019, https://jewishjournal.com/commentary/columnist/301598/the-incred ible-story-of-a-munich-soccer-team-during-the-holocaust-offers-a-lesson/.

147. FC Bayern München, "'Venerated—Persecuted—Forgotten' at the Capitol in Washington," July 20, 2022, https://fcbayern.com/en/news /2022/07/touring-exhibition-goes-international---venerated-persecuted -forgotten-at-the-capitol-in-washington.

148. FC Bayern US (@FCBayernUS), "To commemorate International Holocaust Remembrance Day, FC Bayern presented the Venerated, Persecuted, and Forgotten Exhibit at Columbia University for a Discussion dedicated to remembrance . . .," X, January 27, 2023, https:// twitter.com/FCBayernUS/status/1618999284271321089; PennState,

"Venerated—Persecuted—Forgotten," Jewish Studies Program, February 15, 2023, https://jewishstudies.la.psu.edu/news-and-events/venerated-persecuted-forgotten/.

149. Peter Burke, "From 'History as Social Memory,'" in *The Collective Memory Reader*, ed. Jeffrey K. Olick, Vered Vinitzky-Seroussi, and Daniel Levy (New York: Oxford University Press, 2011), 190–91.

150. "Es war die Fangruppe Schickeria, die Kurt Landauer der Welt wieder in Erinnerung rief" (my translation; *Landauer—Der Präsident*).

151. "Der FC Bayern und ich gehören nun einmal zusammen und sind untrennbar voneinander" (my translation).

152. A video of the impressive sight and the meticulous work that went into its preparation is available on YouTube (Südkurve München, "Kurt Landauer Choreografie FC Bayern—Frankfurt," posted on YouTube, February 5, 2014, https://www.youtube.com/watch?v=OEeHTHbJGk4).

153. Gabriel Duttler and Boris Haigis, eds., *Ultras: Eine Fankultur im Spannungsfeld unterschiedlicher Subkulturen*, Kulturen der Gesellschaft, Band 17 (Bielefeld, Germany: Transcript, 2016); Jonas Gabler, *Die Ultras: Fussballfans und Fussballkulturen in Deutschland*, 5th erweiterte Auflage, Neue kleine Bibliothek 156 (Cologne, Germany: PapyRossa, 2010); Doidge, Kossakowski, and Mintert, *Ultras*.

154. Pavel Brunssen and Robert Claus, "Wessen Kurve? Hooligans und Ultras in den Fanszenen," in *Hooligans: eine Welt zwischen Fussball, Gewalt und Politik*, by Robert Claus (Göttingen, Germany: Die Werkstatt, 2017), 156–62.

155. Schickeria München, "Die (vergessene) Geschichte des 'Judenclub' Bayern München," *Gegen den Strom*, June 2005, 17, Archiv der Jugendkulturen. "Wir als Gruppe stehen zu und hinter der Geschichte des Judenclubs FC Bayern München" (my translation).

156. Schickeria München, cover, *Gegen den Strom*, June 2005, Archiv der Jugendkulturen.

157. "Davidsstern [in the original] und rote Hosen . . . Kurt Landauer und die Erfolgsgeschichte des 'Judenklubs' Bayern München" (my translation; Schickeria München).

158. Schickeria München, "Die (vergessene) Geschichte."

159. Schickeria München, "125 Jahre Kurt Landauer," *Gegen den Strom*, November 2010, 33–34, Archiv der Jugendkulturen.

160. Schickeria München, "125 Jahre Kurt Landauer," 34. Willi O. Hofmann was the club's president from 1979 to 1985. Other speakers were

the author Dietrich Schulze-Marmeling, vice president of the Bavarian Football Association Alfred Fackler, and Robby Rajber, who represented the Jewish sports club Maccabi München.

161. "On the walk to the church, Karl-Heinz Rummenigge and Karl Hopfner were approached by members of our group. We told them that we would welcome it if the FC Bayern board would finally deal with its history and would take a public stand on it. Of course, this can only be the beginning!" ("Auf dem Fußweg zur Kirche wurden Karl-Heinz Rummenigge und Karl Hopfner von Mitgliedern unserer Gruppe angesprochen und mitgeteilt, dass wir es begrüßen, wenn sich der Vorstand des FC Bayern endlich auch mit seiner Geschichte auseinandersetzte und hier öffentlich Stellung beziehe. Dies kann natürlich nur der Anfang sein!") (my translation).

162. Schickeria München, 34. "Dass der FC Bayern sich viel zu spät und immer noch in viel zu geringem Maße mit seiner Geschichte auseinandersetze, obwohl man als Verein besonders Stolz auf seine Historie sein kann" (my translation).

163. Andreas Rüttenauer, "Die ungeliebten Bayern-Fans," Die Tageszeitung: taz, March 26, 2010, https://taz.de/!460080/.

164. Pavel Brunssen, "Der lange Weg der 'Aachen Ultras,'" Transparent— Magazin für Fußball und Fankultur, no. 4 (2013): 18–21; Pavel Brunssen, "Recht der Stärkeren? Der Kampf um die Kurven geht weiter," Transparent— Magazin für Fußball und Fankultur, no. 22 (2017): 46–49; Pavel Brunssen and Robert Claus, "Rechtsextremismus und Fanszenen—ein analytischer Blick auf die gesellschaftlichen Strukturen," in Zurück am Tatort Stadion: Diskriminierung und Antidiskriminierung in Fussball-Fankulturen, ed. Martin Endemann et al. (Göttingen, Germany: Die Werkstatt, 2015), 179–94; Brunssen and Claus, "Wessen Kurve?"

165. Such fanzines are among the holdings of the Archiv der Arbeiterjugend in Oer Erkenschwick and the Archiv der Jugendkulturen in Berlin.

166. In 1988, one of the fanzines included a report from a visit to the game between Tottenham and Arsenal in London. In disgust, the fans wrote: "Quickly, it became clear that we were in the Tottenham fan section, although we were more inclined toward Arsenal, since Tottenham is known as a J** club (and other rabble)" ("Schnell wurde klar, daß wir uns in der Tottenham Kurve befanden, obwohl wir eher für Arsenal waren, da Tottenham ja als Juxxx-Verein bekannt ist [und sonstiges Gesocks]") (FC Bayern Muenchen Fan-Club Niederrhein, Niederrhein News, 1988, ZF89, Archiv der Arbeiterjugend).

167. Gerd Dembowski, "Zur Dialektik der Ultras. Potenziale und Konflikte eines Jugendphänomens zwischen Aufrühren und Partizipation," *Unsere Jugend 66*, no. 6 (2014): 260–70; Gerd Dembowski and Robert Claus, "'Lamm oder Hähnchen?'—Ethnizität und Weißsein in Fankulturen: Interview mit dem Kölner Ultra V.," in Endemann et al., *Zurück am Tatort Stadion*, 142–51; Doidge, Kossakowski, and Mintert, *Ultras*; Duttler and Haigis, *Ultras*; Gabler, *Die Ultras*; Judith von der Heyde, *Doing Gender als Ultra—Doing Ultra als Frau: Weiblichkeitspraxis in der Ultrakultur: Eine Ethnographie*, 2nd korrigierte Auflage, Sportfans im Blickpunkt sozialwissenschaftlicher Forschung (Weinheim, Germany: Beltz Juventa, 2018); Tobias Jones, *Ultra: The Underworld of Italian Football* (London: Head of Zeus, an Apollo Book, 2019); Gunter A. Pilz and Franciska Wölki, "Ultraszene in Deutschland," in *Wandlungen des Zuschauerverhaltens im Profifußball*, ed. Gunter A. Pilz et al., Schriftenreihe des Bundesinstituts für Sportwissenschaft 114 (Schorndorf, Germany: Hofmann, 2006), 63–238.

168. Schickeria München, "Kurt-Landauer-Turnier 2008," *Gegen den Strom*, September 2008, 46, Archiv der Jugendkulturen. "Aufgrund dieser weltoffenen, kosmopolitischen und toleranten Tradition unseres Vereins, sehen wir uns als Bayernfans verpflichtet, uns gegen Rassismus und Diskrimierung in den Stadien und in der Gesellschaft auszusprechen und zu engagieren" (my translation).

169. *Schickeria* is a term associated with someone with celebrity status. Schwabing's Schickeria scene of the late 1970s and early 1980s became famous for the embodiment of Schickeria, a concept that became linked to Munich through the television series *Monaco Franze* (1983), and the song "Schickeria" by Spider Murphy Gang (1981). The group's logo imitates the city's symbol Münchner Kindl. "Both the name and the logo should illustrate the connection to the city of Munich, and finally everyone should see: MUNICH—THAT'S US" ("Sowohl der Name als auch das Logo sollen die Verbindung zur Stadt München verdeutlichen, schließlich soll jeder sehen: MÜNCHEN—DAS SIND WIR!") (my translation; Schickeria München, "Wer wir sind," Schickeria München, accessed February 6, 2023, https://schickeria-muenchen.org/pico/infos/ueber_uns/wer_wir_sind).

170. My translation; Schickeria München, "Südkurve 72: Symbolik der Gruppe," *Gegen den Strom*, September 2008, 4, Archiv der Jugendkulturen. "SÜDKURVE MÜNCHEN—72—Ursprung und Zukunft."

171. Pavel Brunssen and Peter Römer, "Feindbild Polizei: Eine verfahrene Situation," *Transparent—Magazin für Fußball und Fankultur*, no. 3 (2012): 10–15; Melissa Schiefer and Torben Stichling, "Misstrauen

gegenüber der Polizei im Fußball: Eine empirische Untersuchung zu Verbreitung und Ursachen," in *Fanverhalten im Sport: Phänomene, Herausforderungen und Perspektiven*, ed. André Schneider, Julia Köhler, and Frank Schumann (Wiesbaden, Germany: Springer, 2017), 77–91, https://doi.org/10.1007/978-3-658-15900-9.

172. Only one year after the group's foundation, they were interviewed by the national fanzine *Erlebnis Fussball* and already complained that repression was a significant topic for the group ("Interview mit Mark Johanni," *Erlebnis Fussball*, April 2003).

173. Fabian Jonas, "Die Süd schweigt—Grabesstimmung in Fröttmaning," *11 Freunde*, June 13, 2007, https://11freunde.de/artikel/die-süd-schweigt/358149.

174. "20 Jahre Schickeria München: Choreografie & Zaunfahnen-Comeback," Faszination Fankurve, 2022, https://www.faszinationfankurve.de/news/48366/20-jahre-schickeria-muenchen-choreografie-zaunfahnen-comeback. Stadium bans are usually issued for three years and prohibit entrance to any game of Germany's top three leagues.

175. "'Schickeria München': Bewährungsstrafen für Fan-Überfall," *Frankfurter Allgemeine Zeitung*, January 31, 2008, https://www.faz.net/aktuell/sport/fussball/schickeria-muenchen-bewaehrungsstrafen-fuer-fan-ueberfall-1514745.html.

176. Jonas, "Die Süd schweigt." "Für die Gruppe . . . dürfte dies das Ende bedeuten" (my translation).

177. "Interview Schickeria München," *Erlebnis Fussball*, August 2008. "Im Endeffekt war Würzburg nur ein weiterer willkommener Vorwand um mal wieder gegen die aktive Fanszene in München zu schießen, in der Hoffnung dieser den Todesstoß versetzen zu können" (my translation).

178. Brunssen and Claus, "Wessen Kurve?"; Chucky Goldstein, "Ultras und Hooligans sind nicht das Gleiche," *Vice*, April 14, 2015, https://www.vice.com/de/article/ezyd87/ultras-und-hooligans-sind-nicht-das-gleiche-567.

179. Schickeria München, "Quo vadis Ultras? Über die Zukunft der deutschen Ultrà-Gruppen," *Blickfang Ultra*, December 2007, 8. "Ist es möglich, über geschickte Präsentation seiner Themen, über eigene Medien und die Presse die Akzeptanz für unsere Subkultur Ultrà in der breiten Öffentlichkeit zu schaffen?" (my translation).

180. Schickeria München, 80. "All diese Fragen sind mit dem Vorfall auf dem Rasthof Würzburg mit einem Knall für uns zentral für unser Überleben als Gruppe geworden" (my translation).

181. Schickeria München, 80. "Organisierte gemeinsame Auswärts-
fahrten, meist mit dem Bus, und ein möglichst geschlossenes Auftreten
der Gruppe haben für unser Verständnis von einer Ultrà-Gruppe immer
eine große Rolle gespielt.... Bei nahezu jedem Auswärtsspiel wurden
unsere Busse von einem massiven Polizeiaufgebot in Empfang genommen,
eingekesselt und oft alle Mitfahrer kontrolliert, ohne dass vorher etwas
vorgefallen ist. Aufgrund dieser massiven Verfolgung unserer Gruppe
sehen wir uns bis auf weiteres nicht mehr in der Lage, als Gruppe Aus-
wärtsfahrten mit dem Bus zu organisieren" (my translation).

182. "20 Jahre Schickeria." "Ausgesperrte immer bei uns" (my
translation).

183. Schickeria München, "Quo vadis Ultras? Über die Zukunft der
deutschen Ultrà-Gruppen," 81. "Mach Euch Gedanken, findet Euren Weg"
(my translation).

184. The 2014 film about Landauer brought this change of perspective to
the whole country. It said, "It was the fan group Schickeria that reminded
the world of Kurt Landauer."

185. "Many historians have argued that the legacy of the Third Reich
can never be fully come to terms with (if such a concept implies a point of
termination where the past ceases to serve as a matter of exceptional interest)" (Rosenfeld, *Munich and Memory*, 312).

186. Rosenfeld, 312.

187. Rosenfeld discusses the controversies around the NS-
Dokumentationszentrum in the German translation of his book, which appeared in 2004, four years after the first English edition (Rosenfeld, *Architektur und Gedächtnis*, 451–57).

188. Young, *Texture of Memory*, particularly, chapter 6, "The Biography of
a Memorial Icon: Nathan Rapoport's Warsaw Ghetto Monument," 155–84.

189. *Gegenwartsbewältigung* is the title of a book by Max Czollek. See
Max Czollek, *Gegenwartsbewältigung* (Munich: Carl Hanser, 2020).

190. Schickeria München, "SK-Aktionstag FUSSBALL OHNE
GRENZEN—REFUGEES WELCOME," accessed April 29, 2021, https://
schickeria-muenchen.org/pico/blog/109_News; Schulze-Marmeling, *Der
FC Bayern, seine Juden und die Nazis*, 330.

191. Schulze-Marmeling, *Der FC Bayern, seine Juden und die Nazis*, 330.

192. Fabian Scheler, "Kurt Landauer: Der vergessene Erfinder des FC
Bayern," Die Zeit, October 14, 2014, https://www.zeit.de/sport/2014-10
/kurt-landauer-fc-bayern-film/komplettansicht. "Auch Schulze-

Marmeling wurde mal eingeladen und rechnete mit bierseligen und grölenden Fußballfans: 'Ich saß in einem Bierzelt vor 300 Leuten, es war komplett still', sagt er, 'so ein Interesse an meiner Lesung habe ich nirgendwo sonst gespürt'" (my translation).

193. The Julius Hirsch Prize is an award established by the DFB to honor individuals and organizations who promote freedom, tolerance, and humanity. The prize commemorates the life of Julius Hirsch, a former German national player who was expelled from his club, Karlsruher FV, in 1933 because of his Jewish heritage and was later murdered in the Auschwitz concentration camp in 1943.

194. tz, "Julius-Hirsch-Preis an Münchner Ultra-Gruppierung 'Schickeria,'" October 14, 2014, https://www.tz.de/sport/fc-bayern/julius-hirsch -preis-muenchner-ultra-gruppierung-schickeria-zr-4118941.html.

195. "Landauer ist ein Vehikel, um Botschaften zu transportieren," Nino Duit, "Die Erinnerungsarbeiter," February 1, 2018, https://ballesterer .at/2018/05/16/die-erinnerungsarbeiter/.

196. Michael Rothberg, *Multidirectional Memory: Remembering the Holocaust in the Age of Decolonization*, Cultural Memory in the Present File (Stanford, CA: Stanford University Press, 2009).

197. Kurt Landauer Stiftung, "Satzung des 'Kurt Landauer Stiftung e.V.' vom 16. Juni 2017," June 16, 2017, https://www.kurt-landauer-stiftung .de/_files/ugd/adea3a_9ab9f00bd77946d38d4168c24141c42a.pdf. "Insbesondere sollen Projekte im Sinne einer weltoffenen, fortschrittlichen, liberalen und antirassistischen Gesellschaft und eines friedlichen und gleichberechtigten Zusammenlebens aller Menschen unabhängig von ihrer Nationalität, Staatsangehörigkeit, ethnischen und kulturellen Herkunft gefördert werden" (my translation).

198. The official FC Bayern fan shop offers—to give but one example— the article "Sweatshirt Heimat." The photo print shows the Allianz Arena, the office of FC Bayern, the Rathausplatz and the Münchner Kindl. The photos are accompanied by the text "FC Bayern München: Meine Heimat. Mein Verein" (FC Bayern München, "Sweatshirt Heimat," FC Bayern Store, accessed April 28, 2021, https://fcbayern.com/shop/de/sweatshirt -heimat/24967/).

199. The phrase *Mia san Mia* goes back to the nineteenth-century Austro-Hungarian Empire and was used by German politician Franz Josef Strauss, the chairman of the Christian Social Union in Bavaria from 1961 until 1988, before being adopted by FC Bayern in the 1980s (Hans Kratzer,

"Ursprung des FC Bayern-Mottos: Woher das Mia san Mia stammt," *Süddeutsche Zeitung*, August 9, 2013, https://www.sueddeutsche.de/bayern/ursprung-des-fc-bayern-mottos-wer-san-mia-1.1742394).

200. Lahm, "Vorwort," 7. "Was den FC Bayern ausmacht, lässt sich in dem Leitspurch 'Mia san mia' zusammenfassen. Diese drei Wörter bringen Heimatverbundenheit und Traditionsbewusstsein zum Ausdruck. Diese neun Buchstaben stehen für Identifikation, drücken Zusammengehörigkeit und auch einen gewissen Stolz aus. Einen Stolz auf den bayerischen Vereinscharakter, die Bewahrung der eigenen Wurzeln und nicht zuletzt natürlich auf die errungenen Erfolge und Titel. Ein Stolz, der oft auch als Überheblichkeit ausgelegt wird, der polarisiert und dadurch eine Gemeinschaft erzeugt" (my translation).

201. Simon Müller, interview by Pavel Brunssen, January 31, 2023.

202. Veronica Baena, "Global Marketing Strategy in Professional Sports. Lessons from FC Bayern Munich," *Soccer & Society* 20, no. 4 (May 19, 2019): 660–74, https://doi.org/10.1080/14660970.2017.1379399.

203. Since 2015, the revenue of FC Bayern München AG has been between 628 and 750 million euro per year (Statista, "FC Bayern München AG: Konzernumsatz," accessed November 6, 2024, https://de.statista.com/statistik/daten/studie/246557/umfrage/umsatz-fc-bayern-muenchen-ag-konzern/).

204. Club Nr. 12, "Infos zum aktuellen Geschehen in Katar—Club Nr. 12," February 8, 2021, https://clubnr12.org/news/206-infos-zum-aktuellen-geschehen-in-katar. The club publicly claims to have a positive influence on human rights in Qatar. See, for instance, Florian Kinast, "FC Bayern München und Katar: Eine problematische Partnerschaft," *Der Spiegel*, February 11, 2021, https://www.spiegel.de/sport/fussball/fc-bayern-muenchen-und-katar-eine-problematische-partnerschaft-a-7889d38d-3c82-4d8c-9aea-e4b259861846.

205. Club Nr. 12, "Infos zum aktuellen Geschehen in Katar—Club Nr. 12."

206. Sebastian Fischer, "Jahreshauptversammlung des FC Bayern: Revolte bis nach Mitternacht," *Süddeutsche Zeitung*, November 26, 2021, https://www.sueddeutsche.de/sport/fc-bayern-jahreshauptversammlung-hainer-kahn-katar-ott-antraege-1.5473760.

207. Michael Ott, "Antrag zur Jahreshauptversammlung: Beendigung des Katar-Sponsorings beim FC Bayern," accessed November 6, 2024, http://katar-antrag.de/.

208. David M. Herold, C. Keith Harrison, and Scott J. Bukstein, "Revisiting Organizational Identity and Social Responsibility in Professional Football Clubs: The Case of Bayern Munich and the Qatar Sponsorship," *International Journal of Sports Marketing and Sponsorship* 24, no. 1 (2023): 56–73.

209. Giulianotti and Robertson, *Globalization and Football*.

210. *FC Bayern—Behind the Legend*, episode 3 (Amazon Prime, 2021), min. 33:30.

211. *FC Bayern—Behind the Legend*, episode 2, min. 34:25.

212. Schulze-Marmeling, *Der FC Bayern, seine Juden und die Nazis*, 359. "It remains to be seen whether the commitment to the 'Jewish heritage' and an active memory culture will be compatible with FC Bayern's efforts in Asia in the future. Indeed, Qatar, host of the 2022 World Cup, a financier of Hamas who describes the Holocaust as a 'Zionist falsification of history' and makes no secret of its intention to destroy the State of Israel and expel the Jews" ("Allerdings bleibt abzuwarten, wie sich in Zukunft das Bekenntnis zum ‚jüdischen Erbe' und eine aktive Erinnerungskultur mit dem geschäftlichen Engagement des FC Bayern in Asien vertragen. Namentlich mit Katar, Ausrichter der WM 2022, einem Finanzier der Hamas, die den Holocaust als 'zionistische Geschichtsfälschung' bezeichnet und aus ihrer Absicht, den Staat Israel zu zerstören und die Juden zu vertreiben, keinen Hehl macht") (my translation).

213. Global media suggested that the deal was ended because of the fan protests. (For instance, see ESPN's headline: "Bayern Munich end deal with Qatar Airways after fan protests.") Instead, however, it was Qatar's emir who intervened, being unhappy with the German perception of Qatar and behavior at the 2022 World Cup (Reuters, "Bayern Munich End Deal with Qatar Airways after Fan Protests," ESPN.com, June 28, 2023, https://www.espn.com/soccer/story/_/id/37926383/bayern-munich -end-deal-qatar-airways-fan-protests; Süddeutsche Zeitung, "FC Bayern verlängert umstrittenes Katar-Sponsoring nicht," June 28, 2023, https:// www.sueddeutsche.de/sport/fc-bayern-qatar-airways-katar-sponsoring -vertrag-1.5976393).

214. Ronny Blaschke, *Machtspieler Fußball in Propaganda, Krieg und Revolution* (Göttingen, Germany: Die Werkstatt, 2020), 178–98.

215. "Ich freue mich sehr: Meine Gemeinde und mein Verein zusammen!" (my translation).

216. "Der große Kurt Landauer wäre stolz gewesen, das seine Bayern sich so einsetzen" (my translation).

217. "Thank you very much for the words of praise about FC Bayern. I could not have said it any better" ("Vielen Dank für die lobenden Worte über den FC Bayern. Ich hätte es nicht besser sagen können") (my translation).

218. Hofmann, *Mitspieler der "Volksgemeinschaft."* "Die Studie hat ganz klar gezeigt, dass es auch beim FC Bayern Täter gab" (my translation).

219. "Es geht darum, die Vergangenheit aufzuarbeiten. Nicht, sie zu bewältigen" (my translation).

220. "Erinnern alleine reicht nicht" (my translation).

221. FC Bayern München, *Our Club*, 32–33; FC Bayern München, *Unser Verein. Unsere Geschichte. Seit 1900* (Munich: FC Bayern München, 2022), 33. The framing of the third question in the German edition suggests even stronger that the club is questioning its own (former) historical narrative. It asks, "To what extent was FC Bayern even considered a 'Jew club'?" ("In-wiefern galt der FC Bayern überhaupt als 'Judenklub'?") (my translation).

2. FK AUSTRIA VIENNA

1. Although widely ignored in Austria, the event was noted by international newspapers like the *Jerusalem Post*: Jeremy Sharon, "Austrian Football Association Adopts IHRA Antisemitism Definition," *Jerusalem Post*, November 11, 2021, https://www.jpost.com/diaspora/antisemitism/austrian-football-association-adopts-ihra-antisemitism-definition-684724.

2. IHRA's Working Definition of Antisemitism is a nonlegally binding statement that aims to define antisemitism. It was adopted by IHRA in May 2016 (International Holocaust Remembrance Alliance, "Working Definitions & Charters: Working Definition of Antisemitism," accessed November 22, 2021, https://holocaustremembrance.com/resources/working-definitions-charters/working-definition-antisemitism). The high-ranking guests included Karoline Edtstadler, Austrian federal minister for the EU; Werner Kogler, Austrian vice-chancellor and sports minister; and Oskar Deutsch, president of the Israelitische Kultusgemeinde. Representatives of the Austrian and the Israeli football governing bodies and nation states spoke. So did Marcus Franz, district mayor of the tenth district of Vienna.

3. Volkov, "Antisemitism as a Cultural Code"; Michael John and Matthias Marschik discuss the concept of antisemitism as a cultural code in the context of Austrian sport: Michael John and Matthias Marschik,

"Ortswechsel: Antisemitismus im österreichischen Sport nach 1945," in *Antisemitismus in Österreich nach 1945: Ergebnisse, Positionen und Perspektiven der Forschung*, ed. Heinz P. Wassermann, Schriften des Centrums für Jüdische Studien 3 (Innsbruck, Austria: StudienVerlag, 2002), 198–200.

4. "Wer zusammenhält, gewinnt! *(Dionys Schönecker)*." The whole plaque reads, "Dionys Schönecker 1888–1938. Spieler, Trainer und Sektionsleiter des SK Rapid. Vater des Rapidgeists."

5. The museum is divided into three parts: Gemeinsam, Kämpfen, and Siegen (Together, Fighting, and Winning).

6. Interview with FAK player and coach Karl Geyer, quoted in Michael John and Albert Lichtblau, *Schmelztiegel Wien—Einst und jetzt*, 2nd ed. (Vienna: Böhlau, 1993), 437. "Burschen, passt's auf, heute geht's gegen die Juden. Ihr wisst's, haut's es eini, dann sind's dort, wo's hing'hören" (my translation).

7. Andreas Hafer and Wolfgang Hafer, *Hugo Meisl, oder, Die Erfindung des modernen Fussballs: Eine Biographie* (Göttingen, Germany: Die Werkstatt, 2007), 268.

8. Domenico Jacono, "'Hauts es eini, die Juden!,'" *Ballesterer* 49 (2010): 39.

9. John Bunzl, ed., *Hoppauf Hakoah: Jüdischer Sport in Österreich von den Anfängen bis in die Gegenwart* (Vienna: Junius, 1987), 43; Jakob Rosenberg and Georg Spitaler, *Grün-weiß unterm Hakenkreuz: Der Sportklub Rapid im Nationalsozialismus (1938–1945)* (Vienna: Dokumentationsarchiv des österreichischen Widerstandes, 2011), 47–56.

10. Daniel Shaked, interview by Pavel Brunssen, March 10, 2022.

11. Adam Sutcliffe, "Symptoms at Play: Soccer, Austria, and the Jewish Question," *Journal of Sport and Social Issues* 24, no. 3 (2000): 251–59, https://doi.org/doi:10.1177/0193723500243003.

12. Shaked, interview.

13. Silverman, *Becoming Austrians*; Anderson, *Imagined Communities*.

14. Michael John, "'Körperlich ebenbürtig'—Juden im österreichischen Fußball," in *Davidstern und Lederball: Die Geschichte der Juden im deutschen und internationalen Fussball*, ed. Dietrich Schulze-Marmeling (Göttingen, Germany: Die Werkstatt, 2003), 235. The Wunderteam is what people called the Austrian national football team of the 1930s. Under its manager Hugo Meisl and led by its captain Matthias Sindelar, it had an unbeaten streak of fourteen games in 1931–32. The team was famous for its modern style of football. Hugo Meisl's brother Willy acted as FAK's goalkeeper

after World War I and became one of the most renowned sports journalists before escaping from Nazism into British exile.

15. Bernhard Hachleitner et al., "Raum," in *Sportfunktionäre und jüdische Differenz: Zwischen Anerkennung und Antisemitismus—Wien 1918 bis 1938*, ed. Bernhard Hachleitner, Matthias Marschik, and Georg Spitaler (Berlin: De Gruyter Oldenbourg, 2018), 125.

16. Roman Horak, *Ein halbes Jahrhundert am Ball: Wiener Fußballer erzählen* (Vienna: Löcker, 2010), 56. "Als ich zu den Amateuren kam, war die eine Hälfte der Mannschaft Juden und die andere Hälfte 'Arier.' Aber das hat keine Rolle gespielt. Man hat es gewusst, aber keiner hat darüber gesprochen, das war uninteressant! . . . Es gab keinen Wirbel. Man hat nicht gesagt: 'Du Saujud,' Du'" (my translation). Karl Geyer (1899–1998) played for FAK from 1920 until 1928, and he played seventeen games for the Austrian national team. Not much is known about his life during Nazism, but he took on important roles in Austrian football after the liberation, when he led the Austrian young players' academy and even coached the men's national team (1955–56). Geyer was married to Margarethe Mahler, who counted as Jewish for the Nazis although she had left the Israelitsche Kultusgemeinde in 1936. After a short time in Norwegian exile, the Geyers returned to Vienna where Karl took on important roles in the club, which he allegedly coached until 1945 (his exact role is unknown) (Bernhard Hachleitner et al., *Ein Fußballverein aus Wien: Der FK Austria im National-sozialismus 1938–1945* [Vienna: Böhlau, 2019], 130–33).

17. The Wiener Sport-Club was Austria's only football club that did not admit Jews (Bernhard Hachleitner, "Arierparagrafen und andere Aus-schlussmechanismen," in Hachleitner, Marschik, and Spitaler, *Sportfunk-tionäre und jüdische Differenz*, 40, 42).

18. Bernhard Hachleitner and Georg Spitaler, "Demografie jüdischer SportfunktionärInnen," in Hachleitner, Marschik, and Spitaler, *Sportfunk-tionäre und jüdische Differenz*, 94.

19. Hachleitner et al., "Raum," 125.

20. Part of FAK's club culture were the Jewish journalists Friedrich Tor-berg and Willy Meisl, brother to Hugo Meisl, as well as the essayists Alfred Polgar and Anton Kuh.

21. The founding of the Deutsch-Österreichische Turnverein, for instance, was a reaction to the "Aryan clause" introduced by the Erste Wiener Turnverein in 1887. The newly founded club was open to those excluded by or opposed to the "Aryan clause." Twelve years later, in 1899, the Turnverein jüdischer Hochschule was founded, later renamed the Erster

Wiener Jüdischer Turnverein (Alexander Juraske, "Die jüdische Sportbewegung im Wien der Zwischenkriegszeit," in Hachleitner, Marschik, and
Spitaler, *Sportfunktionäre und jüdische Differenz*, 71–88).

22. Juraske, 75.

23. Juraske, 76.

24. Max Nordau, "II. Kongressrede," in *Reden und Schriften zum Zionismus* (Boston: De Gruyter, 1898), 50–60.

25. Juraske, "Die jüdische Sportbewegung," 77.

26. Horak, *Ein halbes Jahrhundert am Ball*, 58. "Aber um auf die Hetz
auf der Tribüne zurückzukommen, die haben da 'Du Saujud,' Du' ge-
schrieen, ein Jude zu einem anderen Juden, es waren ja allesamt Juden.
Raufer sind sie ja keine, die schimpfen nur. Es ist etwas anderes, wenn die
Leute zu Raufen beginnen und mit allem möglichen hinhauen, bis Blut
fließt. Aber die haben nur geschimpft: 'Du Saujud,' Du dreckiger!,' oder
'Isidor, scheußlich, pfui!' Und so war es lustig auf der Tribüne fallweise,
wenn es zu laut, oder der Ball im Out war, haben wir hinaufgeschaut" (my
translation).

27. Horak, 56.

28. John and Lichtblau, *Schmelztiegel Wien*, 437. "Ich war sozusagen
beim Judenklub, wir haben ja auch Judenklub geheißen, obwohl ich Arier
war. Wir waren die Juden, genauso wie Hakoah. . . . Und da war natürlich
folgendes, wenn Hakoah gegen Amateure gespielt hat, da war immer Ri-
valität" (my translation).

29. Hakoah's men's football team became world-famous for beating
West Ham United during the team's trip to England in 1923 with a score of
5–1 (although they played against West Ham's B team).

30. Schulze-Marmeling, "Einführung."

31. Schulze-Marmeling, 17. "Metropole unter den Metropolen des
Donaufußballs war Wien" (my translation).

32. Among them were the two brothers Jenő and Kálmán Konrád, two
world-class players known for their technical style of playing.

33. Horak, *Ein halbes Jahrhundert am Ball*, 33.

34. Bernhard Hachleitner, "Publikumsausschreitungen," in Hachleitner, Marschik, and Spitaler, *Sportfunktionäre und jüdische Differenz*, 214;
Bernhard Hachleitner et al., *Der Wiener Fußball im Nationalsozialismus:
Sein Beitrag zur Erinnerungskultur Wiens und Österreichs*, Wiener Vorlesungen 192 (Vienna: Picus, 2019), 44.

35. Quoted in Hachleitner et al., *Der Wiener Fußball im Nationalsozialismus*, 45. "Die Violetten repräsentieren eine eigene Marke im Wiener,

ja im österreichischen Fußballeben. Sie waren nie das, was man eine harte Mannschaft nennt, wohl weil ihr Verein lange Zeit in mindestens demselben Maße darauf bedacht war, Gesellschafts- wie Fußballklub zu sein. . . . An der Spitze stand ganz unabsichtlich fast stets ein Doktor oder ein Professor" (my translation).

36. Hachleitner et al., 44, 46.

37. Dieter Chmelar, *Ballett in violett: 75 Jahre Fussballklub Austria* (Vienna: Jugend und Volk, 1986). "Tore nie gewaltsam schießen" (my translation).

38. "He always plays and never fights" is a reference to a poem by the Jewish author Friedrich Torberg ("Auf den Tod eines Fußballspielers"), Torberg, Friedrich. "Auf den Tod eines Fussballspielers." In *Lebenslied: Gedichte aus 25 Jahren*, by Friedrich Torberg (Wien, Berlin: Medusa, 1983), 47–48 (my translation).

39. Beppo Mauhart, "Vorwort," in *Wiener Austria: Die ersten 90 Jahre*, by Matthias Marschik (Vienna: Funtoy, 2001), 9. "Austria ist nicht die Geschichte einer Mannschaft von fleißigen Fußballarbeitern, sondern von kreativen Fußballkünstlern" (my translation).

40. Shaked, interview.

41. Hachleitner et al., *Ein Fußballverein aus Wien*, 46–50.

42. Hachleitner et al., 47.

43. A "Hirnfußballer," literally "brain player" is a smart player.

44. Wolfgang Maderthaner, "Die lange Reise des Fußballdoktors Emanuel 'Michl' Schwarz," in *Sportler im "Jahrhundert der Lager": Profiteure, Widerständler und Opfer*, ed. Diethelm Blecking and Lorenz Pfeiffer (Göttingen, Germany: Die Werkstatt, 2012), 124.

45. Hachleitner et al., *Ein Fußballverein aus Wien*, 43.

46. FAK's president from 1932 to 1938 and from 1946 to 1955.

47. Maderthaner, "Die lange Reise," 124.

48. Roman Horak, "Kaffeehaus und Vorstadt, Feuilleton und Massenvergnügen: Über die doppelte Kodierung des Fußballs im Wien der Zwischenkriegszeit," in *Global Players: Kultur, Ökonomie und Politik des Fussballs*, ed. Michael Fanizadeh, Gerald Hödl, and Wolfram Manzenreiter (Frankfurt: Brandes and Apsel, 2002), 65–66.

49. Charlotte Ashby, introduction to *The Viennese Café and Fin-de-Siècle Culture*, ed. Charlotte Ashby, Tag Gronberg, and Simon Shaw-Miller (New York: Berghahn Books, 2013), 2; Shachar Pinsker, *A Rich Brew: How Cafés Created Modern Jewish Culture* (New York: New York University Press, 2018).

50. Ashby, introduction, 4.

51. Horak, "Kaffeehaus und Vorstadt."

52. Bernhard Hachleitner, Matthias Marschik, and Georg Spitaler, "(Sport-)Netzwerke," in Hachleitner, Marschik, and Spitaler, *Sportfunktionäre und jüdische Differenz*, 249.

53. Hachleitner, Marschik, and Spitaler, "(Sport-)Netzwerke," 251.

54. Ashby, Gronberg, and Shaw-Miller, *Viennese Café and Fin-de-Siècle Culture*. A 1936 *Sport-Tagblatt* article wrote about a joke that could be heard frequently in the stadium, namely, that "a Hakoah fan just belongs in the coffeehouse" (Hachleitner, Marschik, and Spitaler, "[Sport-]Netzwerke," 250).

55. In 1920s Germany, similar images were painted about clubs such as Eintracht Frankfurt. The historian Rudolf Oswald argues that during the 1920s, some "stereotypes . . . were extended to antisemitism," and he claims that at the end of the decade, "fanatics not only spoke of 'Kaffeehausklubs' but also of 'Judenvereine'" (Rudolf Oswald, "The Image of the 'Judenklub' in Interwar European Soccer: Myth or Reality?" in *Football and Discrimination: Antisemitism and Beyond*, ed. Pavel Brunssen and Stefanie Schüler-Springorum, Critical Research in Football [Abingdon, UK: Routledge, 2021], 42).

56. *Vorstadt* literally translates as "suburb," but the cultural concept is fundamentally different.

57. "Die Vorstadt führt!," *Illustriertes Sportblatt*, October 8, 1927, ANNO/Österreichische Nationalbibliothek.

58. "Rapid wurzelt in der Bevölkerung und vernachlässigt den heimischen Boden nie. Die Grün-weißen sind ein Vorstadtklub im besten Sinne des Wortes" (my translation; *Illustriertes Sportblatt*).

59. "Wie Keulenschläge dröhnten am Sonntag die Goals der Admira im Gehäuse der Austria. Aufstrebende, gesunde Jugend bombardierte die Verteidigungsstellung einer morsch gewordenen Formation. Der Sport hat über das Geschäft triumphiert. Die frische Jedleseer Wiesenluft hat den stickigen Kaffeehausdunst weggeweht. Die Mannschaft der Spieler hat das Team des Gagenfußballs glatt niedergebügelt" (my translation; *Illustriertes Sportblatt*).

60. To be precise, an all-Austrian league competition was de facto also held in the 1937–38 season and the NS-Gauliga was more than just a Viennese football league, too.

61. Silverman, *Becoming Austrians*, 21.

62. Silverman, 21.

63. "Die gesunde, unverbrauchte Vorstadt führt physisch, moralisch und materiell" (my translation; *Illustriertes Sportblatt*, "Die Vorstadt führt!").

64. "Die Vertretung des heimischen Fußballs" (my translation; *Illustriertes Sportblatt*).

65. Silverman, *Becoming Austrians*, 23.

66. One example is Austria's western province Voralberg, which voted in 1919 that it prefers belonging to Switzerland than to the Wiener Judenstaat ("the Jewish state of Vienna") (Silverman, 22).

67. See, for instance, Bodo Kahmann, "Feindbild Jude, Feindbild Großstadt. Antisemitismus und Großstadtfeindschaft im völkischen Denken" (PhD diss., Georg-August-University, Göttingen, 2017), https://doi.org/10.53846/goediss-6157; Arnold M. Rose, "The Study of Man: Anti-Semitism's Root in City-Hatred," *Commentary Magazine* (blog), October 1, 1948, https://www.commentary.org/articles/arnold-rose/the-study-of-man-anti-semitisms-root-in-city-hatred/.

68. Rose, "Study of Man."

69. Rose.

70. Rapid (Hütteldorf), Wacker (Meidling), Vienna (Döbling), FAC (Floridsdorf), Admira (Jedlesee, Floridsdorf), and Sportklub (Dornbach) all had their area of the city.

71. Domenico Jacono, "Von 'Ewigen Juden' und 'Schuldenbeuteln'—Werden, Wachsen und Wesen einer 100-jährigen Gegnerschaft," in *Alles Derby! 100 Jahre Rapid gegen Austria*, ed. Edgar Schütz, Domenico Jacono, and Matthias Marschik, 2. durchgesehene Auflage (Göttingen: Die Werkstatt, 2012), 27–28.

72. Matthias Marschik and Bernhard Hachleitner, "'Bodenständigkeit' als Metapher," in Hachleitner, Marschik, and Spitaler, *Sportfunktionäre und jüdische Differenz*, 137.

73. Marschik and Hachleitner, 140.

74. *Die Neue Welt*, November 3, 1937, 1, quoted in Marschik and Hachleitner, 140. "Das Wort 'bodenständig' ist ein Ersatz für 'antisemitisch' geworden. Wenn man nicht geradeheraus sagen will, daß man gegen die Juden ist, erklärt man, man sei für die Bodenständigen" (my translation).

75. *Sport-Tagblatt*, May 21, 1921, 9, quoted in Marschik and Hachleitner, 142.

76. Hachleitner et al., "Raum," 119.

77. Hachleitner et al., 120.

78. "'Das Kesseltreiben gegen Rapid,'" *Der Montag*, June 11, 1923, 15, ANNO/Österreichische Nationalbibliothek. "Der gewisse gesellschaftliche Anstrich, den sich dieser Verein zu geben wusste, führte ihm auch bald

jenen Anhang zu, der ihn heute noch charakterisiert. Die numerisch wohl verschwindende, finanziell aber recht leistungsfähige Gesellschaft aus dem Kai-Viertel, reichgewordene jüdische Kaufleute, die aber alles leichter verwinden können als mit den Juden der Hakoah in einen Topf geworfen zu werden" (my translation).

79. *Der Montag*, 15. "Vornehm um jeden Preis' ist ihre Marke. . . . mit einer Deutlichkeit, die anderwärts vergeblich gesucht werden wird, stellen die Amateure ihren ganzen Sportbetrieb nur auf die Fülle ihrer Brieftasche ein" (my translation). Although Schidrowitz statements touch on antisemitic tropes, I propose viewing this piece more through the perspective of class, for example, through the competition between FAK and Hakoah, rather than as antisemitic.

80. Silverman, *Becoming Austrians*, 5.

81. Silverman, 8–9.

82. Rapid fans call him the "epitome of the working football player" ("Er war der Inbegriff des Arbeiter-Fußballers," my translation); Thomas Lanz, *SK Rapid Wien Fußballfibel* (Berlin: Culturcon medien, 2019), 19.

83. Roman Horak, "Josef Uridil & Alfréd Schaffer—Der Tank und der Wandervogel," in Schütz, Jacono, and Marschik, *Alles Derby!*, 48.

84. Uridil neglected his NSDAP membership initially but could no longer hide it after applying for a passport in 1948 (Rosenberg and Spitaler, *Grün-weiß unterm Hakenkreuz*, 260).

85. Anderson, *Imagined Communities*.

86. Uridil is, for instance, squeezed into Rapid's identity as a *bodenständiger Vorstadtklub*, although he was crucial to the commodification of football, something that is usually attributed to the Jew Club FAK. Most myths do have some truth in them. Uridil played for Rapid from 1914 to 1926, and Schaffer for FAK only from 1923 to 1925. Is it, as the sociologist Roman Horak claims, "not accidentally" that Schaffer played for FAK and not Rapid? Perhaps, but counterexamples are easy to find: Sindelar played, in fact, longer for FAK than Uridil did for Rapid (1924–39 versus 1914–26).

87. Sascha Bunda, "Fußball: Rapid-Viertelstunde kein Unesco-Kulturerbe," *Die Presse*, March 22, 2011, https://www.diepresse.com/642245/fussball -rapid-viertelstunde-kein-unesco-kulturerbe.

88. Jacono, "Von 'Ewigen Juden,'" 25.

89. Matthias Marschik, "Realität und Mythos," in Schütz, Jacono, and Marschik, *Alles Derby!*, 19.

90. Marschik, 20.

91. "Austria Wien steht für Einsatz, Spielwitz & Magie." The graffiti depicts the club legends Robert Sara, Herbert Prohaska, and Matthias Sindelar.

92. Michael Bonvalot, "Ein 'Judenverein' und seine Neonazis," *Transparent—Magazin für Fußball und Fankultur* no. 18 (2016): 20–25.

93. One sticker displays FAK's club symbol and a beaten swastika. It says, "A real Viennese is not a Nazi. Better dead than *Unsterblich* [immortal]." *Unsterblich* is the name of a far right hooligan group.

94. The name *Kampfastllln Inzersdorf (KAI2000)* originates from the Inzersdorf area in the south of Vienna. *Kampfastln* is an Austrian term akin to *Kampfasseln* in Standard German, referring to arms or upper arms (literally, "branches"). The term *Kampfasseln* consists of *Kampf*, meaning "fight," and *Assel*, referring to a small crustacean. Additionally, *Assel* is colloquially used to describe a person as asocial in a derogatory and discriminatory manner.

95. One of the Jewish fans standing at the outskirts of the fan section is Lia Guttmann, granddaughter to Jakob Guttmann, former president of FAK. In a video displayed at the exhibition *Super Jews. Jewish Identity in the Football Stadium* (July 12, 2023-January 13, 2024), she recounted how the atmosphere in the main fan section gradually became more right wing over time, prompting her to relocate to a more leftist and comfortable area. Guttmann observed recent changes in the fan section, giving her optimism about returning to a more central location, where the atmosphere is more passionate (Jüdisches Museum Wien, *Superjuden. Jüdische Identitäten im Fußball: Ausstellung im Jüdischen Museum*, July 12, 2023—January 14, 2024; see also Barbara Staudinger and Agnes Meisinger, eds., *Superjuden: Jüdische Identität im Fußballstadion: Katalog zur gleichnamigen Ausstellung im Jüdischen Museum Wien* [Vienna: Jüdisches Museum Wien, 2023]).

96. The letter *h* in the word *Schachklub* is also the symbol for "hooligans."

97. Thomas Northoff, "Graffity-Derby—Beobachtungen in Bild und Text abseits der Stadien," in Schütz, Jacono, and Marschik, *Alles Derby!*, 206.

98. John and Marschik, "Ortswechsel," 193.

99. John, "'Körperlich ebenbürtig,'" 255.

100. Roman Horak, "Things Change: Trends in Austrian Football Hooliganism from 1977–1990," *Sociological Review* 39, no. 3 (August 1991): 531–48, https://doi.org/10.1111/j.1467-954X.1991.tb00866.x.

101. Horak, 539. By the 1950s the first fans had founded supporter clubs, known as *Anhängerklubs*.

102. Domenico Jacono, "Die NS-Zeit als Erinnerungsort im Vereins-gedächtnis des SK Rapid," in *Fussball unterm Hakenkreuz in der "Ostmark,"* ed. David Forster, Jakob Rosenberg, and Georg Spitaler (Göttingen, Germany: Die Werkstatt, 2014), 310. "Ich weiß, wovon ich spreche, denn auch ich schrie 'Judenschweine!' mit der bubenhaften Fistelstimme und dem geballten Fäustchen eines 13-Jährigen, damals im Herbst 1980, beim ersten Derby, das ich ohne erwachsene Aufpasser besuchen durfte Mag es sich dabei auch um eine Äußerung gehandelt haben, die um mit dem britischen Verhaltensforscher Desmond Morris zu sprechen, 'not so much anti-racial as anti-rival' war, so sagt sie doch viel aus über das politisch- historische Bewusstsein eines durchaus durchschnittlichen Wiener Jugendlichen der unteren Mittelschicht dieser Jahre" (my translation).

103. Alexia Weiss, "Wenn der Davidstern zum Judenstern wird," WZ Online, May 6, 2021, https://www.tagblatt-wienerzeitung.at/meinung/blogs/juedisch-leben/2103204-Wenn-der-Davidstern-zum-Judenstern-wird.html.

104. Horak, "Things Change," 532. Roman Horak observes that: "the responses to the social contradictions experienced by the members were expressed . . . more and more in the form of direct violence" (540).

105. Horak, 541.

106. Lanz, *SK Rapid Wien*, 103.

107. Horak, "Things Change," 546.

108. Michael Bonvalot, "Das Nazi-Problem der Wiener Austria," Bonvalot.net, December 14, 2016, https://www.bonvalot.net/das-nazi-problem-der-wiener-austria-845/.

109. Bonvalot.

110. Pavel Brunssen, Peter Römer, and Robert Claus, "'Defenders of European Culture': 'Refugee Crisis', Football Hooliganism, and the Right-Wing Shift in Europe," in *Football and Politics*, ed. James Carr et al., Critical Research in Football (Abingdon, UK: Routledge, 2021), 108–25; Bonvalot, "Ein 'Judenverein' und seine Neonazis."

111. Andrew Hodges, "The Politics of 'No Politics' in Pula, Croatia: An Ethnography of the Demons Football Fan Group," *Sport in Society* 27, no. 1 (2024): 111–25.

112. Ultras Rapid proudly declare that the fan scenes apolitical stance persists until today (Lanz, *SK Rapid Wien*, 109).

113. Michael Heffele, "Der Fußballverein SK Rapid, seine Anhänger und Fans im Fokus von Rassismus, Nationalismus und Männlichkeit" (Diploma thesis, Universität Wien, 2006), 78.

114. John and Marschik, "Ortswechsel," 194.

115. Michael Bonvalot, "Überfall mit Antisemitismus auf Austria-Fan," Bonvalot.net, November 2, 2020, https://www.bonvalot.net/ueberfall-mit-antisemitismus-auf-austria-fan-821/.

116. The network Football Against Racism in Europe (FARE) writes in its 2021 report, *Monitoring Guide to Discriminatory Practices in European Football*, "The Celtic Cross is a symbol used by neo-Nazis worldwide and denotes 'the supremacy of the white race.' It is one of the most widely used racist symbols. In football stadiums it often appears on banners, signs, scarves or stickers" (FARE, *Guide to Discriminatory Practices in European Football*, 6th ed. June 2021, 10, https://farenet.org/uploads/files/2021/._Fare_guide_to_discriminatory_practices_UEFA_.pdf).

117. "'Wir sind keine Geschichtsprofessoren,'" *Der Standard*, March 31, 2010, https://www.derstandard.at/story/1269448575040/derstandardat-interview-wir-sind-keine-geschichtsprofessoren.

118. Michael Bonvalot, "Austria würdigt Opfer des Holocaust," Bonvalot.net, November 8, 2018, https://www.bonvalot.net/austria-wuerdigt-opfer-des-holocaust-843/. "Wir treten als Austria Wien sehr entschieden gegen jegliche Form von Rassismus, Diskriminierung oder Homophobie auf. Die jüdische Geschichte ist ein wichtiger Teil der Austria. Deshalb ist es uns als Klub besonders wichtig, dass unsere Spieler auch wissen und verstehen, was diese Geschichte für uns bedeutet und sie sich einige Minuten Zeit nehmen, um dem zu gedenken" (my translation).

119. Simon Wiesenthal, ed., "Vorwort," in *Projekt: Judenplatz Wien: Zur Konstruktion von Erinnerung* (Vienna: Zsolnay, 2000), 27. "In dieser Bibliothek, in der die Bücher geschlossen bleiben, muß der Betrachter seine eigenen Worte finden" (my translation).

120. Judith Beniston, "'Hitler's First Victim'?—Memory and Representation in Post-War Austria: Introduction," *Austrian Studies* 11 (2003): 2.

121. Beniston, 2.

122. Beniston, 3.

123. Furthermore, Austria did not grant Jews special victim status for restitution claims, treating them the same as other Austrian citizens (Sonja Niederacher, "The Myth of Austria as Nazi Victim, the Emigrants and the Discipline of Exile Studies," *Austrian Studies* 11 [2003]: 23, 31).

124. Hachleitner et al., *Ein Fußballverein aus Wien*, 54.

125. Rapid, for instance, was then without its board members Leo Schid-rowitz and Sigmund Ringer (Hachleitner, Marschik, and Spitaler, *Sport-funktionäre und jüdische Differenz*; Hachleitner et al., *Der Wiener Fußball im Nationalsozialismus*; Hachleitner et al., *Ein Fußballverein aus Wien*; Rosenberg and Spitaler, *Grün-weiß unterm Hakenkreuz*).

126. Hachleitner et al., *Ein Fußballverein aus Wien*, 180. The Vienna edi-tion of the *Völkischer Beobachter* reported on the renaming: "The sport club FAK has now become the sport club Ostmark. A formality, that, how-ever, will have no impact on the club's cultivated tradition" ("Jetzt ist aus dem SpK. Austria der SpK. Ostmark geworden. Eine Äußerlichkeit, eine Formalität, die aber die gepflegte Tradition des Vereines nicht beeinflus-sen wird" (my translation, *Völkischer Beobachter*, Wiener Ausgabe, June 18, 1938, 10, quoted in Hachleitner et al., 180).

127. Hachleitner et al., *Ein Fußballverein aus Wien*, 103.

128. Hachleitner et al., 181.

129. *Völkischer Beobachter*, Wiener Ausgabe, June 8, 1938, 11, quoted in Hachleitner et al., 81. "Die beiden Mannschaften werden vielfach als die bestspielenden Teams des deutschen Fußballs angesehen" (my translation).

130. Hachleitner et al., 56–57.

131. Hödl, "Jewish Studies without the 'Other,'" 122.

132. Matti Bunzl, "Resistive Play: Sports and the Emergence of Jewish Visibility in Contemporary Vienna," *Journal of Sport and Social Issues* 24, no. 3 (2000): 232–50.

133. Hachleitner et al., *Ein Fußballverein aus Wien*; David Forster, "Opfer Österreich, Opfer Austria? Der FK Austria und die NS-Zeit," in Forster, Rosenberg, and Spitaler, *Fussball unterm Hakenkreuz in der "Ostmark,"* 106–21.

134. Other forewords, written by the mayor and other prominent indi-viduals, highlight the importance of memory culture in general terms.

135. Wolfgang Katzian, "Vorwort," in *Ein Fußballverein aus Wien: Der FK Austria im Nationalsozialismus 1938–1945*, by Bernhard Hachleitner et al. (Vienna: Böhlau, 2019), 9.

136. Katzian. "Wie alle Fußballklubs und Sportvereine wurde die Aus-tria unter die Verwaltungshoheit des NS-Regimes gezwungen, ein paar Monate lang hieß sie 'SC Ostmark'. Doch sie ließ sich als Klub nicht ver-einnahmen und wahrte Distanz zur Obrigkeit. Manche Fußballer erlagen

opportunistischen Versuchungen, andere passten sich an, der Austria-Läufer und Wunderteam-Spieler Hans Mock ließ sich als Mitglied der SA von den Zeitungen feiern" (my translation).

137. Katzian, 9.

138. "Die Machtübernahme der Nationalsozialisten im Jahr 1938 zerstörte die Selbstständigkeit und die nationale Identität Österreichs und leitete einen dunklen Abschnitt in der Geschichte unseres Landes ein, der Österreich, seine Menschen und seine Kultur an den Rand des Abgrundes trieb" (my translation).

139. "FAK, traditionally the liberal-bourgeois football club in Vienna, with its supporters, some of whom were Jewish, anti-fascist, or both, and loyal to Austria. It was a 'thorn in the side' of the new rulers from the very beginning. Whoever takes away 'Austria's' independence and name could, of course, not stand a club called 'Austria'" ("Austria Wien, der traditionell 'liberal-bürgerliche' Fußballklub Wiens mit seiner, zum Teil jüdisch/antifaschistischen und österreich-treuen Anhängerschaft, war den neuen Machthabern von allem Anfang an ein 'Dorn im Auge.' Wer 'Österreich' seine Selbständigkeit und seinen Namen nimmt konnte natürlich auch einen Klub namens 'Austria' nicht ertragen," my translation).

140. "Die Jahre der Finsternis: Österreich existiert nicht mehr . . . unser Land und unsere Austria werden 'zwangsarisiert', die Austria wird in 'SC Ostmark' umbenannt" (my translation).

141. I visited FAK's museum on November 15, 2021 and again on December 13, 2022. I visited Rapid's museum on November 12, 2021.

142. Rosenberg and Spitaler, *Grün-weiß unterm Hakenkreuz*; Hachleitner et al., *Ein Fußballverein aus Wien*.

143. Hans Fonje and Karl Langer, *Die Wiener Austria - Fußballzauber aus Österreich* (Vienna: Dr. Fonje, 1962); Georg Spitaler, "Populare Erinnerungsorte—die NS-Zeit im österreichischen Sportgedächtnis," 2005, 18–19.

144. FK Austria Wien, ed., *60 Jahre Wiener Austria: Festschrift 1911 bis 1971* (Vienna, 1971); Jo Huber, *Das große Austria-Buch* (Vienna: Mohl Kurt, 1975).

145. I am thankful to Georg Spitaler, who generously shared his research on the *festschriften* with me.

146. Leo Schidrowitz, *Geschichte des Fußballsportes in Österreich* (Vienna, Rudolf Traunau, 1951).

147. Karl Kastler, *Fußballsport in Österreich: Von den Anfängen bis in die Gegenwart* (Linz: Trauner, 1972), 56–103.

148. Peter Linden and Karl H. Schwind, *100 Jahre! Die Highlights des österreichischen Fussballs: Triumphe, Tränen, Schmähs* (Vienna: Axel Jentzsch bei Linde, 2004).

149. Linden and Schwind, 50; Georg Spitaler, "Populare Erinnerungsorte—die NS-Zeit im österreichischen Fußballgedächtnis," in *Hakenkreuz und rundes Leder: Fussball im Nationalsozialismus*, ed. Lorenz Peiffer and Dietrich Schulze-Marmeling (Göttingen, Germany: Die Werkstatt, 2008), 548.

150. Marschik, *Wiener Austria*.

151. Wolfgang Schüssel, "Vorwort," in Marschik, *Wiener Austria*, 7. "A club that was always cosmopolitan since its founding in 1911 and that kept its firm attitude even during the difficult times of the 1930s and 1940s" ("Ein Verein, der seit seiner Gründung 1911 bis heute immer weltoffen war und ist und große Haltung in der schwierigen Zeit der 30er und 40er Jahre bewies," my translation).

152. Marschik, *Wiener Austria die ersten 90 Jahre*, 72.

153. Marschik, 150. "Es handelte sich zwar um ein arisiertes Lokal, aber Sindelar hatte sich das nicht zunutze gemacht, sondern den Vorbesitzern einen anständigen Kaufpreis bezahlt" (my translation).

154. Peter Pelinka, "Die Violetten," in *Die Eleganz des runden Leders: Wiener Fussball 1920–1965*, ed. Wolfgang Maderthaner, Alfred Pfoser, and Roman Horak (Vienna: Die Werkstatt, 2008), 89. "Die Einverleibung Österreichs ins nationalsozialistische Deutschland traf die Wiener Austria von den österreichischen Fußballvereinen am härtesten: Unter den Spielern und Funktionären gab es viele Juden, nicht nur der legendäre Präsident 'Michl' Schwarz musste sofort nach dem Einmarsch emigrieren—aus dieser Zeit rührt noch das Image des 'Judenklubs,' das bis vor kurzem noch durch antisemitische Sprechchöre gegnerischer Anhänger 'gepflegt' worden ist" (my translation).

155. Hachleitner et al., *Ein Fußballverein aus Wien*, 51.

156. "Nationalsozialismus & Wiederaufbau," FK Austria Wien, accessed November 21, 2021, https://fk-austria.at/klub/geschichte/nationalsozialismus.

157. "Austria gedenkt der Opfer der Novemberpogrome," FK Austria Wien, November 9, 2021, https://fk-austria.at/news/austria-gedenkt-der-opfer-der-novemberpogrome.

158. "The president's position was never restaffed. FAK's managing board insisted that this position belonged only to 'Michl' Schwarz and in fact reserved it for him until he returned in the summer of 1945" ("Der Platz des Präsidenten wurde allerdings nicht nachbesetzt: Der Austria-Vorstand

bestand darauf, dass dieser Platz nur dem 'Michl' Schwarz zukomme und hielt ihm sein Präsidentenamt auch tatsächlich bis zu seiner Rückkehr im Sommer 1945 offen," my translation).

159. "Nationalsozialismus & Wiederaufbau." "Das Stadion wies Wunden des Krieges auf und aus den Kabinen der Austria fehlten Schuhe und Dressen. Es war die Stunde null" (my translation).

160. Hachleitner et al., *Ein Fußballverein aus Wien*, 180.

161. Beppo Mauhart, "Ein Leben voll Sehnsucht und Glauben," in *Mister Austria: Das Leben des Klubsekräters Norbert Lopper: Fußballer, KZ-Häftling, Weltbürger*, by Johann Skocek (Vienna: Falter, 2014), 14. "Diese Zweite Republik, in die Norbert Lopper zurückkehrt, ist Wiedergeburt und Neugeburt in einem" (my translation).

162. Mauhart, 14. "Die Erfahrung von Diktatur, Krieg und Gefängnis . . . wird zur harten Schule der Vernunft" (my translation).

163. Mauhart, 17. "Der Fußball erzeugt in all den Mühen der Aufarbeitung einen symbolischen Anschluss an 'bessere Zeiten,'" (my translation, my emphasis).

164. Wolfgang Katzian, "Ein Leben, Ein Klub, Ein Werk," in Skocek, *Mister Austria*, 7. "Eine der Persönlichkeiten, die die Geschichte der Wiener Austria entscheidend und aufopferungsvoll mitgeprägt hat, war Norbert Lopper. Der Fußball hat sein Leben bestimmt, umgekehrt bestimmte er über drei Jahrzehnte den Fußball der Austria. Obwohl die NS-Herrschaft in seinem Leben wie ein Meteor eingeschlagen hatte. . . . Er hatte einen unschätzbar großen Anteil am Erfolg 'seiner' Austria, deren makelloses Ansehen schon immer sein Ziel, Prinzip und Antrieb war" (my translation).

165. Skocek, *Mister Austria*, 28. "Loppers Lebensbericht ist die Geschichte eines geglückten, mit vielen Anekdoten und Begegnungen angereicherten Lebens, das mit dem Zwangsaufenthalt in Auschwitz bloß eine Zäsur erfuhr. Ob er jemanden mit Groll verfolge, fragte ich ihn. Es war eines unser letzten Gespräche für dieses Buch. 'Ich hab in Wien Gott sei Dank niemanden gefunden, der mir Böses getan hat, ich konnte niemandem Böse sein,' sagte Lopper. 'Die "Kristallnacht" in Wien hab ich nicht mitgemacht. Meinen Zorn hätte ich können am Regime auslassen, aber die Menschen? Hätt ich mich sollen erschießen und nicht zurückgehen? Ich habe der Austria so viel zu verdanken," (my translation).

166. Skocek, 25. "Aufhebens von seinen Schmerzen hat er nie gemacht" (my translation).

167. Skocek, 24. "Lopper hat ein Leben hingelegt, das die Zuversicht nicht einmal im Konzentrationslager Auschwitz verloren hat" (my translation).

168. Skocek, 161. "Bis ich 1973 solche Schmerzen gehabt habe, wenn ich einen Revolver gehabt hätte, hätte ich mich daschossen" (my translation).

169. Skocek, 180. "Er verschenkte sein Herz an diesen Klub und erhielt ein erfülltes, gelungenes Leben zurück, das an äußeren Erfolgen überreich war und an innerer Befriedigung nichts zu wünschen übrig ließ" (my translation).

170. Maderthaner, "Die lange Reise."

171. Forster, "Opfer Österreich, Opfer Austria?" 108.

172. Hachleitner et al., *Ein Fußballverein aus Wien*, 203.

173. Georg Spitaler, "Case Study: 'Der Jude soll zahlen.' Die Wiener Austria im März 1938," in Hachleitner, Marschik, and Spitaler, *Sportfunktionäre und jüdische Differenz*, 298–99.

174. Spitaler, 299. Josef Gerö was persecuted by the Nazis as a "half Jew" according to the Nuremberg Laws. Gerö used to play for FC Libertas Wien, for which he would also serve as president.

175. Hachleitner et al., *Ein Fußballverein aus Wien*, 210.

176. Hachleitner et al., 210. "Ein Narrativ, das sehr gut in die allgemeine österreichische Nachkriegserzählung passt: Die (implizit auch 'deutschen') Nazis sind weg, es geht weiter wie zuvor. Es wurde aber ausgeblendet, dass die Juden—bis auf ganz wenige Ausnahmen, siehe Schwarz—immer noch fehlten, weil sie ermordet oder vertrieben worden waren" (my translation).

177. FK Austria Wien, Peter Klöbl, and Wolfgang Winheim, *100 Jahre Austria Wien* (Vienna: FK Austria Wien Merchandising, 2010); Forster, "Opfer Österreich, Opfer Austria?" 115–16.

178. Hachleitner and colleagues criticize the ignorance of the close ties some of FAK's former leaders had, including that of the honorary president Ernst Kaltenbrunner, his secretary, and the club's vice club director Walter Münch (*Ein Fußballverein aus Wien*, 220).

179. Hachleitner et al., 224.

180. Voted on by the International Federation of Football History and Statistics.

181. Hachleitner et al., *Der Wiener Fußball im Nationalsozialismus*, 118.

182. Franz Blaha, *Sindelar* (Vienna: Blaha, 1946).

183. Matthias Marschik, "Der 'Fall' Matthias Sindelar: Szenen einer Erregung," *SportZeiten* 4, no. 1 (2004): 88.

184. David Forster, "Café Sindelar Revisited: Verlauf und Folgen der Sindelaar-Debatte," in Forster, Rosenberg, and Spitaler, *Fussball unterm Hakenkreuz in der "Ostmark*," 324.

185. Forster, "Café Sindelar Revisited"; Marschik, "Der 'Fall' Matthias Sindelar."

186. Marschik, "Der 'Fall' Matthias Sindelar," 82; Peter Menasse, "Parteigenosse Sindelar," *Falter* 31, no. 3 (December 17, 2003), https://www.falter.at/zeitung/20031217/parteigenosse-sindelar/1959040053; Peter Menasse, "Parteigenosse Matthias Sindelar," *NU*, June 30, 2003.

187. Johann Skocek and Wolfgang Weisgram, *Wunderteam Österreich: Scheiberln, wedeln, glücklich sein* (Vienna: Orac, 1996), 75.

188. Hachleitner et al., *Ein Fußballverein aus Wien*, 75.

189. Hachleitner et al., 75.

190. Hachleitner et al., 77.

191. Forster, "Café Sindelar Revisited," 324; Michael Lechner, *"Wie vom anderen Stern"—jüdischer Fußball in Wien (1909–1938): Eine Kultur- und Sportgeschichte* (Saarbrücken: VDM Verlag Dr. Müller, 2010), 106; "Matthias Sindelar und das antifaschistische Märchen," *Der Standard*, December 19, 2018, https://www.derstandard.de/story/2000094341814/matthias-sindelars-und-das-antifaschistische-maerchen.

192. Wolfgang Maderthaner, "Der 'Papierene' Tänzer: Matthias Sindelar, ein Wiener Fußballmythos," in Maderthaner, Pfoser, and Horak, *Die Eleganz des runden Leders*, 213–14. For instance, Wolfgang Maderthaner: "At least he paid the former Jewish owner Leopold Simon Drill, whom he knew well, the remarkable sum of RM 20,000, which is approximately the actual worth of the property" ("Immerhin bezahlte er dem ihm gut bekannten jüdischen Vorbesitzer Leopold Simon Drill die durchaus beachtliche Summe und dem tatsächlichen Wert der Liegenschaft ungefähr entsprechende Summe von RM 20.000" (my translation).

193. Forster, "Café Sindelar Revisited," 322. "Der Sindelar hat den Besitzer Leopold Simon Drill sehr gut gekannt.... Er wollte den Schaden für Drill minimieren" (my translation).

194. Pelinka, "Die Violetten," 89. "A few months after the German invasion, he bought an 'Aryanized' coffeehouse at Luxenburger street, of course for a decent prize" ("Einige Monate nach dem deutschen Einmarsch erwarb er ein 'arisiertes' Kaffeehaus auf der Laxenburgstraße, freilich um einen handelsüblichen Preis," my translation).

195. FK Austria Wien, "FK Austria Wien Museum," accessed November 15, 2021. "Mit dem Kauf eines von den Nazis 'arisierten' Kaffeehauses

verschaffte sich Sindelar ein zweites berufliches Standbein für die Zeit nach seiner aktiven Karriere" (my translation).

196. Wolfgang Weisgram, *Im Inneren der Haut: Matthias Sindelar und sein papierenes Fußballerleben; ein biographischer Roman*, Egoth Biographie (Vienna: Egoth, 2006), 376–79; Forster, "Café Sindelar Revisited," 325.

197. Forster, "Café Sindelar Revisited," 325.

198. Nello Governato, *La partita dell'addio: Matthias Sindelar, il campione che non si piegò ad Hitler*, 2nd ed., Omnibus (Milan: Mondadori, 2007).

199. Forster, "Café Sindelar Revisited."

200. "Als auch Austria-Präsident Michl Schwarz seines Amtes enthoben wurde und man verbot, ihn auch nur zu grüßen, meinte Sindelar: I, Herr Doktor, werd' Ihna oba immer griaß'n" (my translation).

201. Marschik, "Der 'Fall' Matthias Sindelar," 79.

202. Zeugenvernehmung 4. 6. 1946, quoted in Spitaler, "Case Study," 311. "[Haldenwang], for instance, banned the players of FAK from greeting me from now on . . . and I still remember, with absolute certainty, that the famous now deceased Sindelar told me this and accompanied it with the words: 'imagine that this criminal prohibits me from greeting my boss and president, I, however, will always greet you'" ("[Haldenwang] verbot z. B. den Spielern der Austria, mich von jetzt ab . . . zu grüssen und ist mir noch mit absoluter Sicherheit in Erinnerung, dass mir dies der berühmte jetzt verstorbene Sindelar erzählte und mit den Worten begleitete: 'stellen sie sich vor der Verbrecher verbietet mir meinen Chef und Präsidenten zu grüßen, ich werde Sie aber doch grüßen,'" my translation).

203. Skocek, *Mister Austria*, 32, 30. "Sindelar was a popular antifascist"; I will not accept Sindelar being portrayed as right-wing." ("Der Sindelaar war ein populärer Antifaschist"; "Ich lasse Sindelar nicht ins rechte Eck stellen," my translation).

204. Alfred Polgar, "Abschied von Sindelar," *Pariser Tageszeitung*, January 25, 1939, quoted in Roman Horak and Wolfgang Maderthaner, *Mehr als ein Spiel: Fussball und populare Kulturen im Wien der Moderne* (Vienna: Löcker, 1997), 150. "The good Sindelar followed the city, whose child and pride he was, to death. He was so fused with the city that he had to die when it died. Out of loyalty to one's homeland—everything speaks for this—he killed himself; to live and play football in the trampled, broken, tormented city, that meant to betray Vienna with a disgusting ghost of Vienna. . . . But is it possible to play football like that? And live like this when life without football is none?" ("Der brave Sindelar folgte der Stadt, deren Kind und Stolz er war, in den Tod. Er war so verwachsen mit ihr,

dass er sterben mußte, als sie starb. Aus Treue zur Heimat—alles spricht dafür—hat er sich umgebracht; denn in der zertretenen, zerbrochenen, zerquälten Stadt leben und Fußballspielen, das hieß, Wien mit einem abscheulichen Gespenst von Wien betrügen. . . . Aber kann man so Fußballspielen? Und so leben, wenn ein Leben ohne Fußball keines ist?," my translation).

205. Torberg, "Auf den Tod eines Fußballspielers."

206. Pelinka, "Die Violetten," 89.

207. Such an agreement for a draw seems unlikely (Hachleitner et al., *Ein Fußballverein aus Wien*, 58). Karl Sesta unsuccessfully submitted an application to buy Café Lovrana, which belonged to the Jew Josef Schwimmer. Sesta then "Aryanized" a bakery at Alserbachstreet that had belonged to the Jew Josef Brand. The contract was prepared by the lawyer Bruno Eckerl, who at this time was FAK's club director (Hachleitner et al., 74).

208. The political reason for Sindelar's refusal is speculation. The official reason was his (for a football player) advanced age of thirty-five (Marschik, "Der 'Fall' Matthias Sindelar," 79–80).

209. FK Austria Wien, "FK Austria Wien Museum." "Mit dem Einmarsch deutscher Truppen und dem Anschluss an das Deutsche Reich im Jahr 1938, war der österreichische Fußball praktisch am Ende. 'Jüdische Vereine' wie die Austria wurden verboten, ein Großteil der Funktionäre und Spieler floh unmittelbar nach dem Anschluss" (my translation).

210. Hachleitner et al., *Ein Fußballverein aus Wien*, 17.

211. Marschik, "Der 'Fall' Matthias Sindelar," 90. "Was bleibt, ist das Missbehagen, eine der seltenen Möglichkeiten der öffentlichen Diskussion von Arisierung und alltäglichem Nationalsozialismus, von Mitläufertum und Antisemitismus in Österreich vertan zu haben . . . anstatt weiter zwischen Verdrängung und blutleeren Schuldgeständnissen zu verharren" (my translation).

212. Forster, "Café Sindelar Revisited," 326.

213. Photos of all the graffiti at the stadium are available online: "Wohnzimmer Zwa," KAI2000 InfoBlog, November 2, 2020, https://www.kai2000.wien/news/wohnzimmer-zwa-3/; "Wohnzimmer Zwa," KAI2000 InfoBlog, June 27, 2019, https://www.kai2000.wien/galerie/wohnzimmer-zwa/.

214. Shaked, interview.

215. Shaked.

3. AJAX AMSTERDAM

1. Simon Reynolds, *Energy Flash: A Journey through Rave Music and Dance Culture*, new edition (London: Picador, 2008), 214.

2. Bianca Ludewig, *Utopie und Apokalypse in der Popmusik: Gabber und Breakcore in Berlin*, Veröffentlichungen des Instituts für Europäische Ethnologie der Universität Wien 47 (Vienna: Verlag des Instituts für Europäische Ethnologie, 2018), 109–112.

3. Reynolds, *Energy Flash*, 214.

4. Reynolds, 214.

5. The location is named after "The Legion," a nickname for Feyenoord's fans.

6. Ludewig, *Utopie und Apokalypse in der Popmusik*, 111.

7. Craig S. Smith, "A Dutch Soccer Riddle: Jewish Regalia without Jews," *New York Times*, March 28, 2005, sec. World, https://www.nytimes .com/2005/03/28/world/europe/a-dutch-soccer-riddle-jewish-regalia -without-jews.html.

8. David Winner, *Brilliant Orange: The Neurotic Genius of Dutch Soccer* (Woodstock, NY: Overlook Press, 2002), 211.

9. Its numbers put it far ahead of the world-famous Anne Frank House (which attracted "only" 1.3 million), the Amsterdam Museum (460,000), and the Jewish Museum (358,000) ("Netherlands: Johan Cruijff ArenA Visitors 2019," Statista, June 2020, https://www.statista .com/statistics/990128/total-number-of-amsterdam-arena-visitors -in-the-netherlands/; "Top 15 Amsterdam Museums (by 2020 Visitor Numbers)," *AmsterdamTips* [blog], June 15, 2021, https://www .amsterdamtips.com/top-10-amsterdam-museums).

10. The full paragraph reads: "Hard times. Between 1940 and 1965 Ajax became champion a mere three times and failed to reach the level they had during the successful 1930s. In 1943 they did succeed in winning the FA Cup and then the national championship in 1947. After that it was another full ten years before they could celebrate again. Professional football came to the Netherlands in 1954 and Ajax joined the pros. Three years later they crowned themselves Dutch national champion again" (Ajax Amsterdam, "Ajax Amsterdam Museum," May 5, 2022).

11. Dietrich Schulze-Marmeling, *Der König und sein Spiel: Johan Cruyff und der Weltfußball*, 2., aktualisierte Auflage (Göttingen, Germany: Die Werkstatt, 2016), 59.

12. The only remainder of these clubs today is WV-HEDW, a fusion of AED, HEDW, and WV. Non-Jews played for these clubs as well, just as Jews played for non-Jewish teams. Particularly assimilated, bourgeois middle-class Jews played for multireligious or areligious clubs. Predominantly lower-class Jews tended to join explicitly Jewish boxing or football clubs, and some of them also joined socialist clubs (Marjet Derks and Elisa Rodenburg, "A Bastion against Assimilation? Jewish Sport in the Netherlands, 1890–1940," *Aschkenas* 27, no. 1 [2017]: 109–26, https://doi.org/10.1515/asch-2017-0008; Arnd Krüger and Astrid Sanders, "Jewish Sports in the Netherlands and the Problems of Selective Memory," *Journal of Sport History* 26, no. 2 [1999]: 271–86).

13. Ajax's club culture had been shaped by its largely Jewish neighborhood since the club settled at the "Wooden Stadium" in 1906, located at Middenweg, today Christiaan Huggensplein, in East Amsterdam. Likewise, the club moved to the "de Meer" stadium in 1934, also located in East Amsterdam, where the club remained until 1996.

14. Simon Kuper, *Ajax, the Dutch, the War: Football in Europe during the Second World War* (London: Orion, 2011), 105.

15. Derks and Rodenburg, "Bastion against Assimilation?" 110.

16. Evelien Gans, "Why Jews Are More Guilty Than Others! An Introductory Essay, 1945–2016," in Ensel and Gans, *Holocaust, Israel and "the Jew,"* 22.

17. Evert Vermeer, *95 jaar Ajax, 1900–1995* (Amsterdam: Luitingh-Sijthoff, 1996), quoted in Kuper, *Ajax*, 104.

18. Kuper, *Ajax*, 104; Dietrich Schulze-Marmeling, "Fahrräder, Juden, Fußball: Ajax Amsterdam," in *Davidstern und Lederball: Die Geschichte der Juden im deutschen und internationalen Fussball*, ed. Dietrich Schulze-Marmeling (Göttingen, Germany: Die Werkstatt, 2003), 399.

19. Simone Jacobus, "Jubilerend Ajax had altijd een grote joodse supportersschare," *Nieuw Israelietisch weekblad*, March 16, 1990, Dag edition.

20. Menno Pot, *Sporen van Ajax* (Amsterdam: Lebowski, 2012), 81.

21. Gruber, *Virtually Jewish*.

22. Available at www.ajaxmuseum.nl.

23. "Ajax Tattoos," Ajax Museum, accessed June 22, 2022, https://www.ajaxmuseum.nl/fotos/tattoos/.

24. Schulze-Marmeling, "Fahrräder, Juden, Fußball," 413.

25. "De geschiedenis van de Davidster," *De Ajax Ster*, November 22, 1997, Ajax Archief. "De geschiedenes van de Davidster" (my translation).

26. "De geschiedenis van de Davidster," 27. "De Davidster is nu dan ook het symbool van een trotse natie, een teken van hoop voor elke Jood, die bescherming zoekt in een eigen land" (my translation).

27. The "Amsterdamsche Football Club Ajax," Ajax Amsterdam for short, is named after the Greek mythological hero Ajax. Greek mythology is, however, hardly mentioned in fan performances or fanzines.

28. M. A. van Bemmel, "'We Are Superjews, Ajax Is the Name': A Study of the Jewish Identity of Ajax Supporters" (Master's thesis, University of Amsterdam, 2012), 19.

29. R. A. Pieloor, B. van de Meer, and M. Bakker, *F-Side is niet makkelijk!* (Utrecht: Het Spectrum, 2002), 112. "Joden is niet langer een scheldwoord, het is een geuzennaam."

30. Menno Pot, interview by Pavel Brunssen, May 5, 2022.

31. Pieloor, Meer, and Bakker, *F-Side is niet makkelijk!*, 102.

32. Chants were "Ik heb Ajax onlangs bij de gaskamer zien staan" [I have seen Ajax near the gas chamber], "Het is een Jood het is een miet het is een kanker-Ajacied" [It's a Jew, it's a fag, it's a cancerous Ajax-fan]. A banner read "Joden en Honden verboden in de Kuip" [Jews and dogs prohibited in De Kuip (Feyenoord's stadium)].

33. Pieloor, Meer, and Bakker, *F-Side is niet makkelijk!*, 73, 94–95.

34. "By following Ajax and visiting the games, I have seen how in the 1990's the Jewish identity of Ajax came more and more to the foreground. Many chants in the stadium were about Jews, there were Israeli flags, Jewish memorabilia were sold and so on. In that period the Jewish aspect of supporting Ajax had become quite dominant and it is still present in current days" (van Bemmel, "We Are Superjews," 35).

35. "Ingezonden brieven / mail," *De Ajax Ster*, December 13, 1998, 14, Ajax Archief. "Ik stoor me er een beetje aan dat tegenwoordig bijna alle liedjes over 'joden' gaan. Ik hoor bijna nooit meer AJAX" (my translation).

36. "Ingezonden brieven / mail," *De Ajax Ster*, December 13, 1998, 15.

37. "Post," *De Ajax Ster*, May 7, 2000, 38, Ajax Archief.

38. In most parts of Europe, fans looked to the United Kingdom where fan chants developed in the 1960s, often referencing contemporary pop music. Soon, fans looked to Liverpool where the fan section "the Kop" had become "the standard against which fans measured their vocal power" (Back, "Sounds," 320).

39. "Songteksten," *De Ajax Ster*, October 15, 1997, 3, Ajax Archief, https://archief.ajax.nl. "Wat ons betreft moet de F-Side qua songs de

origineelste worden, het hardste en duidelijkst gaan zingen; kortom de meeste sfeervolle side van Nederland worden" (my translation).

40. "Songteksten," 3. "Tegenstanders moeten onder een orkaan van lawaai met knikkende knieën de grasmat betreden" (my translation).

41. "Tribunenliederen," *De Ajax Ster*, March 5, 1997, 19–20, Ajax Archief. "Strijdliederen"; "liederen ... over een achterliggende strijd"; "liederen die een uiting van bewondering ... of trouw ... zijn"; "Che sera sera / whatever will be will be / we're coming from Amsterdam / che sera sera / what will be will be."

42. "Tribunenliederen," 21 (my translation).

43. "Tribunenliederen (2)," *De Ajax Ster*, May 11, 1997, 20, Ajax Archief (my translation).

44. Kluivert went on to have a phenomenal international career after having scored an outstanding seventy goals for Ajax between 1994 and 1997.

45. "Tribunenliederen (3)," *De Ajax Ster*, June 1, 1997, Ajax Archief.

46. "Tribunenliederen (3)," 22.

47. "Tribunenliederen (3)," 22. "Ook hier benadrukken wij dat wij ook met deze songs niemand willen kwetsen en geven slechts bestaande en gezongen teksten weer" (my translation).

48. "Joden worden kampioen, kampioen, kampioen. Joden worden kampioen, 't zullen de Joden zijn."

49. "Joden Joden, Joden Joden, Joden Joden, we worden kampioen."

50. "Wat ruist er door het struikgewas ... Joden, Joden, Joden."

51. Pieloor, Meer, and Bakker, *F-Side is niet makkelijk!*, 159, 173.

52. Pieloor, Meer, and Bakker, 138.

53. Pieloor, Meer, and Bakker, 145, 159.

54. Gruber, *Virtually Jewish*.

55. Hoy, "Joyful Mayhem," 291.

56. Hoy, 291.

57. Hoy, 300.

58. "Jodenstreeken," *De Ajax Ster*, December 1, 1996, Ajax Archief. Unsurprisingly, antisemitic references have a long tradition in other contexts. The expression "Jew it" was, for instance, "used to tell smokers to cut off the top of their cigar" (Evelien Gans, "Pornographic Antisemitism, Shoah Fatigue and Freedom of Speech," in Ensel and Gans, *Holocaust, Israel and "the Jew,"* 316).

59. Winner, *Brilliant Orange*, 211–12. Similarly, "when Israeli transsexual Dana International won the Eurovision Song Contest with the song 'Viva

La Diva', the occasion was celebrated by Ajax's fans with a song of their own: 'We are the champions! Jews win everything!'" (Winner, 212).

60. "Racialized" here refers not to a praxis engaged in by Ajax's fans directed at Menzo but to racism in general.

61. Ala' Alrababa'H et al., "Can Exposure to Celebrities Reduce Prejudice? The Effect of Mohamed Salah on Islamophobic Behaviors and Attitudes," *American Political Science Review* 115, no. 4 (November 2021): 1111–28, https://doi.org/10.1017/S0003055421000423. "If he scores another few / Then I'll be Muslim, too. / If he's good enough for you, / He's good enough for me. / Sitting in a mosque, / That's where I wanna be."

62. Martina Möllering and Eva Schmidt, "The Case of Mesut Özil: A Symbol of (Non-) Integration? An Analysis of German Print Media Discourses on Integration," *Discourse & Communication* 16, no. 3 (June 2022): 326–45, https://doi.org/10.1177/17504813221101823; Stefanie Schüler-Springorum, "Das kurze Glück des Mesut Özil," in *Die Stadt ohne: Juden Ausländer Muslime Flüchtlinge*, ed. Andreas Brunner et al. (Munich: Hirmer, 2019), 196–99; Dietrich Schulze-Marmeling, *Der Fall Özil: Über ein Foto, Rassismus und das deutsche WM-Aus* (Göttingen, Germany: Die Werkstatt, 2018).

63. Other clubs were named Cadets (Velocitas Breda), Militarists ('t Zesde), or Farmers (GVC Wageningen) (Nicholas Peircey, *Four Histories about Early Dutch Football, 1910–1920* [London: UCL Press, 2016], 134).

64. According to the book *F-Side is niet makkelijk!*, every opposing supporter falls into the category of farmer (Pieloor, Meer, and Bakker, *F-Side is niet makkelijk!*, 63).

65. Van Bemmel, "We Are Superjews," 50.

66. The zijden first emerged in the major cities: Amsterdam (F-Side), Rotterdam (Vak S), The Hague (North Side), and Utrecht (Bunnikzijde) (Ramón Spaaij, *Understanding Football Hooliganism: A Comparison of Six Western European Football Clubs* [Amsterdam: Amsterdam University Press, 2006], 92–93).

67. Spaaij, 94.

68. Spaaij, 93.

69. Spaaij, 26, 33.

70. Spaaij, 422.

71. Kuper, *Ajax*, 18.

72. Kuper, 20.

73. Kuper, 20.

74. Susan Smit states that away fans also took the streetcar from Weesperplein after arriving at the nearby Weesperpoort train station ("De

bal bleef rollen: Ajax binnen voetballend Amsterdam tijdens de Tweede Wereldoorlog" [diss., Amsterdam, University of Amsterdam, 1997], http://www.ethesis.net/ajax/ajax.htm#Deel%20I:%20Vooraf).

75. The streetcar must have passed large groups of Jewish Ajax fans who walked to the stadium from the Vrolikstraat and the Pretoriusstraat-Smitstraat. Simon Kuper provides the following vivid description of Amsterdam's Jewish Quarter: "On Friday evenings the Jewish vendors would turn their carts upside-down, sing socialist and Jewish psalms, and then, if they had enough money, go home for Friday-night chicken soup. On Saturday the streets were littered with chicken bones tossed out of windows. It was back to work on Sundays, when gentile shoppers from all over town thronged the Jewish market on the Quarter's Waterloo Square. Rembrandt, a resident of the Quarter, had shopped at one of its predecessors; the market that stands on the square today, selling junk to tourists, is its heir" (*Ajax*, 16).

76. Vermeer, *95 jaar Ajax, 1900–1995*, quoted in Smit, "De bal bleef rollen."

77. Philo Bregstein and Salvador Bloemgarten, eds., *Remembering Jewish Amsterdam* (New York: Holmes & Meier, 2004).

78. Bregstein and Bloemgarten, xvii.

79. Bregstein and Bloemgarten, xxi.

80. Bregstein and Bloemgarten, xxi.

81. Derks and Rodenburg, "Bastion against Assimilation?," 110.

82. Remco Ensel, "'The Jew' vs. 'the Young Male Maroccan': Stereotypical Confrontations in the City," in Ensel and Gans, *Holocaust, Israel and "the Jew,"* 409–10.

83. "Post," *De Ajax Ster*, October 29, 1999, 43, Ajax Archief; "Wij van VAK 0," *Dapp're Strijders*, May 9, 2004, 6, Ajax Archief.

84. Quoted in van Bemmel, "We Are Superjews," 16–17.

85. Among them was the club's chair Jaap van Praag (from 1964) (he was succeeded by his son Michael [1989–2003], who himself was succeeded by the Jewish chair Uri Coronel [2008–2011]), the players Sjaak Swart (1956–1973) and Bennie Muller (1958–1970), the physiotherapist Salo Muller (1959–1973), and the sponsor Maup Caransa.

86. Winner, *Brilliant Orange*, 217.

87. Winner, 217. The player Jacobus Prins was also part of this Jewish club culture. Muller describes him as "a typical Amsterdam player, a real Amsterdam boy. His family worked in the market with many Jewish men who had their Jewish words. He was therefore always using Jewish words.

It was normal. He wasn't Jewish himself, but he was using these words because it was part of Amsterdam, part of the culture." The players "liked to be Jewish although they weren't," concludes Salo Muller about Ajax's club culture at the time (Winner, 217).

88. Stefanie Schüler-Springorum, "Juden, Holländer, Deutsche—Eine kleine Nachkriegsgeschichte," in *Deutsche Zeiten: Geschichte und Lebenswelt: Festschrift zur Emeritierung von Moshe Zimmermann*, ed. Dan Diner, Gideon Reuveni, and Yfaat Weiss (Göttingen, Germany: Vandenhoeck & Ruprecht, 2012), 256.

89. Schüler-Springorum, 257. "Man kannte sich, die Familien heirateten untereinander und die jungen Ajax-Spieler jobbten nebenbei in den Firmen und Läden ihrer jüdischen Förderer" (my translation).

90. Winner, *Brilliant Orange*, 216.

91. Winner, 216.

92. Winner, 216.

93. Pot, interview.

94. Dienke Hondius, "Bitter Homecoming: The Return and Reception of Dutch and Stateless Jews in the Netherlands," in *The Jews Are Coming Back*, ed. David Bankier (Oxford: Berghahn Books, 2005), 131.

95. "After 1945, Jewish football players were, again, confronted with, often very violent, antisemitism on the pitch. In October 1947, *Onze Revue*, the magazine of the predominantly Jewish football club Wilhelmina Vooruit, noted a rise in antisemitism. Jewish football players were also less tolerant than in the 1930s and were more likely to pick a fight after antisemitic abuse, write about it in club magazines or file a complaint with the national football association KNVB" (Evelien Gans, "Jewish Responses to Post-Liberation Antisemitism," in Ensel and Gans, *Holocaust, Israel and "the Jew,"* 131). In 1947, the KNVB held a course for referees on how to respond to antisemitism on the field (Evelien Gans, "'The Jew' as Dubious Victim," in Ensel and Gans, *Holocaust, Israel and "the Jew,"* 79).

96. Hondius, "Bitter Homecoming," 121–22.

97. Kuper, *Ajax*, 209.

98. Kuper, 209–10.

99. Kuper, 106.

100. Kuper, 107.

101. Jaap van Praag wrote a note, published in the club's journal on November 10, 1945, in which he thanked "all Ajax friends who have treated me with such friendliness after my long period in hiding. I would particularly like to thank Cor and Jan Schoevaart again in our Club Journal from the bottom of

my heart for the place I was granted in their hospitable home in the weeks in which the danger for me was the greatest" (quoted in Kuper, *Ajax*, 106).

102.   The club takes part in the annual sports commemoration on May 4, the national Remembrance Day, and it issued a report about Hamel's stumbling stone on its website (AFC Ajax, "'Stolpersteine' for Eddy Hamel: A Reminder of the Tragic Fate of an Ajax Player," November 22, 2021, https://english.ajax.nl/articles/stolpersteins-for-eddy-hamel-a-reminder-of-the-tragic-fate-of-an-ajax-player/; 4 en 5 mei Amsterdam, "Nationale Sportherdenking," May 4, 2022, https://4en5meiamsterdam.nl/events/nationale-sportherdenking-5/; Jurryt van de Vooren, interview by Pavel Brunssen, April 5, 2022).

103.   Kuper, *Ajax*, 114.

104.   Kuper, 110–11.

105.   Kuper, 115.

106.   Kuper provides this quote from the *Ajax-Niuews* edition of August 1941: "What the members of the club do outside the sports field in political or religious regard, we as sports folk must not judge. As club fellows we have to feel as one, that is the overriding demand. This solidarity, which in wartime had aided men like Jaap van Praag and Jack Reynolds, would afterwards protect the collaborators" (118).

107.   Kuper, 181.

108.   Kuper, 181.

109.   Evelien Gans, "'The Jew' in Football: To Kick around or to Embrace," in Ensel and Gans, *Holocaust, Israel and "the Jew,"* 291.

110.   Kuper, *Ajax*, 184.

111.   Gans, "'Jew' as Dubious Victim," 76; Matthijs Kronemeijer and Darren Teshima, "A Founding Myth for the Netherlands: The Second World War and the Victimization of Dutch Jews," in *Reflections on the Holocaust*, ed. Julia Zarankin (New York: Humanity in Action, 2011), 106–17.

112.   James E. Young was one of many scholars arguing that Anne Frank's success lies in the "mixed Dutch self-perception as traditional refuge . . . and as a nation of passive bystanders" ("The Anne Frank House: Holland's Memorial Shrine of the Book," in *Anne Frank: Reflections on Her Life and Legacy*, ed. Hyman Aaron Enzer and Sandra Solotaroff-Enzer [Urbana: University of Illinois Press, 2000], 223).

113.   Kronemeijer and Teshima, "Founding Myth."

114.   Dienke Hondius, "Return and Reception of Survivors: New Research and Findings," 2000; Kronemeijer and Teshima, "Founding Myth," 110.

115. Hondius, "Bitter Homecoming," 111–13.

116. Among these authors were the lawyer and writer Abel Herzberg, the sociologist and social democrat Hilda Verwey-Jonkey, and the historians Jaques Presser and Richter Roegholt (Gans, "'Jew' as Dubious Victim," 68–69).

117. Hondius, "Bitter Homecoming."

118. Gans, "'Jew' as Dubious Victim," 68–69.

119. Gans, 69.

120. Remco Ensel and Evelien Gans, "Historikerstreit: The Stereotypical Jew in Recent Dutch Holocaust Studies," in Ensel and Gans, Holocaust, Israel and "the Jew," 342.

121. Pot, interview.

122. Kuper, Ajax, 231.

123. Later that year, the permanent exhibition was completely renewed.

124. Remco Ensel, "Holocaust Commemorations in Postcolonial Dutch Society," in Ensel and Gans, Holocaust, Israel and "the Jew," 477.

125. Evelien Gans, "'Hamas, Hamas, All Jews to the Gas.' The History and Significance of an Antisemitic Slogan in the Netherlands, 1945–2010," in Perceptions of the Holocaust in Europe and Muslim Communities, ed. Günther Jikeli and Joëlle Allouche-Benayoun (Dordrecht: Springer, 2013), 85–103.

126. Ensel and Gans, Holocaust, Israel and "the Jew."

127. Gans, "Why Jews Are More Guilty," 34.

128. Gans, 41.

129. Gans, 41.

130. Ensel and Gans, Holocaust, Israel and "the Jew." Evelien Gans writes that "the notion of 'nivellering' [leveling] in Holocaust historiography refers to the reduction of the existing differences in circumstances, emotions, dilemmas and motives between Jews and non-Jews, victims and bystanders. This concept indicates that people with divergent connections to the genocide are put under a single denominator without further problematization, and without adequate reflection on the different positions and attitudes of perpetrators, bystanders, collaborators and victims" (Ensel and Gans, "Historikerstreit," 359–60).

131. Kronemeijer and Teshima, "Founding Myth," 109.

132. "If Jews are seen primarily as victims, there is the danger that they will not be seen as individuals, but rather reduced to a generalized conception of victimhood" (Kronemeijer and Teshima, "Founding Myth," 114).

133. Van Bemmel, "We Are Superjews," 47–48.

134. Evelien Gans, "Philosemitism? Ambivalences Regarding Israel," in Ensel and Gans, *Holocaust, Israel and "the Jew,"* 180.

135. Katie Digan, "'The Activist Jew' Responds to Changing Dutch Perceptions of Israel," in Ensel and Gans, *Holocaust, Israel and "the Jew,"* 241.

136. Digan, 242.

137. Remco Ensel, "Transnational Left-Wing Protest and the 'Powerful Zionist,'" in Ensel and Gans, *Holocaust, Israel and "the Jew,"* 184f.

138. Gans, "Why Jews Are More Guilty," 33.

139. Ensel, "Transnational," 213.

140. Evelien Gans, "Israel: Source of Divergence," in Ensel and Gans, *Holocaust, Israel and "the Jew,"* 216.

141. Gans, "Why Jews Are More Guilty," 23.

142. Digan, "'Activist Jew,'" 242.

143. Gans, "Jewish Responses," 149.

144. Jurryt van de Vooren, "Ajax werd in 1970 overspoeld met dreig-brieven," *Sportgeschiedenis*, August 12, 2021, https://sportgeschiedenis.nl/sporten/voetbal/in-1970-werd-ajax-overspoeld-met-dreigbrieven/.

145. Van de Vooren. "Dit joodse, imperialistische sportcomplex zal vroeg of laat door ons worden vernietigd" (my translation).

146. Van de Vooren. "Ze zijn jou en je ouders vergeten te vergassen. De El Fatah zal je gezin binnenkort wel opruimen. Wat de Duitsers hebben vergeten zullen wij niet vergeten" (my translation).

147. Van de Vooren. "Waarom ben je voor een joodse vereniging gaan spelen? Dit kan niet ongestraft blijven" (my translation).

148. "The start was a letter to the Ajax board, because this football club was going to make a trip to Israel" ("Het was begonnen met een brief aan het Ajax-bestuur, . . . omdat deze voetbalclub een reis naar Israël zou maken" [my translation, quoted in van de Vooren]).

149. Jacques Presser, *Ondergang. De vervolging en verdelging van het Nederlandse Jodendom 1940–1945* (The Hague: Staatsuitgeverij, 1965).

150. Gans, "Israel," 233.

151. Evelien Gans, "The Meek Jew—and Beyond," in Ensel and Gans, *Holocaust, Israel and "the Jew,"* 99.

152. As discussed in the previous chapter, Bodenständigkeit is a value, or concept, associated with someone or something deeply rooted in one's Heimat and "down to earth." It stands in stark contrast to cosmopolitanism.

153. Van Bemmel, "We Are Superjews," 58.

154. "Supporting one's team means—almost by definition—trying to impede the opponent's as best one can. One thus tries to get into the opponent's head; one tries to make her/him uncomfortable. That is called 'home field advantage'" (Markovits, "What Is It about Association Football—the Arrogantly Self-Appointed 'Beautiful Game'—That Renders Most [Though Not All] of Its Fan Cultures so Ugly?," in Brunssen and Schüler-Springorum, *Football and Discrimination*, 203).

155. Kuper, *Ajax*, 193.

156. Markovits argues that this is a main factor for discriminatory banter in European fan cultures: "Self-criticism and self-evaluation only exist in the case of losing, never with winners. With the latter, anything goes. Virtually all fans tolerate and excuse any means to attain the ONLY end that counts for them—that of winning" (Markovits, "What Is It about Association Football," 200).

157. "Ajax 0-1 Hapoel Haifa," *De Ajax Ster*, December 15, 1999, 17, Ajax Archief. "Vanavond speelt Ajax helemaal niet. Het ho belt slechts mee. Maar liefst 38.000 toeschouwers krijgen het gevoel dat ze worden belazerd" (my translation).

158. "Ajax 0-1 Hapoel Haifa," 18. "Het publiek schaamt zich voor dit Ajax" (my translation).

159. "Ajax 0-1 Hapoel Haifa," 18. "Ondertussen worden de gezongen liedjes steeds 'harder': 'We krijgen voetballes', 'We willen voetbal zien', 'Johan Cruyff', 'Spelen voor je geld', 'Wouters rot op', 'Litmanen', alles werd gezongen uit frustratie met het vertoonde 'spel'" (my translation).

160. "Ajax 0-1 Hapoel Haifa," 17. "Gelukkig heeft Ajax uit met 0-3 gewonnen en heeft Hapoël Haifa het idee dat ze die score nooit meer kunnen inhalen" (my translation).

161. "Hapoel Haifa 0-3 Ajax," *De Ajax Ster*, December 15, 1999, 16, Ajax Archief. "Eindelijk de wedstrijd om het Joods kampioenschap" (my translation).

162. "'Good Luck Friend, It's Only a Game,'" *De Ajax Ster*, December 15, 1999, 22, Ajax Archief. "Het sprak ons meer aan dan het gewauwel van de Nederlandse schriftgeleerden" (my translation).

163. "Hapoel Haifa 0-3 Ajax," 16.

164. "'Good Luck Friend, It's Only a Game,'" 23. "Volslagen onbekenden wilden handen schudden en wensten ons veel succes" (my translation).

165. "'Good Luck Friend, It's Only a Game,'" 25.

166. "'Good Luck Friend, It's Only a Game,'" 27. Ronald Pieloor, a member of Ajax's F-Side, remembers, "We also wanted to be in a picture with a

rabbi. I was looking for some orthodox person to pose for our publication and if you have this beard, that makes you a rabbi in my books" (Peled, *Superjews*).

167. Van Bemmel, "We Are Superjews," 38.

168. Peled, *Superjews*.

169. Kuper, *Ajax*, 193.

170. Winner, *Brilliant Orange*, 8.

171. Smith, "Dutch Soccer Riddle."

172. Van Bemmel, "We Are Superjews," 75.

173. Van Bemmel, 45.

174. According to Jan Wouters, "In den Niederlanden bekommt man ja ein antideutsches Gefühl mit auf den Weg; in der Schule lernt man alles Mögliche über den Krieg und da kommt dann noch 1974 zu" (my translation, quoted in Schüler-Springorum, "Juden, Holländer, Deutsche," 260).

175. Schüler-Springorum, 260.

176. Schulze-Marmeling, "Fahrräder, Juden, Fußball," 416.

177. Schüler-Springorum, "Juden, Holländer, Deutsche," 264.

178. Schüler-Springorum, 264.

179. Van Bemmel, "We Are Superjews," 45.

180. Evelien Gans, "On Gas Chambers, Jewish Nazis and Noses," in *Racism and Extremism Monitor Ninth Report*, ed. Peter R. Rodrigues and Jaap van Donselaar (Amsterdam: Anne Frank Stichting / Leiden University, 2010), 154.

181. "The 12 June demonstration got out of hand. The Israeli airline El Al received a (false) bomb threat, and protestors marched on its office. Thereupon the office of the Palestine Committee was set on fire and two members were beaten up by unknown persons" (Ensel, "Transnational," 206, 207).

182. Gans, "On Gas Chambers," 155.

183. Gans, "Why Jews Are More Guilty," 54.

184. Holz, *Nationaler Antisemitismus*.

185. Gans, "Why Jews Are More Guilty," 54.

186. Van Bemmel, "We Are Superjews," 50.

187. Although the motif does not refer to Feyenoord Rotterdam, it is almost certain that the stickers were distributed and probably also produced by Feyenoord supporters, as I encountered the motif placed just next to Feyenoord stickers on several spots. The sticker shows the national colors of the Netherlands, the hooligan symbol ("H"), the Dutch Republic Lion, and the "anti-antifa" logo "Good Night Left Side." In addition,

it displays the slogans "Red White Blue," "Hooligans," and "true to red white blue."

188. See chapter 2.

189. Spaaij, *Understanding Football Hooliganism*, 191.

190. Hobsbawm, "Introduction: Inventing Traditions." Ramón Spaaij notes, "The two contrasting play styles largely seem to be an 'invented tradition.' For example, during a match between the two teams in 1921, Feyenoord's sophisticated, technical game was allegedly frustrated by the rough play of their rivals. The Feyenoord team has, in fact, always contained players with exceptional technical skills" (Spaaij, *Understanding Football Hooliganism*, 191).

191. Peircey, *Four Histories*, 28.

192. "Netherlands: Largest Cities 2022," Statista, 2022, https://www .statista.com/statistics/993709/largest-cities-in-the-netherlands-by -number-of-inhabitants/.

193. Peircey, *Four Histories*, 28.

194. Kuper, *Ajax*, 225.

195. Van Bemmel, "We Are Superjews," 49.

196. He did so not only once but twice: at Feyenoord's championship celebration in 1999 and then again three years later during a friendly game against Tottenham Hotspur. (It may be no coincidence that antisemitism appeared during a game against yet another "Jew Club," namely Tottenham Hotspur) (Michael Wulzinger, "Blut und Kugeln," *Der Spiegel*, September 8, 2002, 148).

197. Feyenoord Rotterdam cooperates with the Anne Frank House to educate fans about antisemitism in football. See Joram Verhoeven and Willem Wagenaar, "Appealing to a Common Identity: The Case of Antisemitism in Dutch Football," in Brunssen and Schüler-Springorum, *Football and Discrimination*, 141–51.

198. "Antisemitic Mural Appears after Dutch Football Star Signs with Ajax," *Jewish News*, August 9, 2021, https://jewishnews.timesofisrael.com /antisemitic-mural-appears-after-dutch-football-star-signs-with-ajax/; "Top Dutch Soccer Player Steven Berghuis Targeted by Lurid Antisemitic Mural After Signing for 'Jewish' Club Ajax," *Algemeiner*, July 27, 2021, https://www.algemeiner.com/2021/07/27/top-dutch-soccer-player -targeted-by-lurid-antisemitic-mural-after-signing-for-jewish-club-ajax/.

199. Furthermore, several stickers appeared in Antwerpen (Belgium) after the local football team had played against Feyenoord. The photoshopped stickers displayed Berghuis with sidelocks, a yellow star with

the word "Jud," and an Orthodox appearance ("Opnieuw beledigende afbeelding van Steven Berghuis, nu in Antwerpen," Jonet.nl, February 15, 2022, https://jonet.nl/opnieuw-beledigende-afbeelding-van-steven-berghuis-nu-in-antwerpen/).

200. Wimpietkees, "Joden Lopen Altijd Weg," posted on YouTube, July 13, 2007, https://www.youtube.com/watch?v=Nn4iwf5vzbs; The "FRFC1908" unofficial Feyenoord online fan shop offers a wide range of such products ("Anti-Ajax," FRFC1908.nl, accessed December 22, 2022, https://www.frfc1908.nl/webshop/tag/anti-ajax/).

201. In 2004, for instance, Feyenoord supporters displayed a large banner with the same message when Feyenoord played against Ajax. The banner is discussed in a game report published in the fanzine *Dapp're Strijders*. The same text also mentions the abundance of Palestinian flags shown by the Feyenoord supporters, "which would make even Jassir Arafat jealous" ("11/04: kakkerlaken—AFC Ajax (1-1)," *Dapp're Strijders*, May 9, 2004, 29, Ajax Archief). In 2021, Feyenoord supporters produced a new mural, depicting the now famous logo of the running "Ajax Jew" together with Pinocchio (probably because he has a long nose "like Jews." Or because he is supposedly lying like Jews or Ajax's fans allegedly do), the plane that crashed into Amsterdam, and the symbol of Ikea. Earlier, Feyenoord hooligans had attacked Ajax supporters at an Ikea parking lot, who allegedly ran away (Marcel Wijnstekers, "De strijd van Feyenoord tegen Jodenhaat: 'Supporters lieten tijdens bezoek Auschwitz vele tranen,'" AD.nl, July 27, 2021, https://www.ad.nl/rotterdam/de-strijd-van-feyenoord-tegen-jodenhaat-supporters-lieten-tijdens-bezoek-auschwitz-vele-tranen~ad828570e/).

202. Jasmin Seijbel, Jacco van Sterkenburg, and Gijsbert Oonk, "Expressing Rivalry Online: Antisemitic Rhetoric among Dutch Football Supporters on Twitter," *Soccer & Society*, August 8, 2022, 1–15, https://doi.org/10.1080/14660970.2022.2109800; Jasmin Seijbel, Jacco van Sterkenburg, and Ramón Spaaij, "Online Football-Related Antisemitism in the Context of the COVID-19 Pandemic: A Multi-Method Analysis of the Dutch Twittersphere," *American Behavioral Scientist*, August 26, 2022, https://doi.org/10.1177/00027642221118286.

203. "De Feijenoorder." "Het is niet zo dat iedereen denkt dat joden vergast moeten worden. We praten altijd over 'voetbaljoden'" (my translation).

204. Van Bemmel, "We Are Superjews," 53–54.

205. Florian Schubert, *Antisemitismus im Fussball: Tradition und Tabubruch*, Studien zu Ressentiments in Geschichte und Gegenwart, Band 3 (Göttingen, Germany: Wallstein, 2019).

206. B. David Tyler and Joe B. Cobbs, "Rival Conceptions of Rivalry: Why Some Competitions Mean More than Others," *European Sport Management Quarterly* 15, no. 2 (March 15, 2015): 227–48, https://doi.org/10.1080/16184742.2015.1010558.

207. Tyler and Cobbs, 237.

208. Moishe Postone describes how forms of anticapitalist thinking tend to perceive capitalism only in terms of its abstract side—for example, money as the root of all evil. This form of anticapitalism is, he claims, a "onesided attack against the abstract" in which "Jews" are equated not only with money, but also with capitalism in general; they are not only seen as representatives, but also as personifications of capitalism ("Anti-Semitism and National Socialism").

209. Verhoeven and Wagenaar, "Appealing to a Common Identity," 143.

210. "The educational strategy is based on three pillars: 1 The importance of loyalty toward one's own club, own city, and fellow supporters. 2 The use of one's narrative, the personal perception, and public explanation of what this loyalty means for the supporter involved and for their behavior. 3 The educational power of the encounter, of the act of meeting a person having educational value. In short, meeting one's own" (Verhoeven and Wagenaar, 145).

211. *NL Times*, "Court Orders Men to Visit Holocaust Memorial for Anti-Semitic Graffiti of Dutch Footballer," July 13, 2022. https://nltimes.nl/2022/07/13/court-orders-men-visit-holocaust-memorial-anti-semitic-graffiti-dutch-footballer.

212. For a discussion on education through memory in football see: Pavel Brunssen, "Möglichkeiten und Grenzen der Erinnerungsarbeit im Fußball: Interview mit Juliane Röleke zu den Potenzialen von Gedenkstättenfahrten mit Fußballfans," in *Wie gelingt partizipative politische Bildung für Jugendliche und junge Erwachsene im Fußball?* ed. Fabian Fritz, Markus Zwecker, and Birger Schmidt (Weinheim, Germany: Beltz Juventa, 2024), 198–206; Pavel Brunssen, "Zwischen Gedenken und Aufarbeitung: Fünf Thesen zur Zukunft der Erinnerungskultur im Fußball," in *Wie gelingt partizipative politische Bildung für Jugendliche und junge Erwachsene im Fußball?* ed. Fabian Fritz et al., Sportfans im Blickpunkt sozialwissenschaftlicher Forschung (Weinheim, Germany: Beltz Juventa, 2024), 207–13; Brunssen and Römer, "Erinnern," 2014; Changing the Chants, accessed September 20, 2021, www.changingthechants.eu; Changing the Chants, "Guidelines for Educational Projects Targeting Antisemitic Behaviour in Football," 2021, https://changingthechants.eu/wp-content/uploads/2021/06/guidelinesV2.pdf; Stefano Di Pietro, dir.,

Changing the Chants (Anne Frank House, Borussia Dortmund, Feyenoord, and FARE Network, 2021), https://changingthechants.eu/documentary/; Andreas Kahrs, "A Comment on Several Specific Aspects of Remembrance and Education Projects in Football," in Brunssen and Schüler-Springorum, *Football and Discrimination*, 166–78; Andreas Kahrs, Amelie Gorden, and Daniel Lörcher, "Besonderheiten und Potenziale historisch-politischer Bildung in der Fanarbeit," in *Soziale Arbeit im Fußball: Theorie und Praxis sozialpädagogischer Fanprojekte*, ed. Patrick Arnold and Jochem Kotthaus (Weinheim, Germany: Beltz Juventa, 2022), 188–201; Ullrich Krömer and Theater der Jungen Welt, eds., "Mit Fußballfans in Auschwitz: Interview mit Daniel Lörcher," in *Das Spiel mit den Anderen: Fußball zwischen Integration und Diskriminierung* (Göttingen, Germany: Die Werkstatt, 2017), 77–85; Manuel Neukirchner, ed., *Gedenken an den Holocaust—Fußball und Erinnerung*, Kleine Fußball-Bibliothek 2 (Dortmund: Klartext, 2018); Lorenz Peiffer and Henry Wahlig, "Verspätete Erinnerung," *Transparent—Magazin für Fußball und Fankultur*, no. 8 (2014): 18–21; Thoma and Liepach, "Eintracht Frankfurt Fans and the Museum"; Verhoeven and Wagenaar, "Appealing to a Common Identity."

213. Verhoeven and Wagenaar, "Appealing to a Common Identity," 145.

214. Peled, *Superjews*.

215. Peled.

216. Susanne Engels, "Cap of Keppel," July 15, 2012, https://www.2doc.nl/speel~POW_00496292~cap-of-keppel-zappdoc~.html.

217. Engels. "Ik kann daar gewoon als een echte jood gewoon rondlopen" (my translation).

218. Poulton and Durell, "Uses and Meanings," 728.

219. John Efron, "When Is a Yid Not a Jew? The Strange Case of Supporter Identity at Tottenham Hotspur," in *Emancipation through Muscles: Jews and Sports in Europe*, ed. Michael Brenner and Gideon Reuveni (Lincoln: University of Nebraska Press, 2006), 238.

220. Christopher Hom, "The Semantics of Racial Epithets," *Journal of Philosophy* 105, no. 8 (2008): 428.

221. "We recommend that future policies to combat antisemitism in football focus upon the *real* perpetrators of antisemitic discourse and behaviour, not Tottenham fans, who are the victims" (Poulton and Durell, "Uses and Meanings," 731). "Tottenham supporters are victims of antisemitism" (Bogna Wilczyńska, "'Being a Yid': Jewish Identity of Tottenham Hotspur Fans—Analysis and Interpretation," *Qualitative Sociology Review* 18, no. 3 [July 31, 2022]: 104, https://doi.org/10.18778/1733-8077.18.3.04).

222. A recent attempt to examine the experiences of Jewish Spurs fans concluded that all thirty-nine interviewees reported that their encounters with antisemitism in football were much worse than elsewhere in society. The paper remained, however, within the binary framework that understands these fan performances as "banter" and as a "mutual give-and-take" (Emma Poulton, "'What Have 6 Million Dead People Got to Do with Football?': How Anglo-Jewish Football Supporters Experience and Respond to Antisemitism and 'Banter,'" *Ethnic and Racial Studies*, October 13, 2023, 1–24, https://doi.org/10.1080/01419870.2023.2259447).

223. Claudia Bianchi, "Slurs and Appropriation: An Echoic Account," *Journal of Pragmatics* 66 (May 2014): 42, https://doi.org/10.1016/j.pragma.2014.02.009.

224. Bianchi, 43.

225. Bianchi, 38.

226. Winner, *Brilliant Orange*, 218.

227. Van Bemmel, "We Are Superjews," 39.

228. Pot, interview.

229. The group VAK 410 dissolved in 2016. The same year, the group Ultras Amsterdam was founded.

230. "Vak410 viert vijftienjarig bestaan: 'Het gaat om een stukje trots,'" *Ajax Life*, January 14, 2016, 15, Ajax Archief. "Hier en daar wordt de geuzennaam 'joden' gebruikt zoals in een van eerste liedjes die werd geschreven en hierboven staat. De groepering heeft niets met religie of politiek, en eigenlijk ook niet meer veel met de geuzennaam die geregeld voor discussie zorgt" (my translation).

231. Pot, interview.

232. "'Jude Gang' flags are a regular feature in the stands during Cracovia's home games, and their initials, 'JG', can also be seen sprayed on walls all around the city. However, unlike Tottenham supporters, many Cracovia fans who are not part of the Jude Gang, actually consider being labelled a Jewish club as an insult, due to its incompatibility with their patriotic Polish identity" (Cole, "Holy War in the City of Knives"; Esch, *Die Stadt als Spielfeld*).

233. For more on the case of Cracovia and antisemitism in Polish football see, for instance, Jacek Burski and Wojciech Woźniak, "The Sociopolitical Roots of Antisemitism among Football Fandom: The Real Absence and Imagined Presence of Jews in Polish Football," in Brunssen and Schüler-Springorum, *Football and Discrimination*, 47–64; Cole, "Holy War in the City of Knives"; Esch, *Die Stadt als Spielfeld*; Andreas Prokopf,

"Fußballhooligans in Polen zwischen Papsttreue und Antisemitismus,"
in *Überall ist der Ball rund: Zur Geschichte und Gegenwart des Fußballs in
Ost- und Südosteuropa - die zweite Halbzeit,* ed. Dittmar Dahlmann, Anke
Hilbrenner, and Britta Lenz (Essen: Klartext, 2008), 115–26.

234. "Welkom in Mokum," *Dapp're Strijders,* November 23, 2003, Ajax
Archief.

235. Bruges fans, for instance, attack Anderlecht supporters with the
following slurs: "Fuck the Jews, those dirty Jews, the Bruges fans will
come to kill you . . . Hamas Hamas, all Jews to the gas" (Ensel, "'Jew' vs.
'the Young Male Maroccan,'" 390). A player of FC Bruges, Noa Lang,
who had transferred to the Belgium club from Ajax even joined in when
the club's supporters chanted that they would "rather die than being a
Jew" (Cnaan Liphshiz, "Belgian Soccer Star Defends Chanting He'd
'Rather Die Than Be a Jew,'" *Jerusalem Post,* May 25, 2021, https://www
.jpost.com/diaspora/antisemitism/belgian-soccer-star-defends
-chanting-hed-rather-die-than-be-a-jew-669059). In Den Haag, too,
the antisemitism was not limited to fan performances: "Uri Coronel
also describes one of the incidents in The Hague, in 2010: Coronel:
'Last year we had won in The Hague and after the match you could hear
the players of The Hague in the dressing room and hallways shouting:
Kankerjoden ['cancer Jews'] and so on" (van Bemmel, "We Are Superjews," 49).

236. The 12th Player, "English | 12-ה השחקן," accessed July 22, 2022,
https://12p.co.il/english/.

237. "'We are the Yiddo's,'" *De Ajax Ster,* May 10, 1998, 14, Ajax Archief.
"Tottenham Hotspur heeft veel gemeen met Ajax" (my translation).

238. "'We are the Yiddo's,'" 14. "And Tottenham, like the best club in the
Netherlands, has the reputation of being a 'Jew Club.' Like Amsterdam,
North London used to be home to a large Jewish community. 'Yids' (Jews)
is therefore used in England as a term of abuse for Spurs fans. And just
like the Ajax supporters, the supporters of THFC have also adopted the
title as a kind of nickname" ("En Tottenham heeft, net als de besteclub
van Nederlandde naam een 'jodenclub' te zijn. Noord-Londen herbergde
vroeger net als Amsterdam een grote joodse gemeenschap. 'Yids' [joden]
wordt in Engeland daarom gebruikt als scheldnaam voor Spursfans. En
net als de Ajaxsupporters, hebben ook de aanhangers van THFC de titel
aangenomen als een soort geuzennaam," [my translation]).

239. "'We are the Yiddo's,'" 16.

240. Spaaij, *Understanding Football Hooliganism,* 94, 192.

241. "Ajacieden op bezoek bij Tottenham," *De Ajax Ster,* December 13, 1998, Ajax Archief.

242. "London . . . is the place for me (1)," *De Ajax Ster,* April 18, 1999, Ajax Archief; "London . . . is the place for me (slot)," *De Ajax Ster,* May 13, 1999, Ajax Archief.

243. "Jaarverslagen Vereniging," June 30, 2005, 49, Ajax Archief, https://archief.ajax.nl.

244. "De Discussie: 'Ajax is helemaal geen Joodse club,'" *Ajax Life,* October 1, 2002, Ajax Archief. "Ajax is helemaal geen Joodse club" (my translation).

245. VVD (People's Party for Freedom and Democracy) MP Ulysse Ellian said, "Als we hier geen eind aan kunnen maken gaan we de strijd tegen antisemitisme niet winnen" (my translation, Peter Visser, "VVD-Kamerlid: Ajax Moet in Gesprek Met Achterban over Verwijzingen Naar Joden," WNL, December 1, 2022, https://wnl.tv/2022/12/01/vvd-kamerlid-ajax-moet-in-gesprek-met-achterban-over-verwijzingen-naar-joden/). Ellian issued a memorandum to end antisemitism together with an MP from the party ChristenUnie, in which they also demanded a halt to "Jew Club" performances ("Dutch Football Should Be Forced to Finally Tackle Anti-Semitism: Coalition Parties," *NL Times,* December 1, 2022, https://nltimes.nl/2022/12/01/dutch-football-forced-finally-tackle-anti-semitism-coalition-parties).

4. TOTTENHAM HOTSPUR

1. "Yid. The Man Who Gave Us the Name," *Fighting Cock* (blog), October 22, 2013, https://thefightingcock.co.uk/2013/10/yid-the-man-who-gave-us-the-name/.

2. By capitalizing *White* and *Black,* I seek to emphasize that these concepts are socially and historically constructed (Lori L. Tharps, "The Case for Black with a Capital B," *New York Times,* November 18, 2014, sec. Opinion, https://www.nytimes.com/2014/11/19/opinion/the-case-for-black-with-a-capital-b.html).

3. "Yid. The Man Who Gave Us the Name."

4. Christine Jacqueline Feldman, *"We Are the Mods": A Transnational History of a Youth Subculture,* Mediated Youth 7 (New York: Peter Lang, 2009).

5. "Yid. The Man Who Gave Us the Name."

6. "Yid. The Man Who Gave Us the Name."

7. Richard Elliott, ed., *The English Premier League: A Socio-Cultural Analysis*, Routledge Research in Football 2 (London: Routledge, 2019); Daniel Parnell et al., "'It's a Whole New Ball Game': Thirty Years of the English Premier League," *Soccer & Society* 23, no. 4–5 (July 4, 2022): 329–33, https://doi.org/10.1080/14660970.2022.2059853; Giuseppe Telesca, "The English Premier League and the City of London (1980–2010): A Tale of Two 'Revolutions,'" *Soccer & Society* 23, no. 4–5 (March 31, 2022): 1–13, https://doi.org/10.1080/14660970.2022.2059860.

8. One Jews Spurs fan declares, for instance, that the way he "learnt about the word ['Yid'] is from the abuse" ("Y-Word Focus Group 3," Tottenham Hotspur, February 10, 2022, https://www.tottenhamhotspur.com /the-club/the-why-word/y-word-focus-group-3/).

9. Les Back, Tim Crabbe, and John Solomos, "Beyond the Racist/ Hooligan Couplet: Race, Social Theory and Football Culture," *British Journal of Sociology* 50, no. 3 (September 1999): 419–42, https://doi .org/10.1111/j.1468-4446.1999.00419.x.

10. Back, Crabbe, and Solomos, 428.

11. Author Anthony Clavane noted about his experiences as a Leeds fan in the mid-1970s, "I began to hear anti-Semitic chants and, when we played Spurs, the obligatory concentration camp hissing noises would occasionally be directed towards the West Stand" (*Does Your Rabbi Know You're Here? The Story of English Football's Forgotten Tribe* [London: Quercus, 2012], 118).

12. According to Poulton and Durell, this chant was heard frequently during the 1970s and 1980s and its complete text was "Spurs are on their way to Auschwitz! Sieg Heil! Hitler's gonna gas 'em again! You can't stop them, The Yids from Tottenham, The Yids from White Hart Lane" ("Uses and Meanings," 718). The song is still heard today, although less frequently than in the 1970s and 1980s. Sometimes, the lyrics were varied to "Spurs are on their way to Belsen," and on occasion chanted by nonrival clubs such as Liverpool ("'Belsen' Cry at Anfield," *Jewish Chronicle*, October 17, 1986).

13. Brian Glanville, "Tottenham Chutzpah," *Jewish Chronicle*, May 17, 1991. Similar songs are: "Gas a Jew, Jew, Jew, stick him in the oven gas mark, / Gas a Jew, Jew, Jew, stick him in the oven gas mark, / In his head in his eye, jump up and down on him make him cry, / Gas a Jew, Jew, Jew, stick him in the oven gas mark." David S. Winner provides another example: "Chelsea fans have been known to sing, 'One man went to gas, went

to gas a yiddo,' a corruption of the popular children's counting song, 'One man went to mow, went to mow a meadow'" ("Don't Blame Soccer's 'Jewish' Teams for Anti-Semitism," *Foreign Policy* [blog], May 10, 2019, https://foreignpolicy.com/2019/05/10/dont-blame-for-anti-semitism-in-soccer-tottenham-hotspur-spurs-ajax-amsterdam/).

14. Efron, "When Is a Yid Not a Jew?" 247–48.

15. It is similar to the Dutch chant "Joden lopen altijd weg" directed at Ajax Amsterdam.

16. Daniel Finkelstein, "Time to Tackle Football Racism," *Jewish Chronicle*, February 29, 2008, 31.

17. Sandy Rashty, "'Racist' Badges at Arsenal," *Jewish Chronicle*, September 21, 2012.

18. "Fans Condemn 'Offensive' T-Shirt Showing Harry Kane as a Chasid," *Jewish Chronicle*, February 12, 2016. In the same year, fans of CSKA Moscow produced stickers showing a Spurs fan walking toward a gas chamber, accompanied by the (English) words: "Welcome to Russia" (Emma Poulton, "Collective Identity and Forms of Abuse and Discrimination in Football Fan Culture: A Case Study on Antisemitism," in Brunssen and Schüler-Springorum, *Football and Discrimination*, 22).

19. "Spurs Condemn Spanish Newspaper over Claims the Club Is 'hated' for Jewish Origins," *Telegraph*, October 16, 2017, https://www.telegraph.co.uk/football/2017/10/16/spurs-condemn-spanish-newspaper-claims-club-hated-jewish-origins/.

20. "Partizan Belgrade Apologise for Antisemitic Banner against Spurs," *Guardian*, September 19, 2014, http://www.theguardian.com/football/2014/sep/19/partizan-belgrade-apologise-antisemitic-banner-tottenham-hotspur; Poulton, "Collective Identity," 22.

21. Antisemitism and sexism are intertwined ideologies. See for instance Brunssen, *Antisemitismus in Fußball-Fankulturen: Der Fall RB Leipzig*, 123–41; Sander L. Gilman, *The Jew's Body* (New York: Routledge, 1991); Stefanie Schüler-Springorum, "Gender and the Politics of Anti-Semitism," *American Historical Review* 123, no. 4 (2018): 1210–22; Karin Stögner, "Nature and Anti-Nature: Constellations of Antisemitism and Sexism," in *Internal Outsiders—Imagined Orientals? Antisemitism, Colonialism and Modern Constructions of Jewish Identity*, ed. Ulrike Brunotte, Jürgen Mohn, and Christina Späti, Diskurs Religion, Beiträge Zur Religionsgeschichte Und Religiösen Zeitgeschichte, Band 13 (Würzburg, Germany: Ergon Verlag, 2017), 157–70.

22. Poulton, "Collective Identity," 22.

23. In the past, Lazio ultras displayed a banner directed at their local rival, AS Roma, saying "Auschwitz Is Your Country; The Ovens Are Your Homes." Whether AS Roma is another European "Jew Club" would be another interesting case study. In 2017, stickers appeared near the Stadio Olimpico that displayed Anne Frank in the jersey of AS Roma. In 2021, when it was announced that the manager Jose Mourinho, just sacked by Tottenham, would become AS Roma's manager in the following season, Lazio fans placed a banner on a motorway ahead of their game against AS Roma that referred to Mourinho: "Yesterday Spurs, today AS Roma . . . Tomorrow Maccabi" (Brunssen and Schüler-Springorum, "Introduction"); Alex Milne, "Lazio Supporters Hang Anti-Semitic Jose Mourinho Banner Ahead of Roma Fixture," *Irish Mirror*, May 15, 2021, https://www.irishmirror.ie/sport/soccer/soccer-news /lazio-supporters-hang-anti-semitic-24116164.

24. One year later, similar attacks happened in Lyon, France (Poulton, "Collective Identity," 22). Just one week later, West Ham fans celebrated the attack by singing "Can we stab you every week?," making gas chamber noises, and chanting "Adolf Hitler—he's coming for you" (Marcus Dysch, "Blood, Hate and Football's Shame," *Jewish Chronicle*, September 30, 2012). They also chanted "Viva Lazio" and "Paolo Di Canio," a former West Ham, now Lazio, player, who had shown the Nazi salute in the past (David Hytner, "Section of West Ham United Support Aim Antisemitic Abuse at Spurs Fans," *Guardian*, November 25, 2012, http://www.theguardian.com /football/2012/nov/25/west-ham-united-antisemitism-spurs).

25. *TOI* Staff and AFP, "Chelsea Soccer Fan Jailed for 8 Weeks for Antisemitic Tweets Aimed at Rival," *Times of Israel*, November 5, 2021, https://www .timesofisrael.com/chelsea-soccer-fan-jailed-for-8-weeks-for-antisemitic -tweets-aimed-at-rival/. In 2017, another Chelsea fan tweeted following the victory over Spurs: "Hitler isn't the only one to silence 70,000 Yids" (Poulton, "Collective Identity," 28).

26. Jessica Elgot, "The Herd: We Didn't Mean It in a Racist Way," *Jewish Chronicle*, August 26, 2012.

27. They declared, "This was more meant because our local rivals use this symbol a lot, and what we were saying was that if you don't pay a subscription towards the upkeep of the website, then effectively, you are a Tottenham fan" (Elgot).

28. Back, Crabbe, and Solomos, "Beyond the Racist/Hooligan Couplet," 427.

29. Jews voiced their hope that the measures will lead to a decline of antisemitism (Julian Kossoff, "Team Tackles the Terraces of Hate," *Jewish Chronicle*, March 16, 1990).

30. Anna Kessel, "Alive and Unchecked—a Wave of Anti-Jewish Hate," *Observer*, October 27, 2007, sec. Football, https://www.theguardian.com /football/2007/oct/28/newsstory.sport2.

31. Simon Griver, "Lesson with Vieira," *Jewish Chronicle*, October 22, 2004.

32. Kessel, "Alive and Unchecked."

33. Kick It Out, *The Y-Word*, posted on YouTube, April 12, 2011, https:// www.youtube.com/watch?v=RIvJC1_hKt8.

34. The online search was conducted on December 27, 2022. It included the spellings "Y word" and "Y-word" and the years 1896–2021. The articles were briefly checked to confirm that they concern Tottenham. The archive is available online: https://archive.thejc.com/.

35. David Baddiel produced the film together with his brother, Ivor. It was made by Fahrenheit films and supported by the Shoresh Foundation. The campaign was launched by Kick It Out, Maccabi GB, and the Community Security Trust (CST).

36. Tottenham legend Gary Lineker explains in the film: "Back in the 1930s and 1940s Jewish people all over Europe were rounded up and killed. People called them 'Yids.'" Although the term was frequently used by British fascists, is seems unlikely that the (German) Nazis used the term. German dictionaries have no entries on "Yid," and in topic-specific dictionaries like *Nazi-Deutsch/Nazi German: An English Lexicon of the Language of the Third Reich*, the term "Yid" does not appear, except when used in English to explain German words. (The word *Jud* is explained as "Yid, Jew. More contemptuous name for Jew than Jude" and the word *Jüdlein* as "Little Yid. Contemptuous name for Jews used by their murderers.") (Robert Michael and Karin Doerr, *Nazi-Deutsch/Nazi-German: An English Lexicon of the Language of the Third Reich* [Westport, CT: Greenwood Press, 2002], 222, 230). The word "Yid" is also absent in Nazi books such as Hitler's *Mein Kampf*, 851st–855th ed. (Munich: Zentralverlag der NSDAP, 1925).

37. "Their attitude was entirely doubtful. Their basic position was: does this really matter? There was still abuse going on from the terrace towards black players, and they had a campaign about to start on homophobia. Won't a campaign about anti-Semitism defocus the more important messages?" (David Baddiel, *Jews Don't Count: How Identity Politics Failed One Particular Identity* [London: TLS Books, an imprint of HarperCollins, 2021], 23).

38. David Baddiel repeated on various occasions that the word itself is a race-hate word (David Baddiel, "Yes, David Cameron, 'Yid' Really Is a Race-Hate Word. Here's Why," *Guardian*, September 17, 2013, http://www .theguardian.com/commentisfree/2013/sep/17/david-cameron-yid-really-is -race-hate-word).

39. Other options for comparison would have been words like *gay* and *queer*, which are now commonly used again after a process of linguistic reclamation. See the previous chapter.

40. The release statement positioned Tottenham's endorsement even before all others, among them Chelsea FC, the club whose fans are known for targeting Spurs with antisemitic chants like a few other clubs do (Community Security Trust, "The Y-Word," *CST Blog*, April 14, 2011, https://cst .org.uk/news/blog/2011/04/14/the-y-word).

41. Kick It Out, "Think Again!—Classroom Activities for Challenging Prejudice and Fostering Community Cohesion," 2012, https://www .migrationmuseum.org/wp-content/uploads/2014/08/Think-Again-Y -Word-educational-pack.pdf.

42. Baddiel, *Jews Don't Count*, 23–24.

43. UK Parliament, "Antisemitism and Other Racism in Football," Hansard, vol. 716, June 22, 2022, https://hansard.parliament.uk//commons /2022-06-22/debates/38A9C59A-455F-4DDA-B24E-6615E26582BA /AntisemitismAndOtherRacismInFootball.

44. Cloake and Fisher, *People's History*, 231.

45. Martin Cloake, "'We Are the Yids': Should Spurs Fans Be Prosecuted for Using the Y Word?" *New Statesman*, March 12, 2014, https:// www.newstatesman.com/culture/sport/2014/03/we-are-yids-should -spurs-fans-be-prosecuted-using-y-word; Cloake and Fisher, *People's History*, 231; Poulton and Durell, "Uses and Meanings."

46. "In September 2013, the Football Association decided that the Y-word was 'inappropriate in a football setting' and 'could amount to a criminal offence'" (Charlie Eccleshare and Jack Pitt-Brooke, "Spurs Fans and the Y-Word: What Happens Next?" *Athletic*, November 19, 2021, https:// theathletic.com/2963758/2021/11/19/spurs-fans-and-the-y-word-what -happens-next/).

47. "'Being a Yid . . .'—Spurs FanChants," FanChants, July 18, 2020, https://www.fanchants.com/football-songs/tottenham_hotspur-chants /r09_0079f_f/.

48. Hytner, "Section of West Ham United Support Aim Antisemitic Abuse at Spurs Fans"; James Meikle and Kim Willsher, "Tottenham Fans

Injured in 'Antisemitic' Attack before Europa League Tie in Lyon," *Guardian*, February 21, 2013, http://www.theguardian.com/world/2013/feb/21/tottenham-fans-antisemitic-attack-lyon.

49. The results stated specifically: "74% of non-Jewish respondents and 73% of Jewish respondents were generally in favour of fans being allowed to use the Y-word," while a "number of supporters, (12% of non-Jewish respondents and 18% of Jewish respondents) outlined that they were against allowing fans to continue to use the term with 4% of non-Jewish fans and 6% of Jewish fans specifically stating that they were personally uncomfortable with its use." The fan consultation was commissioned by the independent research consultancy Populus ("Y-Word Consultation—Update," Tottenham Hotspur, March 21, 2014, https://www.tottenhamhotspur.com/news-archive-1/y-word-consultation-update/).

50. The book was Norman Giller's *Lane of Dreams.* The passage in question was "Wigan's Austrian midfielder Paul Scharner blatantly controls the ball with his hand before steering it past Gomes. The Yid Army, in good humour, light up the Lane with chants of, 'Are you Henry in disguise?'" (Norman Giller, "Tottenham Deliver a Kick in the Wrecking Balls," *Sports Journalists' Association* [blog], January 22, 2010, https://www.sportsjournalists.co.uk/the-giller-memorandum/tottenham-deliver-a-kick-in-the-wrecking-balls/).

51. "WhY Word: Time to Think about It," Tottenham Hotspur, 2022, https://www.tottenhamhotspur.com/the-club/the-why-word/.

52. The taking-a-knee initiative goes back to gridiron football (American football) quarterback Colin Kapernick, who, since 2016, has performed the symbolic gesture during the US national anthem before kickoff. The gesture soon became global, with English association football in particular participating. The gridiron football team Washington Commanders was renamed in 2000, after the name "Redskins" was publicly criticized for being derogatory toward Indigenous Americans. Tottenham's statement refers to these developments directly: "We have already seen several sports entities and franchises make appropriate changes to nicknames and aspects of their identities in recognition of evolving sentiment."

53. "WhY Word: Time to Think about It."

54. "WhY Word: Time to Think about It."

55. The three articles are Stephen Pollard, "Why I Changed My Mind on Spurs and The Y Word," *Jewish Chronicle*, February 16, 2022, https://www.thejc.com/lets-talk/all/why-i-changed-my-mind-on-spurs-and-the-y-word

-15wKTwkh7mpnHqHbXKtUqD; Andre Langlois, "I'm a Spurs Fan and We Should Drop the Y-Word—We Don't Need It," Tottenham Hotspur, February 11, 2022, https://www.tottenhamhotspur.com/the-club/the-why -word/im-a-spurs-fan-and-we-should-drop-the-y-word-we-dont-need-it/; and Mark Solomons, "As a Jewish Spurs Fan, I Saw Y-Word Chants as a Form of Solidarity. But They Have to Go," *Guardian*, February 14, 2022, sec. Opinion, https://www.theguardian.com/commentisfree/2022/feb/14 /jewish-spurs-fan-y-word-chants-tottenham-hotspur.

56. Pollard, "Why I Changed My Mind on Spurs and The Y Word."

57. The club presents the survey as compelling evidence, claiming that a third of the respondents "use the Y-word 'regularly' in a footballing context" and that "almost half of all respondents would prefer to see supporters choose to chant the Y-word less or stop using it altogether." The framing of the findings supports the club's desire to break with the Y-identity. The club highlights, for instance, that 33 percent of the respondents use the term regularly, but leaves buried in the details that another 41 percent of the respondents use the term "occasionally." In sum, 74 percent of fans use the term. Other results are presented confusingly: "18% of respondents that do not use the term in a footballing context consider it 'offensive,' with the number rising to 35% among Jewish respondents." It remains unclear how many 18 percent and 35 percent of another percentage (that is, how many people are not using the term in a footballing context?) entails. The underlying message remains that "respondents . . . consider it offensive." The wording forms the message: the club's website indicates that "*nearly* half" prefer to stop using the phrase, rather than "*less than* half" (my emphasis). The poll results can be read in a variety of ways, but because the club does not give more information, we are left with the framing and the club's strong emphasis on eliminating the Y-word, which determined the public discourse.

58. David Newman, "Proud to Be a Tottenham Yid," *Times of Israel*, October 11, 2019, https://blogs.timesofisrael.com/proud-to-be-a -tottenham-yid/.

59. The website states that 95 percent of the more than twenty-three thousand respondents "were either a Season Ticket holder, an Executive Level or One Hotspur Member and 97% of all respondents had attended at least one match per season. A total of 11% stated that they were Jewish" ("Y-Word Consultation Update," Tottenham Hotspur, December 19, 2019, https://www.tottenhamhotspur.com/news/2019/december/y-word -consultation-update/).

60. Tottenham Hotspur Supporters' Trust, "THST News—February 2022," February 27, 2022, https://thstofficial.com/thst-news-february-2022/.

61. The survey's results were as evenly eclectic as the club's survey: in total, 38 percent of THST members wanted to "move on," while 33 percent "disagreed," and 29 percent reported themselves to be indifferent. Interestingly, THST claims that the club's survey "has prompted the biggest uplift in use" of "Yid" among Jewish respondents: "We asked if the Club's request made you more or less likely to use the so-called Y Word when singing or chanting inside the Tottenham Hotspur Stadium. Some 15% of matchgoing fans who identified as Jewish said it had made them more likely to use the word, compared to 9% of all respondents" (Tottenham Hotspur Supporters' Trust, "THST Fan Survey August 2022," August 2022, https://thstofficial.com/wp-content/uploads/2024/02/thst_annual_fans_survey_2022.pdf).

62. David Cesarani, The "Jewish Chronicle" and Anglo-Jewry, 1841–1991 (Cambridge: Cambridge University Press, 1994).

63. Cesarani, ix.

64. Ben Weich, "'If Hope Doesn't Triumph over Experience, Football Isn't for You,'" Jewish Chronicle, May 31, 2019.

65. Weich.

66. "Spurs Wishes," Jewish Chronicle, October 12, 1973. According to Clavane, the club published a "Happy Yom Kippur" message in a match day program the same year, something rather uncommon for the "Day of Atonement" (Clavane, Does Your Rabbi Know You're Here?, 94).

67. Jewish Chronicle, September 10, 1999.

68. Richard Brecker, "Spurs Sorry," Jewish Chronicle, October 9, 1981.

69. "Apology," Jewish Chronicle, September 9, 1983.

70. Wally Leaf, "Arsenal Fans Warned," Jewish Chronicle, October 30, 1987.

71. "Soccer Hate Campaign," Jewish Chronicle, December 12, 1980.

72. Glanville, "Tottenham Chutzpah."

73. Jewish Chronicle, March 1, 1996.

74. Simon Rocker and Jeremy Lester, "The Flip Side of British Jewry," Jewish Chronicle, March 1, 1996.

75. Jeremy Lester, "Fan the Flames," Jewish Chronicle, March 8, 1996.

76. "Other calls," the text continues, "included a student wanting more information for a dissertation on Jewish fandom." It seems Spurs' Y-identity has steered interest in scholars for a long time now.

77. Clavane, *Does Your Rabbi Know You're Here?*, 95. Arsenal, in stark contrast to Tottenham, embraced its Jewish followers early on: "I am happy to think we have a large number of Jews," Arsenal's chair George Allison wrote to the *JC* in 1934—long before Spurs wished their Jewish supporters a happy new year in 1973 (David Dee, *Sport and British Jewry: Integration, Ethnicity and Anti-Semitism, 1890–1970* [Manchester University Press, 2013], 99).

78. Cloake and Fisher, *People's History*, 218.

79. See, for instance, the confusion expressed by the authors of the brilliant book *A People's History of Tottenham Hotspur Football Club*, Martin Cloake and Alan Fisher:

> At some point from the late 1960s onward, opposition fans began to chant abuse at Spurs supporters using the word. It's impossible to date exactly when this began. Most Jewish supporters of that era are convinced they know when it began but probably are recounting the first time they heard it. One told us with certainty that it was started by Charlton fans in the early 1960s. Another saw Spurs win the 1967 FA Cup Final from the Chelsea end and was appalled by the anti-Semitic abuse. Others blame the popular 1960s and 1970s sitcom *Til Death Do Us Part* and its central character, the bigoted West Ham-supporting Alf Garnett, played with gusto by Spurs season ticket holder Warren Mitchell, who referred to Spurs supporters as Yids. However, it's more likely this came from writer Johnny Speight's sharp ear for the East End vernacular. (225)

80. Emma Poulton, "Towards Understanding: Antisemitism and the Contested Uses and Meanings of 'Yid' in English Football," *Ethnic and Racial Studies* 39, no. 11 (September 2016): 1985, https://doi.org/10.1080/014 19870.2016.1140791; Efron, "When Is a Yid Not a Jew?" 236.

81. Wilczyńska, "'Being a Yid,'" 87.

82. Andreas Grau and Martin Winands, "Herausforderungen quantitativer und qualitativer Forschung in (Jugend-)Kulturen und Szenen: Das Beispiel der Fußballfanforschung," in *Sozialwissenschaftliche Perspektiven der Fussballfanforschung*, ed. Andreas Grau et al., Sportfans im Blickpunkt sozialwissenschaftlicher Forschung (Weinheim, Germany: Beltz Juventa, 2017), 67. Cloake and Fisher claim that the proportion of Jewish fans is "likely to be small" and at no more than "5% of the crowd" (*People's History*, 219). According to Poulton and Durrell, 9.97 percent of the 11,389 respondents during a club survey, published in 2014 on the club's website, declared that they were Jewish ("Uses and Meanings," 716). This was indeed the first Y-word consultation by the club, some of its results can still be found online: "Y-Word Consultation—Update."

83. Glanville, "Tottenham Chutzpah." Brian Glanville provides "a brief note about Jewish footballers" in a 1991 article published in the *JC*: "Leon Joseph was probably the best, a fast, clever, dazzling amateur international left winger who played for Leytonstone, had a few games for Spurs in the '40s, but wouldn't turn pro. It wasn't worth it, then. Harry Gilberg actually displaced the illustrious Eddie Baily at inside-forward against Arsenal in a 1949 Cup tie at Highbury. Spurs crashed 3–0, Gilberg disappeared. To QPR. Micky Dulin was a small, gifted winger in the '60s, but a broken leg frustrated him. One would see him limping sadly in the car park." A few years later, Tottenham also signed the Israeli Ronny Rosenthal, who played for Spurs between 1991 and 1997.

84. In 1991, Nat Solomon became the public limited company chair of Tottenham for a few months during a time of financial turbulences in the club. He continued to become the club's Vice President and was a lifelong Tottenham supporter.

85. "Jewish settlements in areas like Tottenham, Hackney, Golders Green and Finchley grew considerably in the interwar years as many second generation, socially mobile and increasingly secularised Jews relocated from the East End" (Dee, *Sport and British Jewry*, 98). The perception of the Jewish migration out of the East End is problematized later in this chapter. On the public transport to the stadium see also Clavane, *Does Your Rabbi Know You're Here?*, 92.

86. "Tottenham were one of the most prominent professional teams in the capital, becoming the first club outside of the Football League to win the FA Cup in 1901" (Dee, *Sport and British Jewry*, 98).

87. Cloake and Fisher, *People's History*, 221.

88. Dr. Monty Curwen, "Letters to the Editor: Boyhood Memories of Spurs Supporter," *Jewish Chronicle*, March 15, 1996.

89. Others described the 1921 FA Cup triumph also as a crucial memory: "Like thousands of us, our families grew up in the East End 100 years ago and could have gone to West Ham but found it a little less than welcoming so they jumped on the tram that, handily, linked Whitechapel to Tottenham and the rest is history. My grandad went to the 1921 cup final, my dad had a season ticket during both the 51 and 61 title winning seasons" (Mark Solomons, "The Thing I Love Most . . ." *Fighting Cock* [blog], December 17, 2018, https://thefightingcock.co.uk/2018/12/the -thing-i-love-most/).

90. Clavane, *Does Your Rabbi Know You're Here?*, 92.

91. Of course, fans who traveled to the games faced the problem of transportation during Shabbat. A "creative interpretation of religious law claimed," according to Cloake and Fisher, "that the Shabbos tradition could be maintained by purchasing a ticket on the Friday morning and going by an electric tram, not a combustion-engine bus" (*People's History*, 221).

92. David Newman's reflection on being Jewish and a Spurs fan further questions the "glory hunting" hypothesis, also related to the post-1960s period. For Newman, there is also a "theological explanation" for why so many Jews follow Spurs, namely, the club's "tendency to underachievement." Spurs fans hope for glory before each season, which has been continually disappointed since the 1960s. This is, for Newman, just like "our Passover yearnings for the messiah," because both will "never come to fruition." Thus "it is Jewish self-suffering and masochism, not experienced by the other famous teams in the UK, which Israelis have a tendency of supporting from afar—the sort of remote control support which we 'true' fans sneer upon" ("Borderline View: A Tottenham 'Yid' in Israel," *Jerusalem Post*, June 15, 2009, https://www.jpost.com/opinion/columnists /borderline-view-a-tottenham-yid-in-israel). Suffering is indeed a pleasurable experience for football fans, who can make claims to being a "real fan" when they stick with a team through hard times. Spurs fans explain with a certain pride that the term *spursy* has been described in the *OED* since 2016 as "to constantly fail to live up to expectations" (Cloake and Fisher, *A People's History*, 194).

93. Monty Curwen's letter furthermore strengthens the impression that there used to be a competition among Tottenham and Arsenal fans about whose club had "the most Jews" or which club a Jew should follow. Curwen's "relief" that he is "not the only Jew so afflicted" with Spurs is "marred only by the knowledge that so many co-religionists, including Chief Rabbi Dr Jonathan Sacks, have deserted to other clubs." Curwen adds "words of wisdom to the Yom Kippur liturgy," which, he hopes might help. These are the remarkable words: "If you jump on a bus from the / Machzike Adath / To watch Arsenal play on a Shabbos, / You will hear a *geshrei* and, from / somewhere on high / Come the words, loud and clear / You're a *lobbos*. / You are breaking the din, and it's / worse than a sin, / It's a *chMul hashem*, it's a chutzpah. / And it's time that you knew that a / really good Jew / Should be following Tottenham / Hotspur" ("Letters to the Editor: Boyhood Memories of Spurs Supporter"). Curwen would have been relieved to learn that Rabbi Sacks's successor, Chief Rabbi Ephraim

Mirvis, is "well known for his strong support of Tottenham" (Newman, "Proud to Be a Tottenham Yid").

94. Glanville, "Tottenham Chutzpah."

95. Hunter Davies, *The Glory Game*, revised and updated edition (Edinburgh: Mainstream, 2021), 227–34.

96. Davies, 227.

97. Glanville, "Tottenham Chutzpah."

98. Glanville.

99. Clavane also offers a vivid description of Spurs' hangers-on:

Jewish support for Tottenham Hotspur had grown rapidly in the immediate post-war period, and the area north of the railway line, roughly between White Hart Lane and the North Middlesex Hospital, became known as Little Russia following the migration of White Russian refugees from the 1917 Revolution. It was an intimidating neighbourhood, the police only venturing there in pairs, and it spawned a subculture of fearless, colourful characters who appeared to have stepped straight out of a Damon Runyan short story. Need a new watch? A diamond ring? Ticket for the Spurs? Then One-Armed Lou, Johnny the Stick and Fat Stan were your men. Johnny 'the Stick' Goldstein, one of the first ticket touts, was a familiar figure outside White Hart Lane in the 1950s and '60s. As hacks huddled together in the big grey car park, waiting for titbits of gossip, they would spot John hanging around Danny Blanchflower, the Spurs captain. (*Does Your Rabbi Know You're Here?* 139)

100. Morris Keston and Nick Hawkins, *Superfan: The Amazing Life of Morris Keston, Football Fan Extraordinaire and Friend of the Stars* (London: VSP, 2010); John Fennely, "Morris Keston RIP," Tottenham Hotspur, August 16, 2019, https://www.tottenhamhotspur.com/news/2019/august/morris-keston/.

101. Davies, *Glory Game*, 228.

102. Davies, 228.

103. Davies, 229.

104. Clavane, *Does Your Rabbi Know You're Here?*, 94.

105. Aubrey Morris was born in 1919 in Bethnal Green into a family of Jewish immigrants, who, like so many others, had fled from czarist Russia. In 1936, he fought against British fascists in the East End during the Battle of Cable Street; he fought against the Nazis in World War II, and he was a candidate for the Communist Party in East London (Martin Cloake and Adam Powley, *We Are Tottenham: Voices from White Hart Lane* [Edinburgh: Mainstream, 2004], 147–54; Cloake and Fisher, *People's History*, 104; Geoffrey Goodman, "Aubrey Morris: Founder of the First Package

Travel Firm for Football Supporters," *Guardian*, January 13, 2009, sec. Travel, https://www.theguardian.com/travel/2009/jan/13/obituary -aubrey-morris).

106. Poulton, "Towards Understanding," 1985.

107. Alan Fisher claims that "the link between the club and the Jewish community . . . stretches back to around 1910, when large numbers of the predominantly working-class, male Jewish community . . . moved to Tottenham and the surrounding areas" ("The Y Word, Spurs and Changing Times," *Tottenham on My Mind* [blog], February 14, 2022, https:// tottenhamonmymind.com/2022/02/14/the-y-word-spurs-and-changing -times/).

108. Rachel Kolsky and Roslyn Rawson, *Jewish London: A Comprehensive Handbook for Visitors and Residents* (London: New Holland, 2012), 199.

109. Efron, "When Is a Yid Not a Jew?" 243, 236.

110. Hannah Ewence, *The Alien Jew in the British Imagination, 1881–1905: Space, Mobility and Territoriality* (Basingstoke, UK: Palgrave Macmillan, 2019).

111. Hannah Ewence, "Moving 'Out' to Be 'In': The Suburbanization of London Jewry, 1900–1939," *Urban History* 50, no. 4 (2022): 1–18, https:// doi.org/10.1017/S0963926822000165.

112. Goodman, "Aubrey Morris"; Davies, *Glory Game*, 227.

113. Ewence, "Moving 'Out' to Be 'In.'"

114. Clavane, *Does Your Rabbi Know You're Here?*, 65.

115. Cloake and Fisher, *People's History*, 223; Dee, *Sport and British Jewry*, 144; Brian Stoddart, "Sport, Cultural Politics and International Relations: England versus Germany, 1935[1]," *Soccer & Society* 7, no. 1 (January 2006): 29–50, https://doi.org/10.1080/14660970500355579. Clavane notes that Tottenham was "the main attraction to football-mad Jews" in London: "In the 1930s, according to a Manchester Guardian report, Jews made up a third of the average crowd at White Hart Lane—equal to about 11,000 supporters regularly attending. At a 1934 north London derby the Daily Express's Trevor Wignall discovered he 'was nearly entirely surrounded by them'" (*Does Your Rabbi Know You're Here?*, 91).

116. Stoddart, "Sport, Cultural Politics and International Relations," 31.

117. John Harding, "When England Played Germany at White Hart Lane in 1935," *Guardian*, June 11, 2020, sec. Football, https://www.theguardian .com/football/2020/jun/11/nazi-germany-played-england-tottenham-white -hart-lane.

118. Clavane, *Does Your Rabbi Know You're Here?*, 65–66.

119. Harding, "When England."

120. P. Hyams, "Will They Play at the 'Spurs'?" *Jewish Chronicle,* October 18, 1935.

121. Harding, "When England."

122. Dee, *Sport and British Jewry,* 161.

123. "They wrote to the Tottenham authorities pointing out that as one third of the club's support came from Jewry they 'would not tolerate' the carrying out of the arrangement. As they controlled and cornered everything else in Britain the Jews naturally saw no reason why they should not control and corner British sport as well" (A. K. Chesterton, "They Have Spoken—the Silent People!," *Blackshirt,* December 13, 1935, 138 ed., British Online Archives).

124. A. G. Findley, "Sport and Race," *Action,* March 19, 1936, British Online Archives.

125. Findley.

126. *The Blackshirt* even reprinted parts of an article from the *JC* about Jews at White Hart Lane with an antisemitic comment ("Noises Off!" *Blackshirt,* September 18, 1935, 229 ed., British Online Archives).

127. Stoddart, "Sport, Cultural Politics and International Relations," 37, 42.

128. Stoddart, 42.

129. Stoddart, 42.

130. Clavane, *Does Your Rabbi Know You're Here?,* 66.

131. Wilczyńska, "'Being a Yid,'" 102.

132. John Harding calls him a "star" in an article published by the *Guardian* in 2020:

> The star, however, was Ernie Wooley, a 24-year-old Shoreditch turner. Wooley was charged with maliciously and willfully doing damage (to the amount of 3/6) by cutting the lanyard which held up the Nazi flag over the East Stand. In evidence, detective sergeant Wilkinson explained: "I was near the turnstiles at the main entrance. I saw prisoner walk to the end of the stand and after loitering about for a few minutes he clambered on to the gutter at the end of the stand and edged his way along the gutter towards the lanyard supporting the German national flag. He produced an open knife from his pocket and cut the lanyard causing the flag to fall on to the roof of the grandstand. He was seized as he climbed down." Upon being arrested, Wooley remarked: "You've got thousands of police about the ground but no one to watch the flag." Wooley claimed: "I did not maliciously cut the rope. I was merely going to unfurl that flag by untying the knot of the lanyard. That Nazi flag is hated in this country." A Spurs official present said there was no evidence that the rope was worth 3/6 nor was the rope produced in evidence. There followed some confusion concerning the exact

knife used (the police had lost the original) and the case was dismissed. Wooley apparently smiled broadly as he left the dock. (Harding, "When England")

133. Clavane, *Does Your Rabbi Know You're Here?*, 66.

134. Wilczyńska, "'Being a Yid,'" 102.

135. Clavane, *Does Your Rabbi Know You're Here?*, 96.

136. Efron, "When Is a Yid Not a Jew?" 254.

137. Alan Fisher, "Spurs and the Y Word: Fans in the Dock," *Tottenham on My Mind* (blog), January 26, 2014, https://tottenhamonmymind.com /2014/01/26/spurs-and-the-y-word-fans-in-the-dock/. Although accusations seem to be rare, a 1973 article also defended the sitcom against similar criticism: "Any writer who uses irony faces the dangers of being taken at face value and admired for believing the exact opposite of what he really believes, but the sheer ridiculousness of much of Alf Garnett's dialogue, for instance the speech in a recent episode where he insisted that all Tottenham Hotspur's supporters are Jewish, makes the danger much less acute than some people think" (Benny Green, "How Dangerous Is Garnett?" *Jewish Chronicle*, February 2, 1973).

138. Tottenham Hotspur (@SpursOfficial), "The Club is saddened to hear of the passing of actor and Spurs fan Warren Mitchell," X, November 14, 2015, https://twitter.com/SpursOfficial/status/665554314031726592; Spurs Community, "Warren Mitchell Has Died," Forum, accessed November 22, 2022, https://www.spurscommunity.co.uk/index.php?threads /warren-mitchell-has-died.122370/.

139. *Cock a Doodle Doo*, Dec. 1997–Jan. 1998, 18 ed., 35, British Library.

140. Spaaij, *Understanding Football Hooliganism*, 124.

141. Back, "Sounds."

142. Eric Dunning, *Sport Matters: Sociological Studies of Sport, Violence and Civilization* (London: Routledge, 1999); Steve Frosdick and Peter Marsh, *Football Hooliganism* (Cullompton, UK: Willan, 2005); Spaaij, *Understanding Football Hooliganism*.

143. Telesca, "English Premier League and the City of London (1980–2010)," 1–2. The 1970s also saw the publication of two important works on British antisemitism: Colin Holmes, *Anti-Semitism in British Society, 1876–1939* (New York: Holmes & Meier, 1979); Gisela C. Lebzelter, *Political Anti-Semitism in England, 1918–1939* (New York: Holmes & Meier, 1978).

144. Back, Crabbe, and Solomos, "Beyond the Racist/Hooligan Couplet," 420.

145. "Y-Word Consultation—Update."

146. Lord John Mann, interview by Pavel Brunssen, August 1, 2022.

147. Mann.

148. Efron quotes an interviewee according to whom the antisemitic chants became popular in 1977: "According to one respondent: The chants from opposition supporters 'Yiddos, does your Rabbi know you're here?' etc. really became prevalent from around '74–'75 onward. Even then it was mostly during local games against West Ham, Chelsea and especially Arsenal. I did not actually hear a Northern team chanting these songs until the relegation match v Man City 1977 by which time the Tottenham lads had taken on the persona themselves. . . . After this it went nationwide, even international" ("When Is a Yid Not a Jew?" 244).

149. Cloake and Fisher, *People's History*, 226.

150. Gerald Smith, "Chelsea Warns off Teeshirt 'Fans,'" *Jewish Chronicle*, April 5, 1985.

151. Neil Silver, "Anger at Fans' Use of Flag," *Jewish Chronicle*, February 13, 1987.

152. Neil Silver, "Chelsea Bans Racist Fans," *Jewish Chronicle*, January 8, 1988.

153. Chelsea FC, "Say No to Antisemitism," accessed April 17, 2024, https://www.chelseafc.com/en/news/type/say-no-to-antisemitism.

154. Daniel Ben-David, "Chelsea FC Create Jewish Supporters Group, Following Arsenal and Watford," *Jewish Chronicle*, September 15, 2023, https://www.thejc.com/life-and-culture/sport/chelsea-fc-create-jewish-supporters-group-following-arsenal-and-watford-vt19kn7v.

155. Efron, "When Is a Yid Not a Jew?" 244. Masculinity and territoriality were characteristic for the hooligan fan culture, for which it "became particularly fashionable . . . to 'take' the opposing fans' section of the ground" (Spaaij, *Understanding Football Hooliganism*, 130).

156. Efron, "When Is a Yid Not a Jew?" 245.

157. Cloake and Fisher, *People's History*, 226.

158. Field notes, August 2022.

159. Cloake and Fisher, *People's History*, 193.

160. I also encountered the "Yid Army" chants in a similar fashion one week later when Spurs played against Chelsea at their stadium Stamford Bridge. Here, the fans engaged in "Yid Army" chants in a performative takeover of their rival's stadium.

161. Wilczyńska, "'Being a Yid,'" 103.

162. Gerald Jacobs, "Why the Y Word Is My Word," *Jewish Chronicle*, April 22, 2011.

163. "Y-Word Consultation—Update."

164. *Oxford English Dictionary*, "New Words List January 2020 Oxford English Dictionary," January 14, 2020, https://www.oed.com/information /updates/previous-updates/2020-2/january-2020/?tl=true; *Oxford English Dictionary*, s.v., "Yid, n.," accessed January 24, 2025, https://www.oed.com /view/Entry/231844; *Oxford English Dictionary*, s.v., "yiddo, n.," accessed September 6, 2021, https://www.oed.com/view/Entry/74901654.

165. Seb Jenkins, "The Y-Word Is Officially in the Oxford English Dictionary—Spurs Are Mentioned," *Spurs Web—Tottenham Hotspur Football News* (blog), February 11, 2020, https://www.spurs-web.com/spurs-news/the -y-word-is-officially-in-the-oxford-english-dictionary-spurs-are-mentioned/.

166. Ben Quinn, "Spurs Criticise OED over Expanded Definition of 'Yid,'" *Guardian*, February 12, 2020, http://www.theguardian.com/football/2020 /feb/12/spurs-criticise-oed-over-expanded-definition-of-yid.

167. Quinn.

168. Quinn.

169. Baddiel, *Jews Don't Count*, 13.

170. Baker, *Jew*, 48.

171. "Y-Word Focus Group 1," Tottenham Hotspur, February 10, 2022, https://www.tottenhamhotspur.com/the-club/the-why-word/y-word -focus-group-1/.

172. The German word *Jude* evokes different emotions and historical links than the English term *Jew*. Daniel Donskoy's wonderful German late-night show *Freitagnacht Jews* (Friday Night Jews) is, interestingly, not called "Freitag Nacht Juden," as David Baddiel wonders during a conversation with Donskoy. Both agree that it feels different, namely, more uncomfortable, to say the word *Jude* than to say the English word *Jew* ("Mit Daniel Donskoy in London (OV)," season 2, episode 1, *Freitagnacht Jews*, aired September 29, 2023, https://www.ardmediathek .de/video/freitagnacht-jews-mit-daniel-donskoy/mit-daniel-donskoy -in-london-ov-s02-e01/wdr/Y3JpZDovL3dkci5kZS9CZWloc mFnLTYxZjliNzYiLTYoMTMtNGJhMyo4MzUzLThhOThlZjRhY WY2Zg).

173. Franz Kafka, *Letters to Milena*, trans. Philip Boehm (New York: Schocken Books, 1990), 46, quoted in Baker, *Jew*, 48.

174. "Y-Word Focus Group 1."

175. Leo Rosten, *The Joys of Yinglish* (New York: Penguin, 1989), 511, and Leo Rosten, *The Joys of Yiddish* (New York: McGraw-Hill, 1968), quoted in Baker, *Jew*, 52–53.

176. Baker, *Jew*, 53.

177. Efron, "When Is a Yid Not a Jew?" 238.

178. Baker, *Jew,* 53.

179. Baker, 53.

180. Baker, 4.

181. Baker, 3.

182. Baker, 9.

183. Baddiel, *Jews Don't Count,* 29.

184. Baker, *Jew,* 1.

185. Robert Burchfield, *Unlocking the English Language* (Hill and Wang, 1992), 17, 113.

186. Burchfield, 109–10.

187. Burchfield, 110.

188. Burchfield, 110.

189. Wilczyńska, "'Being a Yid,'" 94.

190. "But from a personal, emotional perspective, I'd be sad to see the word go out of circulation. My relationship to Spurs, and my Jewish heritage, and the relationship between the two, creates a powerful emotional connection which I'm reminded of every time thousands of our fans sing in proud unison" (Reubs, "It's Happened Again—Is It Time We Dropped the Y-Word?" *Fighting Cock* [blog], January 10, 2019, https://thefightingcock .co.uk/2019/01/its-happened-again-9s-it-time-we-dropped-the-y-word/).

191. "As a Jewish young boy going mostly on my own, I felt comfortable. I felt welcomed. I was not rejected by the response from Spurs fans and that's something that is very important to me. I understand now that there is a history of assimilation and welcome for Jewish people at White Hart Lane that goes way back to the 1900s, 1920s and onwards and that was kind of carried on and that feeling has stayed with me" ("Y-Word Focus Group 1").

192. Pollard, "Why I Changed My Mind on Spurs and The Y Word."

193. "The trouble is I do actually mind if other people do, I find it offensive in the same way if they chanted the N-word or they decided to start chanting Muslims or something like that, it would have the same effect on me" ("Y-Word Focus Group 1").

194. Pollard, "Why I Changed My Mind on Spurs and The Y Word."

195. "WJC and Board of Deputies Stand against Antisemitism in Football: There Must Be No Tolerance for Use of Slur 'Yid,'" World Jewish Congress, January 4, 2019, https://www.worldjewishcongress.org/en /news/wjc-and-board-of-deputies-stand-against-antisemitsm-in-football -there-must-be-no-tolerance-for-use-of-slur-yid-1-5-2019.

196. Ayala Goldmann, "Daumen für die 'Yiddos' oder Warum ich Fan von Tottenham Hotspur bin," *Jüdische Allgemeine*, February 27, 2020, https://www.juedische-allgemeine.de/kultur/der-rest-der-welt-393/.

197. Paul Levene, "Capital Letters: Spurs Not Antisemitic," *Jewish Chronicle*, January 20, 1989, 2.

198. Poulton, "Towards Understanding," 1995–96.

199. Tottenham Hotspur Supporters' Trust, "Tottenham Hotspur Fans and The WhY Word," February 10, 2022, https://thstofficial.com/tottenham -hotspur-fans-and-the-why-word/.

200. "Y-Word Consultation Update."

201. "Y-Word Focus Group 3."

202. "Y-Word Focus Group 2," Tottenham Hotspur, February 10, 2022, 2, https://www.tottenhamhotspur.com/the-club/the-why-word/y-word -focus-group-2/.

203. Take for instance the perspective of this Spurs fan: "I'm Jewish. My partner is black, we have two mixed race kids. My son is a Season Ticket Holder also. I personally have no problem with the use of the Y-word. I have been known on many occasions to chant it myself in the ground. I say in the ground. It's a really tricky one because outside of the ground or if it's used towards us—when I say us, I mean Spurs supporters—by other sup- porters, I take it in a different way" ("Y-Word Focus Group 2").

204. Wilczyńska, "'Being a Yid,'" 97.

205. Wilczyńska, "'Being a Yid,'" 98; "Y-Word Focus Group 2"; "Life Ban for a Racist Fan," *Jewish Chronicle*, November 28, 2008. In 1996, the Spurs fanzine *Spur of the Moment* depicted Tottenham's Israeli player Ronny Rosenthal with a hat and beard in the style Orthodox Jews would wear. On other occasions, fans posted "Orthodox" emojis (*Spur of the Moment*, 1996, 5, British Library; Poulton and Durell, "Uses and Meanings," 728).

206. Efron, "When Is a Yid Not a Jew?" 252.

207. Klinsmann played for Spurs during the 1994–95 season, scoring twenty goals in forty-one appearances. He later returned on loan during the 1997–98 season, scoring nine goals in fifteen games.

208. "It was not only his diving performance but also Jurgen's easygoing attitude, perfect English, and nonclichéd soundbites that had the media over the moon and eating out of his hand" (Alex Fynn and H. Davidson, *Dream On: A Year in the Life of a Premier League Club* [London: Simon & Schuster, 1996], 9).

209. *Cock a Doodle Doo*, 35; Mark Jacob, "Jurgen Klinsmann an Affair to Re- member," *Spur of the Moment*, n.d., British Library; Melissa Oliveck, "Jürgy Bears All . . . ," *Cock a Doodle Doo*, April 1995, 4th ed., 6, British Library.

210. "Jürgen Klinsmann—The Official Inside Story," 1997.

211. A 2008 article, published in the *JC*, explicitly connects the chants for players as "Yids/Jews" to the greetings to Orthodox Jews: "Once the crowd greets a player with the cry of 'yiddo,' he knows he has made the grade and/or had hero status conferred upon him. (In the past, young supporters have been known to issue similar greetings to Strictly Orthodox Jews encountered in Tottenham streets.) And the chant linked to one of Tottenham's most brilliant strikers—Jermain Defoe/He's a yiddo—is deeply imprinted in the collective Spurs consciousness" ("Life Ban for a Racist Fan," *Jewish Chronicle*).

212. Spurs' fans also celebrated other players in chants like "Jermain Defoe / He's a Yiddo." They also embraced the Black French national Louis Noé Pamarot with the following chant: "I see a massive silhouetto of a man, Pamarot, Pamarot he's a f**king big yiddo / Playing down the right he's very very frightening meeee / He's a yiddo (he's a yiddo) / He's a yiddo (he's a yiddo) / He's a yiddo Pamarot—magnificoooooooooo / He's just a French boy bought by Santini / One of the new boys in the yid family / Taking the place of the sulking paddy / Wingers come wingers go, get kicked by Pamarot / Oi scousers! Noé, he even scores us goals—Pamarot / Oi scousers! He even scores us goals—Pamarot / Oi scousers! He even scores us goals—Pamarot / Will not let you go Pamarot / Will not let you go Pamarot / Noé, Noé, Noé, Noé, Noé, Noé" (Jacobs, "Why the Y Word Is My Word"; Jim Duggan, "Classic Tottenham Songs," Topspurs, accessed November 4, 2022, https://www.topspurs.com/thfc-songs%26chants.htm).

213. Efron, "When Is a Yid Not a Jew?" 250.

214. Josh Glancy, "What If Every Jew Wore the Orthodox Clothing?" *Jewish Chronicle*, March 19, 2021.

215. Silverman, *Becoming Austrians*.

216. Hannah Arendt, "'What Remains? The Language Remains': A Conversation with Günter Gaus," in *Essays in Understanding, 1930–1954: Formation, Exile, and Totalitarianism*, by Hannah Arendt, ed. Jerome Kohn, trans. Joan Stambaugh (New York: Schocken Books, 1964), 12.

217. Fisher, "Y Word, Spurs and Changing Times."

218. Shaul Behr, "Opinion: I'm a Jewish Football Fan and I Have Never Been Prouder to Support Spurs." *The Independent*, February 11, 2022, https://www.independent.co.uk/voices/spurs-tottenham-yword -anitsemitism-b2012922.html.

219. Izzy Wasserstein, "Let's Talk about Yids," *Fighting Cock* (blog), January 23, 2013, https://thefightingcock.co.uk/2013/01/lets-talk-about -yids/.

220. "Y-Word Focus Group 3." Another Spurs fan states explicitly how some of the younger fans perceive they Y-identity as a form of anti-antisemitism:

> I would not want the Club to discourage use of the word because, I'm just going to say it, I consider myself a proud Y*d and when I say that, I'm not some sort of antisemite, in fact I'm very active in combatting antisemitism in my local community. I say that as someone who is a proud Jew and a proud Spurs fan actually and I'm very proud of the Club's link with the Jewish community. I'm very proud that as a Jew, I'm supported by my non-Jewish fans, which I know I would not benefit from at many other London clubs. I think it's a great thing that the younger generation is less offended by it. It's fantastic that we have successfully taken the sting out of the word. I think it's great that kids I grew up with did not know that it was offensive and they were only brought up with it in a positive way. I don't think it would be acceptable to label someone like myself an anti-semite just because I proudly use the word in a way that's actively anti-racist and I use it in a way that means people can't use it offensively toward me. When they do it, it doesn't have the same impact. ("Y-Word Focus Group 1")

221. Werner Bergmann and Rainer Erb, "Kommunikationslatenz, Moral und öffentliche Meinung: Theoretische Überlegungen zum Antisemitismus in der Bundesrepublik Deutschland," *Kölner Zeitschrift für Soziologie und Sozialpsychologie* 38, no. 2 (1986): 223–46; Monika Schwarz-Friesel and Jehuda Reinharz, *Inside the Antisemitic Mind: The Language of Jew-Hatred in Contemporary Germany*, Tauber Institute Series for the Study of European Jewry (Waltham, MA: Brandeis University Press, 2017).

222. Newman, "Proud to Be a Tottenham Yid."

223. "It is commonplace to see fans attending the games with kippot, and even some Haredim from the nearby Stamford Hill community—they do not feel any threat, as they would do at other football stadiums, and this is due to the positive way in which the 'yid' term has been adopted by the fans" (Newman, "Proud to Be a Tottenham Yid").

224. Bogna Wilczyńska argues that the Y-identity for Spurs fans is "not a source of shame, but pride as they either declare a positive attitude towards this minority or they are Jewish themselves" ("'Being a Yid'").

225. Fisher, "Y Word, Spurs and Changing Times."

226. Efron, "When Is a Yid Not a Jew?" 245.

227. Todd M. Endelman, *Radical Assimilation in English Jewish History, 1656–1945*, Modern Jewish Experience (Bloomington: Indiana University Press, 1990).

228. Efron, "When Is a Yid Not a Jew?" 237.

229. Clavane, *Does Your Rabbi Know You're Here?*, 48.

230. Baddiel, *Jews Don't Count*, 29–30.

231. "RTR Extra: Philip Spencer," *Rule the Roost—A Tottenham Hotspur Podcast*, July 24, 2017, https://shows.acast.com/ruletheroost/episodes/rtrextra-philipspencer.

232. Daniel Merriman, "Leipzig Away: More than a Football Match," *Football Pink* (blog), February 19, 2021, https://footballpink.net/leipzig-away-more-than-a-football-match/.

233. Fisher, "Y Word, Spurs and Changing Times."

234. Another Spurs fan ("Jewish female, aged 45–54") similarly describes how Spurs' Y-identity connects her to her father as well as her son:

> Interestingly, I've discussed it quite a bit with my father recently, who's 83, also a long time Season Ticket Holder as was his father. I've been able to get a perspective from my dad over the years of when he remembers the chant first starting and the use of the word and how it was changed over the years and the feeling he's had towards it. He feels the same as I do. That for so many years of being persecuted by use of the word, he actually feels pretty good that his daughter and grandson in 2020 are pretty proud to stand on the terraces and shout it proud and loud. ("Y-Word Focus Group 2")

235. Quoted in Robert Philpot, "The True History behind London's Much-Lauded Anti-Fascist Battle of Cable Street," *Times of Israel*, September 15, 2018, https://www.timesofisrael.com/the-true-history-behind-londons-much-lauded-anti-fascist-battle-of-cable-street/.

236. "Y-Word Focus Group 3."

237. Cloake and Powley, *We Are Tottenham*, 148. Historians suggest that the actual battle at Cable Street took place between counterdemonstrators and the police (not the Blackshirts). Morris is a fascinating character whose story in many ways seems to represent how the suburbanization of London's Jews is linked to Tottenham: Morris not only took part in the Battle of Cable Street but also experienced how his family, who migrated to London from Russia, changed their family name from Putajevski to Morris. Aubrey Morris thus experienced both strategies: assimilation and anti-antisemitic action. It was Mosley's 1936 march that "galvanised his politics" (Goodman, "Aubrey Morris").

238. "Y-Word Focus Group 1."

239. "Y-Word Focus Group 3."

240. Eccleshare and Pitt-Brooke, "Spurs Fans and the Y-Word."

241. Baddiel argues that "Yid" is a race-hate word because it was used by Mosley's Blackshirts: "So by calling the film The Y-Word, we were saying maybe the *hate words for Jews—and Yid is one, daubed as it was across the*

East End by Oswald Mosley's blackshirts—need to be considered as equally unmentionable as the hate words for other ethnic minorities" (*Jews Don't Count*, 24 [my emphasis]).

CONCLUSION

1. Hannah Arendt, "The Aftermath of Nazi Rule: Report from Germany," *Commentary* 10 (1950): 345.

2. Arendt, 345.

3. Alexander Mitscherlich and Margarete Mitscherlich, *Die Unfähigkeit zu trauern: Grundlagen kollektiven Verhaltens*, Ungekürzte Taschenbuchausgabe 25, Piper 168 (Munich: Piper, 1977).

4. Hannah Arendt, "Hannah Arendt to Karl Jaspers, August 17, 1946," in *Hannah Arendt/Karl Jaspers Correspondence, 1926–1969*, by Hannah Arendt and Karl Jaspers, ed. Lotte Köhler and Hans Saner, trans. Robert Kimber and Rita Kimber (San Diego: Harcourt Brace, 1992), 54.

5. Arendt, "What Remains?" 14.

6. The Nazis called Munich "Hauptstadt der Bewegung."

7. Diner, *Zivilisationsbruch*.

8. Arendt, "Hannah Arendt to Karl Jaspers, August 17, 1946," 54.

9. Diner, "Negative Symbiose"; Diner, "Negative Symbiosis."

10. Diner, "Negative Symbiosis," 423.

11. Diner, 424.

12. Diner, 423.

13. Diner, 423. The turn to Landauer occurred in the context of a "memory boom" in German football that not only rewrote Jews back into the history of the sports clubs but also celebrated them as "lost heroes," thereby evoking nostalgia for a "German-Jewish symbiosis" (11Freunde, "Verlorene Helden").

14. Diner, "Negative Symbiosis," 423.

15. Diner, 426.

16. Leslie Morris and Jack Zipes, "German and Jewish Obsession," in *Unlikely History: The Changing German-Jewish Symbiosis 1945–2000*, ed. Leslie Morris and Jack Zipes (New York: Palgrave Macmillan 2002), xi.

17. Morris and Zipes, xi–xii.

18. Morris and Zipes, xii.

19. Katja Behrens, "The Rift and Not the Symbiosis," in Morris and Zipes, *Unlikely History*, 42.

20. Behrens, 39.
21. Behrens, 42.
22. Behrens, 36.
23. Diner, "Negative Symbiosis," 437.
24. Diner, 424.

AFTERWORD

1. Frank Hoekman, "F-Side doet dringend verzoek na onrust over Palestijnse vlaggen," FCUpdate, November 8, 2023, https://www.fcupdate .nl/voetbalnieuws/2023/11/f-side-doet-dringend-verzoek-na-onrust-over -palestijnse-vlaggen.

2. Ajax Supporters Delegatie, "Statement Ajax Supporters Delegatie: Geen politiek in ons stadion." *De AFCA Supportersclub* (blog), November 4, 2024. https://afcasc.nl/statement-ajax-supporters-delegatie-geen -politiek-in-ons-stadion/.

3. "Club Statement," Tottenham Hotspur, October 12, 2023, https:// www.tottenhamhotspur.com/news/2023/october/club-statement/.

4. Matt Law, "Tottenham's Charity Chair Resigns over Club's 'Chronic Lack of Moral Clarity' on Israel Terror Attacks," *Telegraph*, October 13, 2023, https://www.telegraph.co.uk/football/2023/10/13/tottenham -spurs-charity-chair-resigns-israel-terror-attacks/.

5. FK Austria Wien (@FKAustriaWien), "Unsere Gedanken sind heute bei den Opfern des Terrorangriffs auf Israel, der sich am 7. Oktober 2023 zugetragen hat. . . ." X, October 7, 2024, https://x.com/FKAustriaWien /status/1843335602194001946.

6. Antisemitismus-Meldestelle der IKG (@AMeldestelle), "Wien 20. Bezirk: Meldung einer antisemitischen Beschmierung. Graffiti in Violett (Farbe des @FKAustriaWien) werden mit Beschimpfungen in Grün (Farbe des @skrapid) übermalt. U.a ist 2x 'JUDEN' zu sehen; Austria wir von bestimmten Fans traditionell als 'Judenverein' verunglimpft," Tweet, *Twitter*, March 1, 2024, https://twitter.com/AMeldestelle/status /1763476631199396027.

7. Pavel Brunssen and Andrei S. Markovits, "From Chants to Change: German Soccer's Unique Response to Antisemitism Post-October 7," ISCA Research Paper, no. 3 (2024), https://isca.indiana.edu/publication -research/research-paper-series/pavel-brunssen-andrei-markovits -research-paper.html.

8. "Solidarity with Hostages—Relatives Visit the Allianz Arena," FC Bayern München, November 11, 2023, https://fcbayern.com/en/news/2023/11/solidarity-with-hostages---relatives-visit-the-allianz-arena.

9. "'Munich against Antisemitism' on 6 October at Munich's Odeonsplatz," FC Bayern München, October 3, 2024, https://fcbayern.com/en/news/2024/10/demo-against-anti-semitism.

10. "Statement of FC Bayern Munich Regarding Noussair Mazraoui," FC Bayern München, October 20, 2023, https://fcbayern.com/en/news/2023/10/fc-bayern-munich-statement-regarding-noussair-mazraoui.

11. "Commemorative Plaque for Kurt Landauer: Herbert Hainer at 140th Birthday Event," FC Bayern München, July 29, 2024, https://fcbayern.com/en/news/2024/07/140th-birthday-of-landauer-foundation.

BIBLIOGRAPHY

PRIMARY SOURCES

1. FC Nürnberg. "Nürnberger Ultras erinnern an Jenö Konrad." November 19, 2012. https://www.fcn.de/news/artikel/nuernberger-ultras-erinnern-an-jenoe-konrad.
12th Player. "English | השחקן ה-12." Accessed July 22, 2022. https://12p.co.il/english/.
4 en 5 mei Amsterdam. "Nationale Sportherdenking." May 4, 2022. https://4en5meiamsterdam.nl/events/nationale-sportherdenking-5/.
11Freunde. "Verlorene Helden," 2014. https://www.dfb.de/fileadmin/_dfbdam/13724-11F_148_beilage_gesamt.pdf.
AFC Ajax. "'Stolpersteine' for Eddy Hamel: A Reminder of the Tragic Fate of an Ajax Player." November 22, 2021. https://english.ajax.nl/articles/stolpersteins-for-eddy-hamel-a-reminder-of-the-tragic-fate-of-an-ajax-player/.
AG Fankultur. "Vor Leipzig. Erklärung der AG Fankultur." 2016. https://fc.de/fc-info/news/detailseite/details/erklaerung-der-ag-fankultur/.
Ajax Amsterdam. "Ajax Amsterdam Museum." May 5, 2022.
———. "Jaarverslagen Vereniging," Ajax Archief, June 30, 2005. https://archief.ajax.nl.
Ajax Life. "De Discussie: 'Ajax is helemaal geen Joodse club.'" Ajax Archief, October 1, 2002. https://archief.ajax.nl.
———. "Vak410 viert vijftienjarig bestaan: 'Het gaat om een stukje trots.'" Ajax Archief, January 14, 2016. https://archief.ajax.nl.

Ajax Museum. "Ajax Tattoos." Ajax Museum. Accessed June 22, 2022. https://www.ajaxmuseum.nl/fotos/tattoos/.

Algemeiner. "Top Dutch Soccer Player Steven Berghuis Targeted by Lurid Antisemitic Mural after Signing for 'Jewish' Club Ajax." July 27, 2021. https://www.algemeiner.com/2021/07/27/top-dutch-soccer-player-targeted-by-lurid-antisemitic-mural-after-signing-for-jewish-club-ajax/.

Ajax Supporters Delegatie. "Statement Ajax Supporters Delegatie: Geen politiek in ons stadion." *De AFCA Supportersclub* (blog), November 4, 2024. https://afcasc.nl/statement-ajax-supporters-delegatie-geen-politiek-in-ons-stadion/; *Amsterdam Tips* (blog). "Top 15 Amsterdam Museums (by 2020 Visitor Numbers)." June 15, 2021. https://www.amsterdamtips.com/top-10-amsterdam-museums.

Antisemitismus-Meldestelle der IKG (@AMeldestelle). "Wien 20. Bezirk: Meldung einer antisemitischen Beschmierung. Graffiti in Violett (Farbe des @FKAustriaWien) werden mit Beschimpfungen in Grün (Farbe des @skrapid) übermalt. U.a ist 2x 'JUDEN' zu sehen; Austria wir von bestimmten Fans traditionell als 'Judenverein' verunglimpft." X, March 1, 2024. https://twitter.com/AMeldestelle/status/1763476631199396027.

Baddiel, David. "Yes, David Cameron, 'Yid' Really Is a Race-Hate Word. Here's Why." *The Guardian*, September 17, 2013. http://www.theguardian.com/commentisfree/2013/sep/17/david-cameron-yid-really-is-race-hate-word.

Bayerischer Rundfunk. "Alpha-Forum: Uri Siegel im Gespräch mit Sybille Krafft." Bayerischer Rundfunk, June 16, 2014. https://www.br.de/fernsehen/ard-alpha/sendungen/alpha-forum/uri-siegel-gespraech-100.html.

———. "Die Bayern in der NS-Zeit: Schwere Zeiten für den 'Judenklub.'" Bayerischer Rundfunk, August 12, 2015. https://www.br.de/themen/sport/inhalt/fussball/bundesliga/fc-bayern-muenchen/fc-bayern-muenchen136.html.

———. "LandauerWalk: Auf den Spuren von Kurt Landauer." Bayerischer Rundfunk, September 23, 2014. https://www.br.de/fernsehen/das-erste/sendungen/kurt-landauer-der-film/die-app100.html.

Behr, Shaul. "Opinion: I'm a Jewish Football Fan and I Have Never Been Prouder to Support Spurs." *The Independent*, February 11, 2022. https://www.independent.co.uk/voices/spurs-tottenham-yword-anitsemitism-b2012922.html.

Ben-David, Daniel. "Chelsea FC Create Jewish Supporters Group, Following Arsenal and Watford." *Jewish Chronicle*, September 15, 2023. https://www.thejc.com/life-and-culture/sport/chelsea-fc-create-jewish-supporters-group-following-arsenal-and-watford-vt19kn7v.

Blackshirt. "Noises Off!" September 18, 1935, 229 ed. British Online Archives.

Bonvalot, Michael. "Austria würdigt Opfer des Holocaust." Bonvalot.net, November 8, 2018. https://www.bonvalot.net/austria-wuerdigt-opfer -des-holocaust-843/.

———. "Das Nazi-Problem der Wiener Austria." Bonvalot.net, December 14, 2016. https://www.bonvalot.net/das-nazi-problem-der-wiener-austria-845/.

———. "Überfall mit Antisemitismus auf Austria-Fan." Bonvalot.net, November 2, 2020. https://www.bonvalot.net/ueberfall-mit-antisemitismus -auf-austria-fan-821/.

Brecker, Richard. "Spurs Sorry." *Jewish Chronicle*, October 9, 1981.

Bunda, Sascha. "Fußball: Rapid-Viertelstunde kein Unesco-Kulturerbe." *Die Presse*, March 22, 2011. https://www.diepresse.com/642245/fussball -rapid-viertelstunde-kein-unesco-kulturerbe.

Changing the Chants. "Guidelines for Educational Projects Targeting Antisemitic Behaviour in Football." 2021. https://changingthechants.eu /wp-content/uploads/2021/06/guidelinesV2.pdf.

Chelsea FC. "Say No To Antisemitism." Accessed April 17, 2024. https:// www.chelseafc.com/en/news/type/say-no-to-antisemitism.

Chesterton, A. K. "They Have Spoken—the Silent People!" *Blackshirt*, December 13, 1935, 138th ed. British Online Archives.

Cloake, Martin. "'We Are the Yids': Should Spurs Fans Be Prosecuted for Using the Y Word?," *New Statesman*, March 12, 2014. https://www .newstatesman.com/culture/sport/2014/03/we-are-yids-should-spurs -fans-be-prosecuted-using-y-word.

Club Nr. 12. "Infos zum aktuellen Geschehen in Katar—Club Nr. 12." February 8, 2021. https://clubnr12.org/news/206-infos-zum-aktuellen -geschehen-in-katar.

Cock a Doodle Doo. December 1997/January 1998, 18th ed. British Library.

Community Security Trust. "The Y-Word." *CST Blog*, April 14, 2011. https://cst.org.uk/news/blog/2011/04/14/the-y-word.

Curwen, Dr. Monty. "Letters to the Editor: Boyhood Memories of Spurs Supporter." *Jewish Chronicle*, March 15, 1996.

Dapp're Strijders. "11/04: kakkerlaken—AFC Ajax (1-1)." May 9, 2004. Ajax Archief.

———. "Welkom in Mokum." November 23, 2003. Ajax Archief.

———. "Wij van VAK 0." May 9, 2004. Ajax Archief.

De Ajax Ster. "Ajacieden op bezoek bij Tottenham." December 13, 1998. Ajax Archief.

———. "Ajax 0-1 Hapoel Haifa." December 15, 1999. Ajax Archief.

———. "De geschiedenis van de Davidster." November 22, 1997. Ajax Archief.

———. "'Good Luck Friend, It's Only a Game.'" December 15, 1999. Ajax Archief.

———. "Hapoel Haifa 0-3 Ajax." December 15, 1999. Ajax Archief.

———. "Ingezonden brieven / mail." December 13, 1998. Ajax Archief.

———. "Jodenstreeken." December 1, 1996. Ajax Archief.

———. "London . . . Is the Place for Me (1)." April 18, 1999. Ajax Archief.

———. "London . . . Is the Place for Me (slot)." May 13, 1999. Ajax Archief.

———. "Post." October 29, 1999. Ajax Archief.

———. "Post." May 7, 2000. Ajax Archief.

———. "Songteksten." October 15, 1997. Ajax Archief.

———. "Tribunenliederen." March 5, 1997. Ajax Archief.

———. "Tribunenliederen (2)." May 11, 1997. Ajax Archief.

———. "Tribunenliederen (3)." June 1, 1997. Ajax Archief.

———. "'We are the Yiddo's.'" May 10, 1998. Ajax Archief.

Der Montag. "'Das Kesseltreiben gegen Rapid.'" June 11, 1923. ANNO/Österreichische Nationalbibliothek.

Der Standard. "Matthias Sindelar und das antifaschistische Märchen." December 19, 2018. https://www.derstandard.de/story/2000094341814/matthias-sindelars-und-das-antifaschistische-maerchen.

———. "'Wir sind keine Geschichtsprofessoren.'" March 31, 2010. https://www.derstandard.at/story/1269448575040/derstandardat-interview-wir-sind-keine-geschichtsprofessoren.

Deutscher Fußball-Bund. "Julius Hirsch Preis." Accessed January 6, 2025, https://www.dfb.de/nachhaltigkeit-2/julius-hirsch-preis; DFB-Kulturstiftung. 'Auf den Spuren von Julius Hirsch: Die Deportation nach Auschwitz im März 1943'; https://www.dfb.de/preisewettbewerbe/julius-hirsch-preis/.

DFB-Kulturstiftung. 'Auf den Spuren von Julius Hirsch: Die Deportation nach Auschwitz im März 1943'; DFB-Kulturstiftung, January 27, 2021. https://www.dfb.de/fileadmin/_dfbdam/234034-Auf_den_Spuren_von_Julius_Hirsch_einz.pdf.

Di Pietro, Stefano, dir. Changing the Chants. Anne Frank House, Borussia Dortmund, Feyenoord, and FARE Network, 2021. https://changingthechants.eu/documentary/.

Donskoy, Daniel. "Mit Daniel Donskoy in London (OV)." Season 2, episode 1. Freitagnacht Jews. Aired September 29, 2023. https://www.ardmediathek.de/video/freitagnacht-jews-mit-daniel-donskoy/mit

-daniel-donskoy-in-london-ov-s02-e01/wdr/Y3JpZDovL3dkci5kZS9C
ZWlocmFnLTYxZjliNzYiLTYoMTMtNGJhMy04MzUzLThhhOThl
ZjRhYWY2Zg.

Duggan, Jim. "Classic Tottenham Songs." Topspurs. Accessed November 4, 2022. https://www.topspurs.com/thfc-songs%26chants.htm.

Dysch, Marcus. "Blood, Hate and Football's Shame." *Jewish Chronicle*, September 30, 2012.

Elgot, Jessica. "The Herd: We Didn't Mean It in a Racist Way." *Jewish Chronicle*, August 26, 2012.

Engels, Susanne, dir. *Cap of Keppel*. Joodse Omroep / Zuidenwind Film-produkties, July 15, 2012. https://www.2doc.nl/speel~POW_00496292~cap-of-keppel-zappdoc~.html.

Erlebnis Fussball. "Interview mit Mark Johanni." April 2003.

———. "Interview Schickeria München." August 2008.

Fanchants. "'Being a Yid . . .'—Spurs FanChants." July 18, 2020. https://www.fanchants.com/football-songs/tottenham_hotspur-chants/r09_0079f_f/.

Faszination Fankurve. "20 Jahre Schickeria München: Choreografie & Zaunfahnen-Comeback." 2022. https://www.faszination-fankurve.de/news/48366/20-jahre-schickeria-muenchen-choreografie-zaunfahnen-comeback.

FC Bayern—Behind the Legend. Amazon Prime, 2021.

FC Bayern Muenchen Fan-Club Niederrhein. Niederrhein News, 1988. ZF89. Archiv der Arbeiterjugend.

FC Bayern München. 50 Jahre F.C. Bayern München e.V. Munich, 1950. https://books.google.de/books/about/Chronik_%C3%BCber_50_Jahre_Fussball_Club_Bay.html?id=I1TFNAEACAAJ&redir_esc=y.

———. "Commemorative Plaque for Kurt Landauer: Herbert Hainer at 140th Birthday Event." July 29, 2024. https://fcbayern.com/en/news/2024/07/140th-birthday-of-landauer-foundation.

———. "FC Bayern enthüllt Kurt-Landauer-Statue an der Säbener Straße." May 22, 2019. https://fcbayern.com/de/news/2019/05/enthuellung-kurt-landauer-denkmal-an-der-saebener-strasse.

———. "FC Bayern to Hans Bermühler." June 16, 1950. MG Karton 4 5 9, Landauer 1955 Liste, Hecker Julius, Bermühler Hans, John Franz, 1947–1952. FC Bayern Munich Club Archive.

———. "FC Bayern to Hans Bermühler." March 2, 1953. MG Karton 4 5 9, Landauer 1955 Liste, Hecker Julius, Bermühler Hans, John Franz, 1947–1952. FC Bayern Munich Club Archive.

———. "FC Bayern to Oberbürgermeister." May 15, 1944. Amt für Leibesübungen (AfL) 151. Stadtarchiv München.

———. "Hans Bermühler to Kurt Landauer." June 1950. MG Karton 4 5 9, Landauer 1955 Liste, Hecker Julius, Bermühler Hans, John Franz, 1947–1952. FC Bayern Munich Club Archive.

———. "'Munich against Antisemitism' on 6 October at Munich's Odeonsplatz." October 3, 2024. https://fcbayern.com/en/news/2024/10/demo-against-anti-semitism.

———. "Neue Seiten der Erinnerung." 51—Das FC Bayern Magazin, January 2023.

———. "Solidarity with Hostages—Relatives Visit the Allianz Arena." November 11, 2023. https://fcbayern.com/en/news/2023/11/solidarity-with-hostages---relatives-visit-the-allianz-arena.

———. "Statement of FC Bayern Munich Regarding Noussair Mazraoui." October 20, 2023. https://fcbayern.com/en/news/2023/10/fc-bayern-munich-statement-regarding-noussair-mazraoui.

———. "Sweatshirt Heimat." FC Bayern Store. Accessed April 28, 2021. https://fcbayern.com/shop/de/sweatshirt-heimat/24967/.

———. "'Venerated—Persecuted—Forgotten' at the Capitol in Washington." July 20, 2022. https://fcbayern.com/en/news/2022/07/touring-exhibition-goes-international---venerated-persecuted-forgotten-at-the-capitol-in-washington.

———. "Von der Idee zum Kurt-Landauer-Denkmal." May 22, 2019. https://fcbayern.com/de/news/2019/05/entstehungsgeschichte-von-der-idee-zum-kurt-landauer-denkmal.

FC Bayern Museum. "Venerated—Persecuted—Forgotten." FC Bayern Museum, March 18, 2016. https://fcbayern.com/museum/en/the-exhibition/touring-exhibition.

FC Bayern US (@FCBayernUS). "To commemorate International Holocaust Remembrance Day, FC Bayern presented the Venerated, Persecuted, and Forgotten Exhibit at Columbia University for a discussion dediated to remembrance. . . ." X, January 27, 2023. https://twitter.com/FCBayernUS/status/1618999284271321089.

Fennely, John. "Morris Keston RIP." Tottenham Hotspur, August 16, 2019. https://www.tottenhamhotspur.com/news/2019/august/morris-keston/.

Fighting Cock (blog). "It's Happened Again—Is It Time We Dropped the Y-Word?" F January 10, 2019. https://thefightingcock.co.uk/2019/01/its-happened-again-9s-it-time-we-dropped-the-y-word/.

———. "Yid. The Man Who Gave Us the Name." October 22, 2013. https://thefightingcock.co.uk/2013/10/yid-the-man-who-gave-us-the-name/.

Findley, A. G. "Sport and Race." *Action*, March 19, 1936. British Online Archives.

Finkelstein, Daniel. "Time to Tackle Football Racism." *Jewish Chronicle*, February 29, 2008.

Fischer, Sebastian. "Jahreshauptversammlung des FC Bayern: Revolte bis nach Mitternacht." *Süddeutsche Zeitung*, November 26, 2021. https://www.sueddeutsche.de/sport/fc-bayern-jahreshauptversammlung -hainer-kahn-katar-ott-antraege-1.5473760.

Fisher, Alan. "Spurs and the Y Word: Fans in the Dock." *Tottenham on My Mind* (blog), January 26, 2014. https://tottenhamonmymind.com/2014 /01/26/spurs-and-the-y-word-fans-in-the-dock/.

———. "The Y Word, Spurs and Changing Times." *Tottenham on My Mind* (blog), February 14, 2022. https://tottenhamonmymind.com/2022/02 /14/the-y-word-spurs-and-changing-times/.

FK Austria Wien, ed. *60 Jahre Wiener Austria: Festschrift 1911 bis 1971.* Vienna, 1971.

———. "Austria gedenkt der Opfer der Novemberpogrome." November 9, 2021. https://fk-austria.at/news/austria-gedenkt-der-opfer-der -novemberpogrome.

———. "Nationalsozialismus & Wiederaufbau." Accessed November 21, 2021. https://fk-austria.at/klub/geschichte/nationalsozialismus.

FK Austria Wien (@FKAustriaWien). "Unsere Gedanken sind heute bei den Opfern des Terrorangriffs auf Israel, der sich am 7. Oktober 2023 zugetragen hat. . . ." X, October 7, 2024. https://x.com/FKAustriaWien /status/1843335602194001946.

Football Against Racism in Europe (FARE). *Guide to Discriminatory Practices in European Football*, 6th ed. June 2021, https://farenet.org/uploads /files/2021_Fare_guide_to_discriminatory_practices_UEFA_.pdf.

Frankfurter Allgemeine Zeitung. "'Schickeria München': Bewährungsstrafen für Fan-Überfall." January 31, 2008. https://www.faz.net/aktuell/sport /fussball/schickeria-muenchen-bewaehrungsstrafen-fuer-fan-ueberfall -1514745.html.

FRFC 1908. "Anti-Ajax." FRFC 1908 online store. Accessed December 22, 2022. https://www.frfc1908.nl/webshop/tag/anti-ajax/.

Fürst, Dominik. "Streit um Nazi-Vergangenheit des FC Bayern." *Süddeutsche Zeitung*, May 24, 2016. https://www.sueddeutsche.de/sport /muenchen-streit-um-nazi-vergangenheit-des-fc-bayern-1.3004904.

Giller, Norman. "Tottenham Deliver a Kick in the Wrecking Balls." *Sports Journalists' Association* (blog), January 22, 2010. https://www.sportsjournalists.co.uk/the-giller-memorandum/tottenham-deliver-a-kick-in-the-wrecking-balls/.

Glancy, Josh. "What If Every Jew Wore the Orthodox Clothing?" *Jewish Chronicle*, March 19, 2021.

Glanville, Brian. "Tottenham Chutzpah." *Jewish Chronicle*, May 17, 1991.

Goldmann, Ayala. "Daumen für die 'Yiddos' oder Warum ich Fan von Tottenham Hotspur bin." *Jüdische Allgemeine*, February 27, 2020. https://www.juedische-allgemeine.de/kultur/der-rest-der-welt-393/.

Goldstein, Chucky. "Ultras und Hooligans sind nicht das Gleiche." *Vice*, April 14, 2015. https://www.vice.com/de/article/ezyd87/ultras-und-hooligans-sind-nicht-das-gleiche-567.

Golüke, Nick, and Michael Müller. *Landauer: Gefeiert, verbannt, vergessen*, documentary film, 2014.

Goodman, Geoffrey. "Aubrey Morris: Founder of the First Package Travel Firm for Football Supporters." *Guardian*, January 13, 2009, sec. Travel. https://www.theguardian.com/travel/2009/jan/13/obituary-aubrey-morris.

Google Maps. "Erinnerung-Fußball." Google My Maps, 2021. https://www.google.com/maps/d/viewer?mid=1iWZWV6xarJ9z5_lu_sryKca3aLOk67QX.

Green, Benny. "How Dangerous Is Garnett?" *Jewish Chronicle*, February 2, 1973.

Griver, Simon. "Lesson with Vieira." *Jewish Chronicle*, October 22, 2004.

Guardian. "Partizan Belgrade Apologise for Antisemitic Banner against Spurs." September 19, 2014. http://www.theguardian.com/football/2014/sep/19/partizan-belgrade-apologise-antisemitic-banner-tottenham-hotspur.

Herrmann, Siegfried. "Herrmann to Jutzi," August 7, 1946. Karton Mitgliederverwaltung ~ 1950 (ausgeschieden) Ginbart-Jutzi. FC Bayern Munich Club Archive.

Hitler, Adolf. *Mein Kampf.* 851st–855th ed. Munich: Zentralverlag der NSDAP, 1925.

Hyams, P. "Will They Play at the 'Spurs'?" *Jewish Chronicle*, October 18, 1935.

Hytner, David. "Section of West Ham United Support Aim Antisemitic Abuse at Spurs Fans." *Guardian*, November 25, 2012. http://www.theguardian.com/football/2012/nov/25/west-ham-united-antisemitism-spurs.

Illustriertes Sportblatt. "Die Vorstadt führt!" October 8, 1927. ANNO/Österreichische Nationalbibliothek.

International Holocaust Remembrance Alliance. "Working Definitions & Charters: Working Definition of Antisemitism." Accessed November 22, 2021. https://holocaustremembrance.com/resources/working -definitions-charters/working-definition-antisemitism.

Jacob, Mark. "Jurgen Klinsmann an Affair to Remember." *Spur of the Moment*, n.d. British Library.

Jacobs, Gerald. "Why the Y Word Is My Word." *Jewish Chronicle*, April 22, 2011.

Jacobus, Simone. "Jubilerend Ajax had altijd een grote joodse supporters-schare." *Nieuw Israelietisch weekblad*, March 16, 1990, Dag edition.

JC Reporter. "Fans Condemn 'Offensive' T-Shirt Showing Harry Kane as a Chasid." *Jewish Chronicle*, February 12, 2016.

Jenkins, Seb. "The Y-Word Is Officially in the Oxford English Dictionary—Spurs Are Mentioned." *Tottenham Hotspur Football News* (blog), February 11, 2020. Spurs Web. https://www.spurs-web.com/spurs-news/the-y-word -is-officially-in-the-oxford-english-dictionary-spurs-are-mentioned/.

Jewish Chronicle. "Apology." September 9, 1983.

———. "'Belsen' Cry at Anfield." October 17, 1986.

———. "Life Ban for a Racist Fan." November 28, 2008.

———. March 1, 1996.

———. September 10, 1999.

———. "Soccer Hate Campaign." December 12, 1980.

———. "Spurs Wishes." October 12, 1973.

Jewish News. "Antisemitic Mural Appears after Dutch Football Star Signs with Ajax," August 9, 2021. https://jewishnews.timesofisrael.com /antisemitic-mural-appears-after-dutch-football-star-signs-with-ajax/.

Jonet.nl. "Opnieuw beledigende afbeelding van Steven Berghuis, nu in Antwerpen." February 15, 2022. https://jonet.nl/opnieuw-beledigende -afbeelding-van-steven-berghuis-nu-in-antwerpen/.

Jüdisches Museum Wien. *Superjuden. Jüdische Identitäten im Fußball: Ausstellung im Jüdischen Museum*. July 12, 2023–January 14, 2024.

"Jürgen Klinsmann—The Official Inside Story." Fanzine, 1997.

Kafka, Franz. *Letters to Milena*. Translated by Philip Boehm. New York: Schocken Books, 1990.

KAI2000 InfoBlog. "Wohnzimmer Zwa." June 27, 2019. https://www .kai2000.wien/galerie/wohnzimmer-zwa/.

———. "Wohnzimmer Zwa." November 2, 2020. https://www.kai2000 .wien/news/wohnzimmer-zwa-3/.

Kämper, Dirk, and Dietrich Schulze-Marmeling. "Der FC Bayern, die Nazis und Herr Herzog." Dietrich Schulze-Marmeling official website.

Accessed January 25, 2023. https://www.schulze-marmeling.com/artikel
/der-fc-bayern-die-nazis-und-herr-herzog.

Kessel, Anna. "Alive and Unchecked—a Wave of Anti-Jewish Hate." *Observer*, October 27, 2007, sec. Football. https://www.theguardian.com
/football/2007/oct/28/newsstory.sport2.

"Kick It Like Kurt": Eine Erinnerung an den legendären Fußballfunktionär Kurt Landauer. 2010.

Kick It Out. "Think Again!—Classroom Activities for Challenging Prejudice and Fostering Community Cohesion." 2012. https://www
.migrationmuseum.org/wp-content/uploads/2014/08/Think-Again-Y
-Word-educational-pack.pdf.

———. *The Y-Word*. Posted on YouTube, April 12, 2011. https://www
.youtube.com/watch?v=RIvJC1_hKt8.

Kinast, Florian. "FC Bayern München und Katar: Eine problematische Partnerschaft." *Der Spiegel*, February 11, 2021. https://www.spiegel.de
/sport/fussball/fc-bayern-muenchen-und-katar-eine-problematische
-partnerschaft-a-7889d38d-3c82-4d8c-9aea-e4b259861846.

Kossoff, Julian. "Team Tackles the Terraces of Hate." *Jewish Chronicle*, March 16, 1990.

Kratzer, Hans. "Ursprung des FC Bayern-Mottos: Woher das Mia san Mia stammt." *Süddeutsche Zeitung*, August 9, 2013. https://www.sueddeutsche
.de/bayern/ursprung-des-fc-bayern-mottos-wer-san-mia-1.1742394.

Krügel, Christian. "Stolz auf die jüdische Vergangenheit." *Süddeutsche Zeitung*, May 26, 2011. https://www.sueddeutsche.de/muenchen/fc
-bayern-muenchen-stolz-auf-die-juedische-vergangenheit-1.1101845.

Kurt Landauer Stiftung. "Satzung des 'Kurt Landauer Stiftung e.V.' vom 16. Juni 2017." June 16, 2017. https://www.kurt-landauer-stiftung.de/_files
/ugd/adea3a_9ab9f00bd77946d38d4168c24141c42a.pdf.

———. "Welcome Back, Kurt Landauer!" Kurt Landauer Stiftung. Accessed January 29, 2023. https://www.kurt-landauer-stiftung.de/kurt?lang=en.

Landauer—Der Präsident. Feature Film. ARD, 2014.

Langlois, Andre. "I'm a Spurs Fan and We Should Drop the Y-Word—We Don't Need It." Tottenham Hotspur, February 11, 2022. https://
www.tottenhamhotspur.com/the-club/the-why-word/im-a-spurs
-fan-and-we-should-drop-the-y-word-we-dont-need-it/.

Leaf, Wally. "Arsenal Fans Warned." *Jewish Chronicle*, October 30, 1987.

Lempkowicz, Yossi. "'Our Parents Were Burning Jews,' Chanted Fans of a Belgian Football Club in an Antisemitic Video." EJP, December 21, 2018.
https://ejpress.org/our-parents-were-burning-jews-chanted-fans-of-a
-belgian-football-club-in-an-antisemitic-video/.

Lenhard, Michael. *Fußballheimat München und Südbayern: 100 Orte der Erinnerung*. Hildesheim: Arete Verlag, 2018.

Lester, Jeremy. "Fan the Flames." *Jewish Chronicle*, March 8, 1996.

Levene, Paul. "Capital Letters: Spurs Not Antisemitic." *Jewish Chronicle*, January 20, 1989.

Liphshiz, Cnaan. "Belgian Soccer Fans Filmed Giving Nazi Salutes, Singing 'Jews to the Gas.'" *Times of Israel*, December 30, 2021. https://www.timesofisrael.com/belgian-soccer-fans-filmed-giving-nazi-salutes-singing-jews-to-the-gas/.

———. "Belgian Soccer Star Defends Chanting He'd 'Rather Die than Be a Jew.'" *Jerusalem Post*, May 25, 2021. https://www.jpost.com/diaspora/antisemitism/belgian-soccer-star-defends-chanting-hed-rather-die-than-be-a-jew-669059.

Mann, Lord John. Interview by Pavel Brunssen, August 1, 2022.

Meikle, James, and Kim Willsher. "Tottenham Fans Injured in 'antisemitic' Attack before Europa League Tie in Lyon." *Guardian*, February 21, 2013. http://www.theguardian.com/world/2013/feb/21/tottenham-fans-antisemitic-attack-lyon.

Menasse, Peter. "Parteigenosse Matthias Sindelar." *NU*, June 30, 2003.

———. "Parteigenosse Sindelar." *Falter* 31, no. 3 (December 17, 2003). https://www.falter.at/zeitung/20031217/parteigenosse-sindelar/1959040053.

Merriman, Daniel. "Leipzig Away: More Than a Football Match." *Football Pink* (blog), February 19, 2021. https://footballpink.net/leipzig-away-more-than-a-football-match/.

Meyhoff, Andreas, and Gerhard Pfeil. "Fußball: Expertenstreit um FC Bayern zur NS-Zeit." *Der Spiegel*, May 24, 2016. https://www.spiegel.de/spiegel/spiegelblog/fussball-expertenstreit-um-fc-bayern-zur-ns-zeit-a-1093975.html.

———. "Münchner Protokolle." *Der Spiegel*, May 20, 2016. https://www.spiegel.de/sport/muenchner-protokolle-a-74482b35-0002-0001-0000-000144886593.

Milne, Alex. "Lazio Supporters Hang Anti-Semitic Jose Mourinho Banner Ahead of Roma Fixture." *Irish Mirror*, May 15, 2021. https://www.irishmirror.ie/sport/soccer/soccer-news/lazio-supporters-hang-anti-semitic-24116164.

NL Times. "Court Orders Men to Visit Holocaust Memorial for Anti-Semitic Graffiti of Dutch Footballer *NL Times*," July 13, 2022. https://nltimes.nl/2022/07/13/court-orders-men-visit-holocaust-memorial-anti-semitic-graffiti-dutch-footballer.

Oliveck, Melissa. "Jürgy Bears All . . ." *Cock a Doodle Doo*, April 1995, 4th ed. British Library.

Ott, Michael. "Antrag zur Jahreshauptversammlung: Beendigung des Katar-Sponsorings beim FC Bayern." 2021. http://katar-antrag.de/.

Oxford English Dictionary. "New Words List January 2020 | Oxford English Dictionary," January 14, 2020. https://www.oed.com/information /updates/previous-updates/2020-2/january-2020/?tl=true.

———, s.v., "Yid, n." Accessed September 6, 2021. https://www.oed.com /view/Entry/231844.

———, s.v., "Yiddo, n." Accessed September 6, 2021. https://www.oed .com/view/Entry/74901654.

Peled, Nirit, dir. *Superjews.* NTR / Viewpoint Productions, 2013.

PennState. *Venerated—Persecuted—Forgotten.* February 2023. Jewish Studies Program. https://jewishstudies.la.psu.edu/news-and-events /venerated-persecuted-forgotten/.

Polgar, Alfred. "Abschied von Sindelar." *Pariser Tageszeitung,* January 25, 1939.

Pollard, Stephen. "Why I Changed My Mind on Spurs and the Y Word." *Jewish Chronicle,* February 16, 2022. https://www.thejc.com/lets -talk/all/why-i-changed-my-mind-on-spurs-and-the-y-word -15wKTwkh7mpnHqHbXKtUqD.

Pot, Menno. Interview by Pavel Brunssen, May 5, 2022.

Quinn, Ben. "Spurs Criticise OED over Expanded Definition of 'Yid.'" *Guardian,* February 12, 2020. http://www.theguardian.com/football /2020/feb/12/spurs-criticise-oed-over-expanded-definition-of-yid.

Rashty, Sandy. "'Racist' Badges at Arsenal." *Jewish Chronicle,* September 21, 2012.

Reuters. "Bayern Munich End Deal with Qatar Airways after Fan Protests." ESPN.com, June 28, 2023. https://www.espn.com/soccer/story/_/id /37926383/bayern-munich-end-deal-qatar-airways-fan-protests.

Rijnmond. "Bestuur supportersvereniging De Feijenoorder verdeeld over antisemitische muurtekening." July 27, 2021. https://www.rijnmond .nl/nieuws/1294346/Bestuur-supportersvereniging-De-Feijenoorder -verdeeld-over-antisemitische-muurtekening.

Rocker, Simon, and Jeremy Lester. "The Flip Side of British Jewry." *Jewish Chronicle,* March 1, 1996.

Rule the Roost—A Tottenham Hotspur Podcast. "RTR Extra: Philip Spencer." Accessed November 5, 2022. https://shows.acast.com/ruletheroost /episodes/rtrextra-philipspencer.

Rüttenauer, Andreas. "Die ungeliebten Bayern-Fans." *Die Tageszeitung,* March 26, 2010. https://taz.de/!460080/.

Schickeria München. "125 Jahre Kurt Landauer." *Gegen den Strom,* November 2010. Archiv der Jugendkulturen.

———. Cover. *Gegen den Strom*, June 2005. Archiv der Jugendkulturen.

———. "Die (vergessene) Geschichte des 'Judenclub' Bayern München." *Gegen den Strom*, June 2005. Archiv der Jugendkulturen.

———. "Erinnerungen, Erzählungen, Anekdoten zur Deutschen Meisterschaft 1932." *Gegen den Strom*, November 2010. Archiv der Jugendkulturen.

———. "Kurt-Landauer-Turnier 2008." *Gegen den Strom*, September 2008. Archiv der Jugendkulturen.

———. "Quo vadis Ultras? Über die Zukunft der deutschen Ultrà-Gruppen." *Blickfang Ultra*, December 2007.

———. "SK-Aktionstag FUSSBALL OHNE GRENZEN—REFUGEES WELCOME." Accessed April 29, 2021. https://schickeria-muenchen.org/pico/blog/109_News.

———. "Südkurve 72: Symbolik der Gruppe." *Gegen den Strom*, September 2008. Archiv der Jugendkulturen.

———. "Wer wir sind." Accessed February 6, 2023. https://schickeria-muenchen.org/pico/infos/ueber_uns/wer_wir_sind.

Schöffel, Robert, and Uli Köppen. "LandauerWalk: Das Making-Of zur Augmented-Reality-App," September 19, 2014. https://www.br.de/fernsehen/das-erste/sendungen/kurt-landauer-der-film/die-app-making-of-100.html.

Schulze-Marmeling, Dietrich. "Der FC Bayern München in der NS-Zeit: Eine Enthüllung, die keine ist." *Der Tagesspiegel*, May 25, 2016. https://www.tagesspiegel.de/sport/eine-enthullung-die-keine-ist-4884679.html.

Shaked, Daniel. Interview by Pavel Brunssen, March 10, 2022.

Sharon, Jeremy. "Austrian Football Association Adopts IHRA Antisemitism Definition." Jerusalem Post, November 11, 2021. https://www.jpost.com/diaspora/antisemitism/austrian-football-association-adopts-ihra-antisemitism-definition-684724.

Sightseeing Munich. "FC Bayern—Humble Beginnings Tour in Munich." Accessed February 5, 2023. https://sightseeing-munich.tours/en/fc-bayern-bescheidene-anfaenge/.

Silver, Neil. "Anger at Fans' Use of Flag." *Jewish Chronicle*, February 13, 1987.

———. "Chelsea Bans Racist Fans." *Jewish Chronicle*, January 8, 1988.

Smith, Craig S. "A Dutch Soccer Riddle: Jewish Regalia without Jews." *New York Times*, March 28, 2005, sec. World. https://www.nytimes.com/2005/03/28/world/europe/a-dutch-soccer-riddle-jewish-regalia-without-jews.html.

Smith, Gerald. "Chelsea Warns off Teeshirt 'Fans.'" *Jewish Chronicle*, April 5, 1985.

Smith, Stephen. "The Incredible Story of a Munich Soccer Team During the Holocaust Offers a Lesson." *Jewish Journal*, July 16, 2019. https://jewishjournal.com/commentary/columnist/301598/the -incredible-story-of-a-munich-soccer-team-during-the-holocaust -offers-a-lesson/.

Solomons, Mark. "As a Jewish Spurs Fan, I Saw Y-Word Chants as a Form of Solidarity. But They Have to Go." *Guardian*, February 14, 2022, sec. Opinion. https://www.theguardian.com/commentisfree/2022/feb/14 /jewish-spurs-fan-y-word-chants-tottenham-hotspur.

———. "The Thing I Love Most . . ." *Fighting Cock* (blog), December 17, 2018. https://thefightingcock.co.uk/2018/12/the-thing-i-love-most/.

Sporting Statues Project official website. Accessed July 2, 2024. http:// offbeat.group.shef.ac.uk/statues/.

Spruchkammer München I. "Protokoll der öffentlichen Sitzung am 28. November 1946 14 Uhr." November 28, 1946. SpK K 1000. Staatsarchiv München.

———. "Spruch I-410/46." November 28, 1946. SpK K 1000. Staatsarchiv München.

Spur of the Moment, 1996. British Library.

Spurs Community. "Warren Mitchell Has Died." Forum. Spurs Community. Accessed November 22, 2022. https://www.spurscommunity.co.uk/index .php?threads/warren-mitchell-has-died.122370/.

Stadtamt für Leibesübungen. March 14, 1944. Amt für Leibesübungen (AfL) 151. Stadtarchiv München.

Statista. "FC Bayern München AG: Konzernumsatz." 2023. https://de .statista.com/statistik/daten/studie/246557/umfrage/umsatz-fc -bayern-muenchen-ag-konzern/.

———. "Netherlands: Johan Cruijff ArenA Visitors 2019." June 2020. https://www.statista.com/statistics/990128/total-number-of-amsterdam -arena-visitors-in-the-netherlands/.

———. "Netherlands: Largest Cities 2022." 2022. https://www.statista .com/statistics/993709/largest-cities-in-the-netherlands-by-number-of -inhabitants/.

Süddeutsche Zeitung. "FC Bayern verlängert umstrittenes Katar-Sponsoring nicht." June 28, 2023. https://www.sueddeutsche.de/sport/fc-bayern -qatar-airways-katar-sponsoring-vertrag-1.5976393.

Südkurve München. "Kurt Landauer Choreografie FC Bayern—Frankfurt." Posted on YouTube, February 5, 2014. https://www.youtube.com/watch?v =OEeHTHbJGk4.

Telegraph. "Spurs Condemn Spanish Newspaper over Claims the Club Is 'Hated' for Jewish Origins." October 16, 2017. https://www.telegraph .co.uk/football/2017/10/16/spurs-condemn-spanish-newspaper-claims -club-hated-jewish-origins/.

Tharps, Lori L. "The Case for Black with a Capital B." *New York Times,* November 18, 2014, sec. Opinion. https://www.nytimes.com/2014/11/19 /opinion/the-case-for-black-with-a-capital-b.html.

TOI Staff and AFP. "Chelsea Soccer Fan Jailed for 8 Weeks for Antisemitic Tweets Aimed at Rival," November 5, 2021. https://www.timesofisrael .com/chelsea-soccer-fan-jailed-for-8-weeks-for-antisemitic-tweets -aimed-at-rival/.

Torberg, Friedrich. "Auf den Tod eines Fussballspielers." In *Lebenslied: Gedichte aus 25 Jahren,* by Friedrich Torberg (Wien, Berlin: Medusa, 1983), 47–48.

Tottenham Hotspur. "Club Statement," October 12, 2023, https://www .tottenhamhotspur.com/news/2023/october/club-statement/.

———. "The WhY Word | The Club." 2022. https://www.tottenhamhotspur .com/the-club/the-why-word/.

———. "Y-Word Consultation—Update." March 21, 2014. https://www .tottenhamhotspur.com/news-archive-1/y-word-consultation-update/.

———. "Y-Word Consultation Update." December 19, 2019. https://www .tottenhamhotspur.com/news/2019/december/y-word-consultation -update/.

———. "Y-Word Focus Group 1." February 10, 2022. https://www .tottenhamhotspur.com/the-club/the-why-word/y-word-focus-group-1/.

———. "Y-Word Focus Group 2." February 10, 2022. https://www .tottenhamhotspur.com/the-club/the-why-word/y-word-focus-group-2/.

———. "Y-Word Focus Group 3." February 10, 2022. https://www .tottenhamhotspur.com/the-club/the-why-word/y-word-focus-group-3/.

Tottenham Hotspur (@SpursOfficial). "The Club is saddened to hear of the passing of actor and Spurs fan Warren Mitchell." X, November 14, 2015. https://twitter.com/SpursOfficial/status/665554314031726592.

Tottenham Hotspur Supporters' Trust. "THST Fan Survey August 2022." August 2022. https://thstofficial.com/wp-content/uploads/2024/02 /thst_annual_fans_survey_2022.pdf.

———. "THST News—February 2022." February 27, 2022. https:// thstofficial.com/thst-news-february-2022/.

———. "Tottenham Hotspur Fans and The WhY Word." February 10, 2022. https://thstofficial.com/tottenham-hotspur-fans-and-the-why-word/.

tz. "Julius-Hirsch-Preis an Münchner Ultra-Gruppierung 'Schickeria,'" October 14, 2014. https://www.tz.de/sport/fc-bayern/julius-hirsch-preis -muenchner-ultra-gruppierung-schickeria-zr-4118941.html.

UK Parliament. "Antisemitism and Other Racism in Football." Hansard, vol. 716, June 22, 2022. https://hansard.parliament.uk//commons /2022-06-22/debates/38A9C59A-455F-4DDA-B24E-6615E26582BA /AntisemitismAndOtherRacismInFootball.

Visser, Peter. "VVD-Kamerlid: Ajax Moet in Gesprek Met Achterban over Verwijzingen Naar Joden." WNL, December 1, 2022. https://wnl.tv /2022/12/01/vvd-kamerlid-ajax-moet-in-gesprek-met-achterban-over -verwijzingen-naar-joden/.

Vooren, Jurryt van de. Interview by Pavel Brunssen, April 5, 2022.

Wasserstein, Izzy. "Let's Talk about Yids." Fighting Cock (blog), January 23, 2013. https://thefightingcock.co.uk/2013/01/lets-talk-about -yids/.

Weich, Ben. "'If Hope Doesn't Triumph over Experience, Football Isn't for You.'" Jewish Chronicle, May 31, 2019.

Weinthal, Benjamin. "Belgian Jews Demand Soccer Club Stop Antisemitic Chants in the Stands." Jerusalem Post, December 17, 2017. https://www .jpost.com/diaspora/belgian-jews-demand-soccer-club-stop-antisemitic -chants-in-the-stands-518330.

Weiss, Alexia. "Wenn der Davidstern zum Judenstern wird." WZ Online, May 6, 2021. https://www.tagblatt-wienerzeitung.at/meinung/blogs/juedisch -leben/2103204-Wenn-der-Davidstern-zum-Judenstern-wird.html.

Wijnstekers, Marcel. "De strijd van Feyenoord tegen Jodenhaat: 'Supporters lieten tijdens bezoek Auschwitz vele tranen.'" AD.nl, July 27, 2021. https://www.ad.nl/rotterdam/de-strijd-van-feyenoord -tegen-jodenhaat-supporters-lieten-tijdens-bezoek-auschwitz-vele -tranen~ad828570e/.

Wimpietkees. "Joden Lopen Altijd Weg." Posted on YouTube, July 13, 2007. https://www.youtube.com/watch?v=Nn4iwf5vzbs.

Winner, David S. "Don't Blame Soccer's 'Jewish' Teams for Anti-Semitism." Foreign Policy (blog), May 10, 2019. https://foreignpolicy.com/2019/05/10 /dont-blame-for-anti-semitism-in-soccer-tottenham-hotspur-spurs-ajax -amsterdam/.

World Jewish Congress. "WJC and Board of Deputies Stand against Anti-semitsm in Football: There Must Be No Tolerance for Use of Slur 'Yid.'" January 4, 2019. https://www.worldjewishcongress.org/en/news/wjc -and-board-of-deputies-stand-against-antisemitsm-in-football-there -must-be-no-tolerance-for-use-of-slur-yid-1-5-2019.

SECONDARY SOURCES

Adorno, Theodor W. "The Meaning of Working through the Past." In *Critical Models: Interventions and Catchwords*, 89–103. New York: Columbia University Press, 1959.

Alrababa'H, Ala', William Marble, Salma Mousa, and Alexandra A. Siegel. "Can Exposure to Celebrities Reduce Prejudice? The Effect of Mohamed Salah on Islamophobic Behaviors and Attitudes." *American Political Science Review* 115, no. 4 (November 2021): 1111–28. https://doi.org/10.1017/S0003055421000423.

Améry, Jean. *Essays on Antisemitism, Anti-Zionism, and the Left*. Edited by Marlene Gallner. Translated by Lars Fischer. Studies in Antisemitism. Bloomington: Indiana University Press, 2021.

Anderson, Benedict. *Imagined Communities: Reflections on the Origin and Spread of Nationalism*. Rev. ed. London: Verso, 2006.

Arendt, Hannah. "The Aftermath of Nazi Rule: Report from Germany." *Commentary* 10 (1950): 342–53.

———. "Hannah Arendt to Karl Jaspers, August 17, 1946." In *Hannah Arendt/Karl Jaspers Correspondence, 1926–1969*, edited by Lotte Köhler and Hans Saner, translated by Robert Kimber and Rita Kimber, 51–56. San Diego: Harcourt Brace, 1992.

———. "'What Remains? The Language Remains': A Conversation with Günter Gaus." In *Essays in Understanding, 1930–1954: Formation, Exile, and Totalitarianism*, edited by Jerome Kohn, translated by Joan Stambaugh, 1–23. New York: Schocken Books, 1964.

Ashby, Charlotte. Introduction to *The Viennese Café and Fin-de-Siècle Culture*, edited by Charlotte Ashby, Tag Gronberg, and Simon Shaw-Miller, 1–8. New York: Berghahn Books, 2013.

Ashby, Charlotte, Tag Gronberg, and Simon Shaw-Miller, eds. *The Viennese Café and Fin-de-Siècle Culture*. New York: Berghahn Books, 2013.

Back, Les. "Sounds in the Crowd." In *The Auditory Culture Reader*, edited by Michael Bull and Les Back, 311–27. Sensory Formations Series. Oxford: Berg, 2006.

Back, Les, Tim Crabbe, and John Solomos. "Beyond the Racist/Hooligan Couplet: Race, Social Theory and Football Culture." *British Journal of Sociology* 50, no. 3 (September 1999): 419–42. https://doi.org/10.1111/j.1468-4446.1999.00419.x.

Baddiel, David. *Jews Don't Count: How Identity Politics Failed One Particular Identity*. London: TLS Books, an imprint of HarperCollins, 2021.

Baena, Veronica. "Global Marketing Strategy in Professional Sports. Lessons from FC Bayern Munich." *Soccer & Society* 20, no. 4 (May 19, 2019): 660–74. https://doi.org/10.1080/14660970.2017.1379399.

Baker, Cynthia M. *Jew*. Key Words in Jewish Studies. New Brunswick, NJ: Rutgers University Press, 2017.

Baumann, Zygmunt. "Allosemitism: Premodern, Modern, Postmodern." In *Modernity, Culture, and "the Jew,"* edited by Bryan Cheyette and Laura Marcus, 153–56. Cambridge: Polity Press, 1998.

Behrens, Katja. "The Rift and Not the Symbiosis." In *Unlikely History: The Changing German-Jewish Symbiosis 1945–2000*, edited by Leslie Morris and Jack Zipes, translated by M. J. Walker, 31–45. New York: Palgrave Macmillan US, 2002.

Bemmel, M A van. "'We Are Superjews, Ajax Is the Name': A Study of the Jewish Identity of Ajax Supporters." Master's thesis, University of Amsterdam, 2012.

Beniston, Judith. "'Hitler's First Victim'?—Memory and Representation in Post-War Austria: Introduction." *Austrian Studies* 11 (2003): 1–13.

Benjamin, Walter. "Über den Begriff der Geschichte." In *Walter Benjamin— Gesammelte Schriften, Band 1.2.*, edited by Rolf Tiedemann and Hermann Schweppenhäuser, 691–706. Frankfurt: Suhrkamp, 1991.

———. "Über den Begriff der Geschichte—Anmerkungen." In *Walter Benjamin—Gesammelte Schriften, Band 1.2.*, edited by Rolf Tiedemann and Hermann Schweppenhäuser, 1223–66. Frankfurt: Suhrkamp, 1991.

Bergmann, Werner, and Rainer Erb. "Kommunikationslatenz, Moral und öffentliche Meinung: Theoretische Überlegungen zum Antisemitismus in der Bundesrepublik Deutschland." *Kölner Zeitschrift für Soziologie und Sozialpsychologie* 38, no. 2 (1986): 223–46.

Bernett, Hajo. *Der jüdische Sport im nationalsozialistischen Deutschland 1933–1938*. Schorndorf: Hofmann, 1978.

———. *Der Weg des Sports in die nationalsozialistische Diktatur*. Schorndorf: Hofmann, 1983.

———. *Nationalsozialistische Leibeserziehung: eine Dokumentation ihrer Theorie und Organisation*. Schorndorf: Hofmann, 1966.

———. *Sportpolitik im Dritten Reich*. Schorndorf: Hofmann, 1971.

Betz, Susanne Helene, Sema Colpan, Bernhard Hachleitner, Alexander Juraske, Matthias Marschik, and Georg Spitaler. "Jüdischer Sport in Metropolen: Einleitende Bemerkungen." *Aschkenas* 27, no. 1 (January 27, 2017): 1–8. https://doi.org/10.1515/asch-2017-0001.

Beyer, Bernd. *Der Mann, der den Fußball nach Deutschland brachte: Das Leben des Walther Bensemann; Ein biografischer Roman.* Erweiterte Neuausgabe. Göttingen, Germany: Die Werkstatt, 2014.

Bianchi, Claudia. "Slurs and Appropriation: An Echoic Account." *Journal of Pragmatics* 66 (May 2014): 35–44. https://doi.org/10.1016/j.pragma.2014.02.009.

Blaha, Franz. *Sindelar.* Vienna: Blaha, 1946.

Blaschke, Ronny. *Machtspieler Fußball in Propaganda, Krieg und Revolution.* Göttingen, Germany: Die Werkstatt, 2020.

Bodemann, Y. Michal. *Gedächtnistheater: die jüdische Gemeinschaft und ihre deutsche Erfindung.* Hamburg, Germany: Rotbuch, 1996.

Bonvalot, Michael. "Ein 'Judenverein' und seine Neonazis." *Transparent— Magazin für Fußball und Fankultur* no. 18 (2016): 20–25.

Bregstein, Philo, and Salvador Bloemgarten, eds. *Remembering Jewish Amsterdam.* New York: Holmes & Meier, 2004.

Brenner, Michael, and Gideon Reuveni. "Introduction: Why Jews and Sports." In *Emancipation through Muscles: Jews and Sports in Europe,* edited by Michael Brenner and Gideon Reuveni, 1–9. Lincoln: University of Nebraska Press, 2006.

Brunssen, Pavel. "Antisemitic Metaphors in German Soccer Fan Culture Directed at RB Leipzig." In *Football Nation: The Playing Fields of German Culture, History, and Society,* edited by Rebeccah Dawson, Bastian Heinsohn, Oliver Knabe, and Alan McDougall, 218–39. Spektrum: Publications of the German Studies Association 25. New York: Berghahn Books, 2022.

———. "Antisemitic Ressentiment-Communication Directed at RB Leipzig in German Football Fan Culture: The Third Other." In *Football and Discrimination: Antisemitism and Beyond,* edited by Pavel Brunssen and Stefanie Schüler-Springorum, 81–94. Critical Research in Football. Abingdon, UK: Routledge, 2021.

———. *Antisemitismus in Fußball-Fankulturen: Der Fall RB Leipzig.* Weinheim, Germany: Beltz Juventa, 2021.

———. "Der lange Weg der 'Aachen Ultras.'" *Transparent—Magazin für Fußball und Fankultur,* no. 4 (2013): 18–21.

———. "Hitler's American Countermodel: The United States and the Making of Nazi Ideology." *German Politics and Society* 41, no. 3 (Autumn 2023).

———. "Möglichkeiten und Grenzen der Erinnerungsarbeit im Fußball: Interview mit Juliane Röleke zu den Potenzialen von

Gedenkstättenfahrten mit Fußballfans," in *Wie gelingt partizipative politische Bildung für Jugendliche und junge Erwachsene im Fußball?* edited by Fabian Fritz, Birger Schmidt, Simon Walter, and Markus Zwecker, 198–206.

————. "Recht der Stärkeren? Der Kampf um die Kurven geht weiter." *Transparent—Magazin für Fußball und Fankultur,* no. 22 (2017): 46–49.

————. "Zwischen Gedenken und Aufarbeitung: Fünf Thesen zur Zukunft der Erinnerungskultur im Fußball." In *Wie gelingt partizipative politische Bildung für Jugendliche und junge Erwachsene im Fußball?*, edited by Fabian Fritz, Birger Schmidt, Simon Walter, and Markus Zwecker, 207–13. Sportfans im Blickpunkt sozialwissenschaftlicher Forschung. Weinheim, Germany: Beltz Juventa, 2024.

Brunssen, Pavel, and Robert Claus. "Rechtsextremismus und Fanszenen—Ein analytischer Blick auf die gesellschaftlichen Strukturen." In *Zurück am Tatort Stadion: Diskriminierung und Antidiskriminierung in Fussball-Fankulturen,* edited by Martin Endemann, Robert Claus, Gerd Dembowski, and Jonas Gabler, 179–94. Göttingen, Germany: Die Werkstatt, 2015.

————. "Wessen Kurve? Hooligans und Ultras in den Fanszenen." In *Hooligans: Eine Welt zwischen Fussball, Gewalt und Politik,* 156–62. Göttingen, Germany: Die Werkstatt, 2017.

Brunssen, Pavel, and Andrei S. Markovits. "From Chants to Change: German Soccer's Unique Response to Antisemitism Post-October 7." ISCA Research Paper, no. 3 (2024). https://isca.indiana.edu/publication -research/research-paper-series/pavel-brunssen-andrei-markovits -research-paper.html.

————. "Soccer in America: From Pele's Periphery to Messi's Semi-Periphery! But Will There Be an Entry into Football's Core?" *Soziopolis* (blog), June 12, 2024. https://www.soziopolis.de/soccer-in-america -from-peles-periphery-to-messis-semi-periphery-but-will-there-be-an -entry-into-footballs-core.html.

Brunssen, Pavel, and Peter Römer. "Erinnern, um nicht zu vergessen." *Transparent—Magazin für Fußball und Fankultur,* no. 8 (2014): 10–16.

————. "Feindbild Polizei: Eine verfahrene Situation." *Transparent—Magazin für Fußball und Fankultur,* no. 3 (2012): 10–15.

Brunssen, Pavel, Peter Römer, and Robert Claus. "'Defenders of European Culture': 'Refugee Crisis,' Football Hooliganism, and the Right-Wing Shift in Europe." In *Football and Politics,* edited by James Carr, Martin J. Power, Stephen Millar, and Daniel Parnell, 108–25. Critical Research in Football. Abingdon, UK: Routledge, 2021.

Brunssen, Pavel, and Stefanie Schüler-Springorum. Introduction to Brunssen and Schüler-Springorum, *Football and Discrimination*, 1–7.

Bunzl, John, ed. *Hoppauf Hakoah: Jüdischer Sport in Österreich von den Anfängen bis in die Gegenwart*. Vienna: Junius, 1987.

Bunzl, Matti. "Resistive Play: Sports and the Emergence of Jewish Visibility in Contemporary Vienna." *Journal of Sport and Social Issues* 24, no. 3 (2000): 232–50.

Burchfield, Robert. *Unlocking the English Language*. New York: Hill and Wang, 1992.

Burke, Peter. "From 'History as Social Memory.'" In *The Collective Memory Reader*, edited by Jeffrey K. Olick, Vered Vinitzky-Seroussi, and Daniel Levy, 188–92. New York: Oxford University Press, 2011.

Burski, Jacek, and Wojciech Woźniak. "The Sociopolitical Roots of Antisemitism among Football Fandom: The Real Absence and Imagined Presence of Jews in Polish Football." In Brunssen and Schüler-Springorum, *Football and Discrimination*, 47–64.

Cesarani, David. *The Jewish Chronicle and Anglo-Jewry, 1841–1991*. Cambridge: Cambridge University Press, 1994.

Chmelar, Dieter. *Ballett in violett: 75 Jahre Fussballklub Austria*. Vienna: Jugend und Volk, 1986.

Claus, Robert, Cristin Gießler, and Franciska Wölki-Schumacher. "Geschlechterverhältnisse in Fußballfanszenen." 2016. https://library.fes.de/pdf-files/dialog/12993-20170522.pdf.

Claussen, Detlev. "Fussball mit dem Hitlergruss." *indirekter freistoss* (blog), October 24, 2005. https://www.indirekter-freistoss.de/2005/10/24/nachschuss/.

Clavane, Anthony. *Does Your Rabbi Know You're Here? The Story of English Football's Forgotten Tribe*. London: Quercus, 2012.

Cloake, Martin, and Alan Fisher. *A People's History of Tottenham Hotspur Football Club: How Spurs Fans Shaped the Identity of One of the World's Most Famous Clubs*. Seaford, UK: Pitch, 2016.

Cloake, Martin, and Adam Powley. *We Are Tottenham: Voices from White Hart Lane*. Edinburgh: Mainstream, 2004.

Coddington, Anne. *One of the Lads: Women Who Follow Football*. London: HarperCollins, 1997.

Cole, Michael. "Holy War in the City of Knives: Anti-Semitism and Football on the Streets of Krakow." openDemocracy, November 17, 2020. https://www.opendemocracy.net/en/countering-radical-right/holy-war-city-knives-anti-semitism-and-football-streets-krakow/.

Czollek, Max. *Gegenwartsbewältigung*. Munich: Carl Hanser Verlag, 2020.

Davies, Hunter. *The Glory Game*. Revised and updated. Edinburgh: Mainstream, 2021.

Dee, David. *Sport and British Jewry: Integration, Ethnicity and Anti-Semitism, 1890–1970*. Manchester: Manchester University Press, 2013.

Degele, Nina. *Fussball verbindet—durch Ausgrenzung*. Wiesbaden, Germany: Springer VS, 2013.

Degele, Nina, and Caroline Janz. "Homosexualität im Fußball—Zur Konstruktion von Normalität und Abweichung." In *Spielen Frauen ein anderes Spiel?*, edited by Gabriele Sobiech and Andrea Ochsner, 195–214. Wiesbaden, Germany: VS Verlag für Sozialwissenschaften, 2012.

Deloria, Philip Joseph. *Playing Indian*. Yale Historical Publications. New Haven, CT: Yale University Press, 1998.

Dembowski, Gerd. "Zur Dialektik der Ultras. Potenziale und Konflikte eines Jugendphänomens zwischen Aufrühren und Partizipation." *Unsere Jugend* 66, no. 6 (2014): 260–70.

Dembowski, Gerd, and Robert Claus. "'Lamm oder Hähnchen?'—Ethnizität und Weißsein in Fankulturen: Interview mit dem Kölner Ultra V." In *Zurück am Tatort Stadion: Diskriminierung und Antidiskriminierung in Fussball-Fankulturen*, edited by Martin Endemann, Robert Claus, Gerd Dembowski, and Jonas Gabler, 142–51. Göttingen, Germany: Die Werkstatt, 2015.

Derks, Marjet, and Elisa Rodenburg. "A Bastion against Assimilation? Jewish Sport in the Netherlands, 1890–1940." *Aschkenas* 27, no. 1 (2017): 109–26. https://doi.org/10.1515/asch-2017-0008.

Digan, Katie. "'The Activist Jew' Responds to Changing Dutch Perceptions of Israel." In Ensel and Gans, *Holocaust, Israel and "the Jew,"* 241–57.

Diner, Dan. "Negative Symbiose—Deutsche und Juden nach Auschwitz." In *Jüdisches Leben in Deutschland nach 1945*, edited by Micha Brumlik, Doron Kiesel, Cilly Kugelmann, and Julius H. Schoeps, 243–57. Frankfurt: Jüdischer Verlag bei Athenäum, 1986.

———. "Negative Symbiosis: Germans and Jews after Auschwitz." In *The Holocaust: Theoretical Readings*, edited by Neil Levi and Michael Rothberg, 423–30. Edinburgh: Edinburgh University Press, 2003.

———, ed. *Zivilisationsbruch: Denken nach Auschwitz*. Frankfurt: Fischer Taschenbuch, 1988.

Doidge, Mark, Radosław Kossakowski, and Svenja Mintert. *Ultras: The Passion and Performance of Contemporary Football Fandom*. Manchester: Manchester University Press, 2020.

Duit, Nino. "Die Erinnerungsarbeiter." *Ballesterer,* February 1, 2018.
https://ballesterer.at/2018/05/16/die-erinnerungsarbeiter/.

Dunn, Carrie. *Female Football Fans: Community, Identity and Sexism.*
Houndmills: Palgrave Macmillan, 2014.

Dunning, Eric. *Sport Matters: Sociological Studies of Sport, Violence and
Civilization.* London: Routledge, 1999.

Duttler, Gabriel, and Boris Haigis, eds. *Ultras: eine Fankultur im Spannungsfeld unterschiedlicher Subkulturen.* Kulturen der Gesellschaft, Band
17. Bielefeld, Germany: Transcript, 2016.

Ebeling, Knut. "The Art of Searching: On 'Wild Archaeologies' from Kant
to Kittler." *Nordic Journal of Aesthetics* 25, no. 51 (January 10, 2017): 7–18.
https://doi.org/10.7146/nja.v25i51.25152.

———. "Die Flut des Raums: Eine Archäologie der Masse." In *Stadien:
Eine künstlerisch-wissenschaftliche Raumforschung,* edited by Knut Ebeling and Kai Schiemenz, 107–59. Berlin: Kadmos, 2008.

Eccleshare, Charlie, and Jack Pitt-Brooke. "Spurs Fans and the Y-Word:
What Happens Next?" *Athletic,* November 19, 2021. https://theathletic
.com/2963758/2021/11/19/spurs-fans-and-the-y-word-what-happens-next/.

Eder, Jacob S., Philipp Gassert, and Alan E. Steinweis, eds. *Holocaust
Memory in a Globalizing World.* Beiträge zur Geschichte des 20. Jahrhunderts 22. Göttingen, Germany: Wallstein, 2017.

Efron, John. "When Is a Yid Not a Jew? The Strange Case of Supporter
Identity at Tottenham Hotspur." In Brenner and Reuveni, *Emancipation
through Muscles,* 235–56.

Elias, Norbert. Introduction to *Quest for Excitement: Sport and Leisure in
the Civilizing Process,* by Norbert Elias and Eric Dunning, 19–62. Oxford:
Basil Blackwell, 1986.

Elliott, Richard, ed. *The English Premier League: A Socio-Cultural Analysis.*
Routledge Research in Football 2. London: Routledge, 2019.

Endelman, Todd M. *Radical Assimilation in English Jewish History, 1656–
1945.* Modern Jewish Experience. Bloomington: Indiana University
Press, 1990.

Ensel, Remco. "Holocaust Commemorations in Postcolonial Dutch Society." In Ensel and Gans, *Holocaust, Israel and "the Jew,"* 475–98.

———. "'The Jew' vs. 'the Young Male Maroccan': Stereotypical Confrontations in the City." In Ensel and Gans, *Holocaust, Israel and "the Jew,"*
377–413.

———. "Transnational Left-Wing Protest and the 'Powerful Zionist.'" In
Ensel and Gans, *Holocaust, Israel and "the Jew,"* 181–213.

Ensel, Remco, and Evelien Gans. "Historikerstreit: The Stereotypical Jew in Recent Dutch Holocaust Studies." In Ensel and Gans, *Holocaust, Israel and "the Jew*," 341–73.

———, eds. *The Holocaust, Israel and "the Jew": Histories of Antisemitism in Postwar Dutch Society*. NIOD Studies on War, Holocaust and Genocide 4. Amsterdam: Amsterdam University Press, 2017.

Erll, Astrid. *Memory in Culture*. London: Palgrave Macmillan UK, 2011.

Esch, Michael G. *Die Stadt als Spielfeld: Raumbegriffe, Raumnutzungen, Raumdeutungen polnischer Hooligans*. Göttingen, Germany: Wallstein, 2016.

Eshel, Amir. "Layered Time: Ruins as Shattered Past, Ruins as Hope in Israeli and German Landscapes and Literature." In *Ruins of Modernity*, edited by Julia Hell and Andreas Schönle, 133–50. Politics, History, and Culture. Durham, NC: Duke University Press, 2010.

Ewence, Hannah. *The Alien Jew in the British Imagination, 1881–1905: Space, Mobility and Territoriality*. Basingstoke, UK: Palgrave Macmillan, 2019.

———. "Moving 'Out' to Be 'In': The Suburbanization of London Jewry, 1900–1939." *Urban History* 50, no. 4 (2022): 1–18. https://doi.org/10.1017/S0963926822000165.

Faller, Heike. "Onkel Kurt und die Bayern." *Die Zeit*, May 28, 2003. https://www.zeit.de/2003/23/Sport_2flandauer.

FC Bayern München. *Our Club. Our History. Since 1900*. Munich: FC Bayern München, 2022.

———. *Unser Verein. Unsere Geschichte. Seit 1900*. Munich: FC Bayern München, 2022.

Feldman, Christine Jacqueline. *"We Are the Mods": A Transnational History of a Youth Subculture*. Mediated Youth 7. New York: Peter Lang, 2009.

Fischer, Gerhard, and Ulrich Lindner. *Stürmer für Hitler: vom Zusammenspiel zwischen Fussball und Nationalsozialismus*. Göttingen, Germany: Die Werkstatt, 1999.

FK Austria Wien, Peter Klöbl, and Wolfgang Winheim. *100 Jahre Austria Wien*. Vienna: FK Austria Wien Merchandising, 2010.

Fleckenstein, Jutta, and Rachel Salamander. *Kurt Landauer—Der Präsident des FC Bayern Lebensbericht und Briefwechsel mit Maria Baumann*. Berlin: Insel Verlag, 2021.

Fonje, Hans, and Karl Langer. *Die Wiener Austria—Fußballzauber aus Österreich*. Vienna: Dr. Fonje, 1962.

Forster, David. "Café Sindelar revisited: Verlauf und Folgen der Sindelaar-Debatte." In *Fussball unterm Hakenkreuz in der "Ostmark*," edited by David Forster, Jakob Rosenberg, and Georg Spitaler, 314–30. Göttingen, Germany: Die Werkstatt, 2014.

———. "Opfer Österreich, Opfer Austria? Der FK Austria und die NS-Zeit." In Forster, Rosenberg, and Spitaler, *Fussball unterm Hakenkreuz in der "Ostmark,"* 106–21.

Frosdick, Steve, and Peter Marsh. *Football Hooliganism.* Cullompton, UK: Willan, 2005.

Fynn, Alex, and H. Davidson. *Dream on: A Year in the Life of a Premier League Club.* London: Simon & Schuster, 1996.

Gabler, Jonas. *Die Ultras: Fussballfans und Fussballkulturen in Deutschland.* 5., Erweiterte Auflage. Neue kleine Bibliothek 156. Cologne: PapyRossa, 2010.

Gans, Evelien. "'Hamas, Hamas, All Jews to the Gas.' The History and Significance of an Antisemitic Slogan in the Netherlands, 1945–2010." In *Perceptions of the Holocaust in Europe and Muslim Communities,* edited by Günther Jikeli and Joëlle Allouche-Benayoun, 85–103. Dordrecht, Netherlands: Springer, 2013.

———. "Israel: Source of Divergence." In Ensel and Gans, *Holocaust, Israel and "the Jew,"* 215–40.

———. "'The Jew' as Dubious Victim." In Ensel and Gans, *Holocaust, Israel and "the Jew,"* 61–82.

———. "'The Jew' in Football: To Kick around or to Embrace." In Ensel and Gans, *Holocaust, Israel and "the Jew,"* 287–314.

———. "Jewish Responses to Post-Liberation Antisemitism." In Ensel and Gans, *Holocaust, Israel and "the Jew,"* 127–49.

———. "The Meek Jew—and Beyond." In Ensel and Gans, *Holocaust, Israel and "the Jew,"* 83–105.

———. "On Gas Chambers, Jewish Nazis and Noses." In *Racism and Extremism Monitor Ninth Report,* edited by Peter R. Rodrigues and Jaap van Donselaar, 74–87. Amsterdam: Anne Frank Stichting / Leiden University, 2010.

———. "Philosemitism? Ambivalences Regarding Israel." In Ensel and Gans, *Holocaust, Israel and "the Jew,"* 153–80.

———. "Pornographic Antisemitism, Shoah Fatigue and Freedom of Speech." In Ensel and Gans, *Holocaust, Israel and "the Jew,"* 315–40.

———. "Why Jews Are More Guilty than Others! An Introductory Essay, 1945–2016." In Ensel and Gans, *Holocaust, Israel and "the Jew,"* 17–58.

Gillmeister, Heiner. "The Tale of Little Franz and Big Franz: The Foundation of Bayern Munich FC." *Soccer & Society* 1, no. 2 (June 2000): 80–106. https://doi.org/10.1080/14660970008721266.

Gilman, Sander L. *The Jew's Body.* New York: Routledge, 1991.

Giulianotti, Richard, ed. *Routledge Handbook of the Sociology of Sport.* London: Routledge, 2015.

Giulianotti, Richard, and Roland Robertson. *Globalization and Football.* Los Angeles: SAGE, 2009.

Goethe, Johann Wolfgang von. *Italian Journey [1786–1788].* Translated by Wystan H. Auden and Elizabeth Mayer. Penguin Classics. San Francisco: North Point Press, 1982.

Governato, Nello. *La partita dell'addio: Matthias Sindelar, il campione che non si piegò ad Hitler.* 2nd ed. Omnibus. Milan: Mondadori, 2007.

Grau, Andreas, and Martin Winands. "Herausforderungen quantitativer und qualitativer Forschung in (Jugend-)Kulturen und Szenen: Das Beispiel der Fußballfanforschung." In *Sozialwissenschaftliche Perspektiven der Fussballfanforschung,* edited by Andreas Grau, Judith von der Heyde, Jochem Kotthaus, Holger Schmidt, and Martin Winands, 56–74. Sportfans im Blickpunkt sozialwissenschaftlicher Forschung. Weinheim, Germany: Beltz Juventa, 2017.

Gruber, Ruth Ellen. *Virtually Jewish: Reinventing Jewish Culture in Europe.* S. Mark Taper Foundation Imprint in Jewish Studies. Berkeley: University of California Press, 2002.

Guiliano, Jennifer. *Indian Spectacle: College Mascots and the Anxiety of Modern America.* Critical Issues in Sport and Society. New Brunswick, NJ: Rutgers University Press, 2015.

Győri Szabó, Róbert. "Football and Politics in Twentieth-Century Hungary." *International Journal of the History of Sport* 36, no. 2–3 (February 11, 2019): 131–48. https://doi.org/10.1080/09523367.2019.1629583.

Hachleitner, Bernhard. "Arierparagrafen und andere Ausschlussmechanismen." In Hachleitner, Marschik, and Spitaler, *Sportfunktionäre und jüdische Differenz,* 23–46.

———. "Publikumsausschreitungen." In Hachleitner, Marschik, and Spitaler, *Sportfunktionäre und jüdische Differenz,* 206–15.

Hachleitner, Bernhard, Matthias Marschik, Sema Colpan, and Georg Spitaler. "Raum." In Hachleitner, Marschik, and Spitaler, *Sportfunktionäre und jüdische Differenz,* 107–34.

Hachleitner, Bernhard, Matthias Marschik, Rudolf Müllner, and Johann Skocek. *Der Wiener Fußball im Nationalsozialismus: Sein Beitrag zur Erinnerungskultur Wiens und Österreichs.* Wiener Vorlesungen 192. Vienna: Picus, 2019.

———. *Ein Fußballverein aus Wien: Der FK Austria im Nationalsozialismus 1938–1945.* Vienna: Böhlau, 2019.

Hachleitner, Bernhard, Matthias Marschik, and Georg Spitaler, eds. *Sportfunktionäre und jüdische Differenz: Zwischen Anerkennung und Antisemitismus—Wien 1918 bis 1938.* Berlin: De Gruyter Oldenbourg, 2018.

————. "(Sport-)Netzwerke." In Hachleitner, Marschik, and Spitaler, *Sportfunktionäre und jüdische Differenz*, 233–66.

Hachleitner, Bernhard, and Georg Spitaler. "Demografie jüdischer Sport-funktionärInnen." In Hachleitner, Marschik, and Spitaler, *Sportfunk-tionäre und jüdische Differenz*, 89–106.

Hafer, Andreas, and Wolfgang Hafer. *Hugo Meisl, oder, Die Erfindung des modernen Fussballs: Eine Biographie*. Göttingen, Germany: Die Werk-statt, 2007.

Halbwachs, Maurice. *The Collective Memory*. Translated by Francis J. Dit-ter and Vida Yazdi Ditter. Harper Colophon Books, CN/800. New York: Harper & Row, 1980.

Harding, John. "When England Played Germany at White Hart Lane in 1935." *Guardian*, June 11, 2020, sec. Football. https://www.theguardian.com/football/2020/jun/11/nazi-germany-played-england-tottenham-white-hart-lane.

Havemann, Nils. *Fussball unterm Hakenkreuz: Der DFB zwischen Sport, Politik und Kommerz*. Frankfurt: Campus, 2005.

Heffele, Michael. "Der Fußballverein SK Rapid, seine Anhänger und Fans im Fokus von Rassismus, Nationalismus und Männlichkeit." Diploma thesis, Universität Wien, 2006.

Heinrich, Arthur. *Der Deutsche Fussballbund: Eine Politische Geschichte*. Cologne: PapyRossa, 2000.

Hell, Julia. *The Conquest of Ruins: The Third Reich and the Fall of Rome*. Chicago: University of Chicago Press, 2019.

Hell, Julia, and Andreas Schönle. Introduction to Hell and Schönle, *Ruins of Modernity*, 1–14.

Herold, David M., C. Keith Harrison, and Scott J. Bukstein. "Revisiting Or-ganizational Identity and Social Responsibility in Professional Football Clubs: The Case of Bayern Munich and the Qatar Sponsorship." *International Journal of Sports Marketing and Sponsorship* 24, no. 1 (2023): 56–73.

Herzog, Markwart. "Das Selbstbild des FC Bayern als 'Opfer' des Natio-nalsozialismus: Ein Beitrag zum Einfluss der Medien auf Konstruktion und Widerlegung eines populären Geschichtsmythos." In *Zwischen-räume: Macht, Ausgrenzung und Inklusion im Fußball*, edited by Siegfried Göllner, Andreas Praher, Robert Schwarzbauer, and Minas Dimitriou, 228–38. Beiträge zur 2. Salzburger Fußballtagung. Göttingen, Germany: Die Werkstatt, 2019.

————. "Die drei 'Arierparagrafen' des FC Bayern München: Op-portunismus und Antisemitismus in den Satzungen des bayerischen Traditionsvereins." In *Die "Gleichschaltung" des Fussballsports im nationalsozialistischen Deutschland,* edited by Markwart Herzog and Berno Bahro, 1. Auflage, 75–113. Irseer Dialoge 20. Stuttgart, Germany: Verlag W. Kohlhammer, 2016.

———. "FC Bayern Munich as a 'Victim' of National Socialism? Construction and Critique of a 'Heroic Myth.'" *Sport in History* 41, no. 1 (January 2, 2021): 131–52. https://doi.org/10.1080/17460263.2020.1766548.

Hess, Jonathan M. *Germans, Jews, and the Claims of Modernity.* New Haven, CT: Yale University Press, 2002.

Heyde, Judith von der. *Doing Gender als Ultra—Doing Ultra als Frau: Weiblichkeitspraxis in der Ultrakultur: Eine Ethnographie.* 2., Korrigierte Auflage. Sportfans im Blickpunkt sozialwissenschaftlicher Forschung. Weinheim, Germany: Beltz Juventa, 2018.

Hobsbawm, Eric J. "Introduction: Inventing Traditions." In *The Invention of Tradition,* edited by Eric J. Hobsbawm and Terence Ranger, 1–14. Cambridge: Cambridge University Press, 2015.

Hodges, Andrew. "The Politics of 'No Politics' in Pula, Croatia: An Ethnography of the Demons Football Fan Group." *Sport in Society* 27, no. 1 (2024): 111–25.

Hödl, Klaus. "Jewish Studies without the 'Other.'" In *The Future of the German-Jewish Past: Memory and the Question of Antisemitism,* edited by Gideon Reuveni and Diana Franklin, 121–34. Purdue University Press, 2021.

Hoekman, Frank. "F-Side doet dringend verzoek na onrust over Palestijnse vlaggen." FCUpdate, November 8, 2023. https://www.fcupdate.nl/voetbalnieuws/2023/11/f-side-doet-dringend-verzoek-na-onrust-over-palestijnse-vlaggen.

Hofmann, Gregor. *Mitspieler der "Volksgemeinschaft": Der FC Bayern und der Nationalsozialismus.* Göttingen, Germany: Wallstein, 2022.

Holmes, Colin. *Anti-Semitism in British Society, 1876–1939.* New York: Holmes & Meier, 1979.

Holz, Klaus. *Nationaler Antisemitismus: Wissenssoziologie einer Weltanschauung.* Hamburg, Germany: Hamburger Edition, 2001.

Hom, Christopher. "The Semantics of Racial Epithets." *Journal of Philosophy* 105, no. 8 (2008): 416–40.

Hondius, Dienke. "Bitter Homecoming: The Return and Reception of Dutch and Stateless Jews in the Netherlands." In *The Jews Are Coming Back,* edited by David Bankier, 108–35. Oxford: Berghahn Books, 2005.

———. "Return and Reception of Survivors: New Research and Findings." Paper. "Remembering for the Future" Conference, 2000.

Horak, Roman. *Ein halbes Jahrhundert am Ball: Wiener Fußballer erzählen.*
Vienna: Löcker, 2010.

———. "Josef Uridil & Alfréd Schaffer—Der Tank und der Wandervogel."
In *Alles Derby! 100 Jahre Rapid gegen Austria*, edited by Edgar Schütz,
Domenico Jacono, and Matthias Marschik, 2. durchgesehene Auflage,
48–49. Göttingen, Germany: Die Werkstatt, 2012.

———. "Kaffeehaus und Vorstadt, Feuilleton und Massenvergnügen:
Über die doppelte Kodierung des Fußballs im Wien der Zwischenkriegszeit." In *Global Players: Kultur, Ökonomie und Politik des Fussballs*,
edited by Michael Fanizadeh, Gerald Hödl, and Wolfram Manzenreiter,
57–72. Frankfurt: Brandes & Apsel, 2002.

———. "Things Change: Trends in Austrian Football Hooliganism from
1977–1990." *Sociological Review* 39, no. 3 (August 1991): 531–48. https://
doi.org/10.1111/j.1467-954X.1991.tb00866.x.

Horak, Roman, and Wolfgang Maderthaner. *Mehr als ein Spiel: Fussball
und populare Kulturen im Wien der Moderne.* Vienna: Löcker, 1997.

Horn, Dara. "Auschwitz Is Not a Metaphor." *Atlantic*, June 6, 2019. https://
www.theatlantic.com/ideas/archive/2019/06/auschwitz-not-long-ago
-not-far-away/591082/.

Hoy, Mikita. "Joyful Mayhem: Bakhtin, Football Songs, and the Carnivalesque." *Text and Performance Quarterly* 14, no. 4 (October 1994):
289–304. https://doi.org/10.1080/10462939409366091.

Huber, Jo. *Das große Austria-Buch.* Vienna: Mohl Kurt, 1975.

Jacono, Domenico. "Die NS-Zeit als Erinnerungsort im Vereinsgedächt-
nis des SK Rapid." In Forster, Rosenberg, and Spitaler, *Fussball unterm
Hakenkreuz in der "Ostmark,"* 308–13.

———. "'Hauts es eini, die Juden!'" *Ballesterer* 49 (2010): 36–39.

———. "Von 'Ewigen Juden' und 'Schuldenbeuteln'—Werden, Wachsen
und Wesen einer 100-jährigen Gegnerschaft." In Schütz, Jacono, and
Marschik, *Alles Derby!*, 22–29.

Jakubowska, Honorata, Dominik Antonowicz, and Radosław Kossakowski. *Female Fans, Gender Relations and Football Fandom: Challenging the Brotherhood Culture.* Routledge Research in Sport, Culture and
Society. London: Routledge, 2021.

John, Michael. "'Körperlich ebenbürtig'—Juden im österreichischen
Fußball." In *Davidstern und Lederball: die Geschichte der Juden im
deutschen und internationalen Fussball*, edited by Dietrich Schulze-
Marmeling, 231–62. Göttingen, Germany: Die Werkstatt, 2003.

John, Michael, and Albert Lichtblau. *Schmelztiegel Wien—einst und jetzt.*
2nd ed. Vienna: Böhlau Verlag, 1993.

John, Michael, and Matthias Marschik. "Ortswechsel: Antisemitismus im österreichischen Sport nach 1945." In *Antisemitismus in Österreich nach 1945: Ergebnisse, Positionen und Perspektiven der Forschung*, edited by Heinz P. Wassermann, 188–202. Schriften des Centrums für Jüdische Studien 3. Innsbruck: StudienVerlag, 2002.

Jonas, Fabian. "Die Süd schweigt—Grabesstimmung in Fröttmaning." 11Freunde, June 13, 2007. https://11freunde.de/artikel/die-süd-schweigt /358149.

Jones, Tobias. *Ultra: The Underworld of Italian Football*. London: Head of Zeus, an Apollo Book, 2019.

Juraske, Alexander. "Die jüdische Sportbewegung im Wien der Zwischenkriegszeit." In Hachleitner, Marschik, and Spitaler, *Sportfunktionäre und jüdische Differenz*, 71–88.

Jureit, Ulrike, and Christian Schneider. *Gefühlte Opfer: Illusionen der Vergangenheitsbewältigung*. Stuttgart, Germany: Klett-Cotta, 2010.

Kahmann, Bodo. "Feindbild Jude, Feindbild Großstadt. Antisemitismus und Großstadtfeindschaft im völkischen Denken." PhD dissertation, Georg-August-University, Göttingen, 2017. https://doi.org/10.53846 /goediss-6157.

Kahrs, Andreas. "A Comment on Several Specific Aspects of Remembrance and Education Projects in Football." In Brunssen and Schüler-Springorum, *Football and Discrimination*, 166–78.

Kahrs, Andreas, Amelie Gorden, and Daniel Lörcher. "Besonderheiten und Potenziale historisch-politischer Bildung in der Fanarbeit." In *Soziale Arbeit im Fußball: Theorie und Praxis sozialpädagogischer Fanprojekte*, edited by Patrick Arnold and Jochem Kotthaus, 188–201. Weinheim, Germany: Beltz Juventa, 2022.

Kämper, Dirk. "Geschichte als dritte Halbzeit—eine Replik auf Markwart Herzog." Verlag Die Werkstatt, May 24, 2016. https://www.werkstatt -verlag.de/node/223.

———. *Kurt Landauer: Der Mann, der den FC Bayern erfand*. 2nd ed. Zürich: Orell Füssli Verlag, 2014.

Karady, Victor, and Miklós Hadas. "Soccer and Antisemitism in Hungary." In Brenner and Reuveni, *Emancipation through Muscles*, 213–34.

Kastler, Karl. *Fußballsport in Österreich*. Von den Anfängen bis in die Gegenwart. Linz: Trauner, 1972.

Katzian, Wolfgang. "Ein Leben, Ein Klub, Ein Werk." In Skocek, *Mister Austria*, 7.

———. "Vorwort." In *Ein Fußballverein aus Wien: Der FK Austria im Nationalsozialismus 1938–1945*, by Bernhard Hachleitner, Matthias Marschik, Rudolf Müllner, and Johann Skocek, 9. Vienna: Böhlau, 2019.

Keh, Andrew. "Tomahawk Chops and Native American Mascots: In Europe, Teams Don't See a Problem." *New York Times*, May 7, 2018, sec. Sports. https://www.nytimes.com/2018/05/07/sports/native-american -mascots-europe.html.

Keston, Morris, and Nick Hawkins. *Superfan: The Amazing Life of Morris Keston, Football Fan Extraordinaire and Friend of the Stars*. London: VSP, 2010.

King, C. Richard. *Redskins: Insult and Brand*. Lincoln: University of Nebraska Press, 2016.

Kolsky, Rachel, and Roslyn Rawson. *Jewish London: A Comprehensive Handbook for Visitors and Residents*. London: New Holland, 2012.

Koppehel, Carl. *Geschichte des deutschen Fussballsports. Herausgegeben in Zusammenarbeit mit dem Deutschen Fussballbund*. Frankfurt: W. Limpert, 1954.

Krömer, Ullrich, and Theater der Jungen Welt, eds. "Mit Fußballfans in Auschwitz: Interview mit Daniel Lörcher." In *Das Spiel mit den Anderen: Fußball zwischen Integration und Diskriminierung*, 77–85. Göttingen, Germany: Die Werkstatt, 2017.

Kronemeijer, Matthijs, and Darren Teshima. "A Founding Myth for the Netherlands: The Second World War and the Victimization of Dutch Jews." *In Reflections on the Holocaust*, edited by Julia Zarankin, 106–17. New York: Humanity in Action, 2011.

Krüger, Arnd, and Astrid Sanders. "Jewish Sports in the Netherlands and the Problems of Selective Memory." *Journal of Sport History* 26, no. 2 (1999): 271–86.

Kuper, Simon. *Ajax, the Dutch, the War: Football in Europe during the Second World War*. London: Orion, 2011.

Lahm, Philipp. "Vorwort." In *Kurt Landauer: Der Mann, der den FC Bayern erfand*, by Dirk Kämper, 7–8. Zürich: Orell Füssli Verlag, 2014.

Lanz, Thomas. *SK Rapid Wien Fußballfibel*. Berlin: Culturcon medien, 2019.

Lapidot, Elad. *Jews Out of the Question: A Critique of Anti-Anti-Semitism*. Suny Series, Philosophy and Race. Albany: State University of New York, 2020.

Law, Matt. "Tottenham's Charity Chair Resigns over Club's 'Chronic Lack of Moral Clarity' on Israel Terror Attacks." *Telegraph*, October 13, 2023.

https://www.telegraph.co.uk/football/2023/10/13/tottenham-spurs
-charity-chair-resigns-israel-terror-attacks/.

Lebzelter, Gisela C. *Political Anti-Semitism in England, 1918–1939.* New
York: Holmes & Meier, 1978.

Lechner, Michael. *"Wie vom anderen Stern"—jüdischer Fußball in Wien
(1909–1938): Eine Kultur- und Sportgeschichte.* Saarbrücken: VDM Verlag
Dr. Müller, 2010.

Leischwitz, Christoph. "Ein Weg, sich zu erinnern." *Süddeutsche Zeitung,*
February 26, 2020. https://www.sueddeutsche.de/muenchen/sport
/kurt-landauer-weg-ein-weg-sich-zu-erinnern-1.4822515.

Lendvai, Paul. *Antisemitismus ohne Juden: Entwicklungen und Tendenzen in
Osteuropa.* Vienna: Europaverlag, 1972.

Lenz, Britta. "Wisła und Cracovia im 'Heiligen Krieg' Die Anfänge eines
polnischen Traditionsderbys 1906–1927." In *Überall ist der Ball rund: Zur
Geschichte und Gegenwart des Fußballs in Ost- und Südosteuropa—die
zweite Halbzeit,* edited by Dittmar Dahlmann, Anke Hilbrenner, and
Britta Lenz, 89–114. Essen: Klartext, 2008.

Liedtke, Rüdiger. *111 Orte in München auf den Spuren der Nazi-Zeit.* Cologne, Germany: Emons, 2018.

Linden, Peter, and Karl H. Schwind. *100 Jahre! Die Highlights des österreichischen Fussballs: Triumphe, Tränen, Schmähs.* Vienna: Axel Jentzsch
bei Linde, 2004.

Löffelmeier, Anton. *Die "Löwen" unterm Hakenkreuz: der TSV München
von 1860 im Nationalsozialismus.* Göttingen, Germany: Die Werkstatt, 2009.

———. "Grandioser Aufschwung und Krise: Der Münchner Fußball von
1919 bis 1945." In *München und der Fußball: Von den Anfängen 1896 bis
zur Gegenwart,* by Stadtarchiv München, 51–96. Munich: Buchendorfer
Verlag, 1997.

Ludewig, Bianca. *Utopie und Apokalypse in der Popmusik: Gabber und
Breakcore in Berlin.* Veröffentlichungen des Instituts für Europäische
Ethnologie der Universität Wien 47. Vienna: Verlag des Instituts für
Europäische Ethnologie, 2018.

Maderthaner, Wolfgang. "Der 'Papierene' Tänzer: Matthias Sindelar,
ein Wiener Fußballmythos." In *Die Eleganz des runden Leders: Wiener
Fussball 1920–1965,* edited by Wolfgang Maderthaner, Alfred Pfoser, and
Roman Horak, 203–16. Vienna: Die Werkstatt, 2008.

———. "Die lange Reise des Fußballdoktors Emanuel 'Michl' Schwarz."
In *Sportler im "Jahrhundert der Lager": Profiteure, Widerständler und*

Opfer, edited by Diethelm Blecking and Lorenz Pfeiffer, 124–30. Göttingen, Germany: Die Werkstatt, 2012.

Marin, Bernd. *Antisemitismus ohne Antisemiten: Autoritäre Vorurteile und Feindbilder.* Unveränderte Neuauflage früher Analysen 1974–1979 und Umfragen 1946–1991. Frankfurt: Campus, 2000.

Markovits, Andrei S. "What Is It about Association Football—the Arrogantly Self-Appointed 'Beautiful Game'—That Renders Most (Though Not All) of Its Fan Cultures so Ugly?" In Brunssen and Schüler-Springorum, *Football and Discrimination*, 199–208.

Markovits, Andrei S., and Emily K. Albertson. *Sportista: Female Fandom in the United States. Politics, History and Social Change.* Philadelphia: Temple University Press, 2012.

Markovits, Andrei S., and Simon Reich. *The German Predicament: Memory and Power in the New Europe.* Ithaca, NY: Cornell University Press, 1997.

Markovits, Andrei S., and Lars Rensmann. *Gaming the World: How Sports Are Reshaping Global Politics and Culture.* Princeton, NJ: Princeton University Press, 2010.

Marschik, Matthias. "Der 'Fall' Matthias Sindelar: Szenen einer Erregung." *SportZeiten* 4, no.1 (2004): 79–92.

———. "Realität und Mythos." In Schütz, Jacono, and Marschik, *Alles Derby!*, 19–21.

———. *Wiener Austria: Die ersten 90 Jahre.* Vienna: Funtoy, 2001.

Marschik, Matthias, and Bernhard Hachleitner. "'Bodenständigkeit' als Metapher." In Hachleitner, Marschik, and Spitaler, *Sportfunktionäre und jüdische Differenz*, 135–44.

Mauhart, Beppo. "Ein Leben voll Sehnsucht und Glauben." In Skocek, *Mister Austria*, 13–19.

———. "Vorwort." In Marschik, *Wiener Austria*, 9.

Mendelsohn, Ezra. Preface to *Jews and the Sporting Life*, edited by Ezra Mendelsohn, vii–x. Studies in Contemporary Jewry 23. Oxford: Oxford University Press, 2008.

Michael, Robert, and Karin Doerr. *Nazi-Deutsch/Nazi-German: An English Lexicon of the Language of the Third Reich.* Westport, CT: Greenwood Press, 2002.

Misztal, Barbara A. *Theories of Social Remembering.* Theorizing Society. Maidenhead, UK: Open University Press, 2003.

Mitscherlich, Alexander, and Margarete Mitscherlich. *Die Unfähigkeit zu trauern: Grundlagen kollektiven Verhaltens.* Ungekürzte Taschenbuchausgabe, 25. Piper 168. Munich: Piper, 1977.

Moll, Herbert. "'Der Sport hat alles überdeckt . . .'" In *München und der Fußball: Von den Anfängen 1896 bis zur Gegenwart*, by Stadtarchiv München, 9–10. Munich: Buchendorfer Verlag, 1997.

Möllering, Martina, and Eva Schmidt. "The Case of Mesut Özil: A Symbol of (Non-) Integration? An Analysis of German Print Media Discourses on Integration." *Discourse & Communication* 16, no. 3 (June 2022): 326–45. https://doi.org/10.1177/17504813221101823.

Moltke, Johannes von. "Ruin Cinema." In Hell and Schönle, *Ruins of Modernity*, 395–417.

Morris, Leslie, and Jack Zipes. "German and Jewish Obsession." In *Unlikely History: The Changing German-Jewish Symbiosis 1945–2000*, edited by Leslie Morris and Jack Zipes, xi–xvi. New York: Palgrave Macmillan US, 2002.

Mosse, George L. *German Jews beyond Judaism*. Bloomington: Indiana University Press; Cincinnati: Hebrew Union College Press, 1985.

Müller, Simon. Interview by Pavel Brunssen, January 31, 2023.

Mund, Heike. "Verhoeven: 'Landauer war mein FC Bayern-Präsident.'" *Deutsche Welle*, October 15, 2014. https://www.dw.com/de/verhoeven -landauer-war-mein-fc-bayern-pr%C3%A4sident/a-17997537.

Nerdinger, Winfried. "München—Hauptstadt der Verdrängung: Gedenken auf Sparflamme: Wie in der bayerischen Landeshauptstadt mit den Bauten aus der Zeit des Nationalsozialismus umgegangen wird." *Süddeutsche Zeitung*, November 17, 2001.

Newman, David. "Borderline View: A Tottenham 'Yid' in Israel." *Jerusalem Post*, June 15, 2009. https://www.jpost.com/opinion/columnists /borderline-view-a-tottenham-yid-in-israel.

———. "Proud to Be a Tottenham Yid." *Times of Israel*, October 11, 2019. https://blogs.timesofisrael.com/proud-to-be-a-tottenham-yid/.

NL Times. "Dutch Football Should Be Forced to Finally Tackle Anti-Semitism: Coalition Parties." December 1, 2022. https://nltimes .nl/2022/12/01/dutch-football-forced-finally-tackle-anti-semitism -coalition-parties.

Neiman, Susan. *Learning from the Germans: Race and the Memory of Evil*. New York: Farrar, Straus and Giroux, 2019.

Neukirchner, Manuel, ed. *Gedenken an den Holocaust—Fußball und Erinnerung*. Kleine Fußball-Bibliothek 2. Dortmund, Germany: Klartext, 2018.

Niederacher, Sonja. "The Myth of Austria as Nazi Victim, the Emigrants and the Discipline of Exile Studies." *Austrian Studies* 11 (2003): 14–32.

Nora, Pierre, ed. *Les Lieux de Mémoire*. Paris: Gallimard, 1984.

Nordau, Max. "II. Kongressrede." In *Reden und Schriften zum Zionismus*, 50–60. Boston: De Gruyter, 1898.

———. "Muskeljudentum." In *Reden und Schriften zum Zionismus*, 136–37. Boston: De Gruyter, 1900.

Nordmann, Ingeborg. "Neunzehntes Bild: 'Der Intellektuelle.'" In *Antisemitismus*, edited by Julius H. Schoeps, 252–59. Frankfurt: Zweitausendeins, 1995.

Northoff, Thomas. "Graffity-Derby—Beobachtungen in Bild und Text abseits der Stadien." In Schütz, Jacono, and Marschik, *Alles Derby!*, 206–7.

Olick, Jeffrey K., Vered Vinitzky-Seroussi, and Daniel Levy, eds. *The Collective Memory Reader*. New York: Oxford University Press, 2011.

Oswald, Rudolf. "The Image of the 'Judenklub' in Interwar European Soccer: Myth or Reality?" In Brunssen and Schüler-Springorum, *Football and Discrimination*, 37–46.

———. "Mythos 'Judenklub'—Feindbildkonstruktionen im mitteleuropäischen Fußball der Zwischenkriegszeit." *Aschkenas* 27, no. 1 (January 27, 2017). https://doi.org/10.1515/asch-2017-0010.

Otte, Marline. *Jewish Identities in German Popular Entertainment, 1890–1933*. Cambridge: Cambridge University Press, 2006.

Parnell, Daniel, Joel Rookwood, Alex Bond, Paul Widdop, and Jan Andre Lee Ludvigsen. "'It's a Whole New Ball Game': Thirty Years of the English Premier League." *Soccer & Society* 23, no. 4–5 (July 4, 2022): 329–33. https://doi.org/10.1080/14660970.2022.2059853.

Peiffer, Lorenz, and Henry Wahlig. *Jüdische Fussballvereine im nationalsozialistischen Deutschland: Eine Spurensuche*. Göttingen, Germany: Die Werkstatt, 2015.

———. *Jüdischer Sport und Sport der Juden in Deutschland: Eine kommentierte Bibliografie*. Göttingen, Germany: Die Werkstatt, 2009.

———. "Verspätete Erinnerung." *Transparent—Magazin für Fußball und Fankultur*, no. 8 (2014): 18–21.

Peircey, Nicholas. *Four Histories about Early Dutch Football, 1910–1920*. London: UCL Press, 2016.

Pelinka, Peter. "Die Violetten." In *Die Eleganz des runden Leders: Wiener Fussball 1920–1965*, edited by Wolfgang Maderthaner, Alfred Pfoser, and Roman Horak, 84–92. Vienna: Die Werkstatt, 2008.

Pfister, Gertrud, and Stacey Pope, eds. *Female Football Players and Fans: Intruding into a Man's World*. London: Palgrave Macmillan UK, 2018.

Philpot, Robert. "The True History behind London's Much-Lauded Anti-Fascist Battle of Cable Street." *Times of Israel*, September 15, 2018.

https://www.timesofisrael.com/the-true-history-behind-londons-much
-lauded-anti-fascist-battle-of-cable-street/.

Pilz, Gunter A., and Franciska Wölki. "Ultraszene in Deutschland." In *Wandlungen des Zuschauerverhaltens im Profifußball*, edited by Gunter A. Pilz, Sabine Behn, Andreas Klose, Victoria Schwenzer, Werner Steffan, and Franciska Wölki, 63–238. Schriftenreihe des Bundesinstituts für Sportwissenschaft 114. Schorndorf, Germany: Hofmann, 2006.

Pieloor, R. A., B. van de Meer, and M. Bakker. *F-Side is niet makkelijk!* Utrecht, Netherlands: Het Spectrum, 2002.

Pinsker, Shachar. *A Rich Brew: How Cafés Created Modern Jewish Culture.* New York: New York University Press, 2018.

Pinto, Diana. "A New Jewish Identity for Post-1989 Europe." JPR / Policy Paper, no. 1 (1996).

Plato. *Theaetetus. Sophist.* Translated by Harold North Fowler. Loeb Classical Library 123. Cambridge: Harvard University Press, 1921.

Pope, Stacey. *The Feminization of Sports Fandom: A Sociological Study.* Routledge Research in Sport, Culture and Society 81. New York: Routledge, 2017.

Postone, Moishe. "Anti-Semitism and National Socialism." In *Germans and Jews since the Holocaust: The Changing Situation in West Germany*, edited by Anson Rabinbach and Jack Zipes, 302–14. New York: Holmes & Meier, 1986.

Pot, Menno. *Sporen van Ajax.* Amsterdam: Lebowski, 2012.

Poulton, Emma. "Collective Identity and Forms of Abuse and Discrimination in Football Fan Culture: A Case Study on Antisemitism." In Brunssen and Schüler-Springorum, *Football and Discrimination*, 11–34.

———. "Towards Understanding: Antisemitism and the Contested Uses and Meanings of 'Yid' in English Football." *Ethnic and Racial Studies* 39, no. 11 (September 2016): 1981–2001. https://doi.org/10.1080/01419870 .2016.1140791.

———. "'What Have 6 Million Dead People Got to Do with Football?': How Anglo-Jewish Football Supporters Experience and Respond to Antisemitism and 'Banter.'" *Ethnic and Racial Studies* 47, no. 10 (2023): 1–24. https://doi.org/10.1080/01419870.2023.2259447.

Poulton, Emma, and Oliver Durell. "Uses and Meanings of 'Yid' in English Football Fandom: A Case Study of Tottenham Hotspur Football Club." *International Review for the Sociology of Sport* 51, no. 6 (September 2016): 715–34. https://doi.org/10.1177/1012690214554844.

Presser, Jacques. *Ondergang: De vervolging en verdelging van het Nederlandse Jodendom 1940–1945.* The Hague: Staatsuitgeverij, 1965.

Prokopf, Andreas. "Fußballhooligans in Polen zwischen Papsttreue und Antisemitismus." In *Überall ist der Ball rund: Zur Geschichte und Gegenwart des Fußballs in Ost- und Südosteuropa—die zweite Halbzeit,* edited by Dittmar Dahlmann, Anke Hilbrenner, and Britta Lenz, 115–26. Essen: Klartext, 2008.

Ranc, Julijana. *"Eventuell nichtgewollter Antisemitismus": Zur Kommunikation antijüdischer Ressentiments unter deutschen Durchschnittsbürgern.* Münster: Westfälisches Dampfboot, 2016.

Rein, Raanan. "Struggling to Belong in the Face of Otherness: The Atlanta Fútbol Club of Buenos Aires." In Brunssen and Schüler-Springorum, *Football and Discrimination,* 127–37.

Reynolds, Simon. *Energy Flash: A Journey through Rave Music and Dance Culture.* New edition. London: Picador, 2008.

Roose, Jochen, Mike S. Schäfer, and Thomas Schmidt-Lux. "Fans in theoretischer Perspektive." In *Fans: Soziologische Perspektiven,* edited by Jochen Roose, Mike S. Schäfer, and Thomas Schmidt-Lux, 2nd ed., 19–35. Wiesbaden, Germany: Springer VS, 2017.

Rosaldo, Renato. "Imperialist Nostalgia." *Representations,* Special Issue: Memory and Counter-Memory, no. 26 (Spring 1989): 107–22, 1989.

Rose, Arnold M. "The Study of Man: Anti-Semitism's Root in City-Hatred." *Commentary Magazine* (blog), October 1, 1948. https://www.commentary.org/articles/arnold-rose/the-study-of-man-anti-semitisms-root-in-city-hatred/.

Rosenberg, Jakob, and Georg Spitaler. *Grün-weiß unterm Hakenkreuz: Der Sportklub Rapid im Nationalsozialismus (1938–1945).* Vienna: Dokumentationsarchiv des österreichischen Widerstandes, 2011.

Rosenfeld, Gavriel David. *Architektur und Gedächtnis: München und Nationalsozialismus. Strategien des Vergessens.* Translated by Uli Nickel and Bernadette Ott. Munich; Hamburg: Dölling und Galitz, 2004.

———. *Munich and Memory: Architecture, Monuments, and the Legacy of the Third Reich.* Weimar and Now 22. Berkeley: University of California Press, 2000.

Rosten, Leo. *The Joys of Yiddish.* New York: McGraw-Hill, 1968.

———. *The Joys of Yinglish.* New York: Penguin, 1989.

Roth, Leland M. *Understanding Architecture: Its Elements, History, and Meaning.* 3rd ed. London: Routledge, 2018.

Rothberg, Michael. *Multidirectional Memory: Remembering the Holocaust in the Age of Decolonization*. Cultural Memory in the Present File. Stanford, CA: Stanford University Press, 2009.

Rürup, Reinhard. *Emanzipation und Antisemitismus: Studien zur "Judenfrage" der bürgerlichen Gesellschaft*. Göttingen, Germany: Vandenhoeck & Ruprecht, 1975.

Samuels, Maurice. "Philosemitism." In *Key Concepts in the Study of Antisemitism*, edited by Sol Goldberg, Scott Ury, and Kalman Weiser, 201–14. Cham, Switzerland: Palgrave Macmillan, 2021.

Sartre, Jean-Paul. *Anti-Semite and Jew: An Exploration of the Etiology of Hate*. Translated by George J. Becker. New York: Schocken Books, 1944.

Scheler, Fabian. "Kurt Landauer: Der vergessene Erfinder des FC Bayern *Die Zeit*", October 14, 2014. https://www.zeit.de/sport/2014-10/kurt-landauer-fc-bayern-film/komplettansicht.

Schidrowitz, Leo. *Geschichte des Fußballsportes in Österreich*. Vienna: Rudolf Traunau, 1951.

Schiefer, Melissa and Torben Stichling. "Misstrauen gegenüber der Polizei im Fußball: Eine empirische Untersuchung zu Verbreitung und Ursachen." In *Fanverhalten im Sport: Phänomene, Herausforderungen und Perspektiven*, edited by André Schneider, Julia Köhler, and Frank Schumann, 77–91. Wiesbaden, Germany: Springer, 2017.

Schleich, Erwin, and Eva Dietrich. *Die zweite Zerstörung Münchens*. Neue Schriftenreihe des Stadtarchivs München 100. Stuttgart, Germany: Steinkopf, 1981.

Schubert, Florian. *Antisemitismus im Fussball: Tradition und Tabubruch*. Studien zu Ressentiments in Geschichte und Gegenwart, Band 3. Göttingen, Germany: Wallstein, 2019.

Schüler-Springorum, Stefanie. "Das kurze Glück des Mesut Özil." In *Die Stadt ohne: Juden Ausländer Muslime Flüchtlinge*, edited by Andreas Brunner, Barbara Staudinger, Hannes Sulzenbacher, Mirjam Zadoff, and Ulla-Britta Vollhardt, 196–99. Munich: Hirmer, 2019.

———. "Gender and the Politics of Anti-Semitism." *American Historical Review* 123, no. 4 (2018): 1210–22.

———. "Juden, Holländer, Deutsche—Eine kleine Nachkriegsgeschichte." In *Deutsche Zeiten: Geschichte und Lebenswelt; Festschrift zur Emeritierung von Moshe Zimmermann*, edited by Dan Diner, Gideon Reuveni, and Yfaat Weiss, 252–73. Göttingen, Germany: Vandenhoeck & Ruprecht, 2012.

Schulze-Marmeling, Dietrich. *Der Fall Özil: Über ein Foto, Rassismus und das deutsche WM-Aus*. Göttingen, Germany: Die Werkstatt, 2018.

———. *Der FC Bayern, seine Juden und die Nazis*. 3., Erweiterte Auflage. Göttingen, Germany: Die Werkstatt, 2017.

———. *Der FC Bayern und seine Juden: Aufstieg und Zerschlagung einer liberalen Fußballkultur*. 2., Erweiterte Auflage. Göttingen, Germany: Die Werkstatt, 2013.

———. *Der König und sein Spiel: Johan Cruyff und der Weltfußball*. 2., Aktualisierte Auflage. Göttingen, Germany: Die Werkstatt, 2016.

———. *Die Bayern: Die Geschichte des deutschen Rekordmeisters*. Göttingen, Germany: Die Werkstatt, 2007.

———. *Die Bayern: Vom Klub zum Konzern; Die Geschichte eines Rekordmeisters*. Göttingen, Germany: Die Werkstatt, 1997.

———. "Die gescheiterte Assimilation: Juden und Fußball in Budapest." In Schulze-Marmeling, *Davidstern und Lederball*, 319–46.

———. "Einführung." In Schulze-Marmeling, *Davidstern und Lederball*, 11–27.

———. "Fahrräder, Juden, Fußball: Ajax Amsterdam." In Schulze-Marmeling, *Davidstern und Lederball*, 390–418.

———. "Herzog, der 'Spiegel' und die 'Erinnerungskultur.'" In *Zwischenräume: Macht, Ausgrenzung und Inklusion im Fußball*, edited by Siegfried Göllner, Andreas Praher, Robert Schwarzbauer, and Minas Dimitriou, 239–51. Beiträge zur 2. Salzburger Fußballtagung. Göttingen, Germany: Die Werkstatt, 2019.

———. *Kurt Landauer: Der Vater des modernen FC Bayern*. Jüdische Miniaturen 189. Berlin: Hentrich & Hentrich, 2018.

Schüssel, Wolfgang. "Vorwort." In Marschik, *Wiener Austria*, 7.

Schwarz-Friesel, Monika, and Jehuda Reinharz. *Inside the Antisemitic Mind: The Language of Jew-Hatred in Contemporary Germany*. Tauber Institute Series for the Study of European Jewry. Waltham, MA: Brandeis University Press, 2017.

Seijbel, Jasmin, Jacco van Sterkenburg, and Gijsbert Oonk. "Expressing Rivalry Online: Antisemitic Rhetoric among Dutch Football Supporters on Twitter." *Soccer & Society*, August 8, 2022, 1–15. https://doi.org/10.1080/14660970.2022.2109800.

Seijbel, Jasmin, Jacco van Sterkenburg, and Ramón Spaaij. "Online Football-Related Antisemitism in the Context of the COVID-19 Pandemic: A Multi-Method Analysis of the Dutch Twittersphere." *American Behavioral Scientist* 67, no. 11 (2022), 000276422211182. https://doi.org/10.1177/00027642221118286.

Selmer, Nicole. *Watching the Boys Play: Frauen als Fußballfans.* Kassel, Germany: Agon, 2004.

Silverman, Lisa. *Becoming Austrians: Jews and Culture between the World Wars.* Oxford: Oxford University Press, 2012.

———. "Rethinking Jews, Antisemitism, and Jewish Difference in Postwar Germany." In *The Future of the German-Jewish Past: Memory and the Question of Antisemitism,* edited by Gideon Reuveni and Diana Franklin, 135–46. West Lafayette, IN: Purdue University Press, 2021.

Simmel, Georg. "Exkurs über den Fremden." In *Soziologie. Untersuchungen über die Formen der Vergesellschaftung,* by Georg Simmel, 509–12. Berlin: Duncker & Humblot, 1908.

Skocek, Johann. *Mister Austria: das Leben des Klubsekräters Norbert Lopper: Fußballer, KZ-Häftling, Weltbürger.* Vienna: Falter, 2014.

Skocek, Johann, and Wolfgang Weisgram. *Wunderteam Österreich: Scheiberln, wedeln, glücklich sein.* Vienna: Orac, 1996.

Skrentny, Werner. *Julius Hirsch—Nationalspieler—ermordet: Biografie eines jüdischen Fussballers.* Göttingen, Germany: Die Werkstatt, 2012.

Smit, Susan. "De bal bleef rollen: Ajax binnen voetballend Amsterdam tijdens de Tweede Wereldoorlog." PhD diss., University of Amsterdam, 1997. http://www.ethesis.net/ajax/ajax.htm#Deel%20I:%20Vooraf.

Spaaij, Ramón. *Understanding Football Hooliganism: A Comparison of Six Western European Football Clubs.* Amsterdam: Amsterdam University Press, 2006.

Spaaij, Ramón, Jean-Michel De Waele, Suzan Gibril, and Ekaterina Gloriozova. "Football and Politics: Between the Local and the Global." In *The Palgrave International Handbook of Football and Politics,* edited by Jean-Michel De Waele, Suzan Gibril, Ekaterina Gloriozova, and Ramón Spaaij, 3–17. Cham, Switzerland: Palgrave Macmillan, 2018.

Spector, Scott. "Forget Assimilation: Introducing Subjectivity to German–Jewish History." *Jewish History* 20, no. 3–4 (2006): 349–61. https://doi.org/10.1007/s10835-006-9015-2.

Spitaler, Georg. "Case Study: 'Der Jude soll zahlen.' Die Wiener Austria im März 1938." In Hachleitner, Marschik, and Spitaler, *Sportfunktionäre und jüdische Differenz,* 298–315.

———. "Populare Erinnerungsorte—die NS-Zeit im österreichischen Fußballgedächtnis." In *Hakenkreuz und rundes Leder: Fussball im Nationalsozialismus,* edited by Lorenz Peiffer and Dietrich Schulze-Marmeling, 545–57. Göttingen, Germany: Die Werkstatt, 2008.

———. "Populare Erinnerungsorte—die NS-Zeit im österreichischen Sportgedächtnis." Unpublished report, 2005.

Staudinger, Barbara, and Agnes Meisinger, eds. *Superjuden: Jüdische Identität im Fußballstadion*. Katalog zur gleichnamigen Ausstellung im Jüdischen Museum Wien. Vienna: Jüdisches Museum Wien, 2023.

Stoddart, Brian. "Sport, Cultural Politics and International Relations: England versus Germany, 1935[1]." *Soccer & Society* 7, no. 1 (January 2006): 29–50. https://doi.org/10.1080/14660970500355579.

Stögner, Karin. "Nature and Anti-Nature: Constellations of Antisemitism and Sexism." In *Internal Outsiders—Imagined Orientals? Antisemitism, Colonialism and Modern Constructions of Jewish Identity*, edited by Ulrike Brunotte, Jürgen Mohn, and Christina Späti, 157–70. Diskurs Religion. Beiträge Zur Religionsgeschichte und Religiösen Zeitgeschichte, Band 13. Würzburg, Germany: Ergon Verlag, 2017.

———. "New Challenges in Feminism: Intersectionality, Critical Theory, and Anti-Zionism." In *Anti-Zionism and Antisemitism: The Dynamics of Delegitimization*, edited by Alvin H. Rosenfeld, 84–111. Studies in Antisemitism. Bloomington, Indiana: Indiana University Press, 2019.

Sülzle, Almut. *Fussball, Frauen, Männlichkeiten: Eine Ethnographische Studie Im Fanblock*. Frankfurt: Campus, 2011.

Sutcliffe, Adam. "Symptoms at Play: Soccer, Austria, and the Jewish Question." *Journal of Sport and Social Issues* 24, no. 3 (2000): 251–59. https://doi.org/doi:10.1177/0193723500243003.

Szymanski, Stefan, and Silke-Maria Weineck. *It's Football, Not Soccer (and Vice Versa): On the History, Emotion, and Ideology behind One of the Internet's Most Ferocious Debates*. Independently published, 2018.

Telesca, Giuseppe. "The English Premier League and the City of London (1980–2010): A Tale of Two 'Revolutions.'" *Soccer & Society* 23, no. 4–5 (March 31, 2022): 1–13. https://doi.org/10.1080/14660970.2022.2059860.

Thoma, Matthias. *"Wir waren die Juddebube": Eintracht Frankfurt in der NS-Zeit*. Göttingen, Germany: Die Werkstatt, 2007.

Thoma, Matthias, and Martin Liepach. "Eintracht Frankfurt Fans and the Museum: Football History, Remembrance Culture, and the Fight against Antisemitism." In Brunssen and Schüler-Springorum, *Football and Discrimination*, 152–65.

Toffoletti, Kim. *Women Sport Fans: Identification, Participation, Representation*. Routledge Research in Sport, Culture and Society. New York: Routledge, Taylor & Francis Group, 2017.

Tyler, B. David, and Joe B. Cobbs. "Rival Conceptions of Rivalry: Why Some Competitions Mean More than Others." *European Sport Management Quarterly* 15, no. 2 (March 15, 2015): 227–48. https://doi.org/10.1080/16184742.2015.1010558.

Verhoeven, Joram. "Football-Related Anti-Semitism Compared: Report on the International Conference on Anti-Semitism in Professional Football." Anne Frank House, 2015. https://www.annefrank.org/en/downloads/filer_public/db/2d/db2d8481-5a32-4d4b-b695-498849e71d1e/football-related-anti-semitism-compared_2016.pdf.

Verhoeven, Joram, and Willem Wagenaar. "Appealing to a Common Identity: The Case of Antisemitism in Dutch Football." In Brunssen and Schüler-Springorum, *Football and Discrimination*, 141–51.

Vermeer, Evert. *95 jaar Ajax, 1900–1995*. Amsterdam: Luitingh-Sijthoff, 1996.

Volkov, Shulamit. "Antisemitism as a Cultural Code: Reflections on the History and Historiography of Antisemitism in Imperial Germany." *Leo Baeck Institute Yearbook* 23, no. 1 (1978): 25–46.

Vooren, Jurryt van de. "Ajax werd in 1970 overspoeld met dreigbrieven." *Sportgeschiedenis*, August 12, 2021. https://sportgeschiedenis.nl/sporten/voetbal/in-1970-werd-ajax-overspoeld-met-dreigbrieven/.

Wahlig, Henry. *Sport im Abseits: die Geschichte der jüdischen Sportbewegung im nationalsozialistischen Deutschland*. Göttingen, Germany: Wallstein Verlag, 2015.

Waxman, Dov, David Schraub, and Adam Hosein. "Arguing about Anti-semitism: Why We Disagree about Antisemitism, and What We Can Do about It." *Ethnic and Racial Studies* 45, no. 9 (2022): 1–22. https://doi.org/10.1080/01419870.2021.1960407.

Weisgram, Wolfgang. *Im Inneren der Haut: Matthias Sindelar und sein papierenes Fußballerleben; Ein biographischer Roman*. Egoth Biographie. Vienna: Egoth, 2006.

Wiesenthal, Simon, ed. "Vorwort." In *Projekt: Judenplatz Wien: Zur Konstruktion von Erinnerung*, 7. Vienna: Zsolnay, 2000.

Wilczyńska, Bogna. "'Being a Yid': Jewish Identity of Tottenham Hotspur Fans—Analysis and Interpretation." *Qualitative Sociology Review* 18, no. 3 (July 31, 2022): 86–105. https://doi.org/10.18778/1733-8077.18.3.04.

———. "Makkabi, Jutrzenka, Wisla and Cracovia: Polish-Jewish Krakow from the Perspective of Football." *Aschkenas* 27, no. 1 (January 27, 2017). https://doi.org/10.1515/asch-2017-0007.

———. "Żydzi i Polacy na boiskach międzywojennego Krakowa, czyli co piłka nożna może powiedzieć o społeczeństwie / Polish-Jewish interwar

Kraków from the perspective of football." *Studia Judaica* 2, no. 36 (2016): 293–319.

Winner, David. *Brilliant Orange: The Neurotic Genius of Dutch Soccer.* Woodstock, NY: Overlook Press, 2002.

Wulzinger, Michael. "Blut und Kugeln." *Der Spiegel*, September 8, 2002.

Young, James E. "The Anne Frank House: Holland's Memorial Shrine of the Book." In *Anne Frank: Reflections on Her Life and Legacy*, edited by Hyman Aaron Enzer and Sandra Solotaroff-Enzer, 223–28. Urbana: University of Illinois Press, 2000.

———. *The Texture of Memory: Holocaust Memorials and Meaning.* New Haven, CT: Yale University Press, 1993.

INDEX

PAVEL BRUNSSEN is Research Associate and Alfred Landecker Lecturer at the Research Center on Antigypsyism at Heidelberg University. He is author of *Antisemitsmus in Fußball-Fankulturen*; editor, with Stefanie Schüler-Springorum, of *Football and Discrimination: Antisemitism and Beyond*; and editor of *Antigypsyism and Film: Antiziganismus und Film*.

For Indiana University Press

Sabrina Black, Editorial Assistant
Tony Brewer, Artist and Book Designer
Gary Dunham, Acquisitions Editor and Director
Anna Francis, Assistant Acquisitions Editor
Anna Garnai, Production Coordinator
Katie Huggins, Production Manager
Alyssa Nicole Lucas, Marketing and Publicity Manager
David Miller, Lead Project Manager/Editor
Dan Pyle, Online Publishing Manager
Jennifer L. Wilder, Senior Artist and Book Designer

Printed and bound by CPI Group (UK) Ltd, Croydon, CR0 4YY

07/09/2025

14731131-0001